Business Graphics with the IBM® PC/XT/AT

Business Graphics with the IBM® PC/XT/AT

Gregory R. Glau

DOW JONES-IRWIN   Homewood, Illinois   60430

IBM is a registered trademark of IBM Corporation.
Lotus 1-2-3 is a trademark of Lotus Development Company.

© DOW JONES-IRWIN, 1986

All rights reserved. No part of this publication may be reproduced, stored in a retrieval system, or transmitted, in any form or by any means, electronic, mechanical, photocopying, recording, or otherwise, without the prior written permission of the publisher.

This publication is designed to provide accurate and authoritative information in regard to the subject matter covered. It is sold with the understanding that the publisher is not engaged in rendering legal, accounting, or other professional service. If legal advice or other expert assistance is required, the services of a competent professional person should be sought.

From a Declaration of Principles jointly adopted by a Committee of the American Bar Association and a Committee of Publishers.

ISBN 0-87094-754-0

Library of Congress Catalog Card No. 85-72844

Printed in the United States of America

1 2 3 4 5 6 7 8 9 0 ML 3 2 1 0 9 8 7 6

For Kohl—
I Love You

Contents

Acknowledgments **xi**

Introduction **1**
The Influence of Movement, 1   The Problem with Graphs, 2
The Solution, 2   Cause and Effect, 3   How to Use This
Book, 3   Sorry, No Color, 4   Accounting, 4   Business
Graphics, 5   A Positive Look, 6

Chapter
1 Graph Basics **7**
Business Graphics, 7   A Historical Look, 8   An Analytical
Look, 8   Communication, 10   What Do You Need?, 10
Basic Concepts, 11   Getting Started, 11   The Zero Line, 14
A Closer Look, 20   A Historical Look Using a Line Chart, 21
A Trend Line, 23   Line Charts, 24   Windows, 24   Pie
Charts, 26   Editorials, 26   Bar and Column Charts, 28
Everything's Not Roses, 30   Stacked Columns, 31
Poor Examples, 33   Area Charts, 34   One Monthly
Process, 35   Other Graphs, 36   One Last Limitation,
36   Summing Up, 37

Chapter
2 Total Sales **39**
The Sales Trend, 39   A Long-range Look, 40   What About
Inflation?, 42   Sales and Costs, 44   More Direct Costs, 45
Sales and Salespeople, 47   The Sales Pie, 49   A Closer Look,

51 Another Look at Poor Metro, 53 More of Metro's Problems, 54 Summing Up, 56 Other Ideas, 58

Chapter 3 Sales in Sections 59

Breaking Things Down, 60 A Close Look at Contracts, 61 More Contract Detail, 63 Estimates, 64 In-Shop Work, 69 Labor Problems, 72 Contracting Work, 75 Building Pie, 78 Another Group, 79 Subcontracts, 80 Summing Up, 81 Other Ideas, 83

Chapter 4 Cash Flow 85

Cash Flow, 85 Sales and Cash, 86 Flowing Graphs, 86 Sales Don't Necessarily Equal Cash, 88 Sales Equal Dollars, 89 Receivables and Cash, 90 A Two-Edged Sword, 92 Costs and Overhead, 93 Can We Pay For What We Sell?, 94 Seeing Ahead, 94 Receivables and Payables, 96 Are Things Getting Worse?, 97 The Real Secret, 99 The Quality of Receivables, 101 Charting the Age of Receivables, 103 Searching Assets and Liabilities for Cash, 104 The Acid-Test Ratio, 105 Liquidity Ratio, 105 Summing Up, 107 Additional Ideas, 108

Chapter 5 Bids/Warranty/Finance Charges 109

Bids by Quantity, 110 Bids and Sales, 112 Bidding Dollars, 114 A Historical Look, 115 Warranty Problems, 116 Equipment Warranty, 119 People Problems, 120 Finance Charge Problems, 122 More Finance Charges, 124 On the Good Side, 126 Summing Up, 127 Other Ideas, 129

Chapter 6 Direct Costs 131

What are Direct Costs?, 131 Where to Start, 132 The First Picture, 132 Labor Versus Materials, 135 A Closer Look, 138 The Proper Picture, 139 One at a Time, 139 Zeroing In, 141 Total Costs, 143 Another Way to Look, 145 Summing Up, 146 Other Ideas, 148

Chapter 7 Overhead 149

Wrong Images, 149 The Choice, 150 Overhead Details, 151 Overhead and Sales, 152 A Closer Look, 153 Specifics, 154 Utility Costs, 155 Utilities and Sales, 156

CONTENTS

A Closer Look, 157 The Historical Trend, 159 Office Salaries, 160 Who's Best?, 162 Payroll Pie, 163 Advertising and Sales, 164 Converting the Numbers, 165 A Warning, 167 Inside Percentages, 169 Sales and Overhead, 171 Summing Up, 173 Other Ideas, 173

Chapter 8 Financial Statement Items 175

Financial Statements, 175 A Look at Reports, 176 Assets, 177 The Bottom Line: Profits, 178 A Long-Range Trend, 180 Profits and Assets, 182 Profits and Net Worth, 183 Assets and Liabilities, 184 Liabilities as Assets, 188 Asset Pie, 188 Fixed Assets, 190 Measuring Efficiency, 191 Liabilities and Net Worth, 193 A Worse Look, 195 More Interest Problems, 195 Collecting Cash, 197 Summing Up, 200 Other Ideas, 202

Chapter 9 Payroll 205

Payday Problems, 205 Payroll Comparisons, 206 Sales and Labor, 206 A Problem Picture, 207 The Historical Picture, 207 Any Problems Here?, 208 Direct Payroll Comparisons, 209 Payroll Details, 210 Individual Payrolls, 212 Payroll Pie, 214 Where to Look, 216 Inside Payroll, 216 Our Sad Story, 217 Charting Fringes, 217 A Step Further, 219 Payroll's Relation to Profit, 220 Payroll and Cash Problems, 222 Summing Up, 225 Other Ideas, 227

Chapter 10 Inventory 229

The Nonretailer, 230 Sales and Inventory, 231 Inside Inventory, 231 Moving the Stock, 233 Days of Sales, 236 A Closer Look, 238 You're Out of What?, 239 Sales/Inventory per Square Foot, 241 Summing Up, 243 Other Ideas, 244

Chapter 11 Internal Measurements 247

Sales and Hours, 247 Inside Finances, 248 Walt's Secret Formula, 249 Individual Totals, 251 Break-even Dollars, 252 Debt and Equity, 253 Investment and Depreciation, 256 The Bottom Line, 257 Working Capital as a Form of Control, 258 Old Bills, 260 Summing Up, 262 Other Ideas, 263

Chapter

12 Graphs as a Sales Tool **265**
Where to Start, 266   Savings, 267   A Trend Line, 268
Startup Problems, 270   How Noisy is That?, 271   More on Costs, 273   Payback, 275   More on Efficiency, 276
Where the Dollars Go, 277   Summing Up, 278   Other Ideas, 279

Chapter

13 A Tutorial Using Lotus 1-2-3 **281**
Our Pictures, 282   The Main Process, 282   Cell Sizes, 284   Automatic Percent, 287   The Formula, 288
Copying, 289   Graphics, 291

Appendix

A Available Software Programs **297**
Available Software Programs, 298

Appendix

B Book Bibliography **305**

Appendix

C Magazine Bibliography **309**
Article Citations, 309   Magazine Addresses, 315

Index **319**

Acknowledgments

In any project that takes months to organize and complete, people close to the author necessarily hear about it in considerably more detail than they might like. This isn't a problem for the author's family; after all, they have a vested interest in the book (hopefully, it'll pay part of the food bill next year). For friends and fellow workers, though, it can get old awfully fast.

For *not* complaining during the whole process, for listening graciously as I explained this chapter or that graphic concept, for simply being there to let me think out loud, the following deserve special thanks: Mike Gibson, Ken Kuhnke, Tony Malizio, Bob Porter, Carol and Walt Webb, and Ed Wood. Frank Sobek always had good questions and helpful advice.

I also owe a special debt to Don Beil, a professor and author who also reviewed the manuscript from start to finish. Don always has words of encouragement and can—more often than I—see the forest for the trees. You're a good friend, Don.

My Mom reads everything I publish and seems to have more fun with all this than I do.

As in all my work, I get continuous help from my wife, Courtney Ann.

Gregory Glau
Prescott, Arizona

Introduction

If there's one certain thing in business, it's that nothing remains static. *Everything changes.* Oh, you might not recognize it, as you may see the same faces every day and perform many similar tasks much of the time, but inside, every business owner knows that nothing stays the same. Some changes are minor, of course, while others are more obvious, but the fact is that everything in your business is in constant motion. Cash flows both in and out every day. (Often more seems to go *out* than *in.*) Employees change jobs or leave; new people are added. Some new customers pay like clockwork while others only promise that your check's in the mail. Work is quoted and sold; bids are typed, advertising ordered, problems solved, payroll (somehow) made.

The Influence of Movement

Because much of their work is done in the midst of this state of flux, successful businesspeople must have some way to see where they've been, where they stand right now, and estimate where their business might be headed. Because graphics gives you a snapshot of one moment in time, successive pictures can give you something of a moving record of your data, a visual history of where all your sales came from, a look at where all those dollars were spent.

In addition, certain types of graphs—the line graph in particular—help the business owner *feel* this movement. In any graph, what's important is not to be able to extract the exact data from the graph (you get that from the numerical information itself) but what the chart shows. People relate differently to an image than they do to rows of numbers; *they understand the picture.* Also, while graphs give us more of a look at the overall situation, rather than at the details, they're an ideal way to help us absorb large amounts of information.

The Problem with Graphs

The problem with business graphics is twofold. First, they're something few businesspeople received any training in. If you want to plot sales and advertising, what kind of graph should you use? What scale should it be in? What do you do about the fact that last month's sales were $27,500 while advertising only amounted to $157? How do you label the graph? What data should you examine? Over how long a period? For some reason, once you open a business you're automatically expected to *understand* graphs and ratios and the *acid test* and *Flow of Funds* statement. Many of us don't, but only because we've never been trained for it.

Second, making graphs can be a plain chore. Besides having to figure out what to plot and how to chart it, the act of creating a graph is often difficult and time-consuming. It's something we're just not used to doing.

The Solution

The purpose of this book is to give the businessperson a guide by which he or she can examine various areas of his or her business using graphics. You'll learn what's important about cash flow, what to look for, where to extract the pertinent information, and how to plot it. You'll discover how to examine sales and their components, the best way to focus on your costs, how to dig out the details inside of your payroll that you might think are minor, but can cost major dollars. Through all this, we'll suggest the type of graph best suited to help you understand the specific information you're working with. This book is, we hope, the solution to the first problem with business graphics.

Your IBM PC is the answer to the second difficulty. With an easy-to-use program or two, your microcomputer can take all those figures from inside your books and create intelligent, helpful charts, images that will not only tell you where you've been and where you are now, but give you a peek into the future, at where your business will be if current trends are accurate guides to the months ahead.

That's important because one of the primary differences between businesses that are successful and those that fail is the ability of their managers to analyze trouble areas *in time* to do something about them. There are all sorts of hidden threats to your business, surprises that spring up that you shouldn't have to cope with. Graphs can provide an early-warning system to signal that something might be wrong inside one area or another, often soon enough to allow the business owner to act to solve it.

Many businesspeople know they should look at pictures of their information, to make charts for sales and expenses and costs, but it's next to impossible to keep up with them all, every month. So they don't do it, and the information they could ascertain from this visual data is lost. Your PC is a tool that does all the hard work for you—it truly gives you the power to *understand* your own numbers.

Cause and Effect

Most business conditions occur because one thing causes another. Someone's washing machine stops working, so the customer must get it repaired or replaced. A rise in business prompts the need for a more powerful copying machine, and thus creates a sale. Clothing wears out (causing a purchase of new clothes), automobiles break down (causing parts to be purchased or a new car to be ordered), people get fed up with an uncomfortable home (and so they buy air conditioning). A lot of business analysis and data examination concerns itself with this relationship. After all, if we can find the *cause,* perhaps we can vary the effect. If we can determine the optimal media to advertise in for our business, we should be able to figure out if more advertising will create more sales. If we can find out *why* people use our products or services, perhaps we can extend this knowledge to other prospects, so they, too, will become customers.

How to Use This Book

Each chapter focuses on a specific business area. We did things in this manner because this is the way most businesspeople see their figures. They know (or can quickly find out) how much they spent last month for payroll, they know what their current accounts receivable are, they know what they owe.

The questions for each section vary with the focus. How can you best compare sales last year with sales this year? Can a pie chart be used to compare data sets? When should you use a bar chart? A column graph? Are there business uses for a scatter graph? Can you spot a trend? We want to focus on each chart from the viewpoint of what happens inside the business itself; in other words, we want to start with the business function (payroll, general accounting, inventory, etc.), see how they're handled now and then move to how we can convert all that numerical data into helpful business graphics.

While the fancy overlays and color charts and 3-D images we see in some publications are impressive, the business owner needs and looks more for *clarity* and *comprehension*. We want to show you how business graphics can be a tool to help you understand things, not necessarily a showpiece. Like a budget forecast in a column and row format, the graph or chart is simply a *tool*. The advantage a graph has over all those pages with numbers on them is that you can understand a graph easier and faster. You also get a *feeling* for the movement of the data, a feel for how things happen inside your business.

Sorry, No Color

While many graphs can be created in color, both as a display on your video screen and as a hard copy with a plotter or ink jet printer, we've stayed with simple black-and-white drawings for our illustrations. There are a number of reasons for this, including the fact that many small businesses can't afford either a color monitor of sufficient resolution, or a plotter in addition to the standard printer they already own. The use of color itself also comes with its own set of rules, in that we normally associate *red* with business losses, and not all software programs let you use that particular color only when a data point is a negative figure. Some colors show up better than others and so contribute to the informational picture a user gets (where the data alone should be what determines the effect a graph has). Printing in color is often a slow process, so—after the first blush of doing a graph or two—the charts may not get made at all because of the time and effort involved. But, in addition to those difficulties, the main reason we've stayed with this simple format is that anyone can use it. These graphs are clear and understandable, and the whole idea of using graphs, after all, is to communicate their information.

Accounting

Since almost any financial data you want to examine relates to accounting, we have to touch on it. Our focus, though, will be on the specific ratios that are helpful for various areas of a business, along with some guidelines as to what accounting data to examine. We'll explain the sort of accounting information we'll look at in easy-to-understand terms. For example, the Payroll chapter covers not just total payroll, but other associated payroll costs that sometimes we don't consider, like payroll taxes and fringe benefits. Is a particular payroll item *direct* payroll that's related to sales, or *overhead* payroll, that we have to pay whether we sell anything or not?

Business Graphics

Since your PC will do most of the work for you, there's not a lot you need to know in order to create helpful graphs. However, even some of the best programs don't scale things to meet our needs, or put all the labels and information that we need to really understand them automatically onto the charts. Since graphics let us understand our financial information better than any other method, we need to have a basic understanding of what makes up a good graph. Chapter 1 gives you this.

Chapters 2 through 11 cover specific business areas and examine in detail the financial information associated with each. There are some obvious comparisons we all know we should make—things like sales this year versus last, tracking our utility usage and truck repair costs, comparing sales to payroll, and so on. But there are other, helpful ideas that often aren't widely known, and we touch on many of them. We also chart things over different time periods, as that's what you'll do.

When you examine one area or another in any business, the sort of information you have to work with lends itself to a specific type of graph. While all parts of a business are interrelated, some are closely connected to others, while others *directly* depend on another.

The advertising dollar you spend this month won't affect sales until some date in the future. When is it for your business? A graphic look at things will tell you exactly. Every month you collect "X" number of dollars from your customers. For most businesses, this figure varies directly by the sales volume and/or the month-end total of your accounts receivable. If you sell $50,000 worth of goods and services this month, how much can you expect to collect next month? Once a customer lets an account go for, say, 120 days, what's the probability that you'll collect it? What percentage of your accounts are over 90 days old? Is that what it normally is? Is the percentage growing?

What will happen to your cash position if your sales make a sudden spurt? Will you have enough cash available—are you *liquid* enough—to pay the bills until your customers pay you? With the right selection of business graphic images, you can visually *see* how each item relates to the others.

Chapter 12 gives you some specific sales techniques you can use in association with graphics, all with the idea of producing more sales for your business.

The last section of each chapter will make additional suggestions that might apply to your own business. Obviously, we can't cover every possible thing you may want to examine; our purpose here is to suggest some ideas for you to explore, to help you learn what's important to your own business. You also don't want to go overboard and try to chart all the areas that we cover; there are simply too many. Since we don't know what's vital to you and your operation, we've tried to make enough valid suggestions and explain enough example graphs so you'll know what comparisons make sense and how to make them—once you find what's valuable to you.

Chapter 13 is a tutorial that takes you step-by-step from initial data entry to printing a graph, using the popular Lotus 1-2-3™ package. It starts with putting your information into a 1-2-3 worksheet, runs through a brief manipulation of the data, creates a graph, saves your picture, loads in the PrintGraph disk, and prints a hard copy of the image you created.

Finally, Appendix A lists currently available software programs for your PC. Appendix B and Appendix C are a book and magazine bibliography, respectively.

A Positive Look

Although there are all sorts of things we could use as bad examples, we've tried to stay away from them and stress the positive side of things. The example charts you'll cover are not only clear and simple, but *correct*. Rather than trying to tell you to *not* do this or that, we've left the incorrect thoughts out and tried to show you how your charts and graphs should appear. We want you to know what to look for instead of what to avoid.

The data for all the charts is fictitious. Because there are relationships between data sets for some businesses but not for others, no one enterprise could illustrate all that we have here. The figures are consistent with one another, of course, but are not from a single financial statement.

As you read through each chapter, jot down or mark in the book particular comparisons you feel might be helpful to your own business. Pick out a dozen or so to focus on and chart them monthly. As the year progresses, you'll have a continuing picture of the data that's valid for you. Other ideas will suggest themselves to you as time goes along, so add these new ideas as you find them. Once you start to create these moving pictures of your work, you'll be astonished at the information you'll glean from the images.

Lotus 1-2-3 is a trademark of Lotus Development Corporation

Graph Basics

1

For anyone who struggled back in high school geometry with X and Y plots, a computer program that creates graphs is more than a useful tool, it's a blessing. Once you start working with such a program (and there are many, from the simple and basic to the complex and powerful), you'll find that you don't need to know which axis is the X axis, or which quadrant to put things in. Instead, you can concentrate on exactly what you should be zeroing in on: a study of your own financial information.

Not every graphics program will create perfect graphs for you. That isn't to say the graphs won't be accurate, but rather that there are some design limitations inside of every system, both of the software, which will make your graphs, and of the hardware, which will display and print them for you. For example, not all programs will create bar charts, where the bars run on a horizontal plane. Most will have the capability to make column charts (where columns of information run up and down, like the columns in front of old buildings), and these often can tell the same story as bar charts. The printed charts you get from your system are also hardware-dependent. If you have one of the popular dot-matrix printers, you won't be able to have colored graphs (although you can usually shade your data).

Business Graphics

There are generally considered to be three basic areas involved with business graphics. One is the collection and display (and printing) of historical financial information. The second area is called "analytical graphics" and involves what you'd expect—using graphs to help analyze and understand information. The third area covers ways to use graphs to persuade people to a particular point of view. This can run all the way from explaining to your employees why your labor costs must be cut to using charts to show prospective clients how they can save money if they'll buy what you're selling.

A Historical Look

The first area of business graphics—to gather and summarize financial information—gives the business owner a picture of his or her past history, where the business has been, what it has done, and so on. This approach can embody a broad look at things (total sales on a yearly basis) or focus in very tightly on a specific area (freight costs for just the service department). The main purpose of this examination is the tracking of data, often over a long time frame, with the main thrust to summarize the financial information, to gather it together and make it easier to understand. In many (but obviously not all) cases, this is an ideal use for business graphics, as pictures are often easier to understand than rows and columns of figures.

An Analytical Look

The second area of business graphics is an analytical look at things. Now, rather than just to plot the historical data, you want to use the charts to try to find out *why* things happened. This is a more difficult area to get involved with, but graphs can be particularly useful to help you spot any variations in your data, aberrations caused either by an incorrect entry in a file or more importantly, a *change* in the way your business is doing business.

    For instance, your overhead, as a percentage of your total sales, would be calculated each time you receive a financial statement from your accountant. It might run, on a historical basis, in the 25% to 30% range. You can plot this, and it's easy to plot the average range your overhead amounts to. Once this is done, any aberration in either direction will immediately show up on the chart and serves as a signal to the business owner that something has changed. It might be for the better, of course—if you're charting your overhead as a percentage of your sales, perhaps you've made changes to cause the plotting line to go down. In that case, the graph would show you that whatever steps you took are working. Or, you might see a jump in your overhead percentage, which (hopefully) will motivate you to find out why your overhead is running at a higher percentage of your sales and to do something to correct the situation before it gets worse.

You might want to add a trend line to your information, to translate its data as it relates to the time period on your graph. A trend line indicates the overall direction of the information and will project a continuation of its line into the future, to give you an idea of where the area of your business you're looking at will be in a few months, based on your past history.

One of the nicest things about doing graphs on your microcomputer is that you simply have to ask your plotting program to create and graph a trend line for you (much business software has this capability); you don't have to know or understand the mathematics involved. The basic concept of a trend line is to create a straight line through a group of plotted points to indicate their average direction.

You *do* need to realize the limitations of trend-line forecasting. For example, any trend line you create and plot is based on your past historical data. Current business conditions, however, might be completely different than what happened to you over the last few years. More or better competition, a costly employee contract, a change in your basic market—all contribute to a shift in the state of your business, a change in direction that cannot be foretold with a trend line. The trend line, let's remember, is based only on past information, things that have already happened. As such, it can serve as a guide to what *may* take place in the future, and should be regarded as only that—an indication of future performance, if things stay as they were in the past.

Associated with this is that the more data you have on which to base your trend line, the more accurate it will be in terms of the overall direction of your information. However, if you were to plot your monthly sales totals for the last 20 years, a trend line would be useful to show their average direction, but would be of little value as an indicator of future performance. Much of the information is too old to help you make a projection into the next year. Also, the more information focused on the same subject, the more your trend line will smooth out, or the greater its tendency to be flat. So while the past few years (or accounting periods) won't give you a long base on which to create a trend line, they will serve as a more accurate guide to what you might expect for your sales during the next few months.

Even with all that, however, a trend line is an important piece of statistical data that you need to work with and use. Just as you often can't understand a large array of figures, it's sometimes impossible to examine a graph and learn the general direction the data is moving. There may be so many ups and downs that while you can see the variations, you can't tell if the overall trend is going the way you want it to. A trend line will show you. Also, if you somehow could predict the future of one part or another of your business, it would be a tremendous help, and a trend line at least gives you an indication of where one part of your work may be a few months from now.

Communication

The third major area of business graphics is called "persuasive graphics," and focuses on the use of images to persuade others that a specific course of action should be taken. At first glance it might seem that in most small businesses the only person who needs convincing is the boss—she or he makes all the decisions, so any use of graphs should be directed there. However, any business with employees needs some way to communicate things to those people, to present ideas and concepts over and above what they understand from their paycheck.

For example, if you have more than one location or department, it's worthwhile to spend the time to create graphs to show how one area is performing in relation to the other(s). Who's making money for the business, and who isn't? While you probably wouldn't want to publish profit data on an individual basis, you can do it for each store or department, and your people won't be upset. You might want to put out graphs for your salespeople, to show who's selling the most, both to congratulate your best performer and to encourage your worst. So inside your business are ways you can use graphs to communicate with people. You can take things a step further and use them to tell your sales story to your sales prospects: an individual graph, designed specifically for a prospect, is a powerful selling tool.

What Do You Need?

Each business is different in what it wants to do with business graphics, and that determines how complex (and expensive) your system needs to be. However, you'll find that in most instances, the simpler (and least costly) you can keep things, the more use you'll get out of them.

For internal use, almost any dot-matrix printer that will make graphs is acceptable. While it might be nice to have a better quality of graph to present to your sales prospects and/or employees, more likely than not they haven't seen any fancy computer graphs and so won't think anything else is even available. If you do them on nice paper, the graphs will serve their purpose. All the graphs in this book were made with an EPSON® MX-80F/T (the most popular printer for most microcomputers).

For a large corporation, *presentation quality* graphs might be called for, which means the possible use of a plotter or an ink-jet printer that works in color. Some of these printers aren't super fast, but for someone who wants (or needs) the very best graphic images, they're worth investigating.

The bottom line is simply that you must determine your needs in terms of

EPSON is a registered trademark of EPSON CORPORATION.

software and hardware, and start there. In almost every case, simplicity and speed are a hard combination to beat. If you buy software that's too complex for you and your people to use without constant referral to its manual, and/or hardware that creates beautiful images but takes a half-hour to do just one, you may find you simply won't use the system.

Basic Concepts

A graph is simply a picture of information. For most business applications, we look at *time series data,* where we record, say, sales over a period of time. The whole idea of using a graph is to communicate, to present the information in a more understandable manner than you might with a page filled with figures. Unless the graph does that—communicates with the user in an easy, understandable way—there's no reason even to create it. A graph isn't an end in itself, but rather an aid to our understanding.

The first goal, then, is simplicity. A user should be able to look at a graph and understand it quickly, with little reference to associated data.

One limitation in almost any chart is that a graphed image cannot portray the data to its complete degree of accuracy. No graph allows a reader to look at it and say, "Yes, our sales in May were $56,302.20" (unless the figure is entered on the chart itself). If you must find the exact information, you'll need to go to the data from which the graph was created. A chart gives you a representation of the numerical information, a *feeling* for its quantity, a comparison in relation to other quantities, and an indication of how the information is moving.

Getting Started

Let's begin with a simple line graph, based on this set of data from the records of a fictional business:

SERVICE DEPARTMENT LABOR SALES VOLUME

MONTH	LAST YEAR	THIS YEAR
1	39,503	38,361
2	38,202	34,687
3	42,981	46,602
4	39,027	42,850
5	42,981	49,707
6	48,202	50,981

So that you can see the various stages a graph goes through on your video screen, we'll enter this information into a typical graphics package to see how it handles things. Every program is different, of course, in the way it interacts with the user, so this is something of a generic guide to the basics. The first graph you see will look like this:

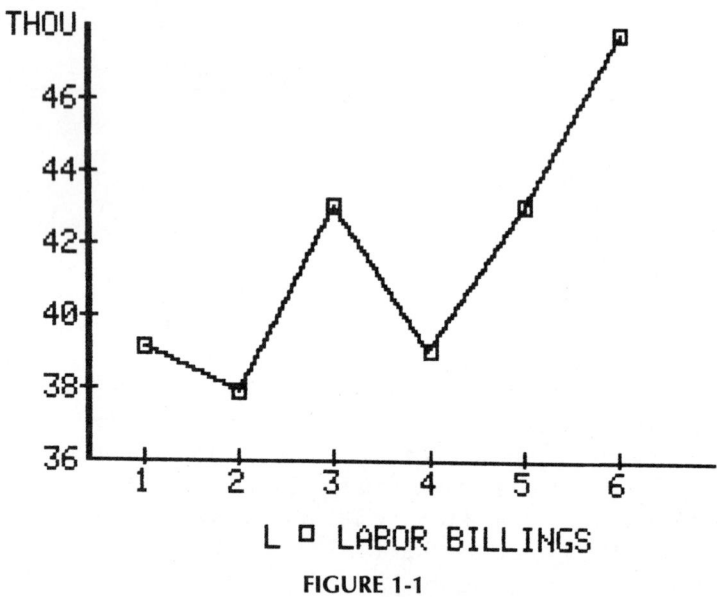

FIGURE 1-1

We'll start with a plot of data from a file called LABOR BILLINGS. The software automatically scales the data and marks the scale points and their descriptions up and down the left side of the picture, in a range from 36,000 to 48,000. The periods between plots run along the bottom of the graph. The bottom of the screen displays a little square box with LABOR BILLINGS after it. This lists the file name the program uses for this set of information on the graph, next to the legend (the square box), to help a user identify it. The "L" in front means that our graph is a line chart.

Unfortunately, the file names we use to keep track of our data don't always make sense to the ultimate user of a graph. In this example, the file name was called LABOR BILLINGS, which doesn't tell whoever looks at the graph what year these figures are from. In most cases, we'll want to change the legend, using the titling capability of our plotting program, rather than use these built-in legends. They can be a little too cryptic.

There are any number of ways you can choose to mark your graphs so they'll properly indicate the frequency of your data. Some software automatically does this for you, although often in a way you didn't intend when you created the chart. If your information has been saved on a yearly basis, for example, most programs list the year and indicate the first letter of each month along the bottom of your picture—J F M A, and so on. This is what people expect to see, after all, and is perhaps the best way to increment time if your charts are on a calendar-year basis—if they start in January and end in the following December.

However, if the information is valuable enough for you to track on a monthly (or quarterly) basis, it's important enough to examine it on a *latest period* basis. That is, you don't want to look at your data only as a calendar year image, but you also need to plot the last 12 months (or whatever you find helpful) of information. Some graphics software gets confused; it can't grasp this concept. For this picture, of the latest *period* of data, it's better to use numbers along the bottom of your graphs, to represent months. The advantage of working with just the numbers is that you can create graphs in the same format, whether the data is for months, quarters, or years. We'll use both the numerical format and the design that puts abbreviations for the period names to indicate the periods charted.

If you were, for example, to save and manipulate your data in a spreadsheet format and then transfer it to a graphics program, you bump into another problem when you save your data on a calendar-year basis. One of the things that does *not* transfer, in many cases, is the periodicity of your data. If you have, for instance, monthly and quarterly information on the same worksheet and save it in the same file, it creates a problem. Often, the graphics package will treat all information in a file exactly the same, and if you have more than one type of data stored there, what do you tell the graph program? It will treat both data sets (quarterly and monthly) the same when it plots them, which (obviously) is not correct.

In effect, then, to overcome this limitation, you're *forced* to save your information in files determined by its periodicity, whether you want to have a large number of files (with the associated added time it'll take to load them) or not. On the other hand, if you compile your information on a simple sequential basis, you can save your files as you want to structure them, rather than being forced into a format dictated by the software. This, as noted, marks your periods as numbers (1 2 3) rather than letters (J F M), but simplifies things greatly.

What may be the best solution to this problem is simply not to rely on the software to put the period indications on your graphs. Instead, use its titling ability to mark your charts in the way they're the most help to you. A good rule of thumb is to use monthly designations (J F M, etc.) when your graph is on a calendar-year basis, and numerical designations (1 2 3, etc.) when its periods are other than that.

If you plan to do a lot of *overlays,* where you'd plot (for example) last year's data compared to current information on the same chart, you need to keep all of your information in the same kind of "blocks" of data. If you like to do things on a yearly basis, then you need to start a file in January and continue it through the following December.

In effect, this means you might want to create more than one file that contains essentially the same data. For example, you might want to examine your sales information on a monthly basis, over the last five years. If you enter it sequentially, with a periodicity of 1 (to keep things simple), most graphics programs won't let you pull out one section and overlay it on another. Since the software doesn't realize you want to compare one year's data to another, it figures it's saving you from a potentially incorrect chart. The obvious solution is to enter each year's data (for this example) on a monthly basis, starting in January and ending in December. Then you can ask for any kind of overlay you find helpful.

For that long-range look at your information, though, you must either have a program that will put each file in sequential order (and thus put the monthly data into a long file) or keep track of the amounts in another file, one that saves the same information, but starts with your first sales figure and ends with your last (even though you might start with data from years ago and end with last month's sales total). Experiment a bit and then you'll know what's right for you.

One problem with using graphs comes at the beginning of the year. Since many data sets are compared on a this-year versus last-year basis, during the early part of the year we don't have much information on which to make a comparison. We have all of last year's data, of course, but at the end of January, we only have one month of the current year to compare that information to. What too often happens is that the graphs don't get made until we're four or five months into the year, so we lose any knowledge we might have gained from our current information.

The answer is, during the early part of a year, to examine the latest 12 months of data. In reality, it's often more useful to examine the latest (whatever period we find helpful) figures, instead of looking at things on just a calendar-year basis. Since your business doesn't start and stop at the end of a year, since it's an ongoing enterprise, why look at things just with a this-year versus last-year approach?

The Zero Line

We also don't want to create a graph without a zero line unless it serves a useful purpose. Often it can (as we'll see), as a narrow focus will help us understand the information on a chart. A graph without a zero line means our data will move differently, as the scale is much tighter. The rise and fall of the lines will be more severe. The one rule is to simply indicate on the graph that it doesn't have a zero line, so the reader knows that the rise and fall of the information will be different than it would be with that zero line in place. So, the first thing we'd want to do with this example is to *rescale* it so we have a zero line. In this case, let's ask the program to scale our graph from 0 to 60,000 to give us a nice range of numbers to work with. This is one of the major benefits of working with graphics on a microcomputer. You can change things instantly, all the way from the number of data points plotted to the scale to the type of graph, and immediately see the effect the new instructions have on your picture.

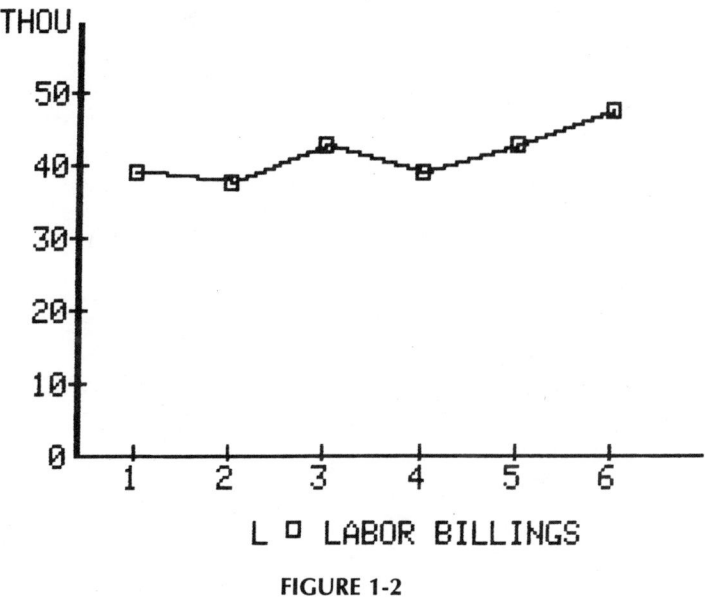

FIGURE 1-2

Now we can see that the line is smoothed out, and the scale, running up and down the left side of the graph, starts at 0 and runs to 60,000. The most obvious difference here is in the rise and fall of the information line of the graph: it's much more even because of the wider scale. Let's add in the second data set.

Figure 1-3 shows both last year's information and the data for the current year. The other addition (besides the plotting line itself) is another legend: L + LABOR LAST. This legend is a bit more descriptive than LABOR BILLINGS was but still doesn't tell the user enough. In fact, in this case the information is unreliable (on purpose, to make a point): LABOR BILLINGS is the file for last year's data, while LABOR LAST was the file name for the current year's information. Since we cannot reliably use file names to indicate which line is which on our graphs, we'll see in a moment how to add more accurate legends and titles.

One difficulty we find here is that although the plotting program uses different legends for each of the data sets (the square box for LABOR BILLINGS and a plus mark for LABOR LAST), it's not really clear as to what's what. We can make things easier to see by asking the software to change the color of the last line we plotted.

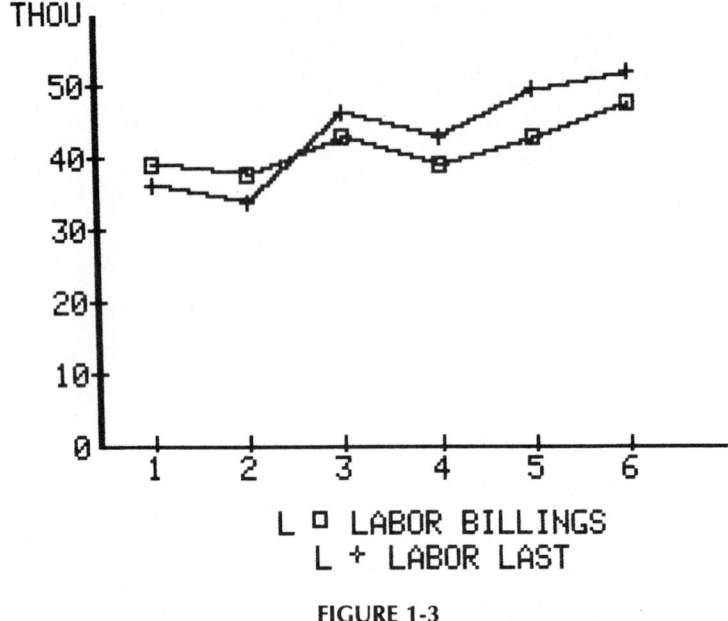

FIGURE 1-3

Figure 1-4 changes the color (in this black-and-white drawing, it looks like a dashed line) of the LABOR LAST data line so it displays and prints as a dashed line, which immediately makes the two lines easier to read and understand. Another legend has been added to the bottom of our graph, without our asking for it—the plotting program does it automatically. That's another weakness in letting the software decide what's *said* on a graph. In this case, since we told the program to overlay the last data set we plotted with a dashed line, it also added a legend, a small circle (○)—that's what the L ○ LABOR LAST means at the very bottom of the graph. Now unless we change the legends to reflect what we want them to say, what will users think? They won't be able to understand this graph, because three legends are listed while only two lines are plotted.

In any case, this change made the desired correction for us, as we can clearly see the two data lines. The next step is to add a border and/or grid lines to help make things clearer. A border on a graph connects it and shows the user where the information starts and stops. You almost always should have a border, and most programs will add one for you automatically. The only reason to add a grid is to make a graph easier to understand.

One disadvantage of using a microcomputer to create your graphic images is that the programs often add *too many* grid lines to a picture. In this case, with only six months of information, grid lines that run both horizontally and vertically probably wouldn't detract from the graph. In many cases, though, particularly

GRAPH BASICS

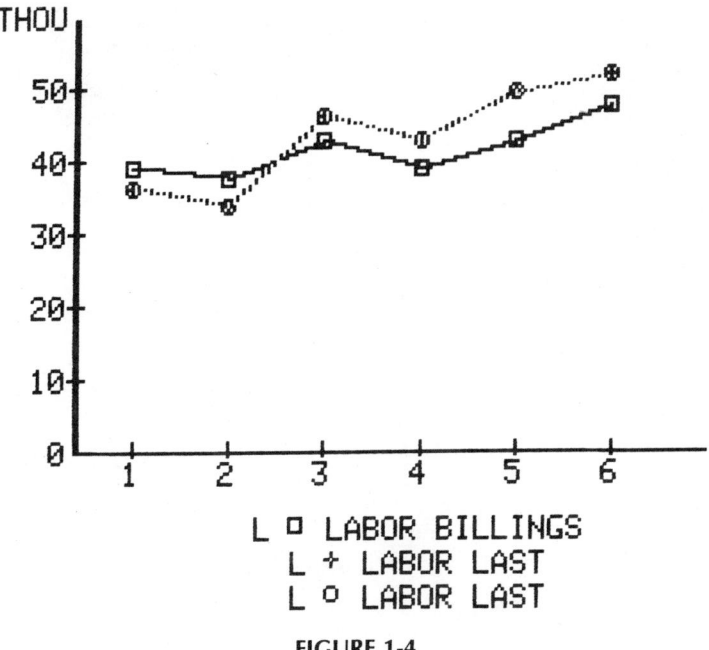

FIGURE 1-4

when you have years and years of data plotted, it doesn't help to have little dots running up and down on the graph to indicate each month. A good rule of thumb is to almost always use horizontal grid lines, because they relate to the numerical data on the chart, but to rarely use vertical lines, because we can usually see, when we need to, where each month or quarter or yearly plot is. Let's add a border and horizontal grid lines to our chart, as shown in Figure 1-5.

For the first time, our picture is starting to look like a real graph. The grid lines make a big difference in our understanding of the information. In this case, it's easy to see that the data represented by these two lines runs in about the 30,000 to 50,000 range. One of the lines crept a bit above the 50,000 mark on its last plot, but overall, the data stayed within the range noted. Horizontal grid lines like these allow the user to spot any real deviation from the average; if one of these plots had dropped to, say, 25,000, it would be more than obvious.

We don't really miss vertical grid lines here; if we want to pick out one month or another, it's easy enough to do so without the additional lines.

Now it's time to put titles and other information on the chart, so the user will know what he or she is looking at.

Figure 1-6 adds two titles: a top line that tells what the information represents, and a side title to let us know what the scale figures mean. Rather than write DOLLARS (or whatever the scale marks indicate, like PERCENT), keep

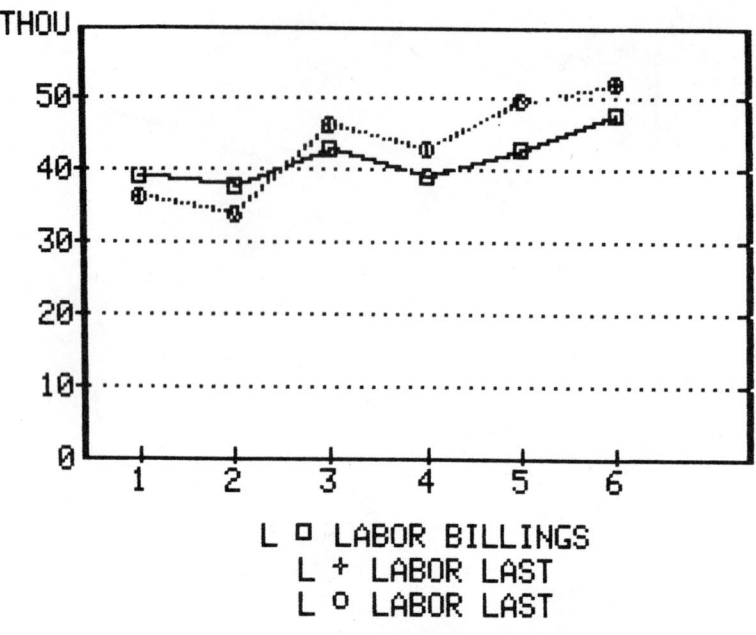

FIGURE 1-5

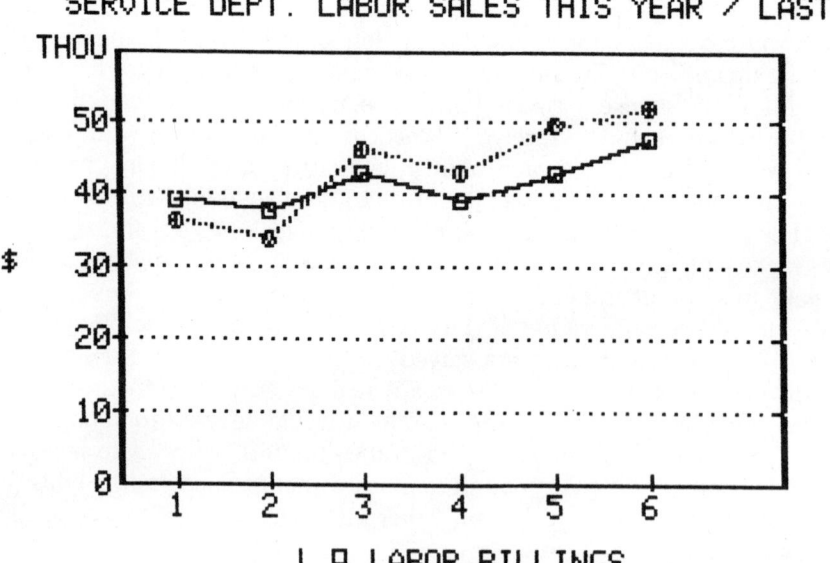

FIGURE 1-6

GRAPH BASICS

things simple whenever you can; the "$" sign here gets the message across and is fast to comprehend. Let's add some information to the body of the chart to help us understand it, as we've done in Figure 1-7.

Rather than to rely just on a legend at the bottom of the graph when we compare two or more data sets, let's indicate what they are on the chart itself. In this case, CURRENT SALES and SALES LAST YEAR are placed by the lines that represent their data, which makes it easy to see what each line means. Finally, let's add some information on the bottom of the graph, again, to help understand things, and see the result in Figure 1-8.

We've now told the user what time period he or she is looking at. The top of the graph indicates that we're comparing data from last year and this year, and at the bottom ← MONTHS → specifies the periods charted. We're using this same format throughout the book; in your own work, you can use whatever you find helpful and mark things where they're the most value to you and your work. As noted above, you may find it more helpful to list the periods you graph by the first letter of their month. If you do charts with varying time frames though, you're probably better off to use the numerical format to mark all periods. All of your images should be constant in terms of what the user sees; the data must be responsible for the changes in what is perceived from the picture.

We added a bit more at the bottom here, too, to explain the difference between the solid line and the dashed line.

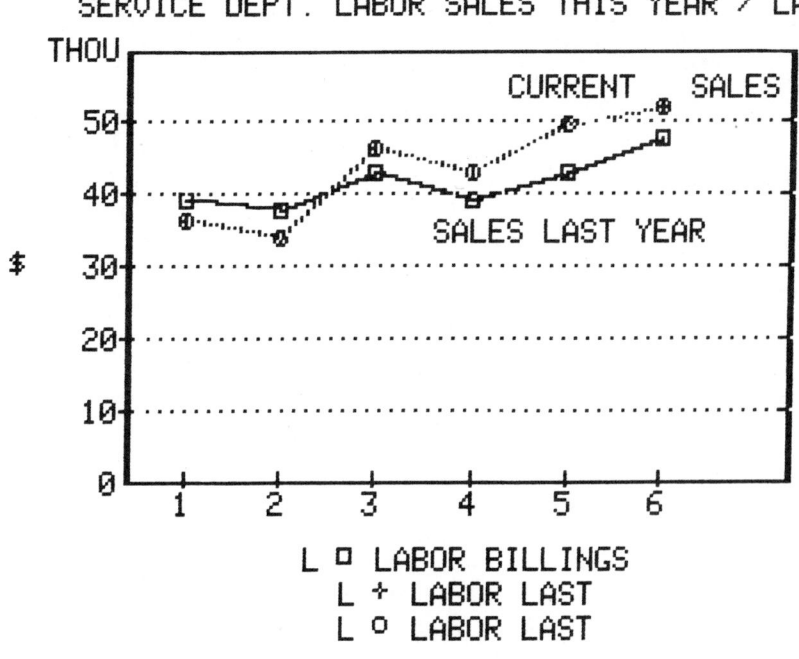

FIGURE 1-7

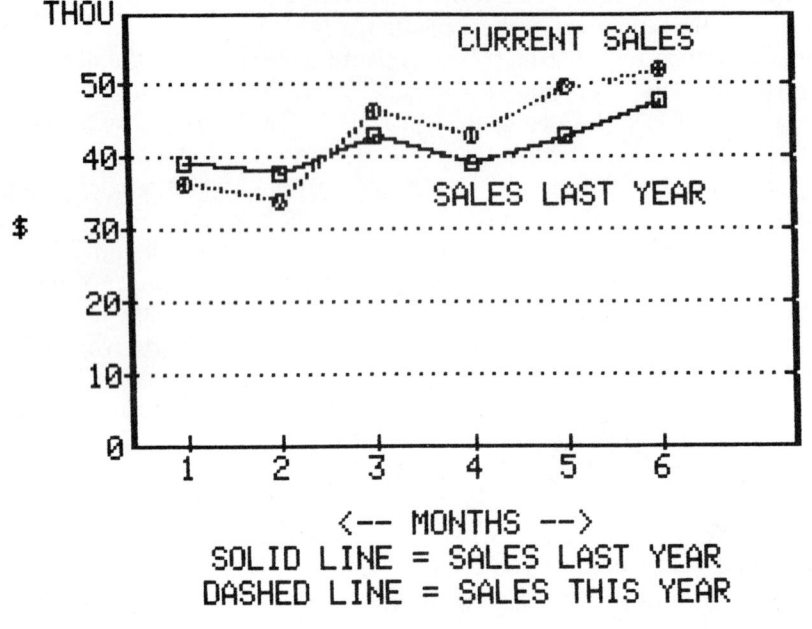

FIGURE 1-8

The steps you go through to create a graph for your own information won't follow this exact sequence—every program is different—but will contain the same basic elements. The important thing—the whole idea, really—is to end up with a chart people can understand quickly, that explains what you want it to cover, and that is clear. A user should be able to look at it and grasp the information without having to ask all sorts of questions like, "What does this line mean?" or "What's that mark, there?"

A Closer Look

A logical extension of this thinking is to eliminate the zero line and plot the data on a much tighter scale. This gives the user the additional advantage of a close look at things and can make the information more understandable. For instance, while we can see where current labor sales and last year's labor sales crossed each other in Figure 1-8, we might be able to understand things better if we examine it with a tighter focus.

Figure 1-9 tightens the scale we've been using to one that runs from $30,000

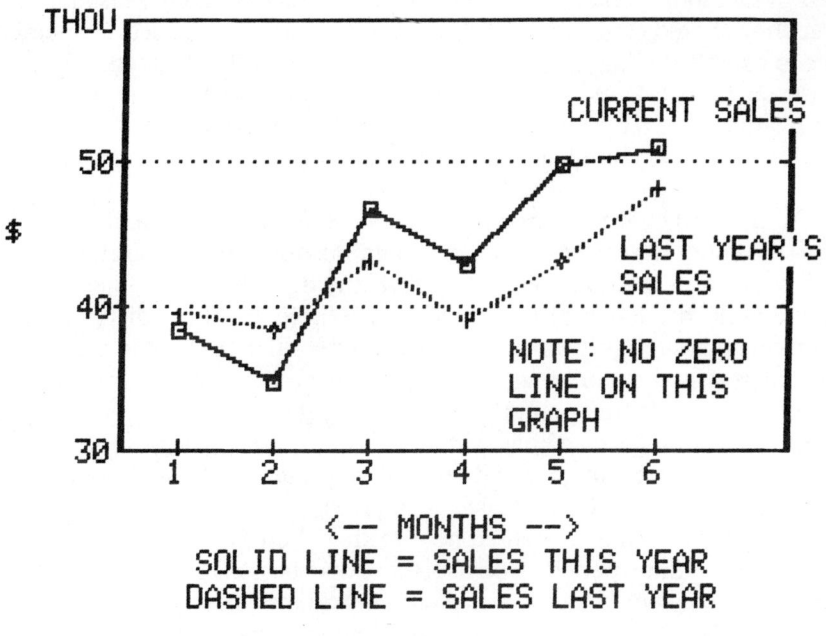

FIGURE 1-9

to $60,000. As such, the information rises and falls much more rapidly. It's also easier to spot where this year's data overtook and passed last year's information. Besides the change in scale, there are two other things different about this graph. One is its small note in the lower right-hand corner, to indicate that there is no zero line. Also, the shading of the lines is reversed for this example—the solid line is for the current information, while the dashed line represents last year's data over the same period of time. The purpose here is to indicate that it really doesn't matter *what* line is what color (or shading), as long as the graph is readable and the information understandable.

A Historical Look Using a Line Chart

One other advantage a line chart gives you is the capability of examining your financial information over a long period of time. Once you have the data in your microcomputer system, you can decide what sections of it to chart, how long a range of data you'd like to examine.

This kind of study lends itself to all sorts of analysis; probably the most obvious are those variations that occur on a seasonal basis. Since the data is plotted over a long period of time, if your business does have seasonal ups and downs, they should come at about the same time each year. Once a general trend has been established it's easy to spot any variations in the data (caused either by an error in the data entry process, or an aberration in the way your operation is doing business). A long-range look at your data is always helpful, just to get an overall feel for how things are going now compared to a historical look at your work.

Figure 1-10 charts the monthly sales volume for our fictional business over the last 36 months. As we know, we could do much the same thing for a 36-month period on a calendar-year basis, if we find that's helpful. While sales appear to stay around the $40,000 per month level, there are three distinct bumps in the information—roughly during months 6-8, months 18-20, and months 30-32. If this chart was done on a yearly basis, with the first plot for January and the last for December (three years later, of course), these correspond to the summer months. As the business owner who created this chart, you'd know what these last 36 months represent, so you'd not only see your sales take those nice jumps, you'd also know *when* the increases took place.

The information is presented here to show how you can create graphs that cover different time periods yet use the same basic format. If this were the information from your business, you'd obviously know when the graph was printed, so you'd know what this 36-month period represented, whether done on a calendar-year basis or started in March (or whenever). The important thing is the

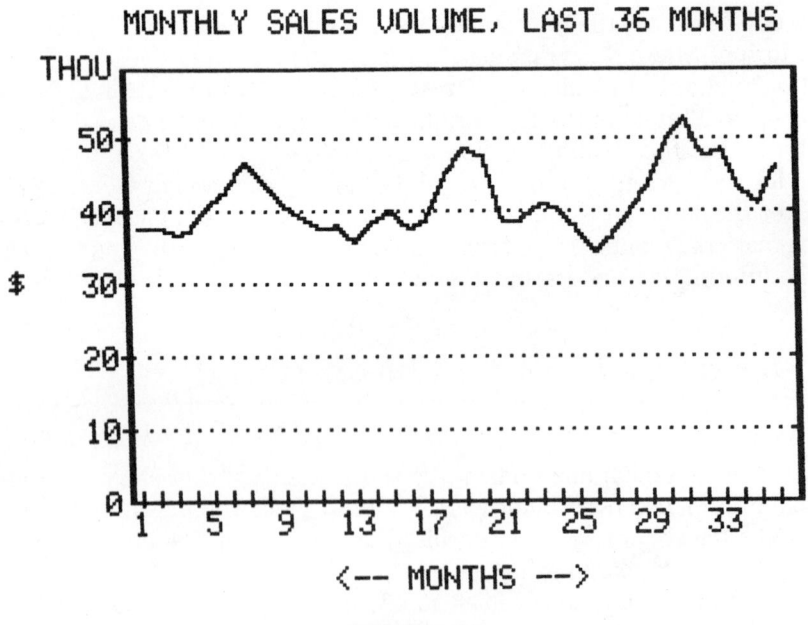

FIGURE 1-10

GRAPH BASICS

basic concept: a historical examination of your business (in this case, its sales) gives you a feel for your own business cycle. In this particular example, too, recent data is heading upward, sales are improving—a good sign.

A Trend Line

You can ask your plotting program to add a trend line to your time series charts to give you an idea of the overall direction the graphed data has been taking and to make a projection into the near future where the information will be, assuming things like business conditions remain the same. With most trend-line information, you shouldn't expect it to predict too far into the future. If you derive your trend line from, say, 12 months of data, you shouldn't request more than about a three-month projection. If you have 24 or more months of data, you can ask for perhaps a six-month projection and still expect to be reasonably accurate. As noted above, if you base your information on a very long period of time, you run the risk of a major change in the business climate that the trend line cannot, of course, know about.

Figure 1-11 plots a trend line (as noted on the graph), based on the 36

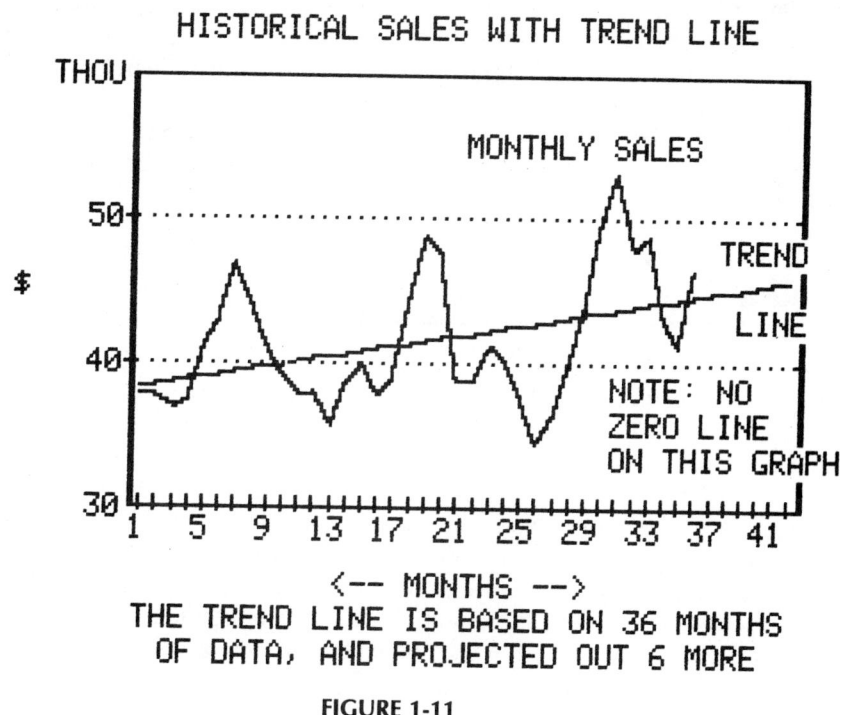

FIGURE 1-11

months of recent information, and projects it for six more months. The data we've been examining is also plotted on the graph. While you really couldn't tell from the information itself (as shown in Figure 1-10) what the overall direction of the data was, the trend line gives you the picture you'd want to see if this were your business. The general trend of monthly sales is rising, which means your sales department (even if that department is just *you*) is doing something right.

You could carry things further and add in an inflation rate to your sales information. Are your sales rising faster than inflation? Or are your sales not keeping pace with the rate of inflation?

Line Charts

From these examples, we can see that a line chart is particularly suited to show the *movement* of changes in the data over a period of time. It's also useful (perhaps the best of all) to show a comparison between two sets of data and for looking at information when it has a trend line calculated and charted. There is a major disadvantage to a line chart in that you can only work with, at best, perhaps three sets of information. More than three lines (and often, more than just two), and the graph cannot be understood. So you're limited in the number of things you can examine at any one time. As with most restrictions, though, you can turn this around and make something good out of it. It gives you the chance to examine the same data in relation to other things, on an *individual* basis—two lines on each chart. This, instead of limiting you, makes things clearer and easier to understand.

Since most business information is done with a comparison of the data to the time that's gone by, a line chart is probably the most useful tool you have in your graphics arsenal.

Windows

Often we're called on to look at data sets that differ widely in terms of their raw numbers. One comparison most businesses like to make is between their advertising and their monthly sales. How are your advertising dollars working? Does more advertising create more sales? The problem when you try to examine these items is that (for example) your sales might run $30,000 or $40,000 per month, while you may spend less than $500 each month on advertising.

There are two solutions to this difficulty. One (we'll examine this in more detail when we run into it) is to multiply or divide one figure or the other, to get them on the same scale so they can be plotted on one graph. Once that's done, it makes it easy to determine if there's any relationship between the figures you chart.

The other solution, and one many graphics programs make available to you, is to create two *windows* on your screen, and plot each item in its own little graph. Then, when the two are compared, you can look for any correlation.

Figure 1-12 illustrates this approach. The top graph covers advertising, on a scale that increments in $200 steps, over a six-month period. The bottom graph shows sales for the same period, although (since the numbers are much larger to start with) each grid line jumps in $20,000 increments.

At first look, there may not seem to be any relationship between these two figures, but we always need to keep in mind exactly what we're comparing. In this case, we really shouldn't expect the advertising we buy now to produce sales *today*. More likely, there will be some lag time before the advertising has its effect, before the sales can be made and recorded. If we look at these charts with that in mind, we get a different impression. The upper graph shows a major increase in advertising in month 3. The sales graph shows a big jump in dollar volume for month 4. Likewise, the advertising graph shows the business spent about the same during the following month (month 4), and the sales chart indicates that sales remained at a high level during its next month (month 5).

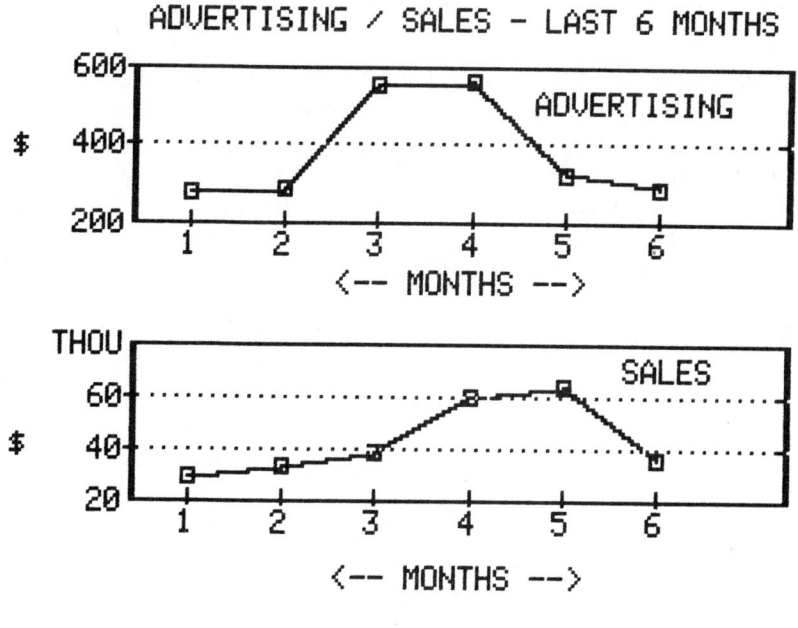

FIGURE 1-12

When advertising was reduced to its original level, in month 5, we can see its effect on the sales the business made during month 6: sales went down. Clearly, this business has a one-month lead time before its advertising starts to work (at least for the period under study).

A more effective way to examine this data is to push one of the figures ahead of the other, so that, for example, the advertising your business does in May will correspond to the sales it records in June. When we look at it later on, that's exactly what we'll do. The purpose of this illustration is twofold. First, we want to show you another kind of line chart, the window chart, and how you might want to use it. Second, we must always know what we're examining and what kind of a result we might expect to see. We won't know what the resulting graphs will tell us, of course, but when we examine advertising and sales, we obviously want to find any correlation between the two, to see if more advertising creates more sales, and to see what kind of a lead time our business should expect before those sales start to come in. As we'll learn when we look closer at this relationship, once we know the lead time our business has, we can test to see what level of advertising we should have—how much we should spend before we reach the point of diminishing returns.

Pie Charts

After that detailed discussion of line graphs, here's an easy one: pie charts. Almost everyone can relate to this kind of graph, as it is such a familiar concept. The ideal use for a pie chart is to compare a number of data items to their combined sum to show how each relates to the total of whatever you're charting. For sales, you might want to know where your sales come from in terms of departments or locations or salespeople. For overhead, you may want to see where your dollars are spent. You can look at a large area (total sales) or an individual item (monthly advertising for March).

Figure 1-13 is a pie chart that covers the sales by the different product lines our fictional business handles. Since a pie chart is ideal to see how each individual item relates to the whole (in this case, our total sales), it lends itself to a percentage breakdown. While we don't know if these percentages are what they should be or not (we'd need more information), this graph shows us the situation for a particular period of time.

With a pie chart, its easy to see how each individual area relates to our total sales for the year. In this case, since retail and contracts are the major areas, we want to highlight them, so we've shaded retail as dark and contracts as plain white, so they'll both stand out.

One major limitation of a pie chart is the number of slices you can display effectively. Any more than about six and the pie starts to look like a wagon wheel; it's simply cut into too many pieces.

SALES BY PRODUCT LINE

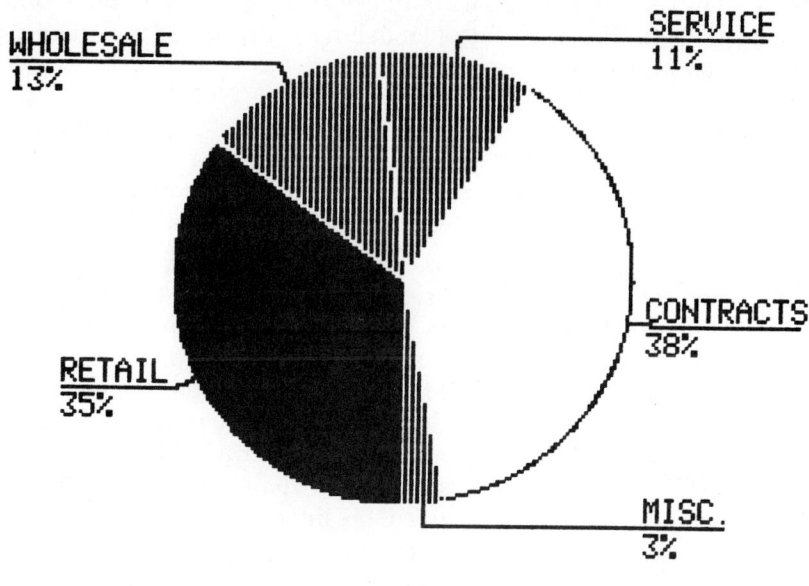

FIGURE 1-13

If your graphics program allows detached slices for your pie charts, take advantage of that capability. It allows you to highlight one specific slice, which is often exactly what you want to do. Along with the colors or shadings you can use, it gives you another way to make your point.

Editorials

Since you can do things like shade a pie chart to your liking or make one line on a line graph thicker or darker than another, this is a good place to mention that graphs, because they're a form of communication, are also a way to get your own views across. Both the selection of the type of graph you use and the information you chart (including the periods graphed), in a sense, *editorialize*. There's nothing particularly wrong with this, and it has its most useful application when you use graphs as a tool to persuade others that a specific course of action is the right thing to do.

For example, if you have one store that's consistently more profitable than your other locations, you might give some thought to the best way to illustrate this fact to your employees. In Chapter 12, where we look at ways to use business graphics as a sales tool, we'll see how to use charts and their information in an effort to get our sales message across. When you examine graphs that someone else creates, always look at them with an eye to determining if the information is being presented in the most objective manner, or if there's a particular point the person is trying to make.

Bar and Column Charts

We like to think of column charts as the columns of old buildings—the columns go up and down. There's a similar chart called a "bar chart" that some graphics programs can provide, where the bars go across your screen or page instead of up and down. In many cases, one chart can substitute for the other.

Bar and column charts are ideal for showing the relationships among items over a brief period of time and for indicating the total quantity of each item in a data set. Whereas line charts are more effective in showing how data moves over time, particularly a long period, bar and column charts are uniquely qualified to give you a feeling for the actual quantity of the information you graph. They don't compare each individual item to the whole (as a pie chart does) but rather concentrate on the numerical value of the data itself.

Figure 1-14 is a column chart that details the truck repair costs for our

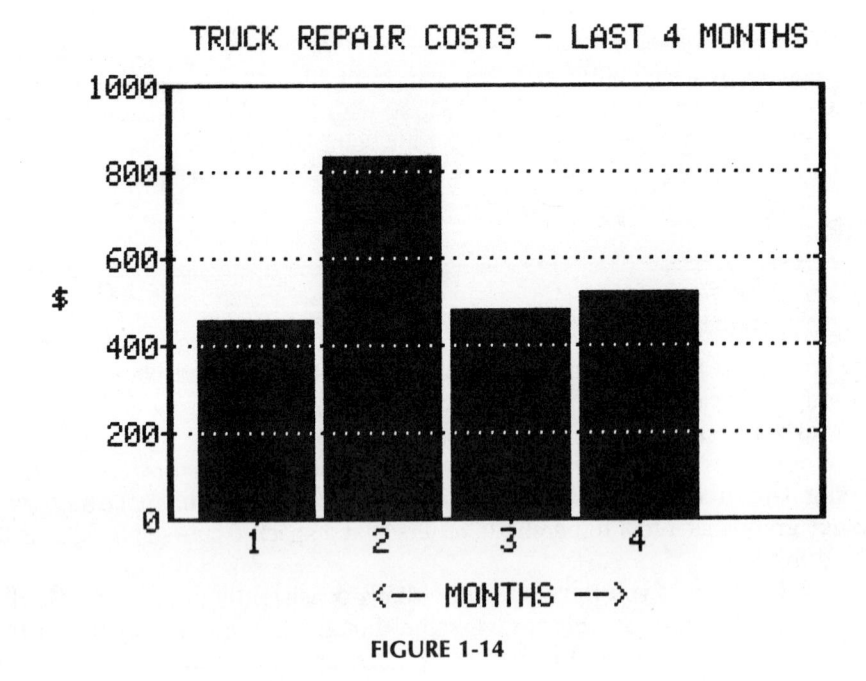

FIGURE 1-14

fictitious business over the last four months. We get a much better feeling for the quantities under study with this graph than we would with, say, a line chart. We can *feel* the dollars we've spent to keep our trucks on the road.

Obviously, there's an unusual rise in month 2. When the business owner spots something like this, she or he will want to dig into the details of the business to find out why costs rose so much during this period. An easy way to do this might be to plot, on this same chart, the number of service calls those trucks handled during each period, to see if there's a relationship between the number of calls people make and the repair costs for their trucks. The same thing could be done, if you had the data, on a per mile basis.

This gives us more information, and there's an obvious correlation between the number of service calls our business took care of during a month and the total it cost our company for truck repairs, as shown in Figure 1-15.

These two charts start an interesting line of thought. First, we may not have paid much attention to our truck repair costs unless we'd graphed them, as we did in Figure 1-14. Once that was done, the jump in the second month's costs indicated a possible problem. After some thought, we broke down our service calls on a monthly basis, and plotted them as a line on the same chart. The more calls, the more repair costs we had.

If we take our thinking a bit further, it looks like there's a relationship in

TRUCK REPAIR COSTS / SERVICE CALLS MADE

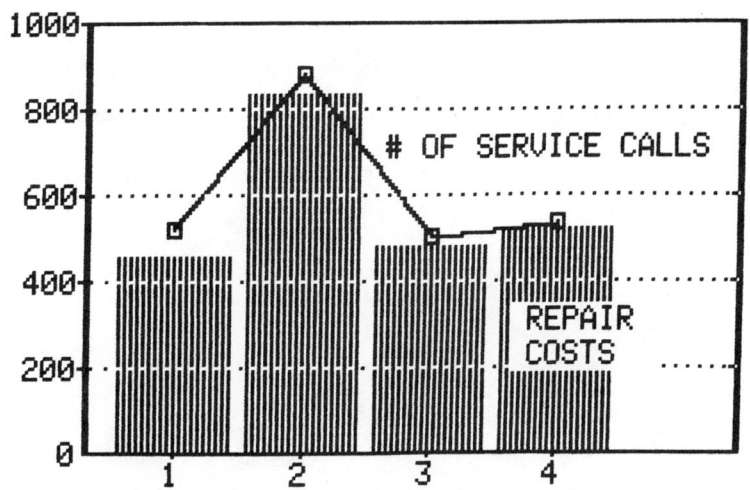

<-- MONTHS -->
THE BARS INDICATE TRUCK REPAIR COSTS
THE LINE IS FOR THE # OF SERVICE CALLS MADE

FIGURE 1-15

terms of the *number* of service calls and the *dollar total* for repair costs. They appear to be about the same. This leads to another idea: let's track both data sets for a period of time to determine if this holds true. If it does, we can predict our truck repair costs each month by the number of service calls we handle during that time. We can track the service calls daily, too, on a cumulative basis, so we'll have a good idea of what our repair bills will be at the end of the month.

All this is noted to illustrate another aspect of graph basics: one idea almost always leads to another. One graph tells you its story, but that gives you an idea about something else, and so on. In this particular example, you might want to study your business even more closely, to see how your truck repair costs compare to the service calls you do (for instance) within a 30-mile radius of your office. Do your trucks start to cost more to repair when you do a lot of long-range service work? Carry the idea even further: are there some preventative maintenance things you could be doing to lower your truck repair costs? How would you chart them so you'd know you were on the right track?

Everything's Not Roses

In any business environment, no one makes money all the time on every product they sell. A column chart can illustrate the rise and fall of our fortunes.

Figure 1-16 is the first graph we've seen with data *below* the zero line. As

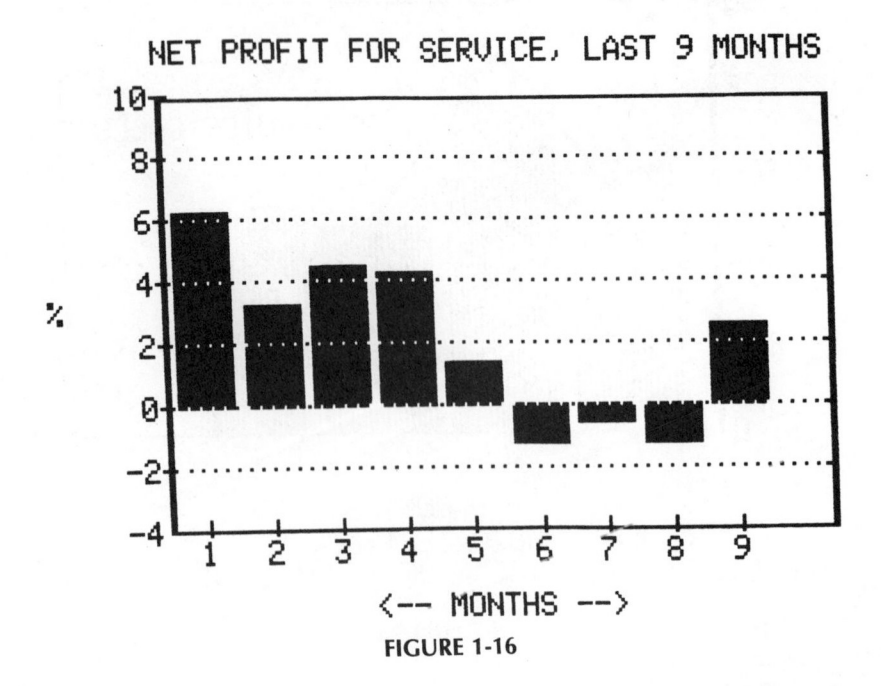

FIGURE 1-16

such, it makes it easy to pick out those months where our business made money and where it operated in the red. The column chart gives us a good grasp for the numerical information itself, too; we can *feel* those good early profits.

Stacked Columns

A stacked column chart (also called a stacked bar chart) takes the information from more than one data set and adds it together. Then it plots each total as a combination of the two, with each separated with different colors or shadings.

Figure 1-17 is a stacked column chart where each column plots two data sets—labor and parts sales for the repair department of our fictional business.

In effect, each bar indicates the combined labor and repair parts sales for each of the nine months plotted. What's obviously different about this chart (as compared to a standard column graph) is that the two individual items each can be seen as well as their combined total.

This approach works particularly well when you have only two items to graph and when one of those remains pretty stable. In this example, the lower data set (labor sales) runs about $10,000 per month—there's very little variation in the repair department labor our fictional business recorded. Thus, when it's combined with the parts sales for the business, the rise and fall we see at the

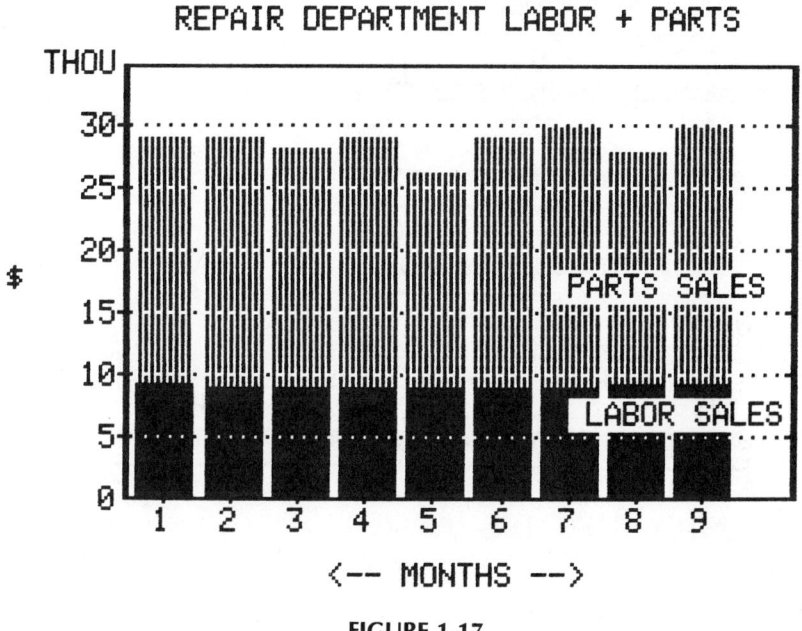

FIGURE 1-17

top of the graph is derived from the *parts sales* area of things, and in fact, we learn that our total each month varies because of the difference in parts sales.

A stacked graph is almost useless when more than one of the data sets has wide fluctuations. While the top of the graph—the total of all the items for each month—will vary in a way you'll be able to see and understand, the individual demarcations of the data will be impossible to grasp. Generally you should use this kind of chart when only *one* of your data sets has significant variations, and put it on top.

Figure 1-18 is called a "bar chart" and uses horizontal bars to illustrate its data. Not all software programs can create such a chart, although if you find you can use its unique view of things, you can put your information into a column chart format, print your graph, and simply turn your paper sideways.

This approach is particularly helpful for data that's growing or shrinking on a regular basis. Figure 1-18 is a good example of this—each figure gets larger as the months run down the page. This format, like its close cousin the column chart, is ideal to use to help you grasp the quantities involved. It's less useful over a long period of time (a line chart would be more effective) and also isn't of much help to compare more than one data set to another.

It's almost always necessary to have a zero line on a bar or column chart.

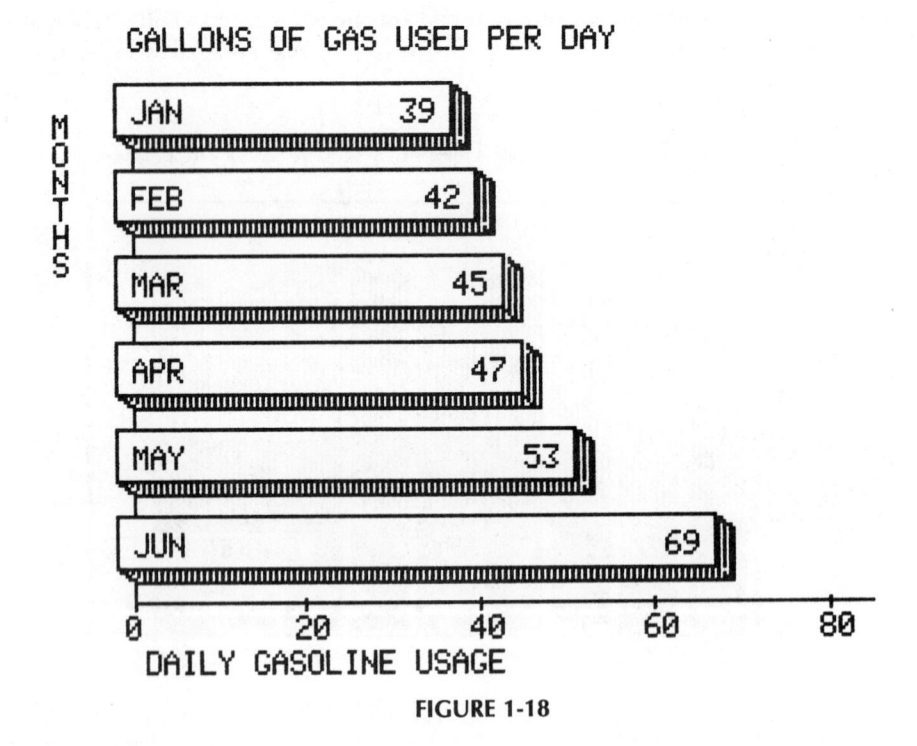

FIGURE 1-18

While a line graph can be used without a zero line to take a closer look at the movement of the information, bar and column charts provide their meaning through the length of their lines. As such, they're close to useless without a zero line.

Poor Examples

Our feeling is that people generally get what they think about but not necessarily what they want. Have you ever picked up something valuable and thought to yourself, "I'd better not drop this," or "My wife will kill me if I break this," and then—inexplicably—drop the darn thing? Part of the reason for our clumsiness is what we had going through our mind at the time—instead of thinking about how we should hold the item to protect it, we were thinking about *dropping it*. So, we did.

There are all sorts of stories about major league baseball pitchers who were told, in a critical game situation, "Don't pitch this batter high and inside," and they went right out and gave the batter that exact pitch. Why? Because they were thinking about it. Lou Tice, a remarkable man who provides all kinds of motivational ideas from his Pacific Institute in Seattle, Washington, tells the story about when he coached high school football. He was telling his young quarterback that he'd better not hold his hands like this, or he wouldn't get a good grip on the ball, and he'd better not hold them like that, or when the center snaps the ball it might sprain a finger, and he shouldn't hold them this way, and he ought not to hold them that way . . . until the quarterback finally turned around and asked, "Well, how the heck *do* you hold them?"

The point is, all the graphs we've used as illustrations in this book are what we believe are examples of what graphs should look like. This isn't to say that the *data* will always be the way a business owner would like it to be; on the contrary, many of the examples use data that tell the businessperson that he or she has a problem with the company, and that something needs to be done to change the situation. But the charts themselves are done as they should be. We didn't use poor examples of charts, because then you might think about the negative side of things and create poor graphs for your own information. We feel it's more helpful to give you positive information, with examples of how to do things right.

If you'd like to see some good examples of poor charts, there's an excellent book that both shows and tells you what *not* to do for graphs. It's called *Statistical Graphics* by Calvin F. Schmid, and it's published by John Wiley & Sons, 605 Third Avenue, New York, NY 10158. Mr. Schmid also has a lot of good information on the overall design of graphics—how wide, for example, each column should be in a column graph, the overall size a line graph should be based on the relationship

Area Charts

One useful graph for showing cumulative data is an area chart. This is basically a line chart, with the area below the line filled in with color or shading. It gives you more of a feeling for the total quantity of the information than a line graph does, and because it's connected together, it gives you a better understanding of the data as a whole than a column chart can.

Figure 1-19 illustrates the cumulative savings you might expect if you implement either Proposal A or Proposal B. The title tells you that you're looking at the product your local utility company sells you in the form of electricity: kilowatt-hours of use. The chart is plotted on a yearly basis, with the information projected for five years.

Since the two proposals are charted in different shades, one is easy to compare to the other. If users have some idea of the cost per kilowatt-hour of

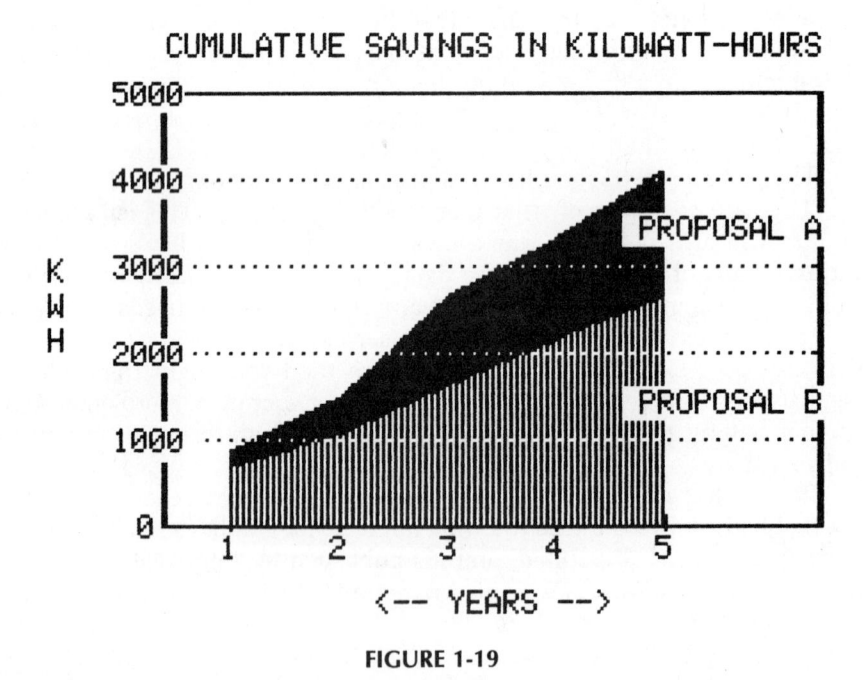

FIGURE 1-19

electricity they have to pay, it's a simple process to translate this data into dollar amounts.

You could do exactly the same thing with a line chart, although you wouldn't get the same feeling for the quantities involved; the area chart helps because its *areas* are painted in.

As such, an area chart is ideal for plotting large quantities of information. It's not as useful as a line chart for charting the movement of that data over a period of time, nor as helpful as a column/bar chart to indicate separate periods of information. For cumulative data, however, it's ideal.

The Monthly Process

Without going into exact detail (since your business is different than anyone else's), it's important to note that graphs are just another tool for businesses to use, but if they're going to help you, they need to be used regularly. It won't do you any good to read this book, pick out six graphs to make, find the information for them from your records, plot and print the graphs, and think about them. You must continue on: just as your business is ongoing, your use of business graphics must also be ongoing. Yes, one thing will lead to another, and one idea will make you pause for a moment and then plot something else another way, so your basic library of graphs might grow for some time. But the main thrust of business graphics is to find those that you find helpful, and then plot their information every month (or quarter, or year—whenever you calculate it). In fact, most software programs are simple enough now that once you know which graphs you want and where the information can be drawn from, you can probably find someone in your office to create them for you every month. You need to keep a running library of your charts, too, so you can compare one thing to another.

All this isn't to say that working with graphs and their associated calculations and printed copies is an altogether easy process. While it's a long way from what you may be doing now—plotting on blue-lined grid paper by hand—it's still work, and still takes time. There's an effort involved, as you need to think about what you want to examine, look at it from various directions until you discover what's important to you, create the graphs, and play with their scales and titles until they're right for you, and so on.

However, once the basic work is done—much like the initial data entry into a file handling system—the rest is downhill. Now, when you know the charts you want every month, you list them and their data, and once the information has been gathered and calculated, you (or your office people) create and print the graphs. More thought and effort will be required when you hit upon a new idea, of course, and pursue it, but for the most part, the hard work will be over. And never forget that even while you're doing the drudge part of the process—

finding the information and playing with it on your video screen until you get the results you need—it's still almost *magic* as you watch your data transformed from rows and columns of figures into a simple, understandable graph.

Other Graphs

There are other graph forms that you should be aware of, but ones we're not going to go into detail about. One is a *scatter graph,* which does basically what a line graph does but without the lines connecting each plotting point. One possible use in business would be to look at warranty claims or the failure rate for a particular item over a period of time. We feel the examples we'll work with in Chapter 12 for this kind of application are more effective than a scatter graph. It might be useful for you if you'd like to see where your customers are coming from, and create a graph with the areas marked to show where your business does its business, and then *scatter* the dots that show the concentration of your customers.

A *high/low graph* is designed to show the movement of prices (particularly those from the stock market). This might be useful to you if you track such things, especially as they relate to your business. For statistical purposes, the high/low chart also can be used to indicate the mean or the average of each plotted point. If you'd find it helpful to chart, for example, the contract sales your business made that showed your highest contract sale, your lowest, and the average amount, you'll find the high/low chart to be a good way to do so.

A *pictorial chart* uses little images of people (or cans of food, or animals) to portray the same data as a bar or column chart. In terms of financial data for your stockholders, a pictorial chart might be useful. Unfortunately, there's little microcomputer software that can handle such things.

There are one or two programs available that will create *map charts,* and while they have some specialized uses, we don't cover them here.

One increasing trend in graphics software is the capability to create charts with a three-dimensional appearance—to give the lines or columns a sense of depth. In many cases, if this is done properly, it's a useful tool and adds to our understanding of the information.

One Last Limitation

Many of the newer, more complex software programs that become available will have the capability of using semilogarithmic charts. These are designed specifically to show proportional changes in your data. A purely arithmetic chart compares absolute differences in the data. If the dollars on a graph rise $10 from one plotting point to the next, they're shown as a $10 increase. The semilogarithmic chart concentrates on the percentage change of the data. If one data point jumps from $10 to $20, it has risen 100%.

In terms of statistical analysis, the semilog chart has some distinct advantages over those that are purely arithmetical. Some include a function that can calculate the percentage difference between numbers within a data set, and we'll use that when we examine advertising and sales. However, it's a long way from the semilogarithmic approach. If the graphics program you use on your PC includes a semilog chart in its graphic arsenal, take advantage of the capability. It gives you a unique and useful new way to look at your numbers.

Summing Up

Because your microcomputer can handle immense amounts of data and quickly convert it into charts and graphs according to your specifications, it serves as an ideal tool for business graphics. Your financial information is constantly being updated and analyzed, checked and projected, all in an effort to help your operation become more profitable. Business graphics go hand in hand with this. You generally want to look at your financial records from a *descriptive* standpoint (to summarize its information), which leads to an *analytical* examination of the data (to search for *why* things happen as they do), and sometimes, to a *persuasive* approach, (to get your ideas across to someone else). Business graphs are an ideal way to help with all three areas.

Making a graph starts with the information itself, and rather than presenting a list of rules to follow, we've included them in the text as ideas to use. You simply start with one plotted line, make sure the scale is one that you want, and build from there. We found it's often helpful to chart things with numbers along the bottom to indicate the passage of time (months, quarters, years), rather than letters of the alphabet, so all the graphs can be done in a consistent format.

Things like grid lines and a border all add to readability and how easy a graph is to understand. Grid lines in particular can be used to highlight an area: if your overhead averages 23% of your sales, why not scale a graph that shows overhead with that 23% mark running across the picture? That way, it's easy to spot any variation. You can widen this approach, too, and scale your graphs (and their resulting grid lines) to mark a *range* of information. If your advertising generally runs between 3% and 4% of your sales, ask your plotting program to mark these figures on any graph that uses advertising as a percentage of sales. You'll instantly spot any aberration.

Titles and legends are also vital to understanding a graph—after all, if the user doesn't know what the lines or plot marks or bars mean, he or she won't have any idea what the graph says. Since many of the file names our plotting program collects its information from might not mean anything to the end user, it's worthwhile to spend the extra time to put the information on the chart, where someone can quickly spot it. Likewise, we want to shade or color the areas we want to highlight to make things clearer. The whole idea is that the difference in graphic images should come from the changes in the data itself, rather than any changes in the format or design of the chart and its titles.

A line chart lends itself to a study of information as that data moves over time—the most common use of business graphics. Whenever you think about a graph you'd like to create, the first step is to consider if a line graph is the best way to portray the information; most of the time, it will be. You want to have no more than two or three lines on each graph. You can adjust the scale of a line graph (be sure to note it on the new picture) to get a closer look at things. Line graphs are also useful for a long-range historical look at your business data; with grid lines to indicate the range something normally travels in, you can quickly pick out anything that's heading out of line.

Line charts also lend themselves to the use of a trend line, which shows you the overall direction your data's been heading, along with a projection of where it'll probably go.

Pie charts are the proper tool to use when you want to examine how a number of items relate to the total of their particular category. Since the pie represents the sum of all its slices, you get an indication of how each individual item relates to the whole.

Bar and column charts are basically the same thing, with the direction of their information changed. Column charts are especially helpful to indicate quantities—the thick columns drive the point home. It's helpful at times to add a line chart as an overlay on a column chart—this can either be a graph that details other information, or a trend line based on the data the column chart plots.

Column charts are less useful than line charts for comparing lots of data over time, as you have a tendency to get too many columns, and the chart becomes confusing. Column charts can also (as line charts can) show data that represents numbers below the zero line. You can also ask for stacked column charts, or one column chart in front of another. The stacked chart shows the total of two or more individual items, while one column chart in front of another is an aid to comparing the two.

If your software program can create a bar chart, where the columns run horizontally (↔), you have an ideal method of looking at things which have an overall progression that naturally leads from the smallest to the largest.

Finally, an area chart is useful to plot cumulative data, as it not only shows the upper range of the information (as a line chart would), but since the area below the line is filled in, you also get a good indication of the quantity of the information itself.

Total Sales

2

There can't be much argument about it: all business starts and ends with *sales*. We're all selling something, and unless we do a good job at it, we won't be in business very long. While sales as a subject to examine is a vital area of anyone's business, it lends itself to a close look, as most businesspeople already track its progress and make comparisons between total sales last year and this year, between the first quarter last year and the same period this year, and so on.

In fact, sales may be the single area most businesses graph on a regular basis, with the "this year-last year" comparison the most prevalent. "How are your sales?" is a common question at any local coffee shop or Chamber of Commerce meeting, and woe to the business owner who doesn't have the answer at his or her fingertips.

Since you probably already have a good idea of how you like to follow your sales, we're not going to spend much time on the big picture of things. A simple line graph that compares monthly sales this year to monthly sales last year—or over the latest 12 months—at least lets you know how you're doing in comparison to the earlier period. It's a worthwhile graph to create, and you should, but we're going to get inside of sales a bit, and suggest some ways to examine this all-important part of your business that perhaps you aren't currently doing.

The Sales Trend

One immediate advantage you have when you put your sales information into microcomputer files is that most graphics programs can perform statistical functions on that data.

```
                MONTHLY SALES WITH TREND LINE
       THOU
                                        TREND LINE

        75

    $   50
                              MONTHLY SALES

        25


         0
              1   2   3   4   5   6   7   8   9
                       <-- MONTHS -->
```

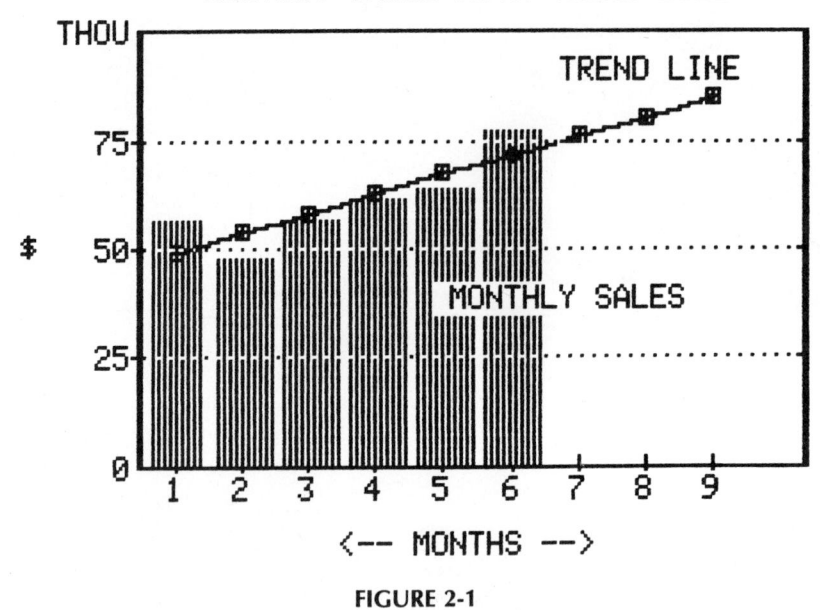

FIGURE 2-1

Figure 2-1 is a column chart that plots the most recent six month's sales figures for our fictional business. It also had the graphics system create a trend line for the data and extend it for three additional months. In effect, this tells the business owner that sales are rising—as shown by the trend line—and that sales for month 9 will be in the $80,000 range. In all, the business is showing strong sales, and the owner should be generally happy with this picture.

Of course, there are ancillary things connected to an increase of this sort in your sales, including the need for more cash to finance their costs. In effect, the business owner should be pleased and warned at the same time by a graph like Figure 2-1: pleased that sales are on the rise (almost always a good sign) but warned that more cash will be required to support those sales.

A Long-range Look

Although it's worthwhile to look at sales from as tight a viewpoint as Figure 2-1 gives us, it's equally beneficial to examine our sales over a period of time.

Figure 2-2 gives us a historical look at the sales for our fictional business over a three-year period—1986 through 1988. A trend line was created, based on the 36 months worth of information and extended to the end of 1989. As

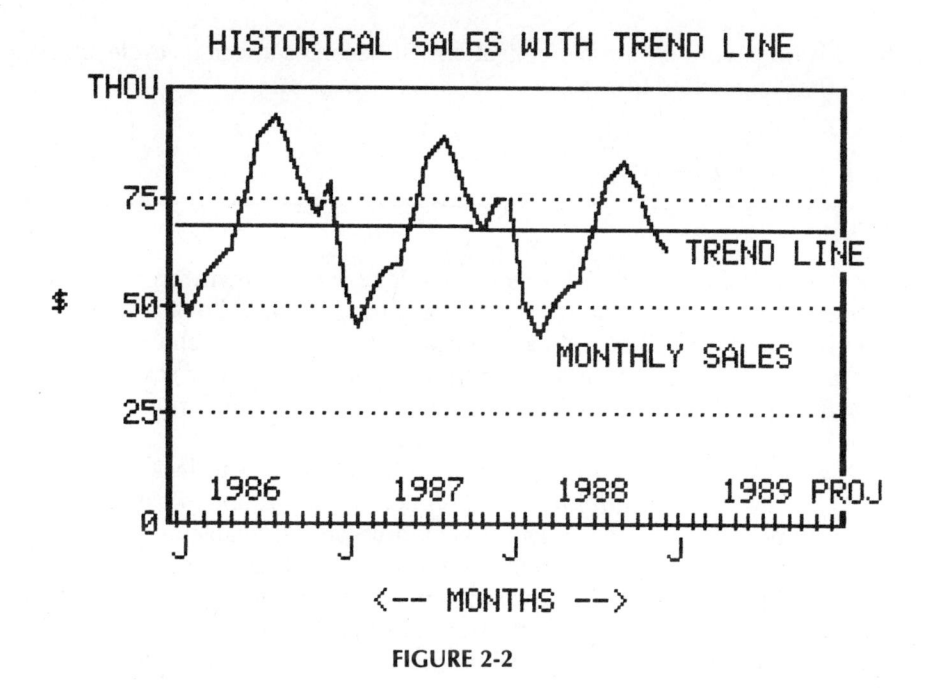

```
              HISTORICAL SALES WITH TREND LINE
     THOU
       ┤
     75┤
         ....................................................
         
       ┤                                         TREND LINE
 $   50┤
         ....................................................
                              MONTHLY SALES
     25┤
         ....................................................
            1986        1987        1988      1989 PROJ
      0 └┴┴┴┴┴┴┴┴┴┴┴┴┴┴┴┴┴┴┴┴┴┴┴┴┴┴┴┴┴┴┴┴┴┴┴┴┴┴┴┴┴┴┴┴┴┴
             J           J           J           J

                         <-- MONTHS -->
```

FIGURE 2-2

noted, this line projects where sales for 1989 will end up, based on the trend of the latest three years of information.

Obviously, this business has a seasonal jump in sales during the summer, followed by an equally severe plunge to a low shortly after the end of the year. The 1988–1989 transition period might be different than past performances would predict, but the business owner who has this graph would be examining it at the end of 1988 and probably could assume—since his or her sales are dropping again—that they would bottom out in two or three months and (hopefully) start to rise a bit later on.

This graph gives us all sorts of information, not the least of which is that we could make a good bet that this business has terrific cash-flow problems. Whenever you get such a wide variance in sales from period to period, you find yourself either without any cash (as a result of your poor sales performance), or with plenty of cash—which encourages purchases that really should not be made.

Often, too, persons who own this sort of business find that they're constantly paying for a "dead horse"—current revenue must be used to pay for advertising or merchandise or services ordered and used long ago. Since there wasn't enough income to support those purchases when they were made, the business owner probably had no choice; however, they hurt the current position, where sales are good and incoming revenue is sufficient to pay all costs and leave a bit in the profit column. The sum of today's profits (and often, cash that should pay current bills) ends up paying on the old obligations. It becomes a vicious cycle, and one that is often impossible to escape.

What About Inflation?

Figure 2-2 also indicates that the general sales *trend* is downward; not a great deal, but there's a little jog to the downside during the middle of 1987. To take a closer look at the trend line (since it appears nearly flat when charted in Figure 2-2), Figure 2-3 plots just the trend line, on a much narrower scale. The zero line for this next example has been eliminated; the scale runs from $60,000 in sales to $70,000 in sales.

Once we expand just this one section of the graph and look at the trend line by itself, we see a disturbing image. Since the trend line is based on three years worth of monthly information, it should be pretty reliable as a forecasting tool. Even if there were no inflation during this period, the general flow of our sales is downward—exactly where we don't want it to go. Of course, some inflation is always present, and so the picture we see in Figure 2-3 is really worse than it appears. Our sales are decreasing while the value of the dollars we receive for

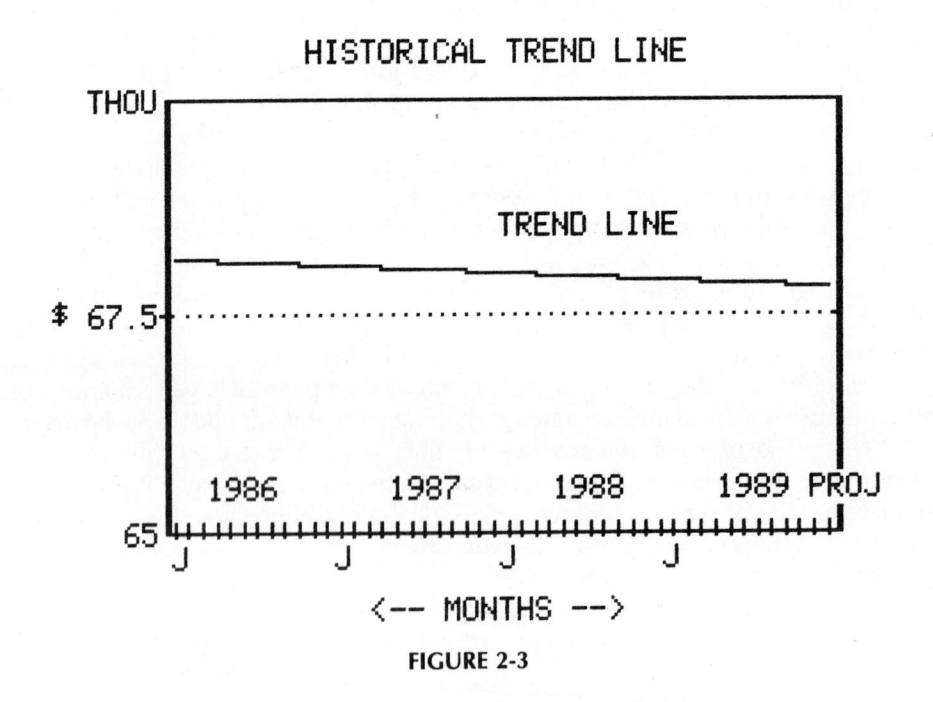

FIGURE 2-3

what we sell is also going down. Our gross sales—which this information is based on—should increase at least at the rate of inflation.

While everyone plots their sales on the basis of the raw data itself, it's often helpful to let your spreadsheet program convert your numbers into percentages and plot them. Now, instead of the rise and fall of your dollar volume, Figure 2-4 shows you the *percentage* increase or decrease of one month's sales to the next. Now, since you look at percentage changes, you can appreciate the severity this particular example illustrates. An awful lot of the lines on this graph are *below* the zero point, and even when the business improved and somehow created an increase in its monthly sales, it soon saw them dropping. The fall in sales around the first of each year is painfully obvious. In the period around January of 1986, sales plunged about 40% *in one month*. It took two months to accomplish the same thing when January of 1987 came along, but the drop was just as steep.

This business has a definite problem in its total sales area. Perhaps this is caused by the changing seasons of the year, or poor management ("business is good now, so we'll take it easy") or poor selling practices. Anyone involved in this enterprise must take steps to eliminate this problem. Perhaps they can diversify into another similar business that'll help smooth things out. Maybe another location—whose sales will come when the main store isn't selling anything—will help. Certainly a tight rein on cash flow will help weather the storms this business suffers.

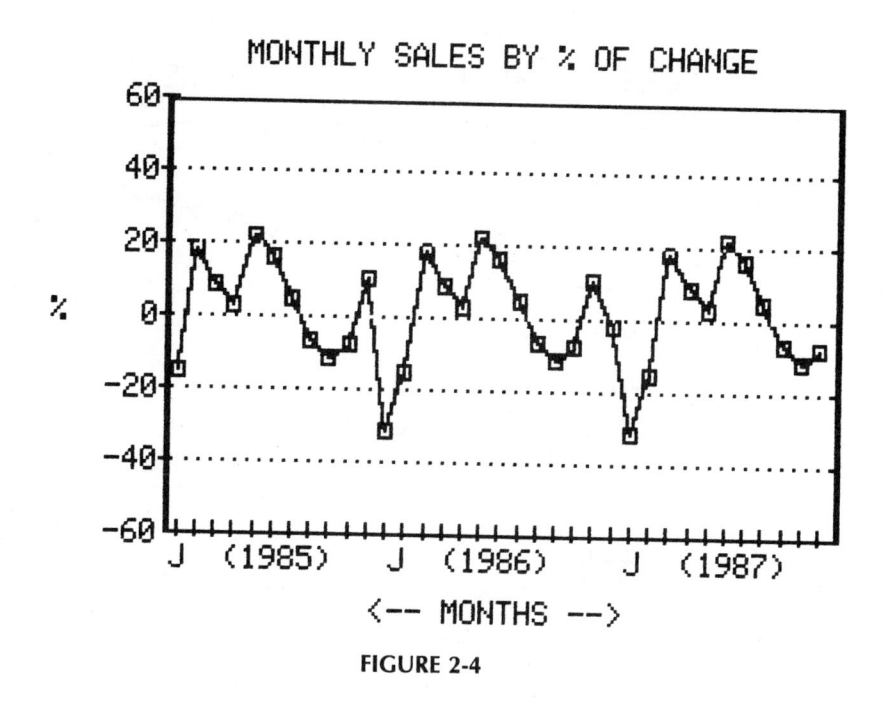

FIGURE 2-4

Sales and Costs

Whatever we sell, we incur costs, often a number of them, to bring the sale to fruition. Costs include the labor and materials directly involved with each particular sale, as well as the overhead costs required to handle the paperwork, and so on. Most often what are called "direct costs" contribute the largest share to anyone's total costs, so they deserve a look here within the context of total sales. While it's useful to plot direct costs as a percentage of sales (which we will, in the chapter on direct costs), it's equally helpful to use their data to create a trend line, to see which way those costs are heading.

Before we look at an example graph, what should we expect? As sales rise, so will our direct costs—that's inevitable. Should they increase at the same rate?

It might seem like they must, but in fact, while we can expect them to grow, they should rise *slower* than sales do, if we work with just the raw figures (rather than percentages). This is because sales are recorded on a *retail* basis, while costs are expenses on a *wholesale* level.

Figure 2-5 plots the trend line for our monthly sales along with another for direct costs, over an 18-month period. The *actual* sales took place (and costs were realized) during the first 12 months. From January of the second year on, the lines are projected, based on the earlier 12 months of data.

Our sales and costs both rise, as they should, and it's also obvious that our

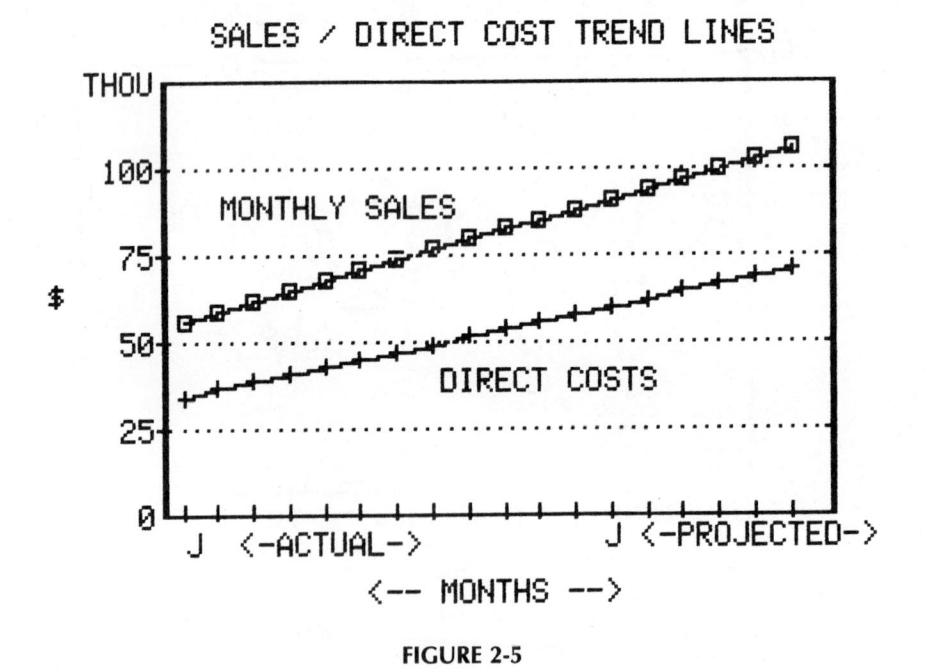

FIGURE 2-5

sales are rising slightly faster than costs are. That's also as it should be. If this graph tells us anything negative, it's that perhaps our costs could be growing slower than they actually are; anything we can do to save on costs helps in the profit end of things. You'll never find that these two lines intersect—let's not forget that *overhead* is also a cost that adds to our total cost picture. That's another data set you might want to chart and follow in terms of trends—sales on one line and the sum of overhead and direct costs on the other. A truly negative picture would find the two lines coming together—total costs starting to meet and exceed sales revenue. All of a sudden, you find your business deep in red ink. A trend line may warn you in time.

More Direct Costs

Though we don't want to dwell on direct costs in this chapter, they need to be examined in relation to total sales, on a percentage-of-sales basis. Figure 2-6 plots direct costs as a percentage of sales over a seven-month time frame. As we know, this can either represent the first seven months of a year or the latest seven-month period—whatever is the most help to you.

Figure 2-6 is presented to show you a danger signal. For the first five months represented here, direct costs as a percentage of sales remained under the 70%

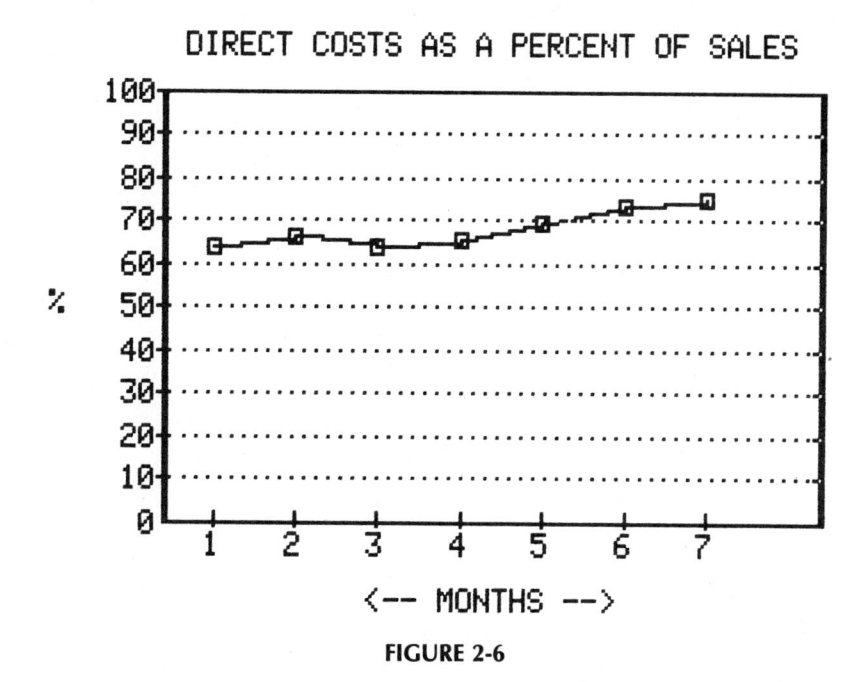

FIGURE 2-6

level. The next two months, however, saw our direct costs as a percentage of sales jump above that 70% figure. Even without a trend line, our direct costs as a percentage of sales are rising—an unhealthy sign.

Now we don't know if that 70% figure has any particular meaning for this business, but if this graph was created along the same line as our others, we should try to indicate important data as part of the chart itself. If our overhead breakeven line is 24%, then we should *scale* the graph to show a grid line at 24%. It makes the information much easier to understand. In this case, perhaps the key is that this business makes money if direct costs total less than 70% of its sales volume, and loses money when the percentage grows higher. In any case, this sort of rise deserves a closer look.

Figure 2-7 eliminates the zero line and puts a tight focus on the information we just examined. Now our scale runs from 60% to 80%, and since the data is plotted on the narrower scale, its rise is much sharper. With this close look at our direct costs as a percentage of our sales, it's obvious we really have a problem. Again, even without the benefit of a trend line, we can see that our direct cost total as a percentge of our sales is taking a tremendous jump. If we plotted this same data on a *percentage of change* basis, it would be even more obvious and disturbing.

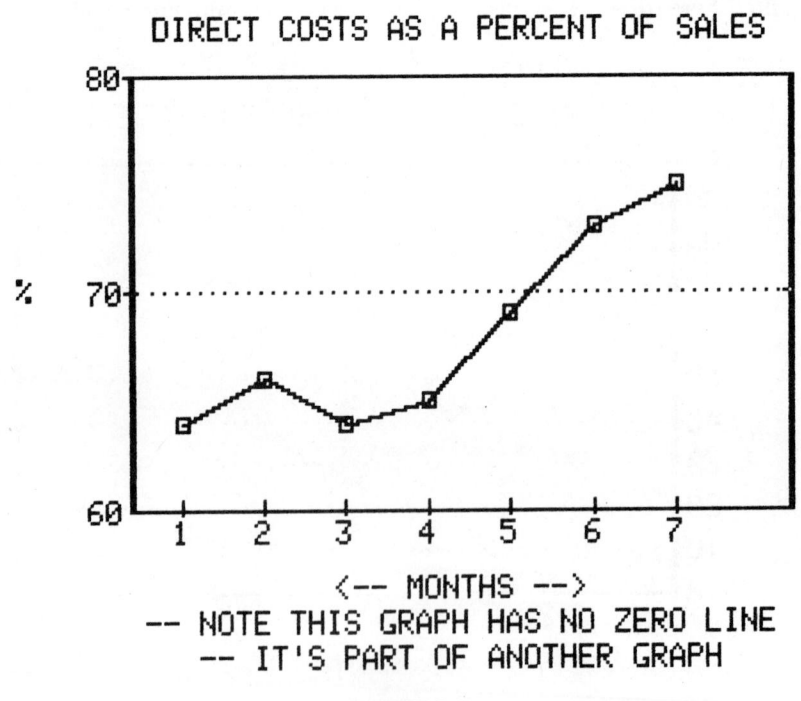

```
               DIRECT COSTS AS A PERCENT OF SALES
          80┐
           │                                          ▫
           │                                       ▫
    %     70┤·····················▫····················
           │             ▫
           │      ▫               ▫
           │  ▫       ▫
          60┴──┼────┼────┼────┼────┼────┼────┼──
              1    2    3    4    5    6    7
                     <-- MONTHS -->
              -- NOTE THIS GRAPH HAS NO ZERO LINE
              -- IT'S PART OF ANOTHER GRAPH
```

FIGURE 2-7

The approach, as always, is that once we find some problem with our data, as we noted in Figure 2-6, it's almost always worthwhile to take a closer look at things, to put the data into a tighter, narrower focus, as we did with Figure 2-7. The information is the same, of course, and the graph without a zero line changes the picture of the data, but it serves its purpose: to show the business owner he or she has a problem and (hopefully) motivate him or her to some action(s) to solve it.

Sales and Salespeople

Businesses vary by how they handle the cost of sales. You might do all the estimating yourself (and you get paid whether you sell anything or not), while the business on the corner might have two outside salespeople (who only get paid on a commission basis), while Walt across the street might have one salesperson, who works on a salary plus an override if they have so much in volume each month.

Associated with the *personal* cost of sales in terms of someone actually spending time out with a prospect, are any number of contributing expenses. Do you have someone in your office who does all the estimating? Who types up the contracts and proposals and sales letters?

However you handle your sales, there are some costs that are associated with each individual sale, expenses it's well worthwhile to track and graph. You may find that one salesperson creates a lot of volume with little profit, because of poor estimating or too many undeliverable promises made to each customer. You might discover that the contractor you thought was your best customer really isn't, because of all kinds of on-the-job changes, or slow payment (that cost you interest expenses), or just because your bids to him are less than they should be because you don't want to lose the work. Perhaps one area of your business consumes an abnormal share of sales costs. You might sell a washer/dryer combination with one simple contract proposal and one visit to the customer, while a complete storm window installation might require five hours of estimating time, plus jobsite visits by your engineering and installation people as well as the salesperson.

The point of all this is to suggest you examine your sales costs and track them, just as you do now with the other costs your business has. Like direct costs and overhead (and pieces of each), sales expenses can be graphed and examined and thought about, either as raw data, on a percentage basis, and with or without a trend line to project where the data is headed.

Figure 2-8 plots eight months of sales cost data, as a percentage of our total sales. The first month, for example, indicates that we spent 5% of our sales dollar to produce the sales we made. This particular set of information shows our figures running under 6% until the latest month, where we had a sharp jump. As always,

SALES COSTS AS A PERCENT OF SALES

<-- MONTHS -->

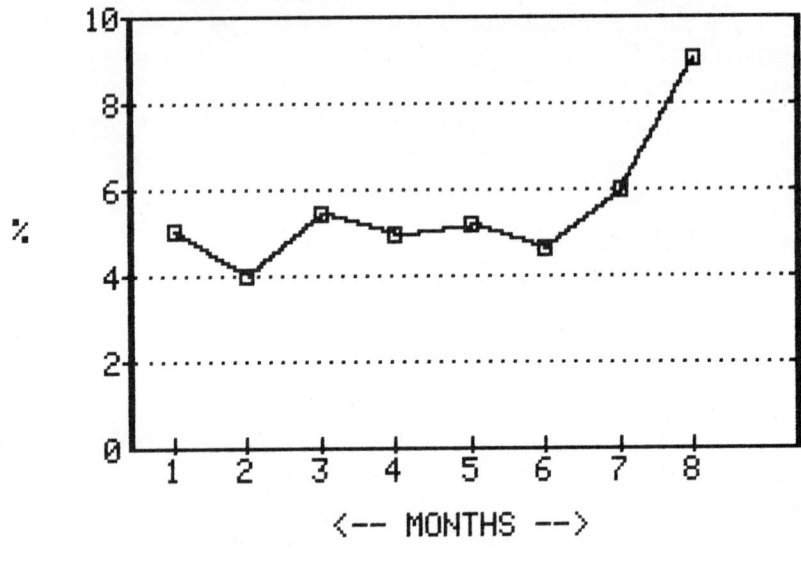

FIGURE 2-8

this is a warning sign that something's not as it should be. Did someone get a larger than usual commission? Another way to examine this set of information would be to plot it on a percentage of change basis—how much did our sales costs, as a percentage of our total sales, rise or fall last month?

The sales figure we use to compare the cost of sales can be refined, too, just as rather than simply lump all of our sales together, we need to total just those sales for which we can attribute some of the cost of our sales department. For example, if we have a retail location with someone on the counter all the time, their labor expense is more of an overhead figure, as they'll likely be paid whether anything is sold or not. So, we wouldn't want to count those sales when we compare our sales total to our sales cost amount.

Figure 2-8 is especially disturbing since it's based on percentages, so it simply means we're spending more of each sales dollar to create our sales. During the first month plotted here, it cost us about a nickel to produce a dollar of sales. During the last month plotted, it cost us almost a dime to create a dollar's worth of sales. Something's obviously wrong. It could be in the sales commissions we're paying or in the sales themselves—are our people selling low-volume/high-commission products? Is one of our people estimating so that jobs lose money yet still collecting a full commission on each job?

To carry things to their logical conclusion, Figure 2-9 shows what our sales cost as a percentage of sales graph should look like, after a few more months have gone by.

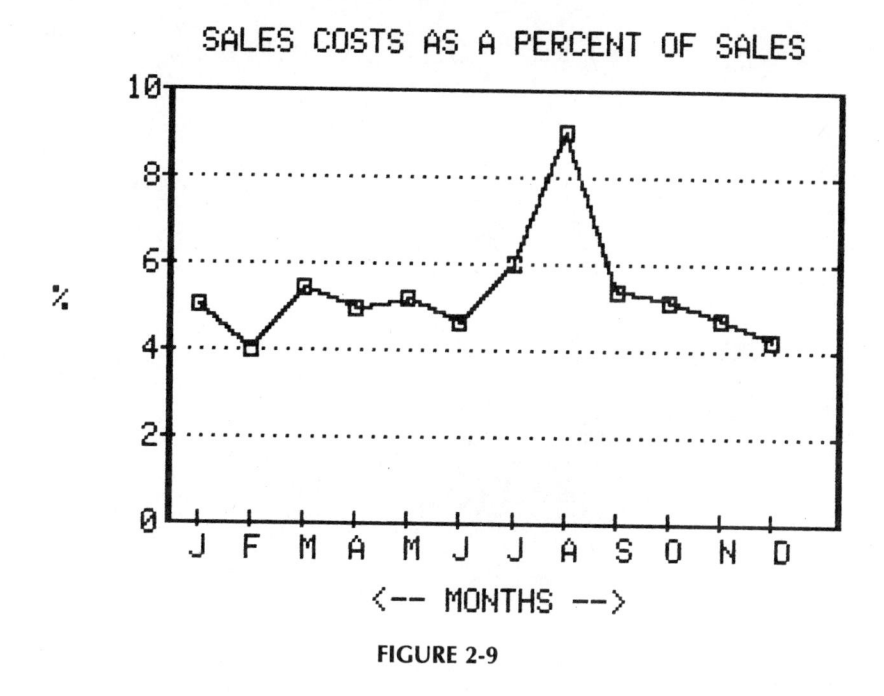

TOTAL SALES

```
        SALES COSTS AS A PERCENT OF SALES
   10┬
    │
    8┤
    │
 %  6┤
    │
    4┤
    │
    2┤
    │
    0┴─┬──┬──┬──┬──┬──┬──┬──┬──┬──┬──┬──┬
       J  F  M  A  M  J  J  A  S  O  N  D
              <-- MONTHS -->
```

FIGURE 2-9

After the sharp jump during months 6–8, this business owner made the right decisions to reduce sales expenses. By the end of this particular period, it cost our business only about four cents for each dollar of sales we recorded, and best of all, the *trend* of the data is downward. Whatever skewed our figures for those few months has been eliminated. This is the graph you should see if your business finds itself as shown in Figure 2-8, with such a rapid rise in the cost of your sales force.

The Sales Pie

If we have more than one location, it's always a good idea to break down total sales based on that and create a pie chart. It's often useful to distribute this graph to our people at each store, so they can see how they're doing in relation to their peers.

It's pretty easy to see from Figure 2-10 that our Central store produces the greatest volume of sales, while Ash Fork is the worst in terms of raw sales volume. With five locations, each should provide 20% of the total, yet that'd be a rare situation for any business.

We want to examine the sales each of our locations produce with a much tighter focus, but it's important to note that even if you only have one store, you

SALES BY LOCATION – JUNE

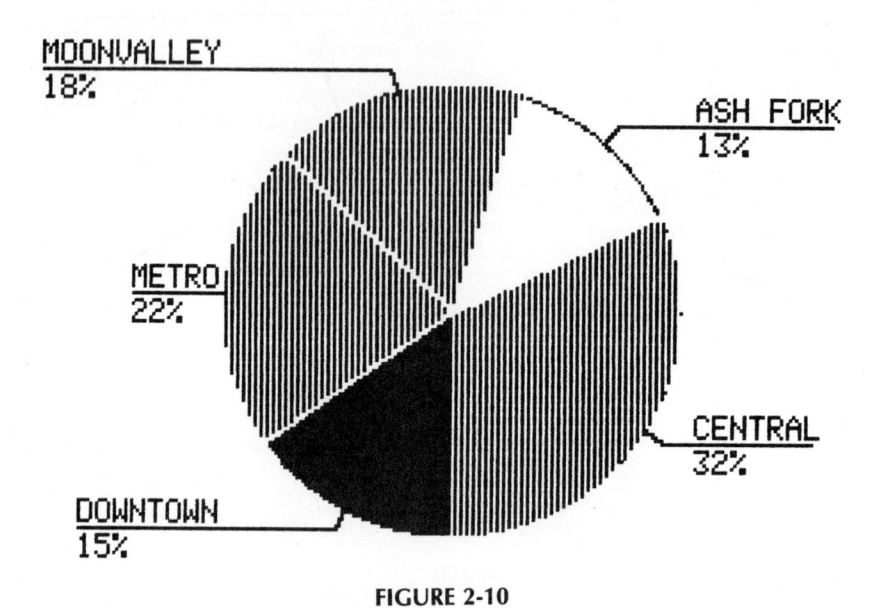

- MOONVALLEY 18%
- ASH FORK 13%
- METRO 22%
- CENTRAL 32%
- DOWNTOWN 15%

FIGURE 2-10

SALES BY DEPARTMENT – JUNE

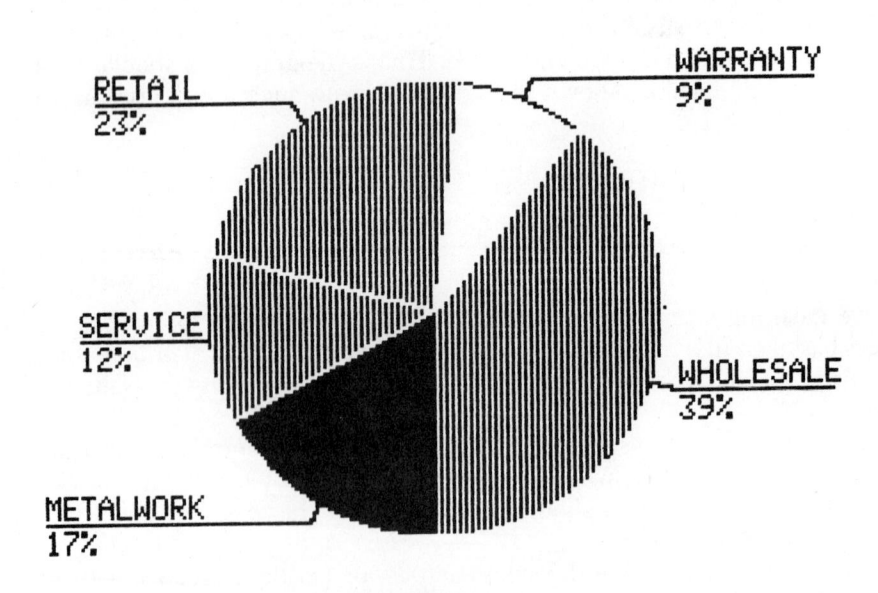

- RETAIL 23%
- WARRANTY 9%
- SERVICE 12%
- WHOLESALE 39%
- METALWORK 17%

FIGURE 2-11

probably have more than one area of your business, more than one department. You can examine sales per department on the same basis as you can sales by location (so the closer look we'll take in a moment will apply to either focus).

Figure 2-11 breaks down our sales for June into five departments; since there are five areas, we could expect each to produce about 20% of our total sales. As with locations, though, it would be an unusual situation (and might even be cause for more worry than the breakdown we actually have). It's obvious from Figure 2-11 that the wholesale end of things creates the greatest sales dollar, while warranty work accounts for the least. Without other figures from other periods, this doesn't tell us a lot, but simply serves as a place to start our close examination of where our sales come from. As noted, we can use the same techniques to look at both our sales by location and by department—the focus is the same.

A Closer Look

One way to narrow our examination of sales data either by location or department is to break it down based on some common focus. For a service-oriented business, that might take the form of looking at each service technician individually—how many calls did he or she perform today? Last month? What was the callback rate for mistakes the technician made? And the bottom line: how many dollars in sales and/or profits did this person contribute to our total?

When we look at our sales based on the individual store locations we have, it's useful to move things along this same direction and compare the sales for each store on a square foot basis. After all, if one store has 2,000 square feet of display area and another only half that, we'd expect the sales of the former to be twice that of the smaller location.

Figure 2-12 is a bar chart that plots the monthly sales our fictitious business produced during June. This is the best type of graph to use to illustrate this information, as we can see at a glance who's best, who's worst, and how the rest happened to do during this particular period. Clearly the Metro store had a poor record, while our Moonvalley location topped sales for June. Naturally, we'd want to have more than one month's worth of data before we made any major decisions, but Figure 2-12 gives us a picture of a point in time, a chance to see each location in relation to the others in a way where they're all on an equal footing.

This is perhaps a more accurate look at things than what we saw in the pie chart of Figure 2-10. While that told its own story—how each store contributed to *total* sales—Figure 2-12 gives us a better feel for how one location compares to all others, based on a low common denominator. It takes into account the size of each store and quite probably the store's staff and its associated costs; the larger the location and the more people you probably have working there, the higher its overhead is (in raw figures), and so on.

```
SALES PER SQUARE FOOT BY LOCATION-JUNE
```

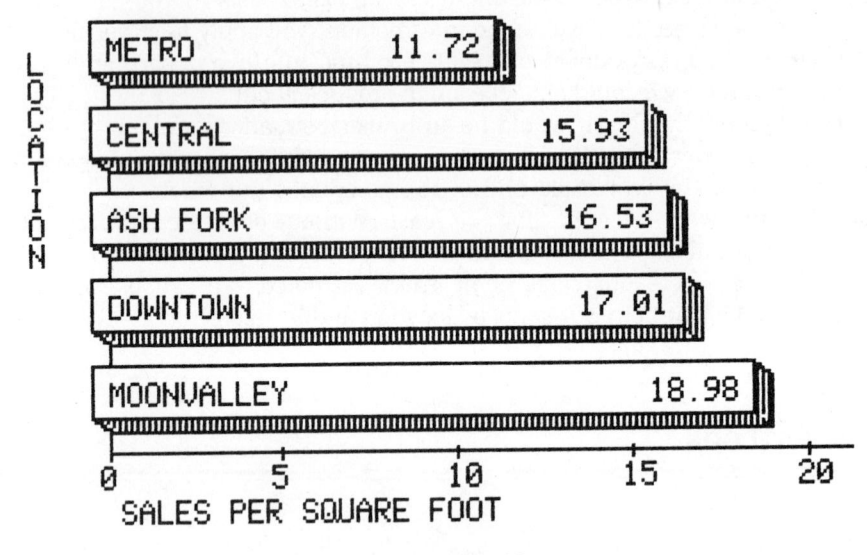

Location	Sales per Square Foot
METRO	11.72
CENTRAL	15.93
ASH FORK	16.53
DOWNTOWN	17.01
MOONVALLEY	18.98

FIGURE 2-12

It seems obvious, too, from Figure 2-12, that the Metro store is lagging far behind not only the best location, but trails all other stores by a wide margin. Why? One month's worth of information on a single chart isn't going to tell you the whole story, but if you create this display every month and find that over a period of time Metro is consistently at the bottom of your sales barrel, you have a definite problem that needs to be corrected. Is it with the people? Merchandise? Location? Displays? Advertising? Can Metro make a go of things with monthly sales of less than $12 a square foot?

If you happen to find that, yes, Metro is always much the worst of any of your locations, then you have to decide whether to change your staff, add to or change the inventory mix, perhaps even eliminate the location completely. The important thing is that you can see, with a graph like Figure 2-12, exactly how one store compares to each of your others. It's a useful tool to hand out to your people at the end of each month, and quarter, too, so they can see how they're performing.

You can examine any individual area inside your sales with this same approach. As Figure 2-11 illustrated the sales per department, you can take that same information and break it down to some common feature to create an accurate comparison among divisions inside your business. You can't do it (obviously) for each data set on a per square foot basis, but there's always a way to see how they compare. Perhaps you can divide sales by the number of people in each department, or the number of hours worked, or sales calls made, or estimates presented. The idea is to get things down to their lowest common denominator.

Another Look at Poor Metro

Since our Metro store is getting the worst of things here, let's take its sales data one step further and see how it looks on a historical basis. This is a logical next step, once we've examined the other charts, particularly when we found that Metro had a problem when we looked at sales on a per square foot basis.

Figure 2-13 gives us a long-range look at what the metro store has contributed to our overall sales, on a percentage of sales basis. This particular graph covers two full years plus eight months of 1988. Like other similar graphs, the scale for this example was designed to add information to the picture and make it easier to understand. It's obvious that the Metro store has been producing between 20% and 24% of our total sales for some time now. Lately, as we move into the fall of 1988, its sales are slowing. The sales line we plot has moved out of its normal range—that historical area between 20% and 24%—and worse, it appears to be heading downward. Why? Are our total sales much higher, while Metro's remained the same in raw dollar figures, which would cause it to have a lower percentage of sales figure? Or is there a problem at the store?

Figure 2-14 plots the sales per square foot data for our Metro store as a

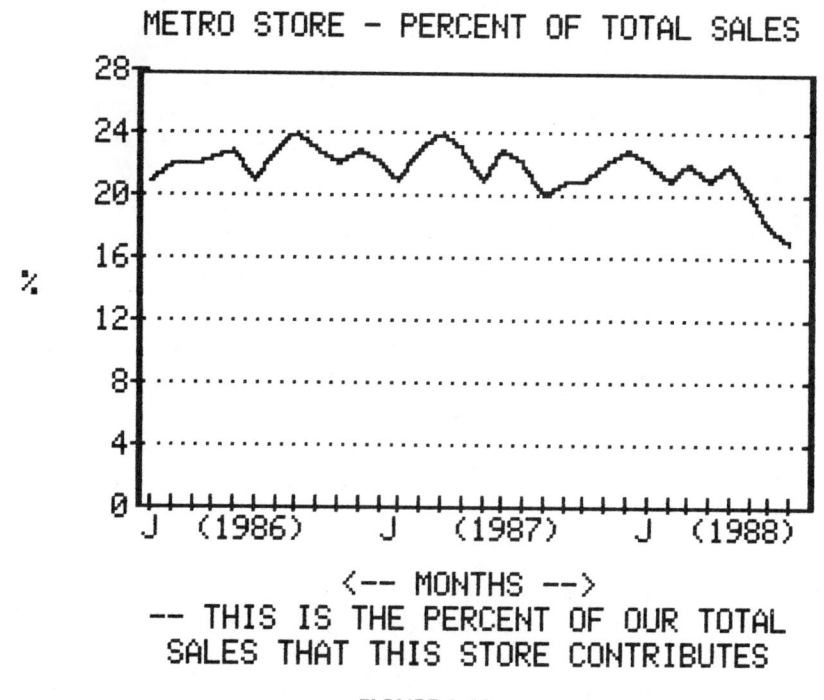

FIGURE 2-13

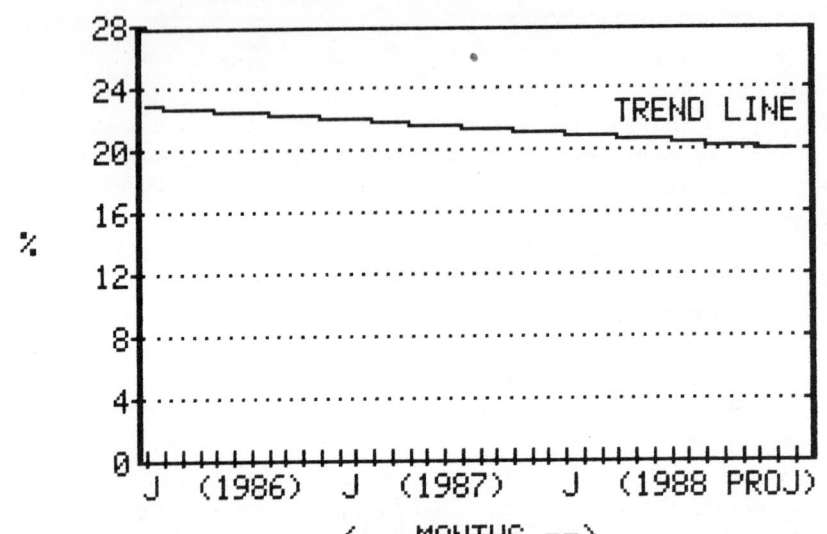

```
              METRO STORE - % OF SALES TREND LINE
    28
    24
                                          TREND LINE
    20
    16
%
    12
     8
     4
     0
       J  (1986)    J   (1987)    J   (1988 PROJ)
                    <-- MONTHS -->
    THIS TREND LINE PROJECTS THE LAST SIX MONTHS
    OF 1988, BASED ON THE PRIOR 30 MONTHS OF DATA
```

FIGURE 2-14

trend line—as noted, it's based on 30 months of information, and projected for six more. While we could see the recent drop in sales for this location in Figure 2-13, this illustration shows us its sales have been falling for some time. On a percentage basis, our trend line projects they'll be down to around 20% of our total volume after just another few months. They were up around 24% back at the start of 1986, so the Metro store's dropped four full percentage points in terms of our overall sales. If we looked at the data for this store alone, the drop as a percentage of *its* sales would be even more severe, as both of these last two illustrations are based on its percentage of total sales, an (obviously) much larger figure than the sales produced by this one store itself.

More of Metro's Problems

Whatever the cause, there's clearly a problem with Metro. Just as we looked at a historical picture of its relationship to our total sales, it's helpful to create a chart for this one store (our problem child) based on a long-range look at its sales on a square foot basis. We want to see if they average within a certain range, get a feeling for any seasonality that might cause wide fluctuations, and so on. While this doesn't make any sort of comparison with our other stores, we could take this data a step further and create a line graph for two or three locations over a long period of time, based on their sales per square foot.

Figure 2-15 plots Metro's sales on a square foot basis over a 30-month period. The June figure we examined earlier in Figure 2-12 is the last item on this graph—if this were your business, you'd be examining this data at the end of June. As always, our scale is plotted to help us understand the information; in this case, sales have been running within the $12–$14 range for some time now, and suddenly we see them dip and fall below the $12 mark. This might be just a passing problem, of course, but still serves as a warning that we need to investigate further.

The easiest way to do this is to narrow our focus, to create a graph without a zero line. This gives us something, as we know, of a false picture of the data, but at the same time serves a purpose: in this case, it should scare the business owner into doing something about the Metro store.

Figure 2-16 eliminates the zero line from the data we just examined; the $11.72 monthly figure we've been following all this time is our latest plot. Since our scale is only between $11.50 and $14, the monthly gyrations in sales per square foot are much steeper. But as we see, they remained within the $12 to $14 range for more than two years, only to recently fall below that $12 figure.

When we couple this information with a trend line, we confirm the problems at our Metro store. Not only are our recent sales down, but the overall trend line

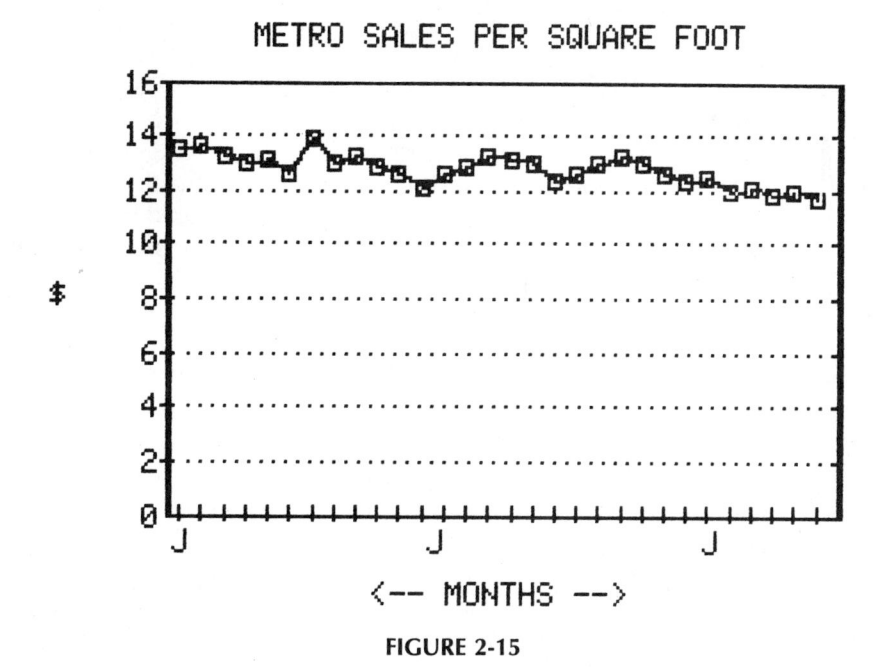

FIGURE 2-15

```
METRO SALES PER SQUARE FOOT WITH TREND LINE
14.00
13.50
13.00
 $
12.50       ACTUAL                          TREND
             SALES                          LINE
12.00
11.50
    J                  J                  J
         <-- MONTHS -->
    -- NOTE THERE IS NO ZERO SCALE ON THIS
       GRAPH - IT IS A CLOSE-UP OF ANOTHER
```

FIGURE 2-16

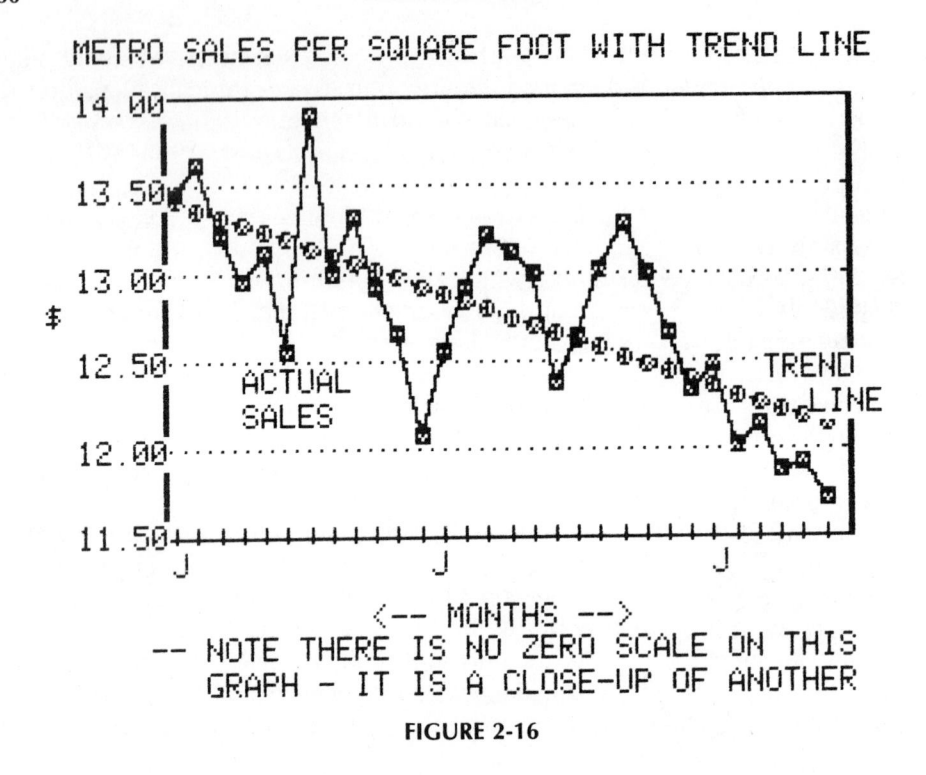

heads lower, and at a pretty severe rate. Another way to examine (and get upset about) this data would be to plot it on a percentage of change basis, where the graph would indicate how much—from a percentage standpoint—the store's sales rose or fell each month, compared to the prior month.

There's obviously a serious problem with the Metro store—all graphs confirm it—and it's up to the business owner to find out what the difficulty is and take steps to correct things. This same kind of examination can be used for any major part of your sales; we just chose to pick on the Metro location for these examples.

Summing Up

It's important to understand that it is vital to plot your total sales this year compared to the same period last year, and just because we didn't provide an illustration here does not mean you shouldn't track that data. On the contrary, that information is vital, and something that should be done every month. But that's obvious (you probably already do it, even by hand), and so we didn't spend time on it here. Another helpful way to look at sales last year versus sales this year is to compare them on a percentage of change basis—how they compare, up or down, on a percentage basis from last year to this. Just as you should plot monthly sales this year compared to last, it's worthwhile to chart things on a "latest 12 month" basis. Knowing what your sales are for the most recent 12 months is often just as valuable as plotting them on a calendar basis.

One thing to apply to any sales information is a trend line, to let your microcomputer calculate and plot the direction things are heading. Too often, monthly sales fluctuations disguise where your sales are really going, and the trend line helps you know. The more data you can base your forecast on, the more accurate its picture will be, so you want to examine sales on a long-term historical basis, and plot a trend line based on that long line of sales volume.

If your trend line appears flat—which it often will, particularly if it's based on a lot of similar figures—you can squeeze the graph down a bit and plot it on a narrower scale. This, as you know, distorts the real figures, but often is the only way to discover if a seemingly flat line has any real trend, any real movement to it. Most often an examination of this sort will show a rise or fall in the line—valuable information.

If you see that the general trend of your sales, based on a historical picture, is downward, you have a definite problem, as they ought to at least keep up with inflation. Although it's a bit of work, you can factor in the inflation rates for whatever periods your data covers and get a picture of your sales data based on a dollar value that doesn't fluctuate.

Another way to examine sales is to plot their monthly change on a percentage basis. While it's sometimes difficult to relate to the raw dollar totals, when you see that sales were down 22% from last month to this, you instantly know the meaning of the information.

You should examine sales in relationship to the costs involved to produce those sales. These involve direct costs (which you can look at on a percentage of sales basis) as well as sales costs (what it costs for the presentation and/or engineering to sell a particular job).

The business owner should also know where his or her sales come from, both in terms of location and department, if there is more than one of either. Is one store or division better than another, sales-wise? Why?

You need to take a closer look at the sales information you gather from your locations and/or departments and often can get a good idea of what the data means by putting it all on some common ground. We chose to examine sales on a per square foot basis, as it puts those sales figures into a form where each store is graded equally.

You can combine your examination of sales on a square foot basis with a comparison for each location, to try to see if any one store or department is consistently worse (or better) than the others.

It's also helpful to examine, on a long-range basis, how each division or location contributes to your total sales, on a percentage basis. Once calculated and charted over a period of time, this percentage should remain stable, and it's a warning sign when one store starts to produce more or less than it has been (if one location provides *more* of your sales, percentage-wise, then another must be contributing less).

Much of this information lends itself to an examination with a trend line, to show both the general direction of the data as well as a projection of where we might expect our business to be a few months from now. Any trend line gains accuracy with more figures on which to base its calculations. It's important to remember, though, that as with any forecast based on past performances, current business conditions may not match those of the past. Thus, it's a good idea when you work with trend-line information to create a forecast based on a historical look at the information, over a long period of time, as well as a trend line based on more current data (with a shorter forecast period, of course).

Other Ideas

One useful comparison to chart is between the sales you make and your outstanding accounts receivable. Generally, you'd expect the two to rise at about the same rate and would worry if they didn't. You might find it useful to use your spreadsheet program to calculate your month-end accounts receivable total as a percentage of your monthly sales, and plot it.

The whole idea of any sale is to create a profit, so it's worthwhile when you get your monthly or quarterly profit/loss statement to plot sales along with profits. Again, one should rise and fall with the other—the more sales, the more profit we'd expect—and it would be cause for alarm if one line on the graph didn't match the other. You may have to do some numerical manipulation to get both figures on the same scale, perhaps by multiplying your profit figures by 10 or 100.

Sales are always directly tied to the salespeople who work for you; without them, there are no sales. Obviously, some businesses are more dependent on sales personnel than others, so this comparison might not be valid for your line of work. If you do have a sales staff, try plotting the sales they produce by salesperson or sales office. You might also want to examine the sales by product and/or product line—perhaps the goods you buy from one wholesaler far outsell those of another. If so, it's important that you're aware of it.

Sales in Sections

3

The average businessperson might know his or her total sales were $55,000 last month, probably can elaborate in terms of any profit that was recorded, and might even be able to describe why their work turned a profit. But the more astute business owner spends the time required to find out where their sales (and thus profits) are generated.

Unless you handle only one product or service, there are subdivisions of your business that you'll find profitable to examine. A bookstore, for example, which handles only books, still will find obvious value in knowing what sort of books sell the best. Your bookstore will have racks of westerns, fiction, cookbooks, computer books, romance titles, and so on. Wouldn't it be beneficial to understand which area(s) produce the most sales? The best gross profit? The fastest inventory turnover?

If you do nothing but service repair work, wouldn't it be interesting to discover which *types* of products you work on are the easiest to service, have the least number of warranty callbacks, have the best record for parts availability, the brand(s) your customers seem the most satisfied with?

If your work requires you to do installations for general building contractors, would you find it helpful to know who you're doing the most work for? The least? Who has the best payment record? The worst? Who has the fewest/greatest number of on-the-job change orders? Which builder calls for the most "minor" adjustments after the sale that seem to take trip after trip before they're finally satisfied?

Within the wide context of *sales* are any number of helpful combinations the business owner can track in an effort not only to learn more about how their business functions, but also—especially since the subject is sales—to examine and think about one area or another in an effort to increase their sales total. What's important to you and your work might be altogether different than it is for other businesses in your town. They might sell a lot of service and repair labor, while you handle parts on a retail basis only. Or you may handle warranty repair claims and have a small wholesale setup for some parts, while the business down the block might sell appliances and farm out any required repair service. Inside of anyone's sales, though, are areas that can be broken down on an individual basis to help the business owner know not just what's going on inside the enterprise but can also point the way to more sales and profits.

Much of the focus inside your sales concerns itself with where they come from. Who are your customers? Even if you work for a wide variety of people over the period of a year, some, and perhaps much of your business will be for people you worked for before, and since you did a good job, they're repeat customers. Who are they? Is there something else you can sell them?

Breaking Things Down

Inside your inventory are products that move better than others, sections that produce more profits than others. You might discover that you've got a substantial investment in the appliance parts section of your inventory, but the darn stuff just doesn't sell. Armed with this information (obviously gathered and studied over a sufficient time period), you'd be ready to decide to eliminate the slow-moving stock and put that cash into the products that consistently contribute the most to sales and profits.

In your service department are technicians who seem to always make money for your business, and others who are marginal. Graphics provides an ideal way to see how your people are performing, with a simple ongoing line graph of the dollar volume a service technician produces, along with a line graph for the same period for their *total costs*. That cost line should include the direct labor expenses, any fringe benefits, any associated taxes you must pay, along with the total cost for any callbacks that must be made because the service technician made a mistake.

Coupled with service are the sales your service people make, simply because they're out there on the job. Prospects (rightly or wrongly) have a tendency to believe a repair person, to put more credence into what they say, compared to what a salesperson might tell them. Since your service people are already on the job, have already spoken to the customer and explained their problem (and, naturally, your solution to it), the customer is more likely to buy from you instead of a competitor (and in many cases, might not even look around for another estimate). So your service department makes sales and profits *over and above* what it produces in simple service work, because of the sales it creates.

A Close Look at Contracts

As with your total sales volume, the first and most obvious approach is to track whatever area(s) you find important on a this-year versus last-year basis. In fact, a basic "this period compared to that" for the most obvious parts of your business is a helpful starting point. As with sales, we're not going to illustrate that approach with a graph here, but that doesn't mean you shouldn't chart this data if you find it useful. Instead, we're going to suggest some graphs that might help you understand an area inside your sales; the *parts* of your business that you want to study (and there might be a number of them) depend on your own interests and needs.

Since a lot of our work depends on what we call contracts, that'll be our focus for much of this section. Contracts, in this context, describes those sales our fictional business makes to contractors, people who build new homes. What's important to you can be examined in exactly the same way, of course; keep that in mind as you look at the examples.

Rather than starting with an obvious look at things, Figure 3-1 illustrates an unusual idea: to analyze and graph the average sales volume for every contract the business records; in this case, over a period of 18 months.

In effect, while this example doesn't tell you the total volume that contracts

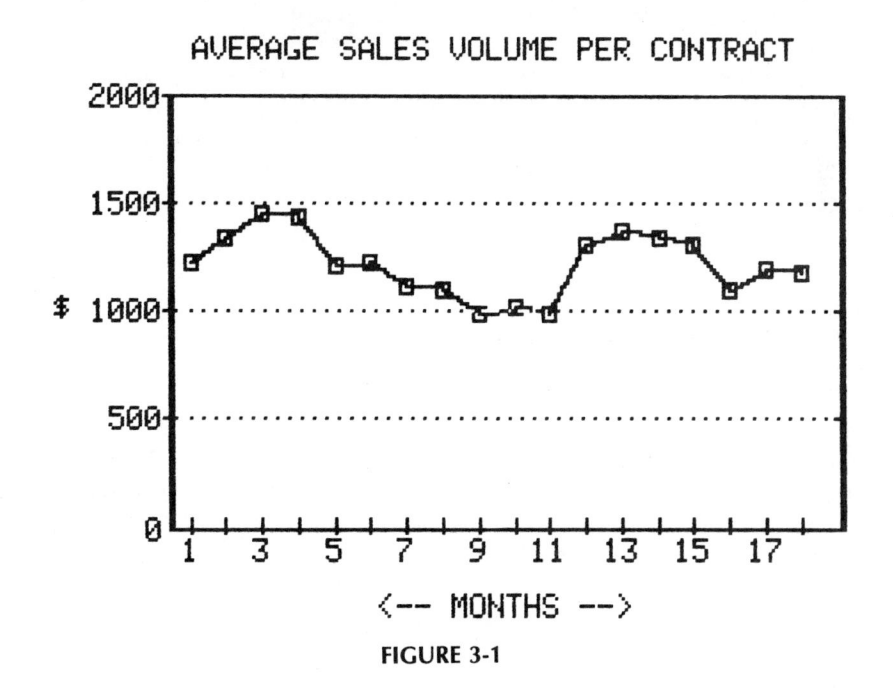

FIGURE 3-1

contribute to your sales total, it indicates instead how they, as a group, are performing, whether the jobs you sell are larger or smaller from month to month. Do you find that you're more successful if you handle a number of smaller sales, or if the same sales total is made up of fewer, but larger items?

Each business is different, and while many companies strive to sell larger jobs, too many big installations can tie up a lot of cash, might force you to hire additional employees (who may or may not be qualified), and if there are problems, they're *big* ones. Most businesses prefer a mix between their large jobs and those that have a smaller sales volume. It's the old question of what you'd rather have: one person who owes you a thousand dollars, or a thousand people who each owe you one dollar. Only business owners can determine what sort of work they'd like to pursue and what their business is best geared for; a graph like Figure 3-1 tells you what the average current volume is for each contract you sell.

Let's take Figure 3-1 a step further and add a trend line to show what direction our fictional business is heading. But let's also notice that—as we've seen in many other cases—the sales on a per contract basis in this example run within a *range* of figures. In this case, over the 18 months plotted, they've consistently been between $1000 and $1500. You can *see* the business cycle at different times of the year.

Figure 3-2 plots the same information we just looked at, with the addition of a trend line that shows the general direction of the data. The trend line extends another six months, to project what our average sales volume per contract will be based on the prior 18 months of information. While we couldn't determine it from Figure 3-1, this example clearly shows a downward trend.

Information of this type isn't necessarily bad, of course; it all depends on where you want your business to go, the jobs you want it to be involved with. More lower-volume installations involve more overhead but perhaps are safer in terms of the severity of on-the-job problems and the collection of your bills. Larger installations generally consume less overhead (on a percentage basis) and raise sales volume to the point where you can bid lower on other jobs, and thus create even more sales.

This is true because much of anyone's overhead total is *fixed* and not dependent on the dollar volume of work in progress. After all, that's what overhead is: what you must pay, whether you sell anything or not. If you are able to make a large sale it won't make your electric bill rise, nor will it necessarily increase the payroll for your office staff. There may be some minor overhead increases (more long-distance phone calls, extra paperwork to be shuffled and filed), but generally your overhead total will remain about the same. This is why many businesses try to sell the largest jobs their people can handle; as sales volume rises, overhead remains about the same, so overhead as a *percent* of sales decreases.

The point is, of course, that graphs like these last two give the business owner a feel for what's happening inside their business, as well as where it's headed.

AVERAGE CONTRACT VOLUME WITH TREND

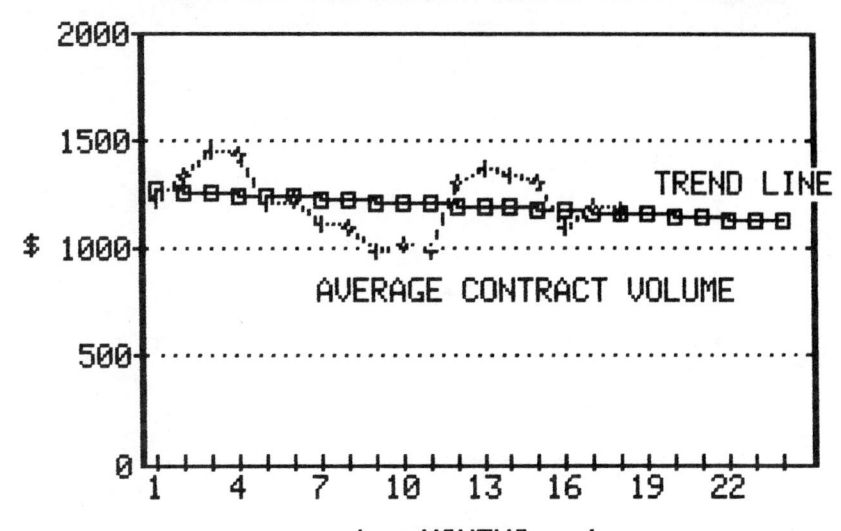

[Chart showing average contract volume with trend line over months 1-22, with dollar values from 0 to 2000. Trend line is labeled, and the average contract volume series is plotted.]

<-- MONTHS -->
THE PLOTTED DATA IS FOR 18 MONTHS, AND THE TREND LINE PROJECTS IT OUT ANOTHER 6 MONTHS

FIGURE 3-2

More Contract Detail

Since we're examining the subject of contracts in detail, let's look at another way to break down the information. Most businesses do work both inside the city where they're located and outside its limits. The main differences are in travel time and associated costs, and sometimes a difference in the sales tax you have to collect. Figure 3-3 charts the sales data for our fictitious business over an 18-month period for the contract work it did outside the city limits.

It's obvious from this illustration how our sales volume for contracts out of the city is decreasing, even without the benefit of a trend line. Why is it going down? Is that a trend we want to continue, or do we need to do something to increase sales in this area? Naturally, we'd want to examine other data for this part of our business, to see if in fact we are making money on these jobs or not, how much they contribute to our total overhead, and so on. We might find that we want to help the current trend continue its downward plunge—perhaps we're not able to properly estimate and/or supervise the work we do outside the city, so we'd be better off to take on only those jobs where we're sure to show a profit. Maybe the contractors we work for out of town are slower to pay than our other customers, or more difficult to track down when they do get behind. Once we

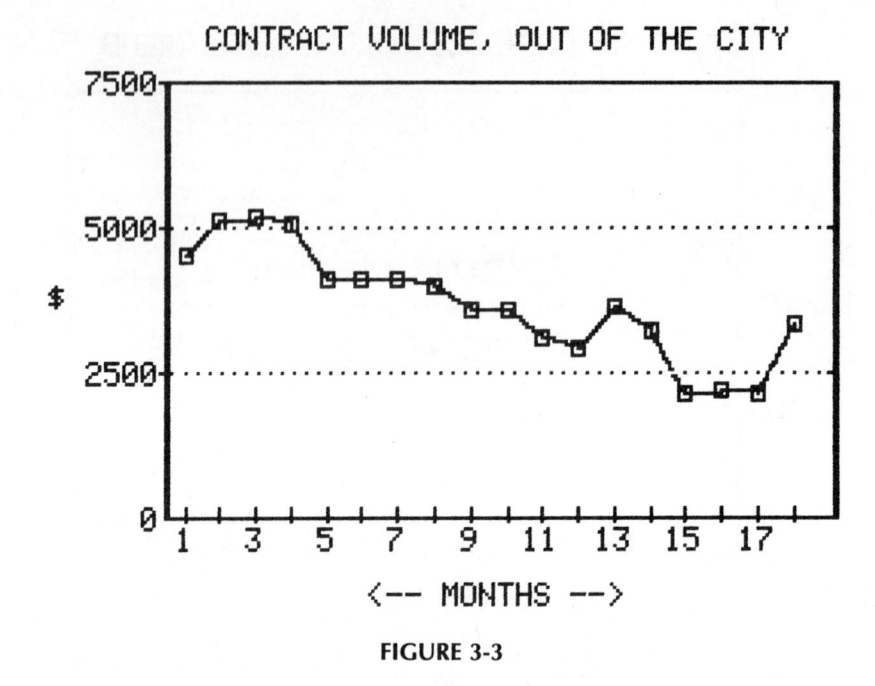

```
             CONTRACT VOLUME, OUT OF THE CITY
    7500
    
    
    5000      ┌┐┌┐
          ┌┐  ┘└┘└┐
$                 └┐ ┌┐┌┐┌┐
    2500           └┘└┘└┘└┐ ┌┐     ┌┐
                          └┐┘└┐ ┌┐ ┘└┐
                           └┐ └┐┘└┐  └┐ ┌┐
                            └┐ ┘  └┐ ┌┘┌┘
                             └┐┌┐  └┘└┐
    0
       1   3   5   7   9   11  13  15  17
                   <-- MONTHS -->
```

FIGURE 3-3

know where our sales are coming from and their dollar value—as we've seen in these first three examples—then we can determine if we're on the right track, or if we want to make an effort to change the direction our business is heading.

Estimates

Most businesses work on a bid basis—even a customer in a retail store examines a product and decides to buy or not based on need, along with a perception of the product's value in relation to the price marked on the item. Someone in the market for a water softening system usually calls around and asks for two or three estimates on the total cost for the installation. Even a lot of the professions are getting into a bidding situation, where hospitals post their daily costs, attorneys advertise their charges for one service or another, and so on. If the work you do involves the presentation of estimates to your customers, then it's an area you can examine graphically, to see where you've been, where you are now, and in what direction your business is headed.

Figure 3-4 gives us a long-range look at the bid volume for our fictional business. Surprisingly, many businesses don't keep track of this data—the potential sales volume their estimates represent—in the same way they do their

BID VOLUME, LAST 48 MONTHS

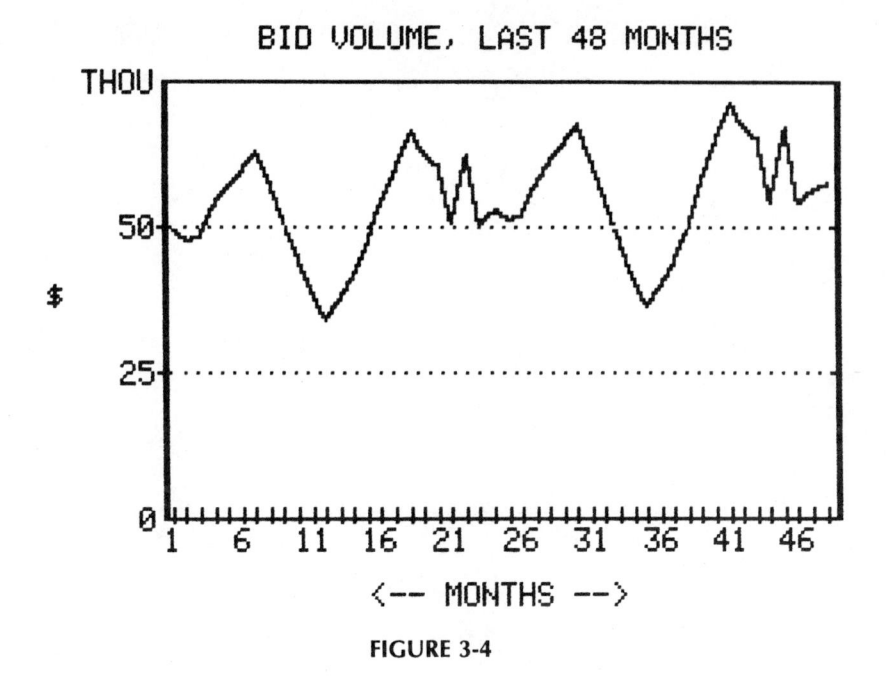

FIGURE 3-4

sales information. It's a helpful way to look at things, as it tells us how much work was available to our business, if we could sell every job we bid on.

Figure 3-4 isn't particularly enlightening, as it covers such a long period of time and doesn't include a trend line or other helpful information to help us understand its data. It's presented here as a starting point for some other ideas, and also to indicate that not every graph has a story to tell. Often, we have to look at our figures from one direction or another before we understand them. One logical way to better examine this information would be to plot both sales and bid volume—to give you an idea of how one relates to the other. Another would be to move one of the figures, so the bids you made during May are plotted along with the sales you recorded in June (you might find there's a two month or even longer time once you start to examine this data). If much of your work is done on a bid basis, then you might want to cull the information even more by plotting only the sales actually produced from the estimates you make, rather than to plot your total sales figure (which will be distorted by sales unrelated to those on which you estimated).

Any look at the bids you make in relation to the sales they produce should be done on a percentage basis, as shown in Figure 3-5.

This example let the spreadsheet program where we store our sales and bid information calculate the percentage of bid volume that actually turned into sales. For example, during one particular month you might present estimates to po-

SALES AS A PERCENT OF TOTAL BID VOLUME

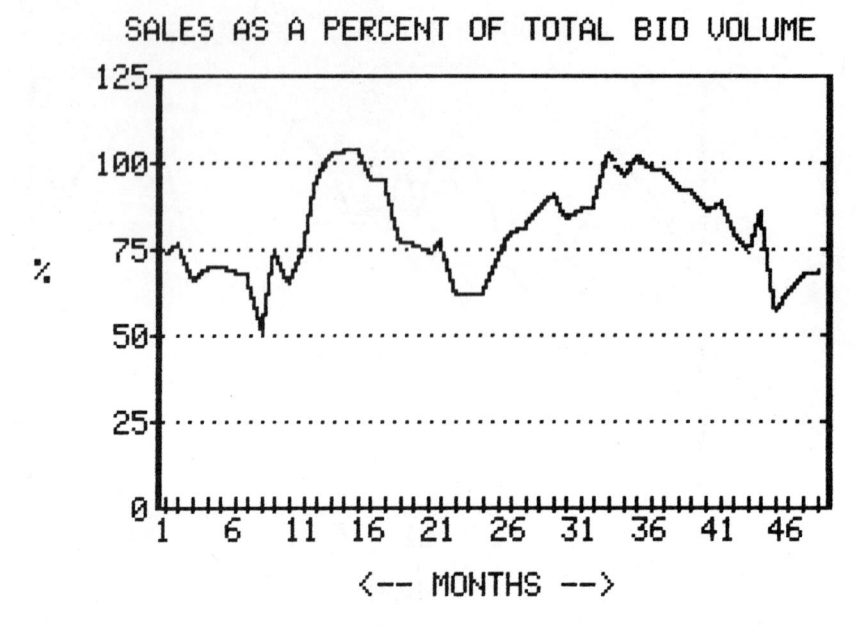

FIGURE 3-5

tential customers with a total value of $50,000. If you eventually closed $40,000 worth of sales from these estimates, this means you sold at an 80% rate. You calculate this by dividing what you sold (40,000) by the total sales volume you estimated (50,000), which comes out to 80%.

This is an interesting long-range look at things (it's over the same 48 months that Figure 3-4 covered for bid volume) and the mathematics involved are simple. You just divide your sales volume by your bid volume, for each monthly figure.

The basic information we can glean from this chart is that we generally get more than 75% of the total we bid on in the form of sales volume. Also, there are months where we get more than 100% of our bid volume, which is to be expected—we'll always get work based on bids we created months ago, so there will be times when the total adds up to more than the potential volume we've bid on during one monthly period.

Another way to look at this data would be to plot the percentage of sales our business records based on how old the quotations are: we get "X" percent during the month the bid was made, for example, less than one month ago; "Y" percent when the bid is between 30 and 60 days old; and so on. Let's add a trend line to the data in Figure 3-5 and see how our sales staff is doing.

Figure 3-6 plots the same 48 months of information we just examined, with the addition of a trend line. This tells us the direction our data's been going, and projects out for 12 more months how our sales will be in relation to our bid volume.

SALES IN SECTIONS

The interesting thing about all this is that once you determine roughly what percentage of your bid volume you normally record as sales and get some idea of the time frame involved, you can make an accurate prediction of what's going to happen to your business. For instance, you might find—with a study of your own bid and sales volume information—that you generally sell about 75% of your bid volume, with a 30-day lag time. If you write $50,000 worth of quotations in March, you can estimate that April's sales will come in at about 75% of that—about $37,500. Once you chart this information for a long enough period to have an accurate base, you can total up the bids you made during the current month and just about know what your sales volume will be next month.

That gives you all kinds of lead time to plan what you'll need in the way of more people, extra cash, material for installations and inventory, and so on.

Figure 3-6 also tells us a comforting story about our sales people (even if the total sales staff is just you): it's doing a good job. Although we couldn't tell from the actual data, the trend line on this picture shows a nice rise: we're recording more and more of our bid volume as sales. While the projection might not prove accurate (it ends up around 90%, which is a worthwhile goal but perhaps not achievable), the overall line is rising. For one reason or another, our business is getting a greater and greater share of the bid volume we're estimating. Isn't that the whole idea?

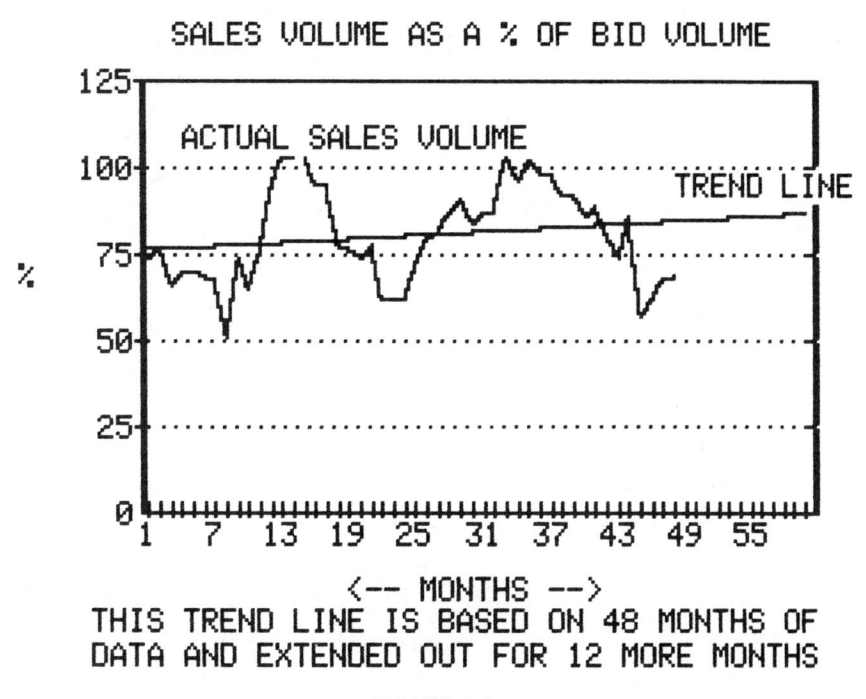

FIGURE 3-6

It's also gratifying to note that we don't even need to reduce the scale for this graph to see how the trend line is rising or falling—we can see that our sales performance is improving even with the wide (from 0 to 125%) scale we have here.

Another way to study this same information is to create trend lines based on both the bid volume your business has and the sales you receive from those estimates.

Figure 3-7 plots both these lines, based on 48 months of data, and projects 12 more months. It's important to mention that these lines are plotted on a dollar basis, where the information we've been examining has been charted on a percentage level, so the images we see are different in what they contain. The first thing we notice in Figure 3-7 is that both lines are growing at a pretty good rate. That's a healthy sign for any business, because unless sales grow, the business stagnates. Since sales are often based on the volume of the estimates a business puts out, we must make sure our bid volume grows; sales, then, will follow. In this example, that is confirmed by the growth of sales; as our bid volume increases, so does our total sales. The trend of the bid volume is a line we want to follow on a regular basis, as if it starts to head downward, it's a sure sign our sales will soon get lower, too—exactly where we don't want them to go.

```
         BID VOLUME / SALES VOLUME TREND LINES
     THOU
      75+ ··················································
                    BID VOLUME TREND
   $  50+─────────────────────────────────
                                       SALES VOLUME TREND
      25+ ··················································

       0 └┴┴┴┴┴┴┴┴┴┴┴┴┴┴┴┴┴┴┴┴┴┴┴┴┴┴┴┴┴┴┴┴┴┴┴┴┴┴┴┴┴┴┴┴┴┴┴┴┴┘
          1    7   13  19   25  31   37  43   49  55
                        <-- MONTHS -->
          THESE TREND LINES ARE BASED ON 48 MONTHS
          OF DATA AND PROJECTED OUT 12 MONTHS MORE
```

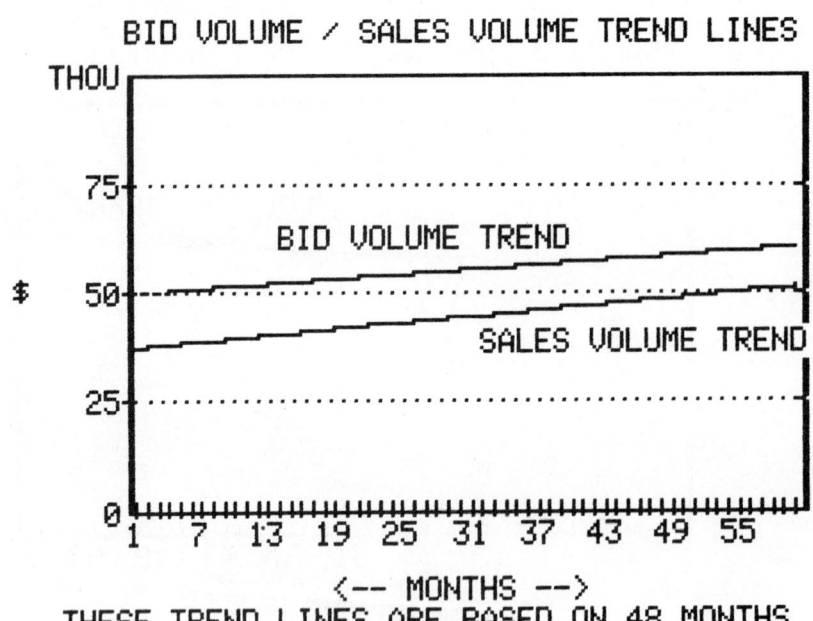

FIGURE 3-7

The lines appear to be growing closer together. That's also a good sign, as it means our sales department is doing its job by converting those estimates into sales dollars. In all, these are the pictures a business owner should see when he or she examines their bid and sales volume.

In-Shop Work

Just as we've looked at contracts as a part of our total sales and examined the bid volume we write in relation to the sales it creates, it's also helpful to look deep inside our sales at any repair work we do. Your business might have service people who go to a customer's home to repair something, and/or you might allow people to bring in their products for you to repair in your office. It depends on the service work your business does as to what you might want to examine, but for purposes of illustration, we'll look at the work done in the shop area of our fictional business. Not all businesses provide this service for their customers, of course, but if yours does, you know it's one of the hardest to control and make any money on.

A lot of businesses post a sign that tells their customers there's a minimum charge for any work done in the shop. While this is a good idea, it's often difficult to enforce: a customer who has bought from you for 20 years comes in and takes ten minutes of a service technician's time is hardly a candidate for a minimum charge. Too often, you just tell the customer that there's "no cost" and let it go at that. A lot of the time, too, you just can't justify your minimum charge for a piddling little job or for finding what's really a piece of scrap material for someone. A customer might call to ask for advice on this or that and ties up one of your people for a half hour; the time's just lost. And, there are times where your service technician spends an hour on something only to find it can't be fixed for one reason or another, or that the customer needs a part he or she simply can't afford. It's difficult—and causes hard feelings—when you try to charge for such things.

Because it's such a difficult area to control, it's an ideal one to examine, all with an eye as to how you might improve or change things to make in-shop service profitable. The first step is to break down both sales and costs as they relate to service. What are your sales for the service work you do in your shop? What are the costs involved for this particular area of your business? You need to have some record-keeping method to track these things, even though you might not currently record this information.

Figure 3-8 shows the data for our fictitious business for its in-shop sales and their costs, calculated by dividing the labor cost figure by its retail total to arrive at a percent. This chart duplicates the graph you might create for your total sales/cost amounts. You probably shouldn't be too surprised that there are times when this part of your business shows a loss. That's the nature of this type

"IN SHOP" COSTS AS A % OF "IN SHOP" SALES

<-- MONTHS -->

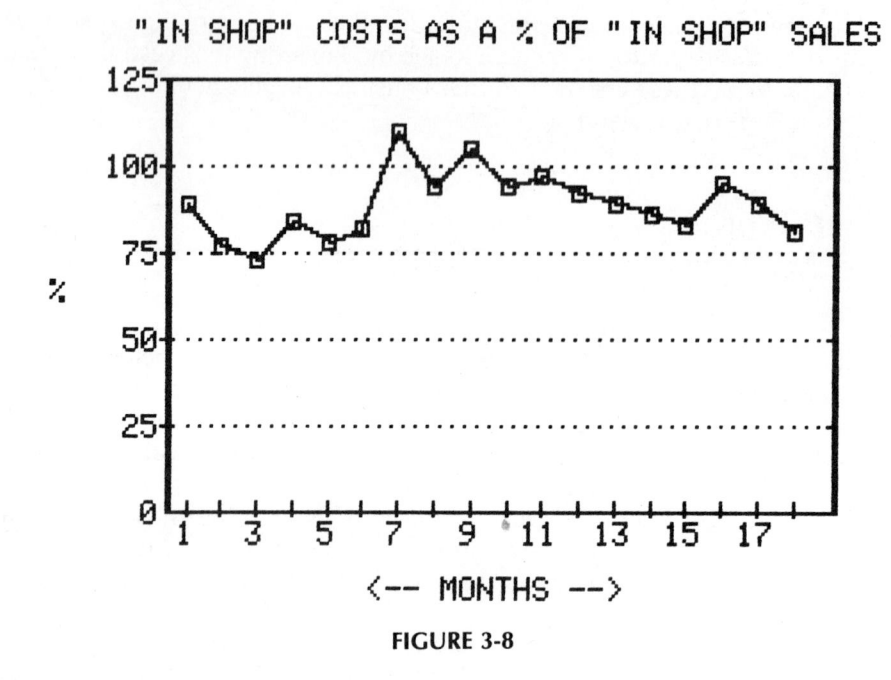

FIGURE 3-8

of service, and while you don't want *any* area of your business to lose money, there may be other considerations that you need to keep in mind. For instance, even though this department isn't profitable part of the time, perhaps it creates other work for your business. If someone brings in a product that you diagnose as defective, the customer might want you to go to their home and replace it. That can lead to major sales, too, as other problems are discovered.

The important thing is that business owners realize that this facet of their work is difficult to make a profit on, and a monthly graph like Figure 3-8 shows exactly how this one area of things is doing. Of course, other parts of your business can be examined the same way, once you take the time to break out their sales and costs, so you can compare one to the other on a graph.

A logical extension of this information is to let your micro create a trend line based on your data and plot it.

Figure 3-9 shows the same information we just graphed, with the addition of a trend line that is projected another six months. As is often the case, while we couldn't tell from a chart of the data itself, the trend line makes it obvious that our in-shop costs as a percentage of their sales are rising. This information should disturb any business owner, as it means this one section of the business is going from bad to worse, in terms of profit.

Another way to examine this information would be to create a graph with a very narrow scale—perhaps between 60% and 120%—as we've done with Figure 3-10.

The trend line shows a steeper rise because of the restricted scale. As always,

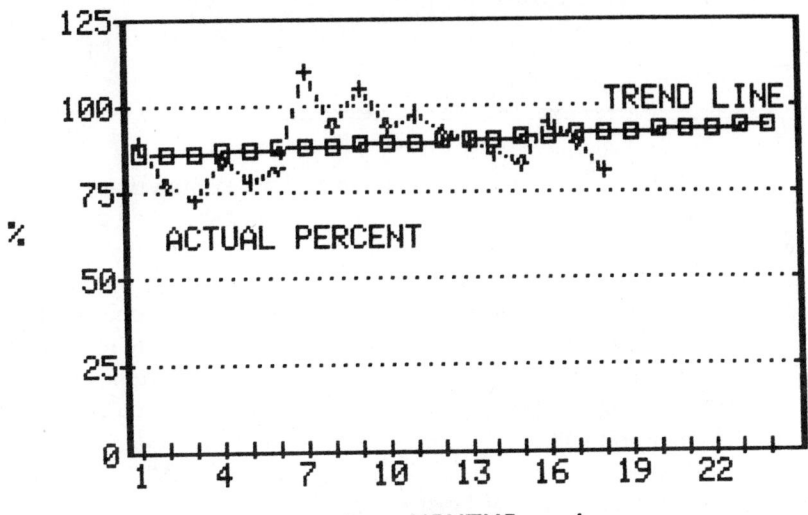

IN SHOP COSTS AS A % OF SALES W/TREND

...TREND LINE

ACTUAL PERCENT

<-- MONTHS -->
THE TREND LINE IS BASED ON 18 MONTHS
OF DATA, AND PROJECTED OUT FOR 6 MORE

FIGURE 3-9

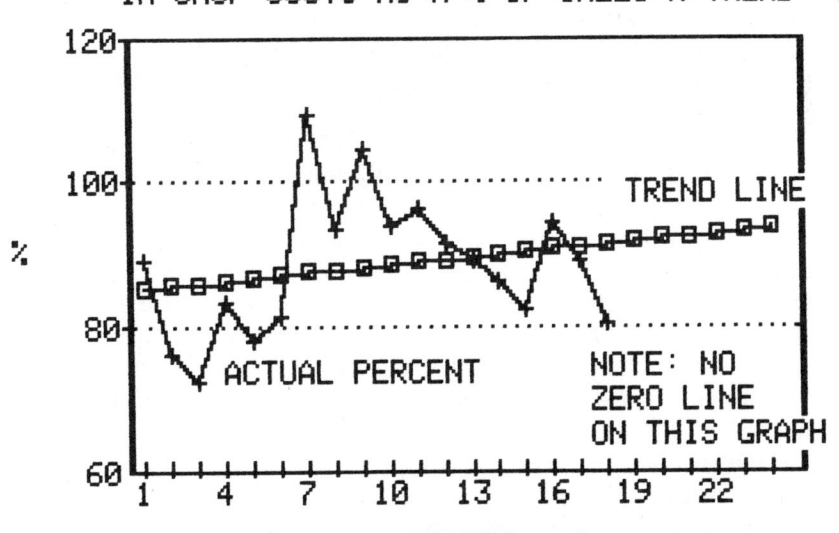

IN SHOP COSTS AS A % OF SALES W/TREND

TREND LINE

ACTUAL PERCENT   NOTE: NO
                  ZERO LINE
                  ON THIS GRAPH

<-- MONTHS -->
THE TREND LINE IS BASED ON 18 MONTHS
OF DATA, AND PROJECTED OUT FOR 6 MORE

FIGURE 3-10

information like this is designed to motivate the manager to do something to correct the situation.

Labor Problems

Now that we've examined in-shop labor repair costs, let's expand that same focus and take a more general look at our repair labor and its associated costs from a businesswide standpoint. Rather than just the repair work we might do at our place of business, let's also include any outside repair labor our business sells. Any business that sells labor, either for service or installation, has one of the more difficult tasks that faces the business owner: it's often impossible to make a profit on labor. There are any number of reasons for this, but the bottom line is that much of the time you simply cannot charge the price you need to receive to come out even on the labor you sell.

There are other costs besides basic salary and fringe benefits that must be considered when you examine your labor expenses. There are times when your people cannot work for one reason or another, and yet they must be paid. There are other times when someone can't fix a customer's problem, so you have to send another service technician or two out, at your expense, to find and correct the problem. Something you buy from a manufacturer comes through and needs repair; your costs to fix it total $150, but the manufacturer only allows (if anything) $50. You absorb the rest. A little rise in insurance costs here, an extra coffee break or two there, and a business can quickly find itself in a money-losing position in respect to its labor sales.

Since we've been working with repair labor, let's stay on that same tack and see how our labor should look when we plot its costs along with the sales it produces.

Figure 3-11 is the picture we see when we plot these two data sets; as labor costs rise, so should their associated sales. If one line runs at a direct variance from the other, we know we've got a situation we need to examine more closely. Note that the title for this chart indicates exactly what it plots: retail labor revenue and the cost of labor that's charged against the retail price. A similar graph might include any material and/or equipment these service people install out on the job, but that would skew the picture. We really want to focus on just labor for this example: its costs and its sales. The cost figure you use for this plot would include, of course, any associated labor expenses such as insurance, fringe benefits, and so on.

While the two lines we see in this example are what we'd expect them to be, it's always worthwhile to take a closer look at things. Even though there doesn't appear to be a problem here, a tighter look might reveal something.

Figure 3-12 plots the trend lines for the two data sets we just examined, and projects them six months into the future. While Figure 3-11 showed us what

RETAIL LABOR REVENUE / COST LABOR

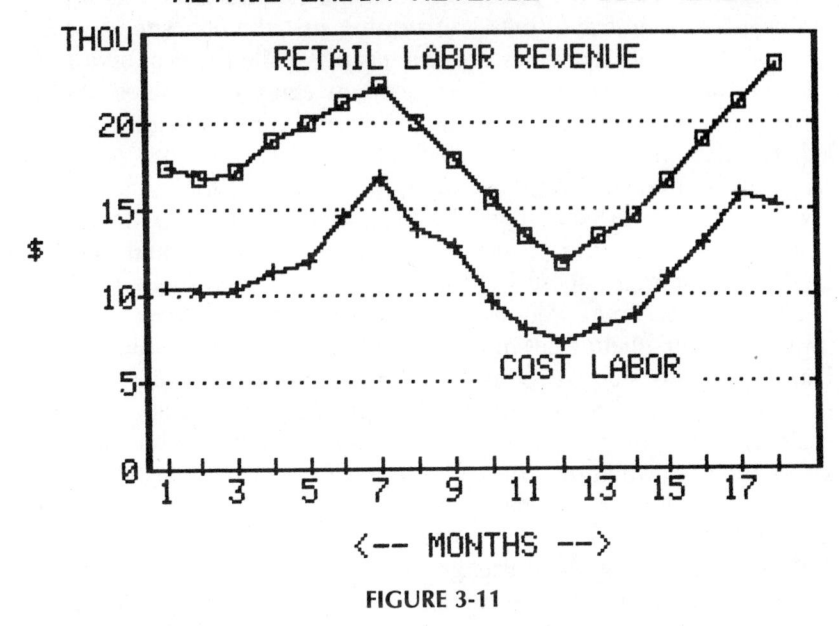

FIGURE 3-11

REPAIR LABOR / COST LABOR TREND LINES

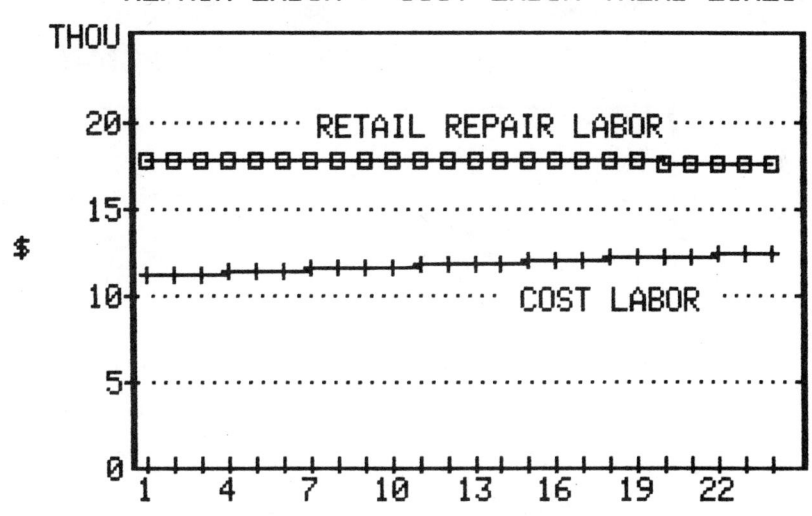

THESE TREND LINES ARE BASED ON 18 MONTHS OF
DATA AND PROJECTED OUT FOR 6 MONTHS MORE

FIGURE 3-12

73

was seemingly a problem-free picture of our labor and its costs, this illustration is cause for alarm. The trend lines are running just the opposite of what we'd hope they would: retail labor sales are decreasing, while the cost of our labor is rising. There's still a considerable difference between the two lines (they're obviously not going to intersect), but that's because our overhead costs are not included. The data plotted here are for actual labor sales and costs only, without any regard to the overhead required to support things. What sort of a picture would we see if our overhead added $2000 a month to our cost total? All of a sudden, the lines would start to meet, and this department would find itself in the red. What's important about Figure 3-12 is that it serves as something like the warning you'd get from a double-barreled shotgun: *both lines* are going the wrong way, and you'd better get into gear and do something about it.

The logical next step when you find a problem like Figure 3-12 illustrates is to look at things on a percentage basis. Figure 3-13 does that, and plots the labor costs as a percentage of the labor sales for our fictitious business over an 18-month period. As we know, these can represent either the last 18 months or 18 months on a calendar-year basis, whatever we feel is most helpful at this particular time.

What's most striking about this graph of the same information we've been examining are all of those plotting marks we see on the 60% line; for fully 10 of the 18 months under study, labor costs amounted to exactly 60% of the retail

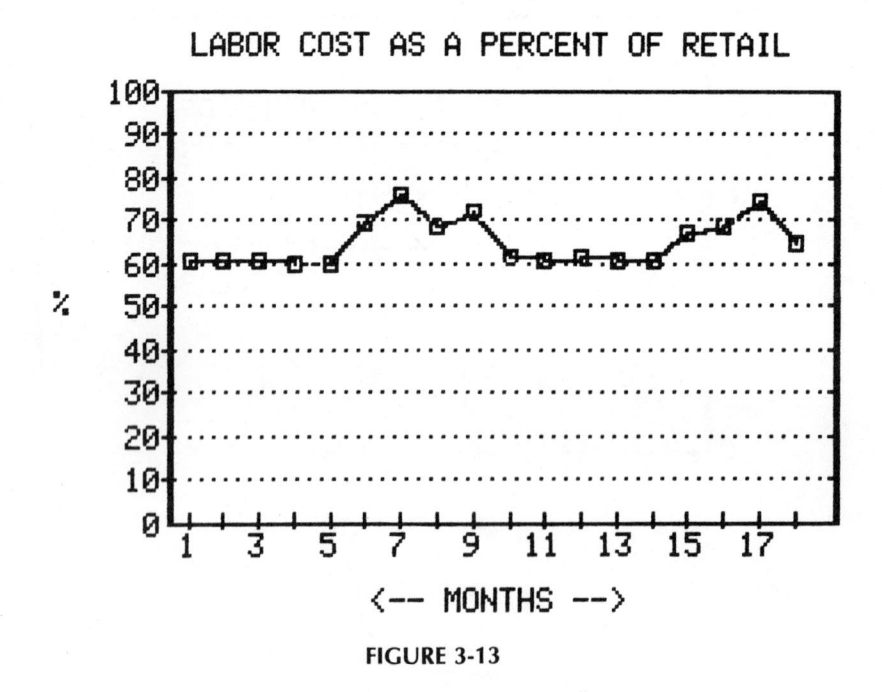

FIGURE 3-13

price our business received for that labor. The other striking thing is that months 6 through 9 of the first yearly period saw a sharp rise in labor costs as a percentage of its sales. Why? On a percentage of change basis (which would be another useful way to look at this data) the rise at this point would be even more severe. At the far end of the graph, the last four months also saw a jump, again getting close to the 80% mark.

From this information, it's impossible to understand the *why* behind these increases. When a series of data points remains so stable over a period of time, it takes quite a jolt to knock them off stride, so to speak. In this example, our labor costs as a percentage of their sales rose almost 20% in a very brief span of time.

The ideal way to discover the reason behind these fluctuations would be to go back and examine our sales during these periods and compare them to our sales when the line was flat. Who were the service technicians on the job? Who supervised things? Were these times of the year when some of our people were standing around, not able to work (but still being paid) because of weather conditions? Were sales very low while our people were kept on the payroll (which changes the percentage figure we're looking at)? There has to be some reason, and now that the business owner knows *when* there was a problem, he or she knows where to look to find out what happened, determine why it took place, and figure out a strategy to see that it doesn't happen again.

Contracting Work

Earlier in this chapter we examined the contracts our fictional business handled, particularly in the way they relate to our sales total. It's also often helpful to get a bit closer to contracting work (or any area, of course, that is important to your business) with an eye to where the work comes from, who we're selling to. Contracts, as you'll recall, is the work our business does for contractors, people who build new homes.

When we want to take a close look at who we're doing work for, the natural starting point is to compare this year's sales to last year's (or the latest monthly period to the same period last year).

Figure 3-14 is a line graph that plots our sales to Bob's Builders over a nine-month period, comparing this year's sales to last year's. It's obvious that early in the year sales were about the same, then split apart in March, where this year's figures fall lower than last year's sales. Once we spot this, we'd want to find out the reason behind it: is Bob simply not building as much as he did last year, or is more of his work going to one of our competitors? If the latter is the case, what can we do to change the situation?

In this example, by July our fictional business turned things around and current sales surpassed those from last year.

```
       SALES VOLUME FOR BOB'S BUILDERS,
   5000┬THIS YEAR COMPARED TO LAST YEAR
       │                        CURRENT YEAR
   4000┤········· ··············· ··········
       │          LAST
       │          YEAR
   3000┤········ ·····················
    $  │
       │
   2000┤········ ·····················
       │
       │
   1000┤··········· ························
       │
       │
      0┴──┼──┼──┼──┼──┼──┼──┼──┼──┼──
          1  2  3  4  5  6  7  8  9
             <-- MONTHS -->
```

FIGURE 3-14

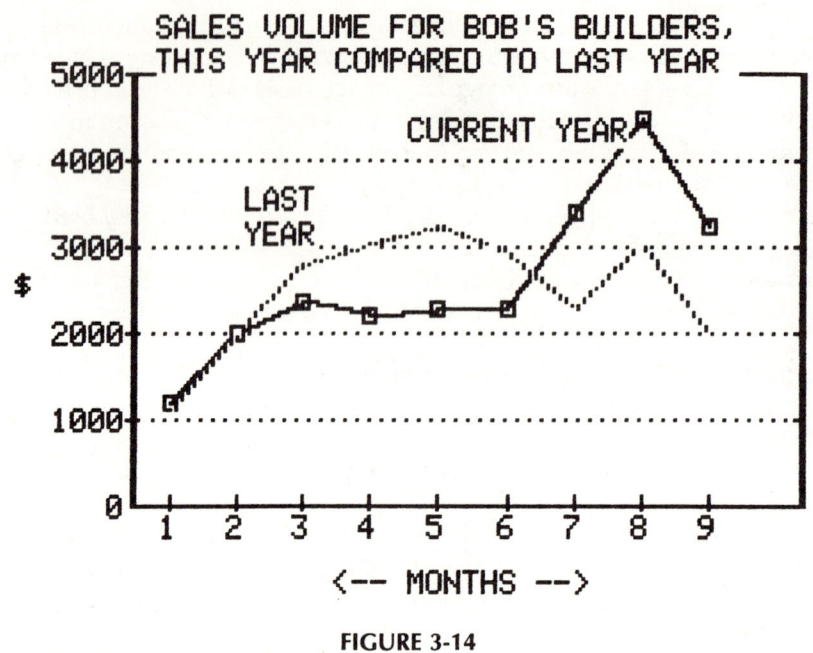

This comparison is something you'd want to do only for your larger volume people (in this example, only for those contractors for whom we do a lot of work).

There are really a number of things this comparison will tell you. In the construction business, for example, where we work with contractors, it gives us a good handle on our pricing policies: unless we're competitive, even the most faithful contractor strays from our fold and buys from the heating and cooling business down the street. A graph like Figure 3-14 helps us know how our prices are. It also gives us a feel for the financial health of the people we work for. Contractors can be funny people: when they owe us money, they seem to have a tendency not to want to come in and tell us they're running behind. Instead, they often shun any contact with us and end up having the competition do their current work. Since we usually have a good idea of who's building how much and where they're building it, Figure 3-14 gives us a feel for how much work our business is getting from the total work a specific contractor has in process.

A logical followup to Figure 3-14 would be to plot a trend line for this year's sales to date and overlay it on a graph of a trend line for last year's sales for the same period for this particular customer. That would give us an indication of how our sales volume for this contractor is heading—lower or higher—and if we project the trend-line information, it even will give us a feeling for how much sales volume we'll do for this customer. If they're slow to pay their bills, this information helps us determine how much cash we may need to borrow; if they pay as each part of a job is completed, it tells us a bit more about the cash we can expect to collect during the coming months.

It might seem to make sense to graph the percentage increase or decrease in the business a contractor gives you. A graph like this doesn't make the figures easier to understand, however. Perhaps you'll find, say, a 10% decrease for three months in a row. On the graph, these 10% decreases will show up as a straight line—each month's sales were 10% less than the prior month's. So, a percentage graph for this sort of data doesn't make it easier to comprehend; you might as well list the percentage increases or decreases on a sheet of paper.

Figure 3-15 plots the picture we've been covering—how the sales our fictional business made to "Ed the Builder" have been doing, on a percentage basis. It's obvious that they've been decreasing at the rate of 10% per month, but the graph we can ask our microcomputer for doesn't do a good job at telling the story. This is because it can only work with raw data, and when we ask it to plot percentage changes, it does its job, but comes up with a flat line—right at the 10% mark.

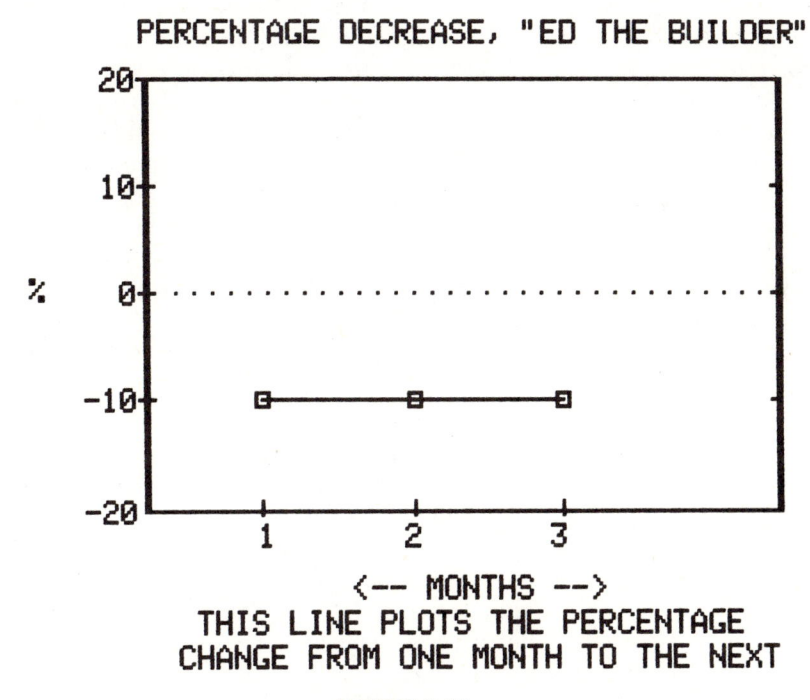

FIGURE 3-15

Figure 3-15 illustrates why a graph of information that changes on a percentage basis isn't as helpful (in this case) as just the raw data itself might be. At the moment, microcomputer programs are limited to standard arithmetic charts, which show simply the movement of the data itself. When we want to show a percentage increase or decrease, we need to use a semilogarithmetic chart, which plots the percentage change as an increment that rises or falls. There's more on this in Chapter 2, and as you can see from Figure 3-15, when we plot the sales we made to "Ed the Builder" on a percentage of change basis, and those sales decreased by 10% each month, we simply get a straight, flat line.

Building Pie

A logical extension of a study of those people you do work for is to show how their sales volume connects to your total through the use of a pie chart. As you know, this will give you a feeling of how each contractor's sales volume relates to the total sales you get from contracting.

This examination can be done every month, although you can run into a fluctuation problem when you do it that often. In most small businesses, sales are recorded as they're billed. For contracting work in particular, invoices sent out don't always match the sales they represent during any given period. This is because a lot of contracting work is done on a draw basis. You estimate how much of a job you've completed at a particular point in time (like the 10th of the month, if that's when you send out invoices), and base the amount of the bill on this estimate. This method lets you collect while a job is in progress rather than having to wait until it's completed. For instance, when 25% of a job is done, it's billed and—hopefully—paid. Often, these percentage figures aren't completely accurate. If you're short of cash, the natural tendency is to inflate your estimate (for billing purposes) of how complete a job is. Also, it sometimes happens that you'll want to record as much dollar volume in sales as possible during a specific period of time (particularly as the end of a year approaches), so you might record invoices that really aren't quite due as of their billing date.

Figure 3-16 represents data for the third quarter of a year, based on the percentage of contract sales that each of five builders contributed to the total our fictional business recorded. Builders Supply gave us the largest share of our volume (almost half), while Allied SW bought the least from our business. Without the same chart over other periods of time, Figure 3-16 doesn't tell us if these percentages will hold true, but once you plot this information over a few quarterly periods, you'll know who's buying from you and who isn't. We'd also want to follow through on Allied SW's purchases—why were they only 3% of our total contract sales? Was it because this particular business simply isn't doing much business, or are we just getting a small piece of their pie?

SALES IN SECTIONS 79

NEW HOMES BY BUILDER – 3RD QUARTER

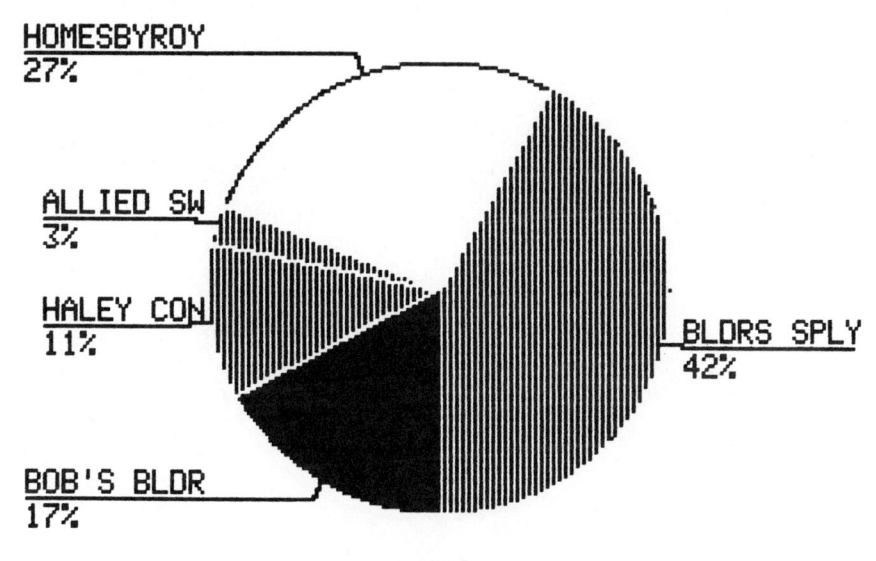

HOMESBYROY
27%

ALLIED SW
3%

HALEY CON
11%

BOB'S BLDR
17%

BLDRS SPLY
42%

FIGURE 3-16

Another Group

It's an obvious comparison to make, but surprisingly, while most businesses break down their sales by department, many business owners don't keep a sales breakdown for the different product groups they handle. When the business manager looks at his or her inventory totals, they'll ask for a breakdown by wholesaler or type of product or department code; it's just as important to extract the data for the different product *groups* you happen to handle.

Figure 3-17 illustrates the sales, on a percentage basis, our fictional business made for the third quarter of a year, for the four major contracting groups it sells from. In this example, New Homes provides nearly 40% of our sales, while the weakest end of the business was our Remodeling group. Why? With four areas to sell to contractors from, we'd expect them each to contribute about 25% of our total contract volume, and the only one right on line is the Plumbing group.

As with any other information, this data is only relevant when you relate it to other periods, other graphs. If Remodeling over a period of time stays at its low level, we need to spend some time in that department to determine the reason for it. Perhaps this one chart is derived from data that showed a good increase in sales for the rest of our product groups, while Remodeling remained about the same—thus causing a decrease in its percentage figure.

SALES BY PRODUCT GROUP – 3RD QUARTER

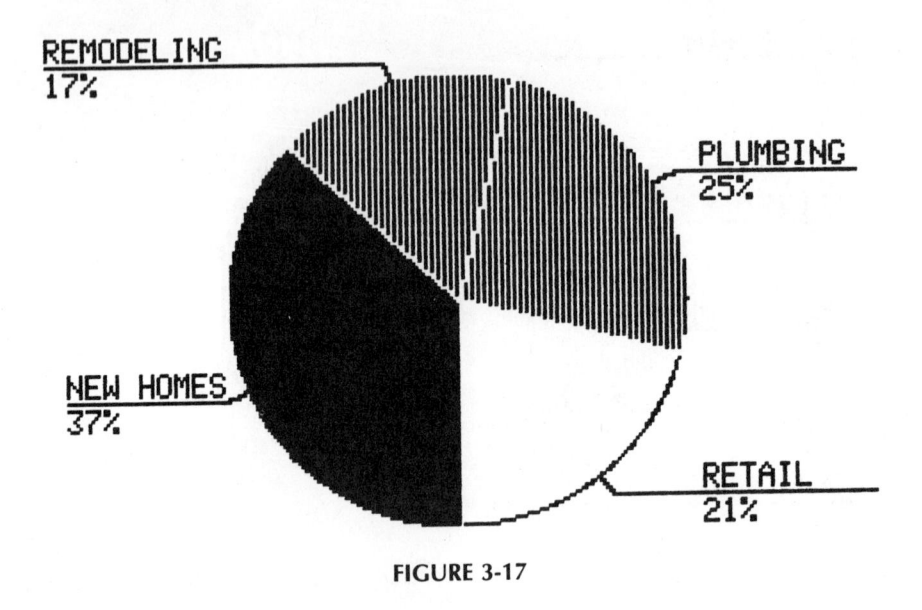

REMODELING 17%
PLUMBING 25%
NEW HOMES 37%
RETAIL 21%

FIGURE 3-17

Subcontracts

One area of contracting work involves what is called "subcontracts." One person—a general contractor—will take on an entire job and hire out parts of it to subcontractors. This can include almost anything, of course, and a new home under construction usually will involve a number of them—a plumbing company, an electrician, a heating contractor, drywall people, a painting crew, and so on.

While we've examined our sales to contractors on an individual basis (for Bob's Builders in Figure 3-14) and in a pie chart (Figure 3-16) so we can see how each company we work for relates to our total contract sales, it's equally useful to plot the data on a monthly basis as a bar chart. This gives us a unique and useful view to help understand where our sales are coming from for the particular period under study.

For the month of June, Figure 3-18 illustrates the contract work we did for six different builders, running from the lowest in volume (Carter's New Homes) to our best customer for this area, Ram Builders. As always, one month of information doesn't tell us a whole lot but needs to be coupled with a continuous study on the same basis. In this case, since the area of contract sales (with our business acting as a subcontractor) is important to us, we'd want to create this chart every month, just so we can see how things are going. If Ram is consistently

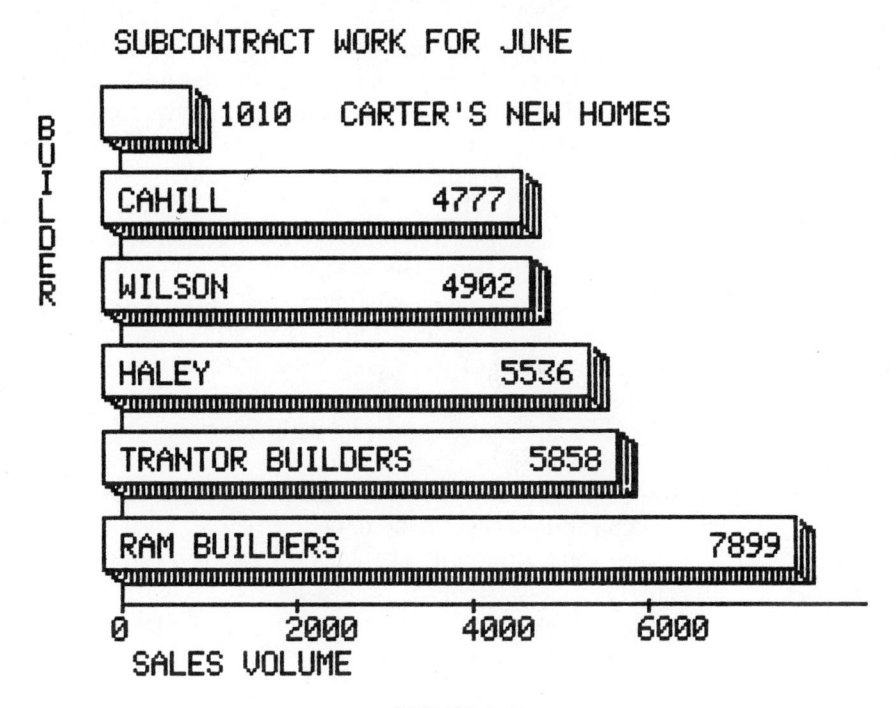

```
               SUBCONTRACT WORK FOR JUNE
  B        ▌ 1010    CARTER'S NEW HOMES
  U
  I   ┌─CAHILL─────────────4777─┐
  L
  D   ┌─WILSON─────────────4902─┐
  E
  R   ┌─HALEY──────────────────5536─┐
      ┌─TRANTOR BUILDERS───────────5858─┐
      ┌─RAM BUILDERS────────────────────────7899─┐
      0      2000      4000      6000
            SALES VOLUME
```

FIGURE 3-18

our best customer, they should be treated as such. If Carter's New Homes is always our lowest-volume buyer, perhaps we need to spend more time with the Carter people in an effort to raise their dollar total. This information, as marked on the graph, is plotted as raw sales totals, instead of on the percentage basis we looked at before.

There's another side to this coin, too. Just as someone who owns a business like ours (heating and air conditioning) is hired by contractors to work on this job or that installation, and so we track our sales by *builder,* a contractor should do the same thing in reverse: by *subcontractor.* The viewpoint is different, of course. For the builder who looks at monthly charts of the people he or she buys from, the idea would be to determine if the supplier who gets most of your business gives you the service this large volume deserves.

Summing Up

Unless your business sells only a single product and/or service, there are sections inside your work that will fall logically into a grouping that makes sense to take a close look at.

Since our business works with contracts—those installations we install for a contractor—we chose to examine them in detail for this chapter. Your work will more than likely be completely different in terms of what you need to look at, but the basic techniques are the same. A good starting point is to break down each item (in our examples, *contracts*) into its average volume. Is it rising or falling for this section of your work? Why? Is the data headed the way you'd like it to be? Add a trend line to the basic information to see its direction and to project where it will take you a few months down the road.

Think about other ways to break down whatever area(s) you want to study. Do you do some of your work inside the city limits, and other work out of the city? In different cities? Is some of your work taxable, while other parts are not? Does some of it involve major equipment, while other work is based entirely on small parts? None of these comparisons might be right for you, of course; the idea is to examine one area or another inside your work and break it down as much as possible. If you find you don't get valid information from such a breakdown, you don't have to continue tracking the data.

Since many companies get a majority of their business from the estimates they create and present to their customers, take a long look at the bids your business makes. You want to know how many quotations you're making and plot the data. You need to know how many of those bids you can turn into sales, on a percentage basis. This same comparison, on a *dollar* basis, is done in Chapter 2. How is your sales department performing? Does the trend of this information make you think they'll sell a greater share of your estimates in the future?

With most of this information, it's helpful to plot a historical picture of the data, to see how things have taken place over a period of time. Your trend lines become more meaningful and accurate, too, when they're spread over a long time frame.

Another area that many business owners have to wrestle with concerns repair labor. Our examples took a look at the work our fictional business performed on its premises, but the same basic techniques hold true for any examination of labor. This section of your business needs to be split away from the main area, both in terms of its costs and in the sales it creates. The addition of a trend line to your graph lets you know where you're heading. Our study found that while labor and its sales moved about the same when the raw data was plotted, when we charted just the two trend lines we found a problem.

Within any group, it's worthwhile to examine the relationship your business has with its best customers, the people who buy the most from you. You'd want to look at each customer (we looked at building contractors) in regard to his or her contribution to your total sales for the group under study, as well as individual figures for every month or quarter. Conversely, if you purchase a lot of materials or services from other people, chart their sales to you in an effort to determine if you're getting your money's worth.

If you know your line of work, you can often glean more information from these graphs than you'd expect, particularly in terms of your own pricing policies and the cash condition of some of your customers.

Other Ideas

Since you can combine any logical group of what you sell, or who you sell to, there are an untold number of combinations you might want to examine. Instead of suggesting some specific areas that you might want to look at, it's probably more helpful to give you some general ideas on how to select groups to consider. Anything that's informative should be charted on a regular basis. When you find an area that perhaps sounded good but doesn't tell you anything, stop tracking its information and making graphs of it.

The key to much of this kind of examination is to break things down to their lowest level. For instance, you might want to look at just the sales your business makes for, say, the Plumbing area. You may also want to break this data down, to the sales per truck this part of your work provides. Or the sales created on a per mile basis. Or per service call. You might do much of your work through mail order, or over the phone. Break those sales down on a per delivery or per call basis. The whole idea is to pick a group of logically related sections of your work, break down their contribution to sales/overhead/profit/costs to the lowest possible level, and examine things. Many times, you'll find the information isn't helpful, and when you do, move on to something else. But inside your work, hidden away somewhere, are three or four groups of things that will give you terrific information when you chart their data.

Cash Flow

4

Cash. It's at the heart of every business transaction, the true bottom line of every company, the way we gauge the health of an enterprise. By any standard, cash is an accurate measurement of our effectiveness as managers: if there's enough left after our sales are totaled and costs paid, we've done well; if not, we've done something wrong. It's as simple as that.

In the old days, it was an easy matter to add up what we had left in the cash drawer at the end of the day. Today we have all sorts of ledgers and journals that we must sort through to find out what we sold, and even more pieces of paper to extract data from to figure out if we made money or not. But the process is the same, and under it all floats (pardon the pun) *cash*. With cash in the bank, we're successful; without it, we're not in business.

Cash *Flow*

It's important to remember that cash flow means just what it says—cash moves *both* in and out of your business, and the businesspeople who look just at what they expect to collect or only what they owe see things from a myopic viewpoint. The movement of dollars in your business has to be examined from both directions—coming and going. And it is a *movement*. Every day you receive cash or sell products that promise future cash. Every day you write checks or purchase things on credit that promise a future outlay of funds. Cash is constantly received and spent, juggled and moved, added and subtracted, and with your computer you can get an accurate estimate of what cash you can expect to receive and how many dollars you'll need next month to pay your bills.

Cash is often confused with *assets,* and while your assets include the cash you have available, cash is a liquid asset, while other things (trucks, office machines, buildings) that are assets are not liquid. Even your inventory isn't fully liquid: you must sell it before you collect the cash. For these reasons, it's important to consider where you put your cash, because if too much is someplace where you can't retrieve it when you need it (like the down payment for a new truck), you have a cash flow problem. Likewise, unless you've got the cash you do have available out there working for you, you might be very liquid but probably won't be in business for a long period of time. There must be a balance in the places you put your cash, to ensure that you have enough for your current needs (payroll, equipment for the job you'll start tomorrow), but still have the proper amount out there working for you.

Sales and Cash

Any study of cash necessarily starts with sales, as they generate all the dollars you'll receive (unless you borrow money or sell stock in your business). The sales you made last month and the month before (and before that, of course) directly determine the cash you'll receive this month. If you let your customers charge their purchases, the total accounts receivable amount has a direct bearing on the cash you can expect to get. Every business has a historical pattern that reflects how well they collect what their customers owe them. On the average, unless the management changes its policies or credit terms, or business conditions change, this ratio will remain steady over a period of time.

It's a fairly simple thing to go back through your monthly sales reports and/or accounts receivable totals and monthly summaries of cash collected to determine this ratio. You'll find that *on the average* you collect, say, 55% of the outstanding receivables, or perhaps 40% of the sales total, and so on. Whatever your average ratio is, it can serve as a guide to what you can expect to collect in the future.

Flowing Graphs

This is where business graphics gives us something of a line on the future based on what we've done in the past, and while we can't predict what will happen, the proper dollar amounts displayed in a helpful graphics format can at least show us a picture of what's taken place with an eye to what we can expect next month. Let's examine the records of a fictional business that's like many in that it records much of its sales during one period of the year. In this case, let's say it's an air conditioning business that records most of its sales during the summer months.

Because line graphs help create a feeling of movement and give a bit more life to the image we receive from them, they form a good basis to examine this particular data.

Figure 4-1 is a line graph of just the sales information for our fictitious business. It's easy to see when summer arrived and when it left. This particular scale, shown running up and down the left side of the chart, isn't the best choice for this graph, because of the large open area below the line; it was done this way so that when we add in things like accounts receivable totals and payments, we have somewhere to put these smaller amounts.

There's nothing particularly fascinating about one line of sales information, and even when we add in the accounts receivable total (Figure 4-2), we see about what we expect. Since the amount our customers owe us will depend in a direct way on our sales volume, we can expect these two lines to approximate one another. This *does* tell us, though, that this particular business can anticipate that its receivables total will vary in direct proportion to sales, except perhaps during the summer months, where the comparison isn't as exact.

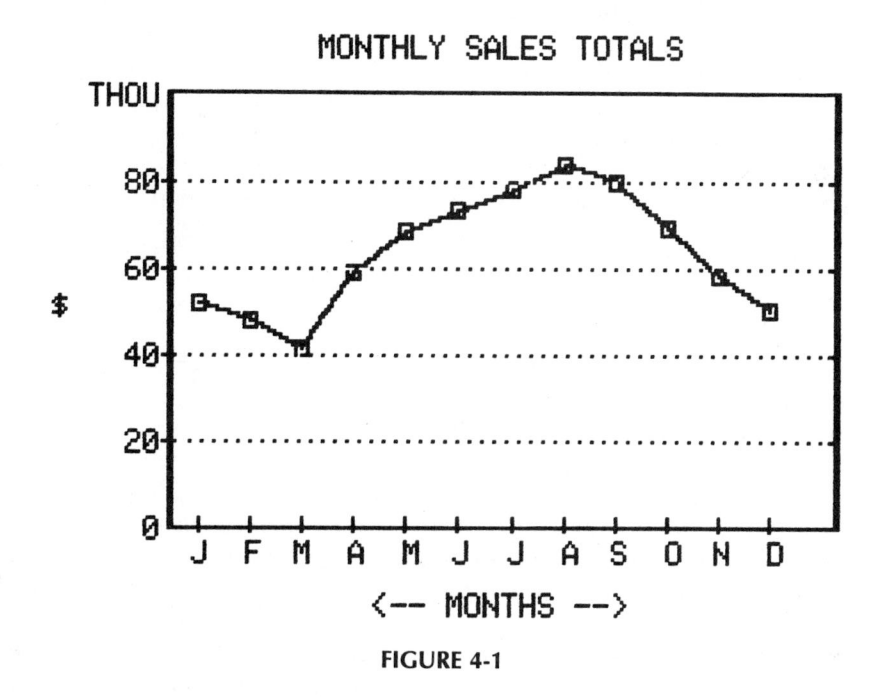

FIGURE 4-1

MONTHLY SALES / ACCOUNTS RECEIVABLE

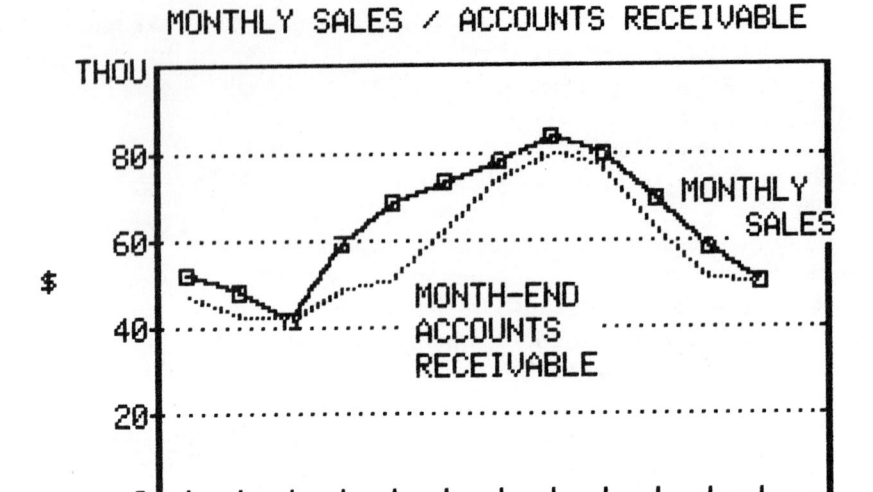

[Figure: Line graph showing monthly sales and month-end accounts receivable from January through December, with values ranging from 0 to 80+ thousand dollars. Both lines peak around August-September.]

FIGURE 4-2

There could be a number of reasons for this, but a logical one is that people who buy summer's big-ticket item (air conditioning) most likely can afford it, and perhaps will send along a check as soon as they receive the invoice. So while the sales can increase dramatically, accounts receivables might not, as a lot of bills are paid before the receivables are totaled at the end of each month. When September came along for this business during this particular year, the receivables started to follow the exact line as sales, confirming the relationship predicted by the graph.

Sales Don't Necessarily Equal Cash

Figure 4-3 again shows the total sales line, but now the lower line represents the cash collected each month. However, there are some major discrepancies between the data sets. While the first three months follow a close pattern (coincidence?), the period from March to April shows a tremendous increase in sales, while the total cash collected *decreased*. As sales continued their rapid climb through June, July, and August, the dollars flowed in at a much slower rate during the same period.

In the September—October period, we find a reversal of what took place early in the summer. Now, sales show a sharp decline, while the amount of cash the business received continued to increase—still not at the same rate that sales

MONTHLY SALES & CASH COLLECTED

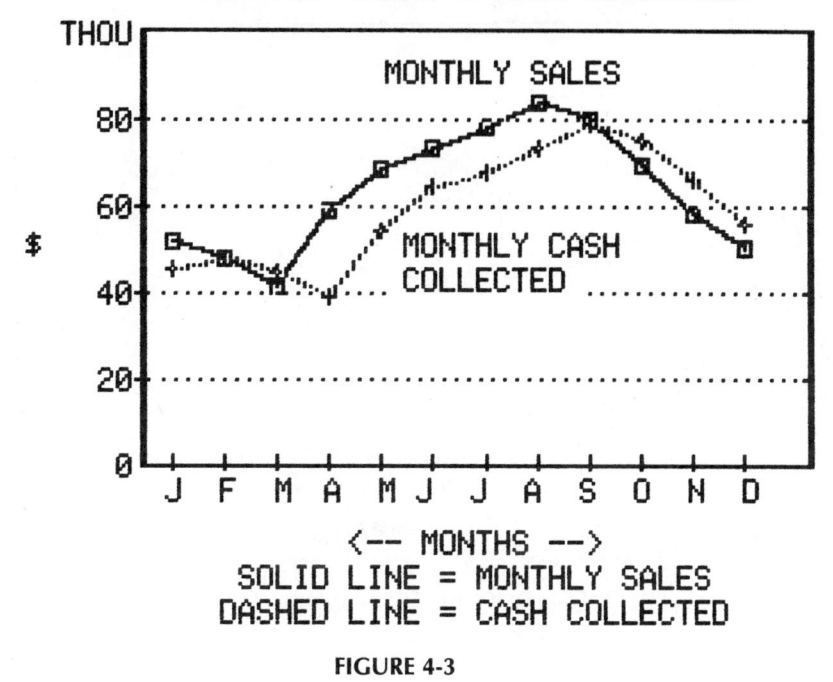

```
THOU
  │              MONTHLY SALES
80┤                        ┌─□─┐
  │                    ┌─□─┘   └─□
  │                  ┌─┘    ╱·····+·····+
60┤              ┌─□─┘  ╱+·┘
$ │          ┌─□─┘  ╱·+┘  MONTHLY CASH
40┤ □──□──□─┘ ╱·+·┘        COLLECTED
  │  +··+··+
  │
20┤
  │
 0└─┬──┬──┬──┬──┬──┬──┬──┬──┬──┬──┬──┬
    J  F  M  A  M  J  J  A  S  O  N  D
         <-- MONTHS -->
      SOLID LINE = MONTHLY SALES
      DASHED LINE = CASH COLLECTED
```

FIGURE 4-3

grew, but in direct opposition to the sales pattern for this period. By the end of the summer, cash starts to catch up with the volume of sales.

During the last three months of the year, sales still continue to drop but the cash inflow increases to more than the sales total.

In almost any graph that looks at related accounting data, you'll find some correlation in spots here and there. Just as you should be suspect of any graph where *everything* matches exactly, you should be equally suspicious of anywhere none of the periods seem to follow one another. In this particular case (Figure 4-3), we find only spots of equal movement.

Sales Equal Dollars

Doesn't it make more sense to assume that the monies we collect should follow sales by some time period? After all, since our fictional business has an accounts receivable system through which it lets people charge their purchases, we shouldn't expect their payments to arrive at the same time as they would if the business handled everything on a purely cash basis.

Figure 4-4 illustrates what happens when we plot the sales figures along with the cash we collected one month later. In other words, sales for March

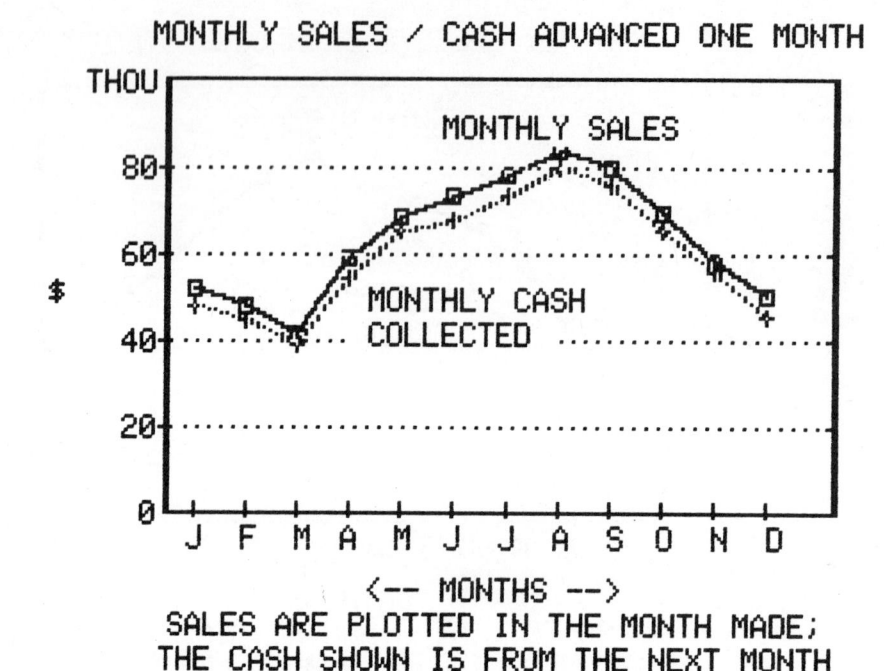

```
         MONTHLY SALES / CASH ADVANCED ONE MONTH
     THOU
                            MONTHLY SALES
      80-
      60-
  $              MONTHLY CASH
      40-        COLLECTED
      20-
       0
         J  F  M  A  M  J  J  A  S  O  N  D
                    <-- MONTHS -->
         SALES ARE PLOTTED IN THE MONTH MADE;
         THE CASH SHOWN IS FROM THE NEXT MONTH
```

FIGURE 4-4

(about $42,000) are plotted where you expect them—over the "M". But the cash collected plotted over that same "M" is the cash this business received during *April*—one month after the sales were made and recorded.

In effect, Figure 4-4 shows how this month's sales affect next month's cash. In this particular business, there's a direct relationship between the two, much more so than between the raw sales and cash totals for each month we examined in Figure 4-3.

Receivables and Cash

If you owned this business, you may be able—based on the information shown in Figure 4-4—to reliably forecast what cash you could expect to collect next month, once you tallied this month's total sales. This has all sorts of implications. Once you know how much cash you'll have available, you can decide what to do with it, when to spend money on this or when to purchase that. But you'd want to take things a step further, to examine the relationship between receivables and cash.

Figure 4-5 shows the accounts receivable totals for each month, along with

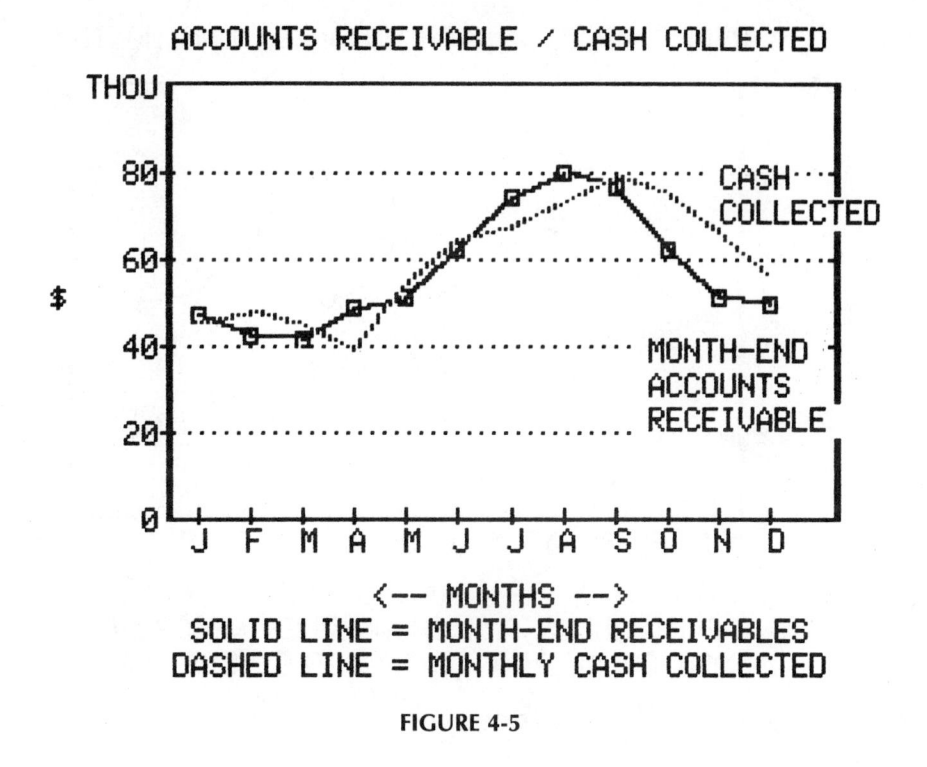

ACCOUNTS RECEIVABLE / CASH COLLECTED

(Graph showing month-end receivables as solid line and monthly cash collected as dashed line, plotted from January through December, with dollar values in thousands ranging from 0 to 80+.)

SOLID LINE = MONTH-END RECEIVABLES
DASHED LINE = MONTHLY CASH COLLECTED

FIGURE 4-5

the cash collected for each monthly period. The relationships here are very similar to what we examined in Figure 4-3 and have a number of instances where one line doesn't match the way the other moves.

Figure 4-6 shows the same figures, with the cash received *advanced* a month in front of the receivable totals. In effect, this confirms what we saw when we looked at sales and cash, when the cash collected amounts ran a month ahead of the sales figures. Again, both lines rise and fall in almost direct proportion to one another. It tells the business owner he or she has about a 30-day collection cycle.

Because sales compared to the cash received, and receivables compared to the cash received, both tell us the same story, this particular business can reliably estimate the cash it will collect next month, based on either its sales or receivables totals, *as long as its policies remain the same.* That's an important qualifier, because, if this were your business, you might suddenly decide to limit the access of credit to your customers, or to be more liberal in whom you allow to charge. Either would change conditions. There's no problem with this—after all, if it *were* your business, you'd know what was happening and wouldn't base your cash expectations on sales or receivables totals once you adjusted the rules of the game. But as long as things remain on the same basis, this business has an accurate method to forecast its cash inflow.

```
        RECEIVABLES / CASH ADVANCED ONE MONTH
     THOU
      ┌─────────────────────────────────────┐
   80─┤  MONTHLY                            │
      │  CASH                               │
      │  COLLECTED                          │
   60─┤                                     │
 $    │              MONTH-END              │
   40─┤              ACCOUNTS               │
      │              RECEIVABLE             │
      │                                     │
   20─┤                                     │
      │                                     │
    0─┴──┬──┬──┬──┬──┬──┬──┬──┬──┬──┬──┬──┬─┘
         J  F  M  A  M  J  J  A  S  O  N  D
               <-- MONTHS -->
     RECEIVABLES ARE SHOWN WHEN RECORDED;
     CASH COLLECTED IS FROM THE NEXT MONTH
```

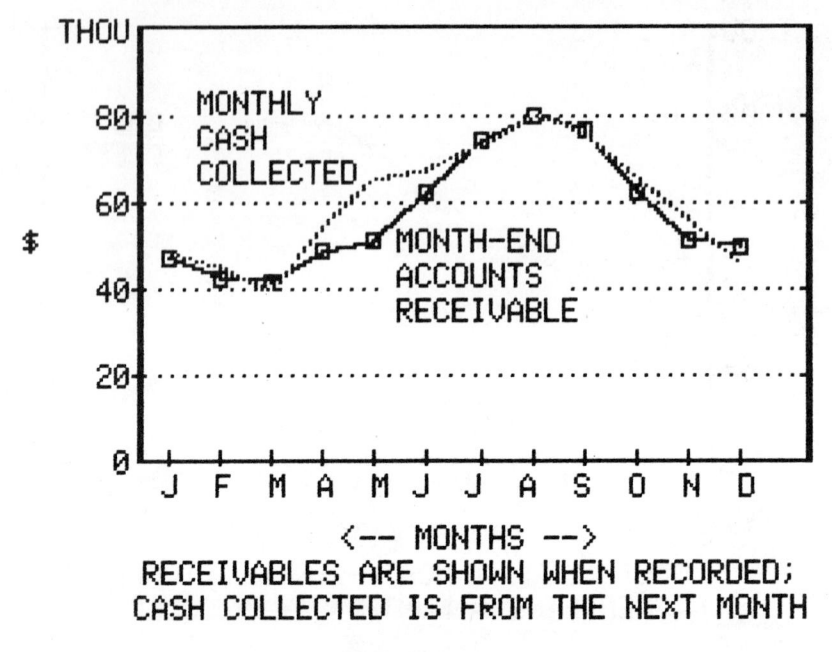

FIGURE 4-6

Your business might be different, of course—your "lag" time might be two months, or three, or longer. It could also be less; while we've examined things only on a monthly basis, you might have weekly information you could take a look at. The whole idea is to examine what data you have under different sets of conditions—move one line or the other forward, over different time frames, so you can see what correlates for you. A line graph examination of cash does exactly that—it gives you a picture of your own data.

A Two-Edged Sword

The movement of cash is an important consideration, because since it flows both in and out of any business, it's a two-edged sword that cuts both ways. Obviously, if you don't have enough money in the bank to meet payroll, you've got a problem. The solution most often used to combat a cash deficiency is to somehow create more sales. While more volume solves many problems, it also cuts both ways. The worst of these comes along when our sales really spurt, while our collections plod along at the same old rate. The dollar amount will rise, of course, as the sales volume goes up, but the problem is that dollars often don't arrive in our mail until long after we've had to pay for the products and/or labor we've sold.

Costs and Overhead

A good illustration of the two-edged sword that cash can become is shown in Figure 4-7. Here we have two new lines, based on the sales and cash collected figures we saw before, and the graph is on the same scale as the earlier line graphs we saw in this chapter.

The solid line is based on costs. Let's imagine that our business operates on a 34% gross profit margin—34 cents out of every dollar we sell (on the average) is left for overhead and profit. Sixty-six percent of our sales dollar, then, goes to pay for the material and labor involved in each sale. Let's also suppose that our business has an overhead that comes to 23% of its total sales.

The bottom line—assuming that these percentages apply to all sales we make during a given period—is this:

DIRECT COSTS	66%
OVERHEAD	23%
TOTAL COSTS	89%

On this basis, our business would have an 11% net profit (11% of its total sales) before taxes.

The solid line in Figure 4-7 shows our monthly costs for both the materials and labor required to produce and distribute our products, plus the overhead

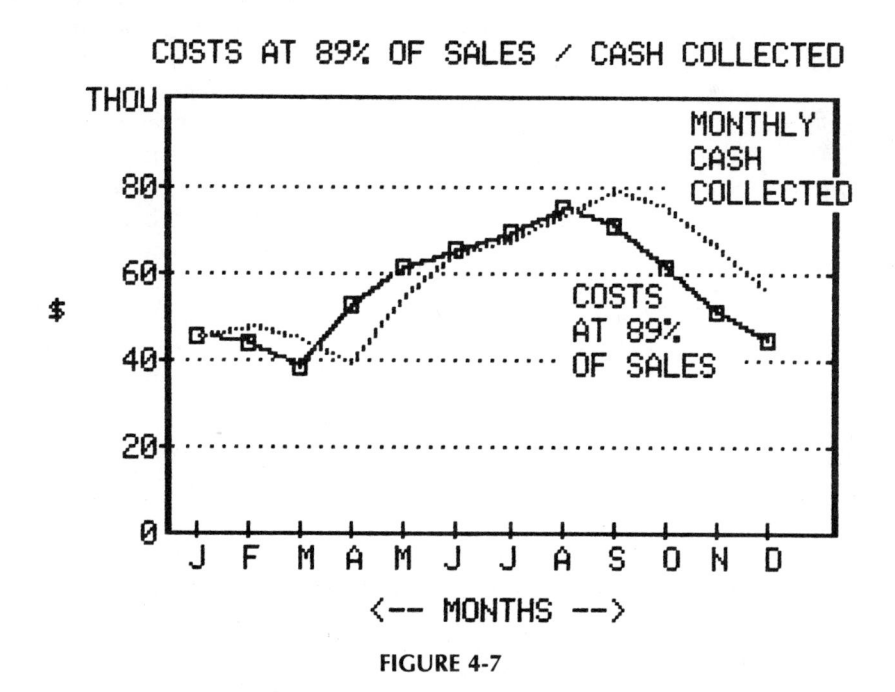

FIGURE 4-7

needed to run the business—a total of 89% of the sales totals. It should leave a more than comfortable margin of 11% for net profit and anything unexpected.

Can We Pay For What We Sell?

In this case, the cash we received more than matched our monthly dollar needs for the first three months of the year. However, in April our summer sales started to skyrocket (and with them, our monthly cost outlay), and although the dollars we received also grew, they didn't arrive in a large enough volume to offset our increased costs.

This isn't a completely accurate image, in that a lot of the purchases we make are on, say, a 30-day net basis, and so we *really* don't have to pay for them during the current month. A more correct picture would plot these figures a month ahead of the others, to *lead* them by a month or two. However, since cash collected should come along *after* the sales are made and payments are required *after* the items are purchased, rather than plot both lines a month in the future, it's almost as accurate (and definitely easier) to plot them both in the same month. It's important to remember that the purpose of this particular graph is to make a point—a huge increase in sales will *eventually* create a greater inflow of cash, but in the meantime, we can find ourselves in a deficit position, as we do here for the April through September period.

These five months were the best for our business both in terms of sales and in the total cash we collected. Our costs, though, grew at the same rate as our sales and because cash didn't flow as fast into the business as it went out, we were cash-poor during the best time of the year. In September the situation reversed itself, and cash once again started to exceed our cost requirements.

What's the lesson here? If you find a similar pattern in your business, it's important to try to *conserve* cash during those times when it exceeds costs, to have it available when it will not. This might seem obvious, but the natural tendency is to think, "we have it, so we'll spend it," without enough thought to the invariable changes in future conditions. And we need to be constantly vigilant in terms of our credit policies and collection terms, as they directly affect the flow of cash into our business.

Seeing Ahead

Where do you spot things like this? While it's helpful to look back over an entire year's figures and think, yes, we should have saved some cash during the spring, it's too late in the game to have any affect on things. For this example, we've used whole-year figures, so let's expand just the first section of Figure 4-7 to see what our position looked like back in May.

Figure 4-8 is the graph we'd have seen in May, if we monitored these two amounts on a monthly basis. It's a close-up view without a zero line, so we can judge more effectively the movement of the data. Early on, we'd probably feel pretty good about things, as the cash for the first three months more than matched costs. However, the situation reversed itself in April, and May finds our costs and cash only a bit closer together. The fact that the two lines *crossed* in the March-to-April period indicates that a significant problem may be right around the corner, and the business owner who is on top of things will immediately take steps to reverse the situation.

While we don't want to slow down the growth of sales, once we realize what's happening to our cash/cost ratio, we can take some measures to improve things. We *know* we'll need cash from somewhere to cover our costs, so we can make plans to borrow it or do something else to raise the money we'll need. We might also want to examine our sales to gauge their quality: perhaps some of the sales growth isn't producing the profits it should—we may just be trading dollars. We'll want to look harder at our costs and overhead with an eye to reducing them. The point is, when we see this pattern on a graph, it alerts us to a potential and growing problem before it becomes overwhelming. That's the whole function of

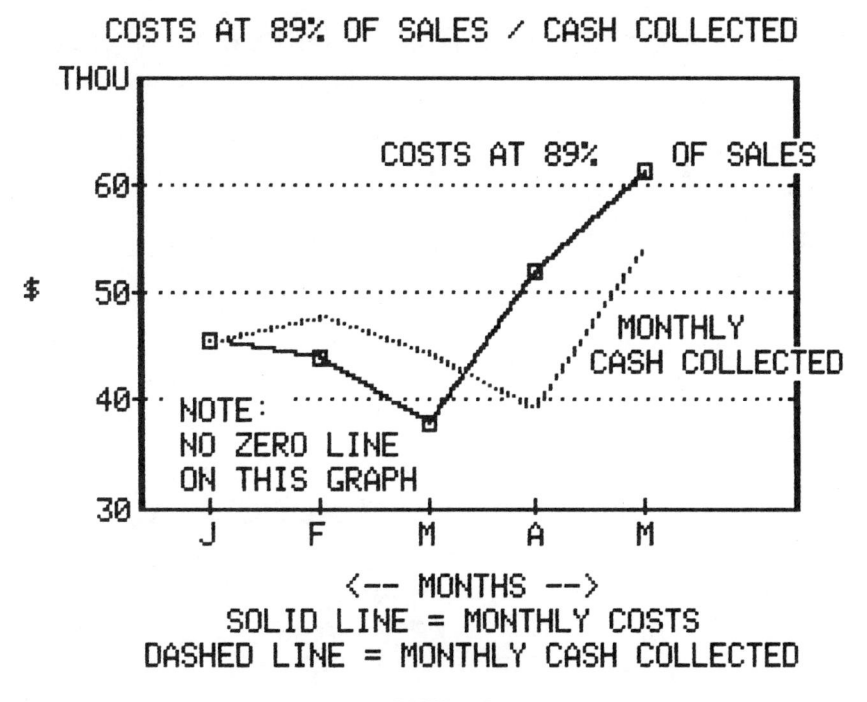

FIGURE 4-8

graphic analysis—to give the business owner an idea of where he or she has been and where the business is headed.

Receivables and Payables

One of the most interesting things we can create with business graphics is an examination of our moving financial picture—how we're doing in one period compared to another. It's almost automatic to do it with sales, as that's one figure we're constantly concerned with. But it's also helpful to take a look at receivables and payables in the same context.

Figure 4-9 charts the month-end figures for accounts receivable for last year, along with the first eight months of the current year. For the first five months of the year, the figures were about the same. However, starting in June the current accounts receivable total began to grow, and by August it was substantially ahead of last year's total.

An increase in accounts receivable is generally viewed as a sign that business is on the upswing. However, as with any data, a variation from what's expected must be closely examined. Is the accounts receivable total greater this year than

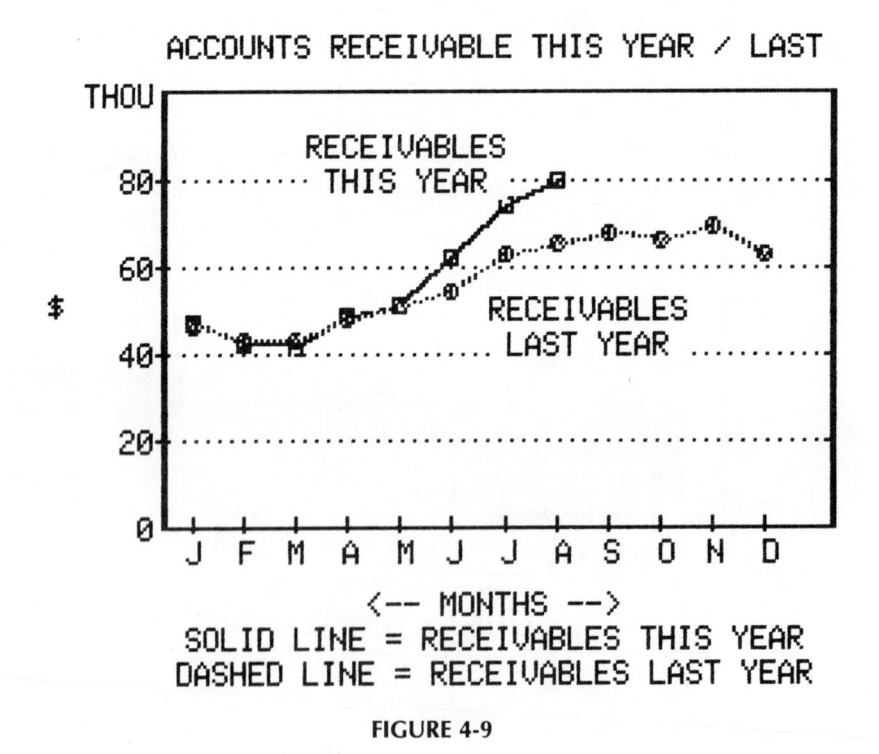

FIGURE 4-9

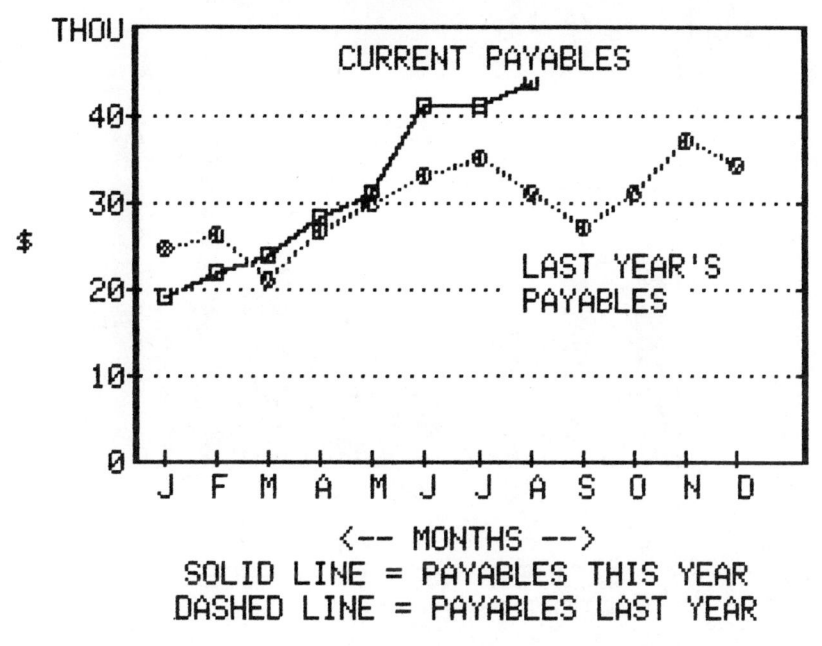

```
        ACCOUNTS PAYABLE THIS YEAR / LAST
   THOU
                    CURRENT PAYABLES
     40
                                  ▫▫▫
                              ▫▫▫▫
                            ▫  ⊙⊙⊙⊙⊙⊙⊙⊙⊙
     30                  ▫  ⊙⊙⊙              ⊙⊙⊙⊙
 $              ⊙⊙⊙⊙▫▫▫⊙⊙⊙                ⊙⊙⊙⊙
           ⊙⊙⊙⊙    ▫▫▫           LAST YEAR'S
     20  ⊙  ▫▫▫                  PAYABLES
        ▫▫

     10

      0
        J  F  M  A  M  J  J  A  S  O  N  D
                 <-- MONTHS -->
         SOLID LINE = PAYABLES THIS YEAR
         DASHED LINE = PAYABLES LAST YEAR
```

FIGURE 4-10

last because of more sales volume or because people aren't paying on time? Has the business eased its credit policies to produce more sales only to have them turn into old accounts receivable? While this particular graph doesn't give you the answer to that problem (one like Figure 4-15 will), it signals you that something *might* be wrong, that there might be a problem on the horizon. It gives you this information while there's time to take corrective action if it's called for.

Along this same line, Figure 4-10 tells the same story for accounts payable. Actually, last year's total was greater only during the first two months of this year, which climbed at an alarming rate all the way through August. The *difference* between the two lines is obvious, and signals that the business is either experiencing a great increase in sales (and thus costs) or isn't paying its bills as it should. In either case, Figure 4-10 gives the business owner a strong message that there might be a serious problem.

Are Things Getting Worse?

The situation is aggravated when you examine Figures 4-11 and 4-12. Figure 4-11 is a column graph for the first eight months of the current year, where the

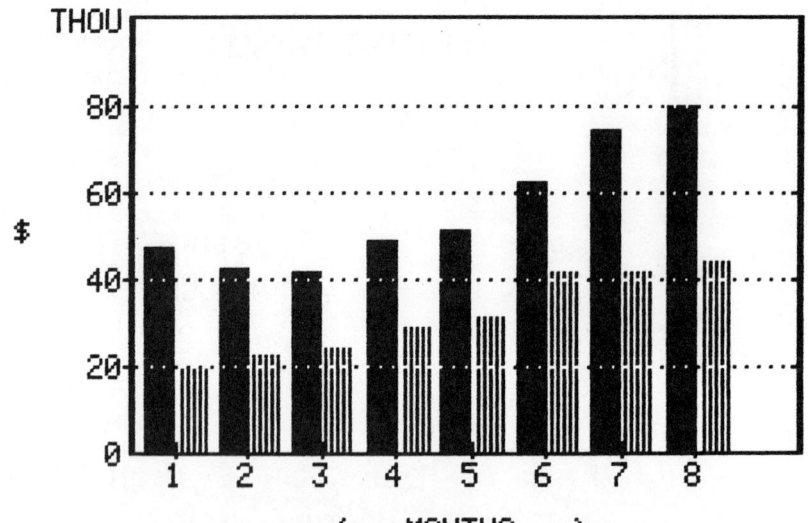

ACCOUNTS RECEIVABLE / PAYABLE

<-- MONTHS -->
LEFT BAR (SOLID) = RECEIVABLES
RIGHT BAR (DASHED) = PAYABLES

FIGURE 4-11

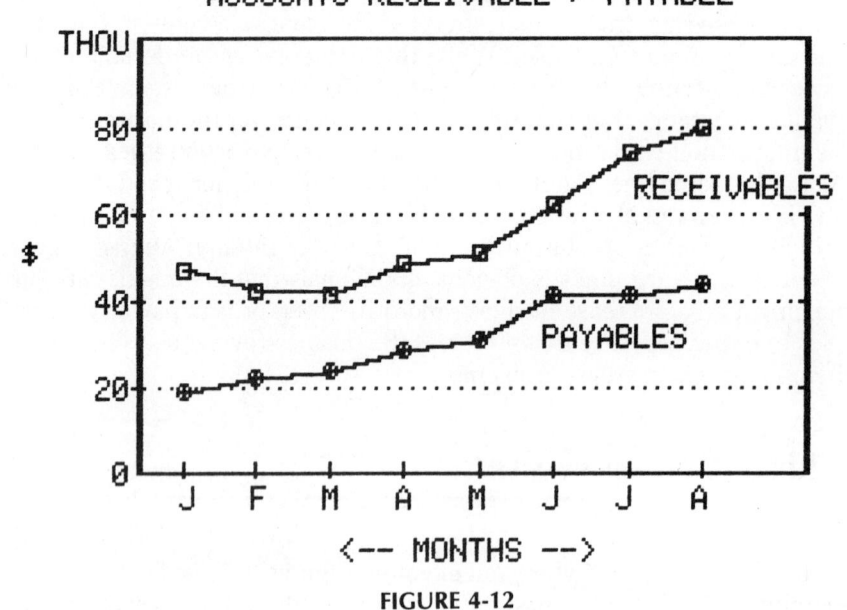

ACCOUNTS RECEIVABLE / PAYABLE

<-- MONTHS -->

FIGURE 4-12

left bar displays the month-end receivables total and the right bar shows the payables total. It's obvious the receivables/payable *ratio* is shrinking. The accepted rule-of-thumb for most businesses tells us this ratio should be 2-1 or greater.

Figure 4-12 displays the same data in a line-graph format. Although generally a column chart gives us a better feeling for the data when we look at two figures like payables and receivables, we sometimes get a better impression of their *rate of change* with a line graph. When the two amounts are plotted as a line graph in Figure 4-12, we get a measure for how one line increases in relationship to the other.

It's usually valid to plot two associated items together (as they are in Figure 4-12). If we just look at the receivables in Figure 4-9 or the payables in Figure 4-10, it *appears* that payables are rising faster than receivables. If that's the case, the business could face serious problems. If receivables and payables increase or decrease at about the same rate, things are probably acceptable. In this case, Figure 4-12 shows us that payables are increasing at a slower rate than the receivables are, but is that what we're really interested in? While Figure 4-12 gives the business owner a feeling for the *rate* of increase for each of the two plotted lines, it's something of a red herring in that what we're looking for is the *ratio* between payables and receivables and not necessarily just their growth rates.

The Real Secret

While all this gives the business owner some good information (and is based on data you'll want to track), it's well worthwhile to take things a step further and have your spreadsheet compute the ratio between your accounts receivable and accounts payable amounts. Generally, graphics programs can't do this sort of math for you, so you must create your own *data files* with the ratio information, rather than just the raw data. It's just as easy—both in your spreadsheet and in your graphics program—to work with a ratio figure as it is to work with a total dollar amount.

If you owned the fictitious business we're examining here and plotted your receivables/payables ratio for the first six months of the year, Figure 4-13 is what you'd see. Since the first of the year (where you had about a 2.4-1 ratio between the two figures), this ratio has steadily deteriorated. It's starting to bump regularly at or below the 2-1 mark. Confronted with these figures, the alert business owner will know to take corrective action of some sort. The logical place to look is, of course, at the accounts receivable area, to see if more cash can be collected. If you get more dollars in payment and apply them to accounts payable, while still making profitable sales, your receivables total will stay where it should and payables will decrease. This is because while those current sales will *add* to both

FIGURE 4-13

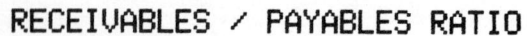

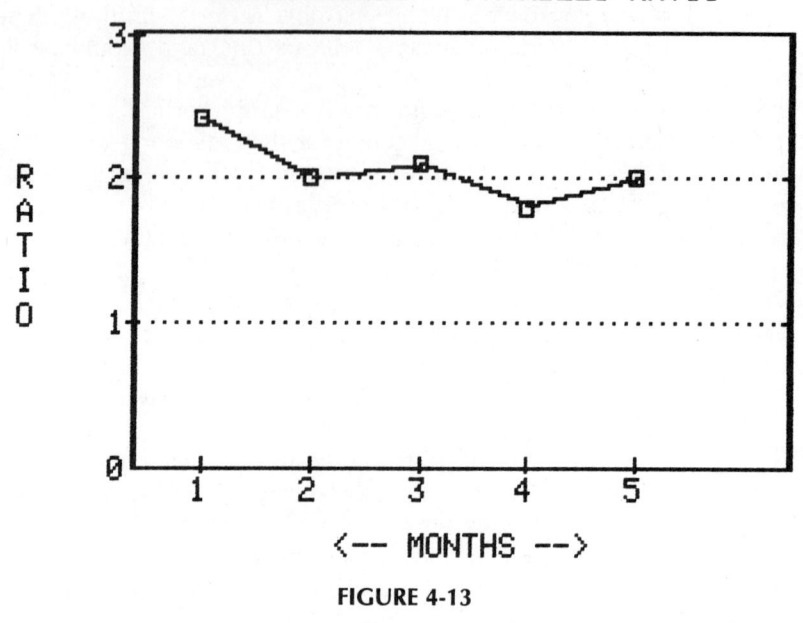

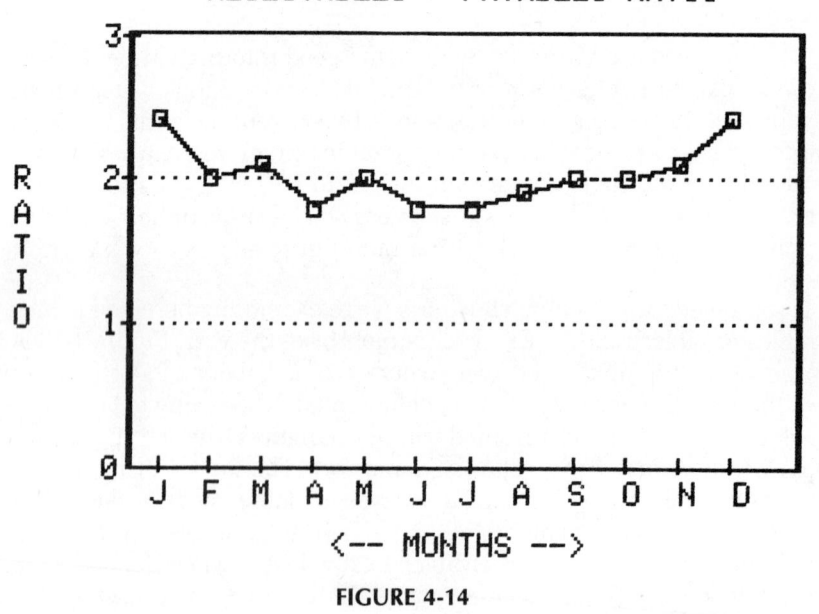

FIGURE 4-14

receivables and payables (more sales generates more costs as well as charge accounts), receivables increase at a *retail* level, while payables increase on a *cost* basis. Receivables must grow more than payables.

Figure 4-14 represents what happened to our fictitious business for the whole year. It assumes the owner made changes in the operation to the extent the receivables/payables ratio made a marked improvement, and in fact they finished the year at about 2.4-1. Although the scale is stretched out to accommodate 12 months worth of figures, we can see the early-year decline in the receivables/payables ratio, a slight improvement in the July-to-October period (probably the results of midterm adjustments being made), and finally, a substantial growth in the ratio during the final two months.

The Quality of Receivables

Any business with customers who owe it money must consider the quality of those receivables—what percentage of the outstanding amount it can expect to collect. Some businesses have better luck than others, due to the nature of the work itself or the people the business associates with. Sadly, the ones that generally have the most at risk when it comes to bad debts are those businesses that can least afford them.

It seems obvious that the older an account becomes, the less likely it is that you'll collect it. Unless your business is on a completely cash basis, it's important to keep track of how old your accounts are, to attempt to control them so you'll eventually get paid. To help this process, almost everyone gets an "aging report," which lists a numerical breakdown of the age, the quality, of their accounts receivable. Often the business owner sees something like this:

AGING REPORT FOR JUNE, 1986
0–30 days old	$31,965.12
30–60 days old	17,306.36
60–90 days old	11,007.99
90 days and older	2,484.01

Often it's helpful to convert the same figures to a percentage format and examine them on a graph. Figure 4-15 shows us just that, with the percentage amounts instead of just the raw dollar figures. You want to use a complete scale for this sort of display (all the way from zero to 100) because it gives you a better feel for the actual size of the data represented. While you can't use this sort of bar chart for monthly comparisons, if you create one every month on a regular basis, you can quickly find out—by leafing through them—if one particular area is getting worse as the months go by.

It's possibly just as useful to examine the same information in a pie-chart

AGED RECEIVABLES BY PERCENT FOR JUNE

- 51%   0 - 30 DAYS OLD
- 27.5%   30 - 60 DAYS OLD
- 17.5%   60 - 90 DAYS OLD
- 4%   90 DAYS AND OLDER

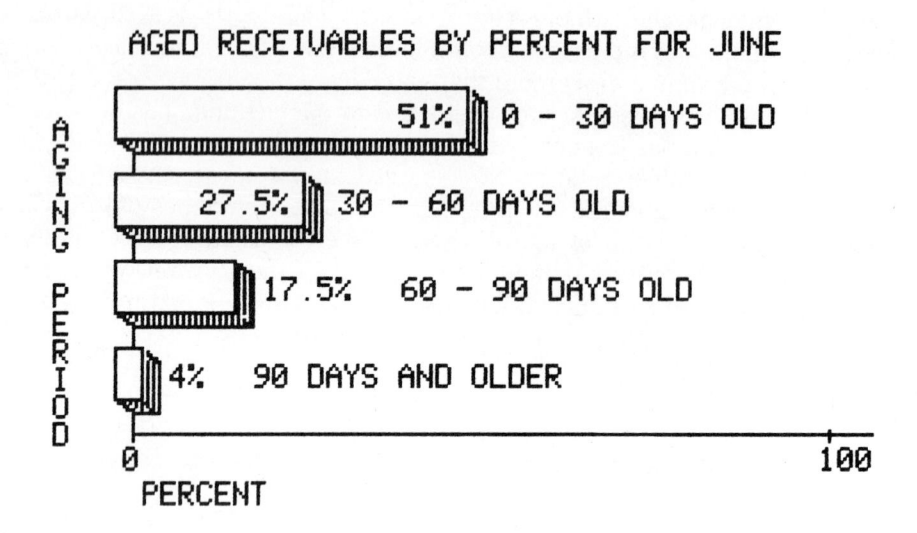

FIGURE 4-15

AGED RECEIVABLES BY PERCENT FOR JUNE

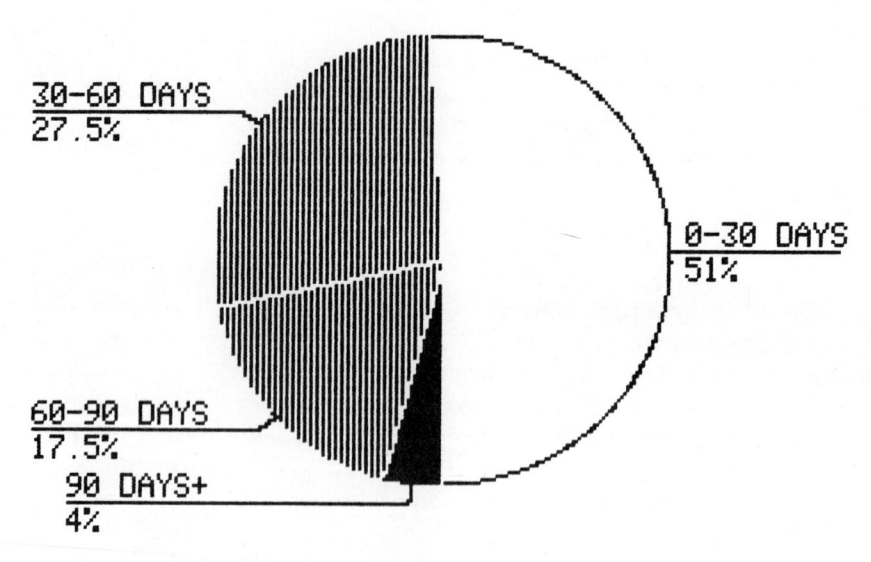

- 30-60 DAYS   27.5%
- 0-30 DAYS   51%
- 60-90 DAYS   17.5%
- 90 DAYS+   4%

FIGURE 4-16

format. While the bar chart of Figure 4-15 shows us how each figure relates to the others, Figure 4-16 illustrates how each part of our accounts receivable relates to our *total* accounts receivable.

Figure 4-16 uses the same percentages we just examined in Figure 4-15 but puts them into the pie-chart format to give us a feeling for how each particular area relates to the total of our accounts receivable. It's obvious that the biggest share—more than half, by a little bit—is in what we'd consider the current area. The smallest slice of this pie is also what we'd expect—the 90 day and older category. The other two slices are where we might be the most disturbed by this chart: almost one-third of our accounts receivable are in the 30-60 day section; nearly one-fifth are in the 60-90 day category. Combined, we find we've got almost half of our outstanding accounts older than 30 days.

You can equate this information with your own ability to pay your bills when they come due. If half of your customers can't pay their bills until they're a month or two old, you should be aware that you're in exactly the same situation: you won't be able to pay *half of your bills* until they're just as old. Unless you can collect the cash, you can't pay your own bills.

Charting the Age of Receivables

You can take things a step further, too. Every business has a historical pattern that a little study can discover. If you go back through your aging reports, you'll soon find out in what range your average figures should be. Let the numbers themselves tell you what's important (and what's not) for your business.

For instance, you might discover that your old accounts (defined as older than 60 days) historically average about 20% of your accounts receivable total. It's a worthwhile project, then, to create a graph like Figure 4-17. This chart displays the percentage of your receivables total that is older than 60 days, on a monthly basis. It's done for the first nine months of the year. With this sort of guide, the owner can see that old accounts were being reduced early in the year, but the situation started to change back in month 4. By month 5, more than 20% of the total showed up in the "old" area and stayed there through September.

It's obvious that the business owner isn't taking the steps needed to reduce this growth in old accounts, and if it remains unchecked it will cause a serious hardship for the business in terms of cash flow. If this trend continues, the amount in *old* accounts receivables will continue to grow every month.

A graph like this one not only makes it easy for the business owner to see the situation, but he or she can instantly do the math to get an approximate value for these old receivables. It's one thing to realize that 20% of your receivables are old, and quite another to multiply that 20% by (for example) total accounts receivable of $70,000, and suddenly figure out there are $14,000 real dollars

```
     OLD ACCOUNTS RECEIVABLE IN PERCENT
  30
     ┌──┐ (PERCENT)
     │  │
     │  │                    ┌──┐┌──┐┌──┐┌──┐
  20 │  │┌──┐          ┌──┐  │  ││  ││  ││  │
     │  ││  │┌──┐┌──┐  │  │  │  ││  ││  ││  │
     │  ││  ││  ││  │  │  │  │  ││  ││  ││  │
     │  ││  ││  ││  │  │  │  │  ││  ││  ││  │
  10 │  ││  ││  ││  │  │  │  │  ││  ││  ││  │
     │  ││  ││  ││  │  │  │  │  ││  ││  ││  │
     │  ││  ││  ││  │  │  │  │  ││  ││  ││  │
     │  ││  ││  ││  │  │  │  │  ││  ││  ││  │
   0 └──┘└──┘└──┘└──┘  └──┘  └──┘└──┘└──┘└──┘
      1   2   3   4    5     6   7   8   9
              <-- MONTHS -->
```

FIGURE 4-17

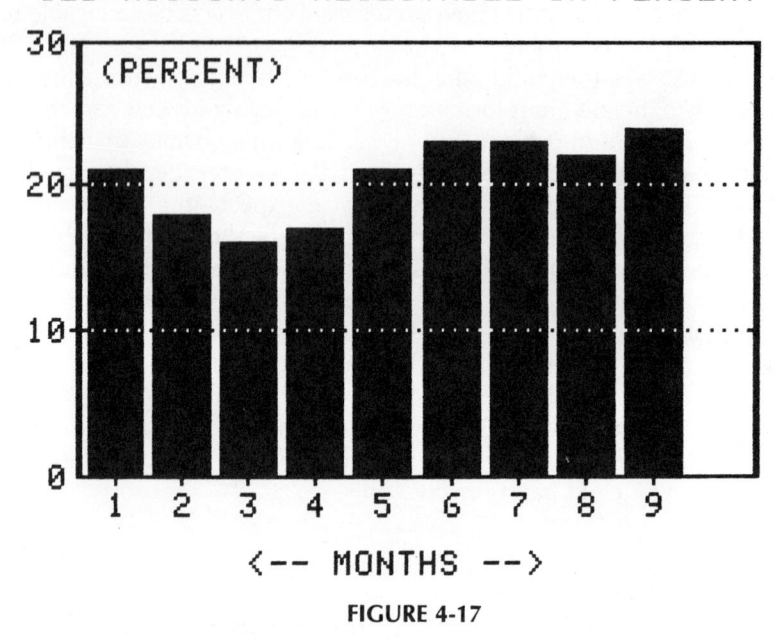

sitting there, getting older by the day. It motivates you to do something to try to collect some of these overdue accounts.

Along this same line, it might be worthwhile to go back over your records to determine exactly what percentage of old accounts your business historically collects. You might discover that once an invoice gets more ancient than 60 or 90 days, it's almost impossible to collect it.

Searching Assets and Liabilities for Cash

While sales and accounts receivable are the logical places to look for cash, the business owners can get a line on their cash position from the balance sheet they receive every month or quarter.

There's a distinct relationship between the amount of available cash (working capital) and the debts (liabilities) a business owes. "Working capital" is the excess of current assets over current liabilities and serves as a measure of the business's ability to pay its current debts. Your balance sheet, for example, may show that you have $100,000 in current assets (generally cash and things that can be quickly converted into cash, including inventory), and $50,000 in current liabilities (debts due now or within one year).

The difference between the two is working capital, the amount of cash you have to *work* with. The "current ratio" reflects the relationship between these two figures. If you *divide* your current assets by your current liabilities, you end up with what accountants call the "current ratio." In this example, you'd divide $100,000 by $50,000, which gives you a 2-1 ratio. Like the comparison between accounts receivable and accounts payable, a 2-1 split indicates that the business is probably in good condition. A ratio less than this is a danger sign: the business might not have enough cash to *do* business.

Like any accounting item converted into a ratio, the unusual must be examined, whatever direction it appears in. For instance (assuming that a 2-1 ratio applies to your line of work), you'll obviously be concerned if you find your business with a 1.5-1 ratio, or a 1.4-1 figure. But you might not be as concerned if this ratio started to grow, and in fact you may be quite pleased if you checked last month's figures and discovered you had a 2.7-1 ratio between current assets and current liabilities.

However, *any* aberration should be examined in detail to find out what caused the change. For instance, that high current ratio might be caused by too many slow-paying customers (current assets include your current accounts receivable total). If that's the case, the ratio indicates a problem, rather than a reason to be content with things as they are.

The Acid-Test Ratio

A harsher look at the current state of your cash examines the ratio between *quick assets* and current liabilities. Inventory and any prepaid expenses are removed from total current assets, and only quick assets are left in the asset account: cash, net receivables, and any marketable securities—only those things we can expect to convert *quickly* into cash. The excluded items (like inventory) are left out because you might not be able to change them rapidly into funds. This ratio tracks the current *pool* of cash, the actual dollars that are available to pay current debts.

One other consideration arises here—the quality of the marketable securities and the net receivables included in the total. How good are the receivables? If you sell the securities, will you incur a loss? As with any financial figure, you often have to look a bit deeper under the surface information to discover the truth about your condition.

Liquidity Ratio

All of this leads to a ratio we feel is important to track. The comparison is a bit different than the usual, and that perhaps is where it gains its validity. Yes, it's necessary to look at the current ratio (current assets divided by current liabilities) and the acid-test ratio (quick assets divided by current liabilities) as both give you a feel for your current cash position.

But in addition, you might also keep monthly tabs on the liquidity ratio of your business. This simply divides your total assets by your current assets. If you have $70,000 in total assets and $35,000 in current assets, you have a .5 (50%) ratio here—exactly one-half of your total assets are in a *liquid* form. If you had only liquid assets, then you'd be *100% liquid*.

Is a lot of liquidity good? Do you need a lot of cash around, or would it be better to have those same funds out working for you? That all depends on your cash requirements, and business graphics can help you know your own. For example, we saw earlier in this chapter how one business experienced a terrific sales growth during the summer months, but at the same time, it didn't have the cash to cover its anticipated costs. The knowledgeable manager looks at his or her liquidity ratio in view of the estimated cash needs of the business. If it appears that business conditions will cause a cash-flow problem, then she or he will want to *increase* the liquidity ratio to compensate. The worst thing that can happen is to have both a deficit in the cash needed *and* a low liquidity rate, where many dollars are tied up in fixed investments of some sort. Those dollars can't come to the rescue, then, when the bills start to accumulate.

Figure 4-18 is a column chart that covers the first half-year of a business,

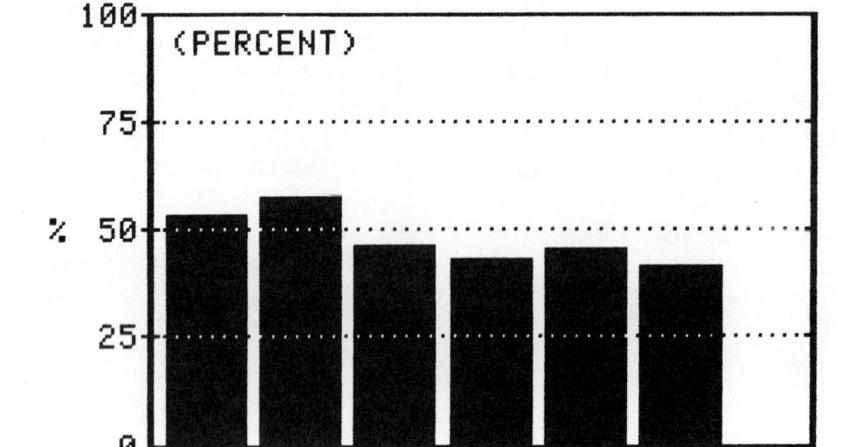

FIGURE 4-18

and shows the month-end liquidity ratio, with the figures multiplied by 100 so they're shown in percentage fashion. The January figure, for example, indicates this business had about 53% of its assets in a *liquid* form—about half its assets were in cash or something that could be quickly converted into cash. However, with some minor fluctuations, this percentage steadily decreased throughout the first half of the year. In June, only about 40% of the business's assets were in a form creditors would accept for invoices—cash or its equivalent.

How do you think this business would fare if it had the same cash-flow problems we examined earlier? Could this business handle a rapid rise in sales? Would it have the cash available to cover the necessary costs? The sad part of all this is that even if the business has the assets to handle a spurt in sales, they're of no use unless they can be easily converted into cash. The wise manager looks at *all* ratios, with a particular eye to his or her liquidity position both now and down the road a bit.

Summing Up

Nothing works without cash, but all too often the business owner thinks of just incoming cash and doesn't pay enough attention to what will be going out the door to pay that stack of bills he or she has accumulated. Cash *flows* in both directions inside every business.

While there's a definite relationship between sales and cash and between accounts receivables and cash, it's different for every company. A graphic look at these figures is often the only way to see what kind of collection cycle your business has. By moving one line on a chart one direction or the other, the business owner can usually determine *exactly* how today's sales or receivables total will affect tomorrow's cash. Once you know how much cash will be available, you can plan properly.

But cash flow is a two-edged sword, since it does move both in and out of any business. It's important to track the cost of sales (including overhead items), as we must have the cash available to pay them. While an increase in sales will raise cash and accounts receivable, it also increases what we owe. Often, those bills will come due before our customers pay us, which puts the business in a deficit position.

This all leads to the fact that it's necessary to examine cash flow not only from both directions, but also with an eye to *when* we'll need a specific amount of money, and whether it will be there at the time it's needed.

We also should chart accounts receivable and accounts payable; it's important to compare this year's totals with last year's, to see if there are any variations. If there are—in either a positive or negative direction—it's a sign to investigate further. We need to look at not only just the rise or fall in these totals, but also at the relationship between the two, the ratio between payables and receivables. And in fact, this is the real secret of any examination of this sort—to plot the *ratio* that's important to our business.

We must look particularly at a growing accounts receivable total to determine *why* it's getting larger. If it's because our sales are higher, that's fine. If it's because more people aren't paying their bills, it's not so good and in fact might pinch our cash position down the road. So the quality of our receivables are important, and we can judge their quality by their age—the older they are, the less likely we are to collect them.

Finally, we need to keep track of our working capital, our current ratio and acid-test ratio, and—perhaps most useful of all—our liquidity ratio. All these must be examined in light of our anticipated cash requirements. The liquidity ratio in particular tells us what shape our dollars are in and gives us the chance to take corrective action before we start to get calls from creditors demanding that they be paid.

Additional Ideas

There are some extra ideas it might make sense for your business to examine on a regular basis. The way to determine this is to look at your own figures for the items suggested to see if they may be valuable for you.

For example, you might want to create a column chart that tracks your working capital. Depending on when you get your financial statements, you can do this monthly or quarterly. A column chart will give you a good feeling for what's happening to your working capital, whether it's increasing or decreasing.

You might want to track sales on one line of a line graph and working capital on another line. If your sales increase, does your working capital? Or does it go down? Why?

We used the example of a business with an 89% total gross cost percentage. From your financial statements over the past few years, gather your own percentages and graph them. Is your gross margin decreasing or increasing? Why?

Another way to look at accounts receivable and accounts payable is not just with their raw totals, but at either the volume of change or percentage of change. An examination of last year's receivables to this year's totals is important, but you might learn more from a look at what the *rate* of change is. Plot the percentage difference for each month and see what it tells you.

Through all this, keep in mind that since cash moves both in and out of your business, it's a primary concern of every business owner. The right selection of cash flow charts for your business can help put cash in the bank.

Bids/Warranty/Finance Charges

5

Inside anyone's business are areas that don't deserve detailed study but still need a look once in a while. Perhaps you don't do much volume in one place or another, or the costs are minimal, or it's simply a part of your business that you haven't thought that much about.

In this chapter we're going to touch on three such areas that might affect your work: bids, warranty repair, and finance charges. Inside your own business will be any number of others, so as you read through how to examine these kinds of data sets, the important thing is not the examples we'll use, but how to apply these techniques to your own work.

Many of us work on a bid basis, and for us, most (if not all) of our sales volume comes directly from estimates we make. To be successful, our prices have to be right, our quotations done in a professional manner, and we have to do our work so the customer will call us the next time he or she needs something in our line. While we took a look at bids and how they relate to sales volume in Chapter 3, in this chapter we'll examine bids from a couple of unusual directions and learn more about how our business functions at the same time.

Whenever you sell anything, there's always an implied warranty, not only as to its quality but also that the product will do what you promise. A tree you sell usually has to be guaranteed to live for a certain time; a boiler you install will probably have a warranty on its lifespan, but also be expected to be large enough to properly heat your customer's home; an office machine must perform the functions you told your customer it could handle.

Whenever there's a sale, then, there are associated warranty considerations, and most businesses put a percentage into their overhead to cover warranty costs. Depending on what your line of work happens to be, your warranty expenses might be just the freight costs to return defective merchandise to a manufacturer. In our business, we also have labor expenses—when we install an air conditioning system for your home, we guarantee the labor for one year.

Wouldn't it be helpful to know which equipment brand you sell has the fewest breakdowns? The worst repair record? Which brand(s) are the easiest to work on? The most difficult? Which brands *should* you sell? The same questions often apply to the service technicians you use—who's making money for you, and who's only drawing a salary?

While we all have an idea in our mind that one particular brand is good while another causes more than its share of problems, too often this feeling is based on incomplete information. We're most likely to remember the *worst* installation we had, the one that cost us the most in terms of dollars and aggravation. There may be another brand—totally unrelated to the one bad case that sticks in our mind—that costs our business much more over the period of a year, but we haven't made the effort to dig out the data and plot it. We'll make some suggestions in this chapter on what to look for in your warranty repair records, and how to examine it.

The third area we'll touch on, again, might not relate to your business at all. If you operate on a purely cash and carry basis, then you might not have customers who owe you any money. However, most small businesses still allow some customers to charge their purchases, and once you do that, you'll have a certain percentage of them who simply won't pay. There can be any number of reasons for this, including dissatisfaction with the work you did. Unless your business has some way to monitor how your people are paying (not only who is and who isn't, but when the cash is sent), you have problems with accounts receivable. We'll look at accounts receivable in its wide context as a balance sheet item in Chapter 8, but in these days where "Your check is in the mail" is the byword of many customers, you need all the help you can get when it comes to watching how people pay. We'll cover some graphic techniques here on how you can do just that by looking at the finance charges you can add to your past-due accounts.

Bids By Quantity

While it's vital to examine the estimates you make in terms of how they relate to the sales those estimates produce, it's often equally helpful to look at the raw number of bids you write from a couple of directions.

Figure 5-1 is a line chart that plots a 12-month picture of the number of quotations our fictitious business created. While this illustration doesn't tell us

FIGURE 5-1

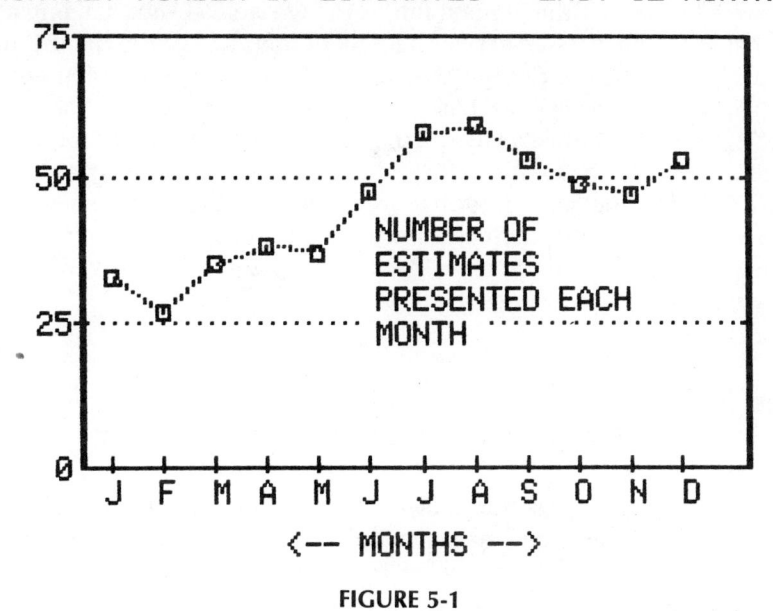

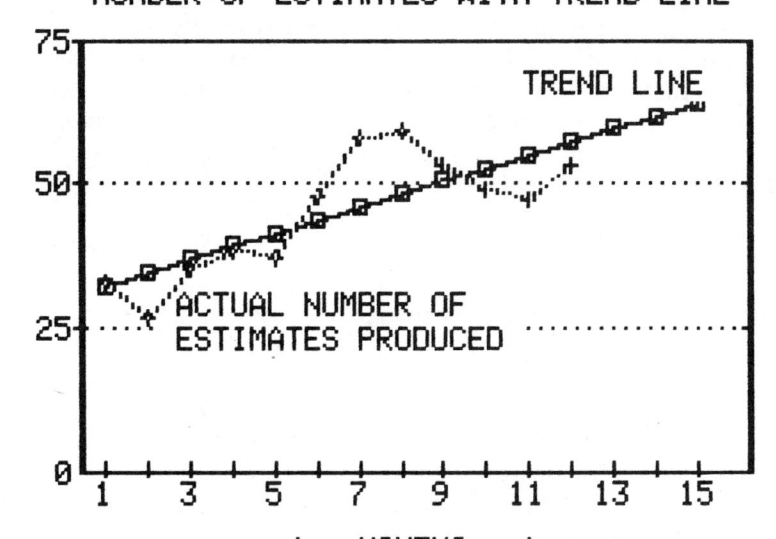

FIGURE 5-2

anything about the quality of those bids (How many did we sell? What was their volume?), we can see that the general line is rising—a good sign. It's important to realize that many businesses derive the bulk of their sales from the estimates they put out. If we study the right information, we can get a pretty accurate idea of what our upcoming sales will be, based on the bids we write during the current period. Let's take this example a step further and have our plotting program add a trend line.

Figure 5-2 plots the same information we just examined and adds a trend line to show the direction of the data, plus a projection of where our business will be three months from now. It's a good picture, and the kind we'd hope to see when we examine our own information.

Bids and Sales

Another useful way to look at the total number of bids you produce is to link them to the number of sales you make from those estimates. If, during one month, you write 30 quotations and eventually sell 15 jobs, you had a 50% success rate for that particular group of bids. You can have your spreadsheet do the calculations for you and ask your graphics package to keep a running visual total of your sales success.

Figure 5-3 covers the data for our fictitious business over a three-year period and plots the percentage of quotations that eventually turned into sold jobs. The range our business shows on this historical basis appears to be between about 60% and 75%—that's the number of jobs we sold out of each 100 quotations we presented. It's interesting to note that at no time during this period did we do better than 75%. Why not? Perhaps that would be a good goal to work toward. It's equally interesting that we never hit the 50% mark, either, so we always (during this time) sold more than half of the estimates we created.

The logical next step is to have our plotting program add a trend line to this information, to see if our overall percentage is rising or falling.

Figure 5-4 narrows the scale of our graph considerably, and plots the information we just examined within a 40% to 80% range, along with a trend line. The trend line, as noted on the chart, is based on 36 months of information and projected for six more.

While it's nothing to shout about, the general trend of the percentage of bids we're selling is on the upswing, growing slightly as time goes along. It's not a really rapid rise, but this steady growth is probably preferable and indicates that we're on the right track, that our sales methods are working.

With this much information, the trend line should be accurate, and so should its projection. Again, this is exactly the picture we'd want to see when we examined our actual data.

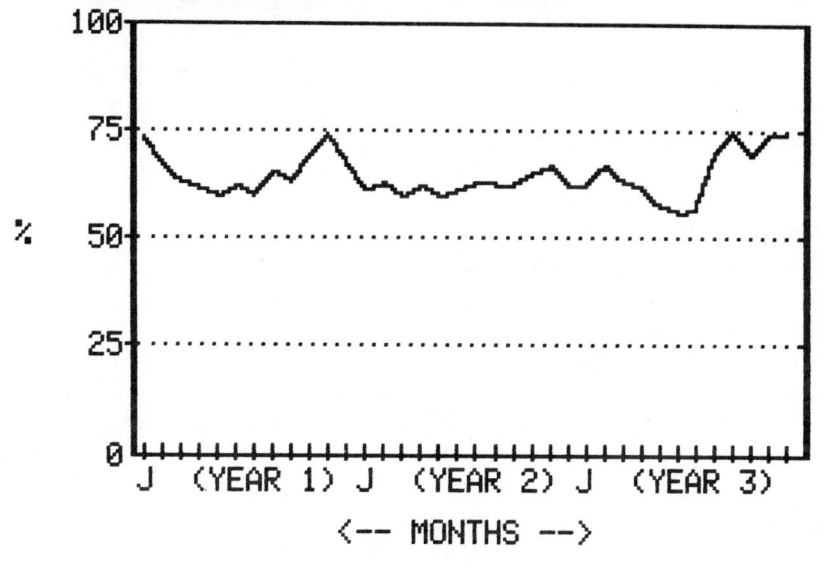

FIGURE 5-3

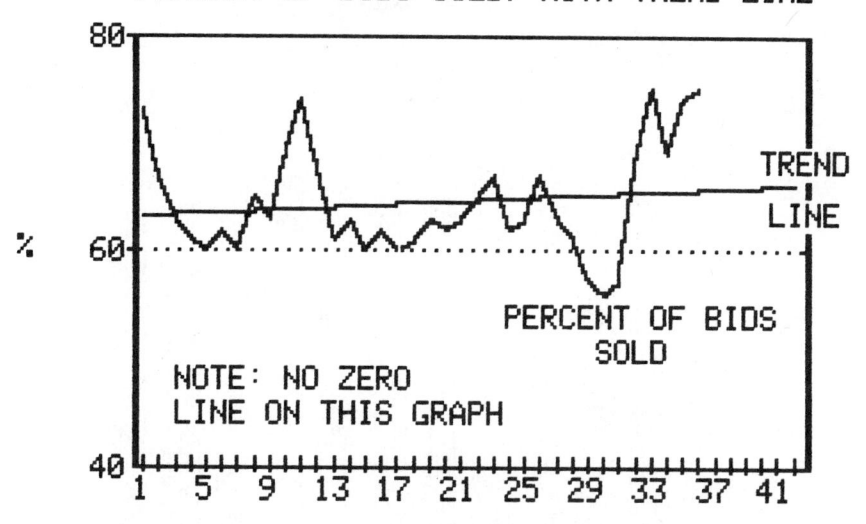

The percentage of bids sold, for 36 months.

FIGURE 5-4

Percent of bids sold, with trend line. Note: no zero line on this graph. The trend line is based on 36 months of data and projected out for six more.

113

Bidding Dollars

While a close examination of the number of estimates we make is good, and is better when we relate that information to the number of sales it produces, it's equally useful to take the same basic information and look at it from a dollar standpoint. You can have your spreadsheet program take the number of bids you make during a specific period and divide it into the total bid *value*. This will tell you the average amount for each estimate you make. Once you have that information and plot it over a period of time, you'll know if your quotations are just rising in terms of quantity—the raw number of bids you type up and present—or if they're also increasing in dollar value. Generally, of course, the more quotations you make, the more jobs you'll sell. Likewise, the greater the value of those bids, the greater your sales volume will be.

This example takes the number of quotations our business made over the latest 12 months, and divides that figure into the total dollar value those bids represent. Since we saw in earlier graphs the total number of bids we presented were on the increase, we should expect that their average value might decrease. Naturally, we'd hope for a rise in value along with a rise in quantity, but it would be unusual if that really happened.

There are two things you'll notice in Figure 5-5. The first is that our average quotation ranges between $1500 and $2000. Secondly, the recent drop in value

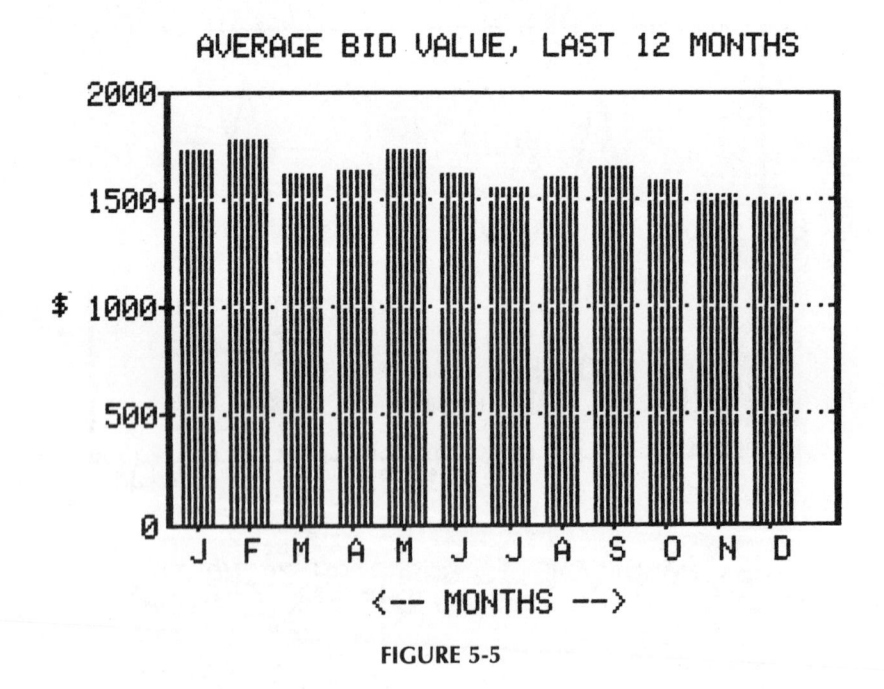

FIGURE 5-5

is obvious, even without a trend line. We get a feeling from the entire graph that the dollar value is decreasing. However, to really understand what's going on between our bids and the sales they produce, we need to back up historically a bit and examine things from a longer viewpoint.

A Historical Look

Figure 5-6 plots the amounts, on a monthly basis, of the average dollar value for estimates our fictitious company presented to its customers over a 36-month period.

As we saw when we examined just the most recent twelve month's worth of information, this historical picture finds our average bid running in the same $1500–$2000 range. We can also see the latest drop to the $1500 level, and might be a bit comforted to note that two other times in the past, our average estimate value dropped to the same low. Even without the benefit of a trend line, though, the general information seems to be heading downward; let's add a trend line to see what it tells us (see Figure 5-7).

We've tightened up the scale to estimate the zero line, so, as we know, the picture of our data is a bit changed, and the line that charts our average bid volume rises and falls much more sharply. However, the process serves its purpose

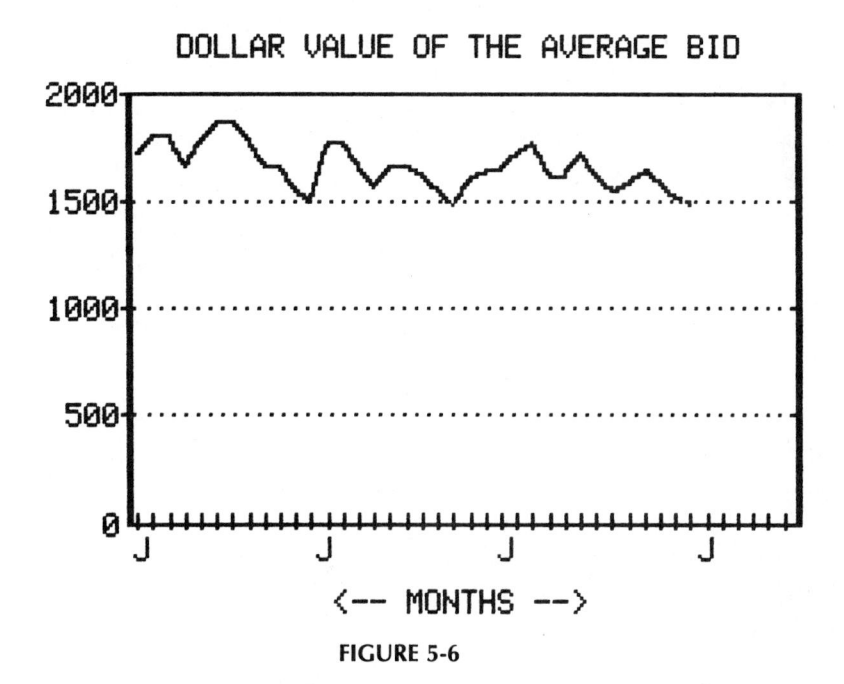

FIGURE 5-6

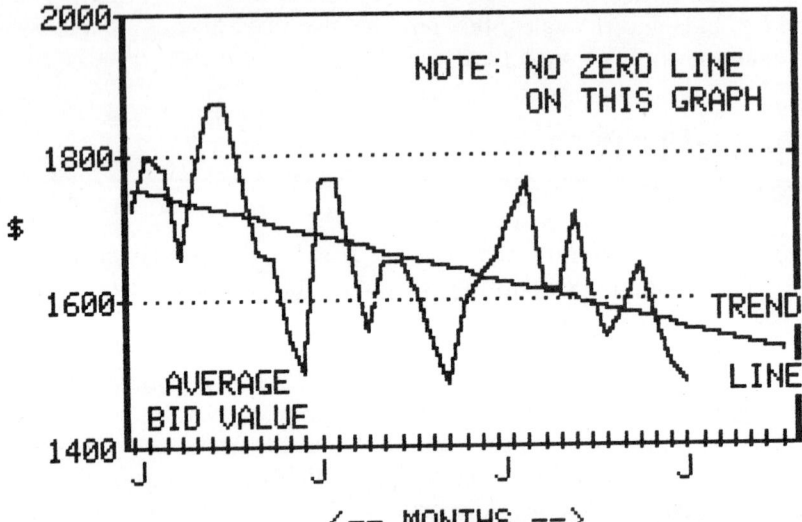

```
                    AVERAGE BID VALUE, WITH TREND LINE
      2000┐
          │                    NOTE: NO ZERO LINE
          │                          ON THIS GRAPH
      1800┤
   $      │
          │
      1600┤                                      TREND
          │       AVERAGE                        LINE
          │       BID VALUE
      1400┴┼┼┼┼┼┼┼┼┼┼┼┼┼┼┼┼┼┼┼┼┼┼┼┼┼┼┼┼┼┼┼┼┼┼┼┼
           J        J        J        J
                    <-- MONTHS -->
         THE TREND LINE IS BASED ON 36 MONTHS OF
         DATA, AND PROJECTED OUT FOR ANOTHER SIX
```

FIGURE 5-7

as we see that the trend line representing the value of our average bid has been dropping for some time, and at an alarming rate.

As noted on the graph, the trend line is based on 36 months of information and projected for another six months. The information Figure 5-7 gives us may not be disturbing; we in fact might want our business to work with lower volume jobs, and, at the same time, hope to sell more of them. The important thing is not whether the trend line rises or falls, but that it heads in the direction you feel is right for your own business. In this case, Figure 5-7 tells the owner that the average dollar value of each estimate the company makes is dropping, and fast. That's going to mean a drop in sales volume, unless the business can convert a greater percentage of its bids into sales.

Warranty Problems

Whatever we sell, we have to provide some guarantee on it, often on both the material itself and on the labor it might take to repair the product during its warranty period.

It's important to realize that all warranty costs we might incur may not be a total loss. Instead, by taking the best possible care of our customers that we can, we improve our chances for future business from these same people. So it pays for any company to go out of its way to ensure that its customers are happy, even if that means it has to absorb in-warranty expenses that it really shouldn't have to.

For instance, you might provide first-year in-home service for the products you sell. Any parts are probably guaranteed by the manufacturer, so during the warranty period, you have to pay the freight to get the new parts to your store, the freight to send the bad items back to your supplier, and pay your cost labor (and its fringe benefits) to handle any warranty problems.

This data is fairly easy to track. If you don't have much warranty repair, you can even keep it on a legal pad, with columns for the information. A larger business might want to use a simple file-handling system on its microcomputer to track the costs of the information along with other data—what items cause the most problems, what product groups have the greatest warranty expense totals, and so on. When your billing people find a warranty situation, the work order is voided (since you won't send a bill to your customer), and the data transferred to your record-keeping system.

The important thing here is to track all the information. Often, labor is so obvious that we keep a record of its cost, but we also need to list freight, phone call expenses, the cost of equipment we loan to our customer while we're waiting for parts, as well as any other costs that might be involved. Once we have an accurate picture of our warranty expenses, we can start to examine them with an eye not just to understanding where the dollars went, but to make an attempt to lower their total.

The first comparison to make is to relate your total warranty costs to your sales volume. Each business will vary, of course, but once you track this data over a period of time, you'll have a good idea what yours should average. In this case, Figure 5-8 plots a nine-month picture of the warranty costs on a percentage of sales basis for our fictional company. As always, we need some supporting information to determine how things look on a long-term basis, but at least for the nine months shown in Figure 5-8, we know that our warranty costs ran at about 2% of our gross sales volume.

If we know—from enough study of our warranty information—that 2% of our sales is about what we should expect to spend on warranty costs, then Figure 5-8 tells us we may have an upcoming problem, as our warranty costs jumped a bit over the past four months and currently are running away from the 2% level.

To help put things into perspective, if the owner of our fictional business examined these nine months of information and knew that 2% of sales was the maximum he or she should spend for warranty repairs, the logical thing is to do something to correct the problem. Perhaps one brand of equipment is causing

FIGURE 5-8

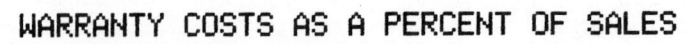

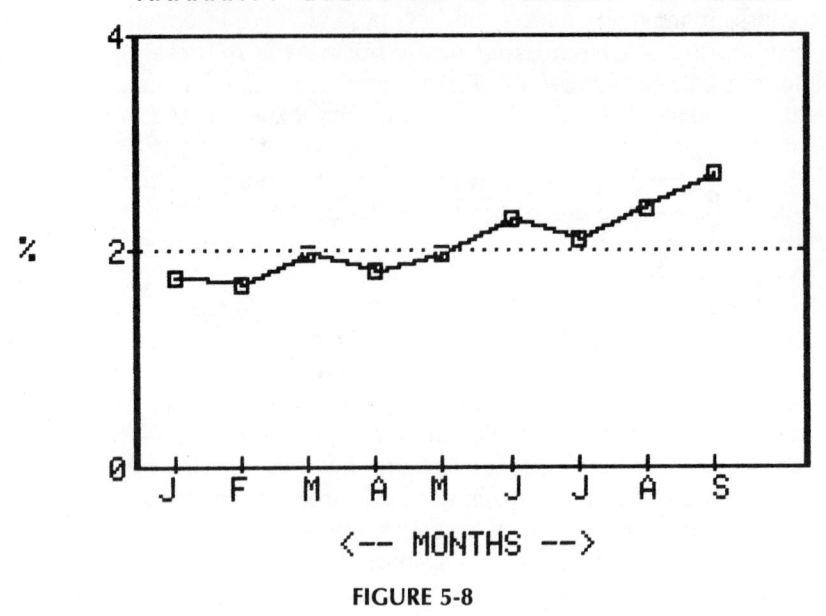

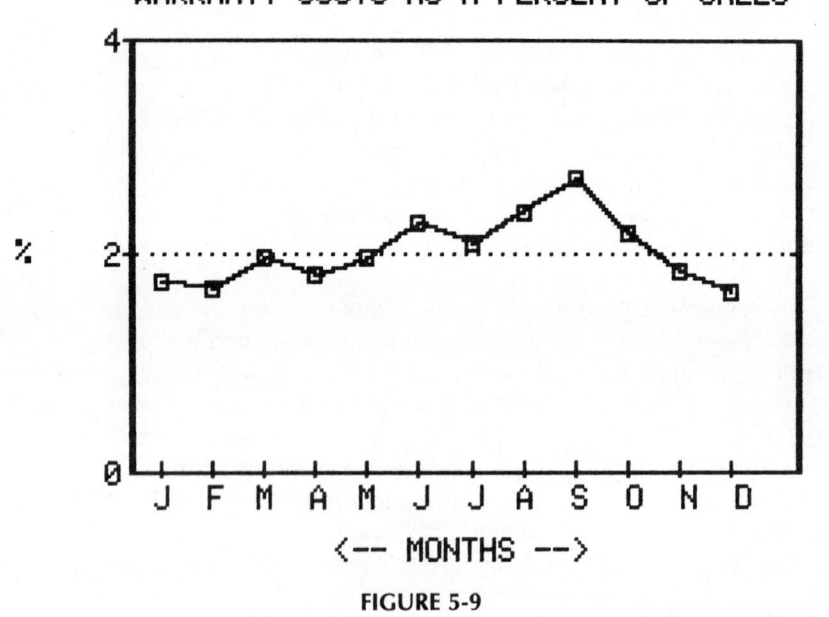

FIGURE 5-9

the most difficulty: let's stop selling it. Perhaps one grade of equipment *inside* of a brand we handle is where most of the problems start: let's find out where and at least not continue to sell those specific products.

Once we found ourselves with a terrific brand of equipment, except for its line of heat pumps. Unknown to us (and probably most others in the dealer network), these particular units were not built by the company we purchased them from. Instead, they had another manufacturer build this line of units for them, put their name tags on, and sold them as their own equipment. Once we discovered where all our problems were coming from, we stopped selling that specific unit.

Figure 5-9 illustrates what the warranty repair cost graph should look like, once the business owner found the problem and took the proper measures to correct things. By the end of the 12 months shown, warranty costs as a percentage of sales were lower than the 2% mark. As always, with all graphs, these were created so the scale marks will help us understand the information. In these examples, 2% was the (fictional) figure the business wanted to keep its warranty repair costs under. So, we asked our plotting program to scale with that 2% figure in mind, so it would show up as a grid line of the chart.

Equipment Warranty

Most major brands of equipment, whether in our line (furnaces, air conditioners) or another (washers and dryers, appliances, electrical equipment, and so on) have a factory warranty. As anyone in business knows, some brands are better than others at how they support their dealers when it comes to first-year (or even first-month) warranty repair labor. Some manufacturers don't say a word when you charge them for sending a service technician out to fix a factory defect, while others complain and may only reluctantly agree to pay part of your bill to them. What this means is that you'll end up absorbing some of the warranty repair labor the factory should reimburse you for.

A logical thing to examine, then, is your cost of repair for each brand of equipment you handle. It might be worthwhile to use the examination for total warranty costs (including those the manufacturer pays for), but it means a bit more if you work only with the dollars that come out of your pocket.

Figure 5-10 uses a bar chart to show the warranty repair costs for each of the four brands of equipment our fictional business handled during the month of June. The figures shown, as noted on the graph, are not raw dollar amounts. Doing that might distort our graph, because if we sell twice as much of one brand as we do another, we should expect to have double the in-warranty costs for the first than for the second.

In this case, the dollar amounts shown are the warranty costs our business had to put out for every $10,000 in sales for each brand of equipment. That's an

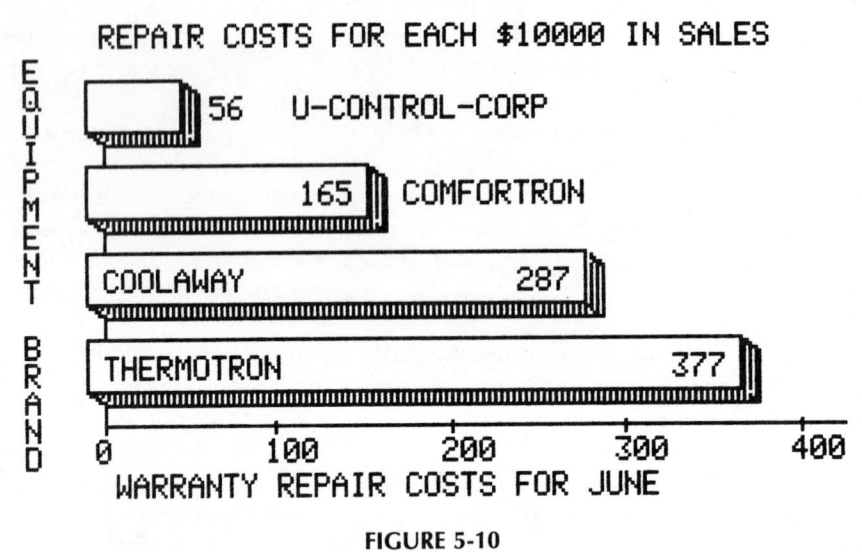

```
                REPAIR COSTS FOR EACH $10000 IN SALES
  E
  Q
  U  ┌──────┐
  I  │  56  │   U-CONTROL-CORP
  P  └──────┘
  M  ┌───────────────────┐
  E  │       165         │  COMFORTRON
  N  └───────────────────┘
  T  ┌──────────────────────────────────┐
     │ COOLAWAY                    287  │
  B  └──────────────────────────────────┘
  R  ┌────────────────────────────────────────────┐
  A  │ THERMOTRON                            377  │
  N  └────────────────────────────────────────────┘
  D  0        100       200       300       400
           WARRANTY REPAIR COSTS FOR JUNE
```

FIGURE 5-10

easy calculation to make and puts each brand on the same basis, so our comparison is more meaningful. The equipment we bought from U-Control Corporation performed well during June. The Thermotron equipment, on the other hand, cost us almost seven times as much for in-warranty repair. Why? Was it because we had many more problems with Thermotron, or because the U-Control Corporation people paid for nearly all the calls we had to make to repair factory defects? Whatever the case, we obviously need some supporting information to know if we have a problem or not, and that data can be as simple as creating this chart over a period of time. If Thermotron is consistent in its warranty costs, we'd better do something to change the situation (sell less of it, add more when we bid to use it on a job, fight with the factory for the money they should pay, etc.). If, over a period of time, U-Control equipment is consistently best, maybe we should start to use more of it. If this data holds true over a few years, it's obvious when we specify U-Control material that we'll have lower costs. Why not use more U-Control equipment, so we can bid a little lower and perhaps sell a bit more?

People Problems

We've looked at warranty repair costs in the context of total sales and in light of the equipment we handle, but it's also important to take a look at your people and how they're performing. Since this section is about warranty repair work, the people who will do it for you are your service technicians, so we'll examine their performance.

BIDS/WARRANTY/FINANCE CHARGES

From a labor standpoint, it's worthwhile to calculate the total sales each service technician produces, as well as total cost (including any fringe benefits and callbacks for mistakes made). From a warranty viewpoint, it's helpful to simply track the callback rate per service technician. You don't want to look at the raw data, as one service technician might make more calls over the period under study than his or her counterparts do. So, like the warranty repair costs we looked at for each brand of equipment our fictional business sold, let's break down the number of callbacks each of our service people had for every 100 calls made during June.

It's important to keep track of each callback based on the original person on the job. Often, a different service technician will go back to correct the problem, but the cost of the callback must be charged to the technician who originally went out to the customer's home.

It's also interesting to note that this information (as contrasted to simply a study of the dollars a service person produces or costs) gives us something of a feeling for how well our people are doing from a customer satisfaction standpoint. The more callbacks, the more dissatisfied customers we've got out there.

While Figure 5-11 covers only one month, each person in our service department is on the same basis—the callback rate is per 100 calls they made during the month. Al obviously did very well, while Janet and Bob show rates three times as high. Why? A bar chart is used for this comparison, as we want to see how each person is doing in relation to his or her peers. It also gives us a good feeling for the quantitive difference between the technicians shown.

As always, more information over a longer period of time is needed before you decide to give Al a raise or let Bob and Janet go, but the basic concept is what we want to illustrate here. With any of these studies you can, of course,

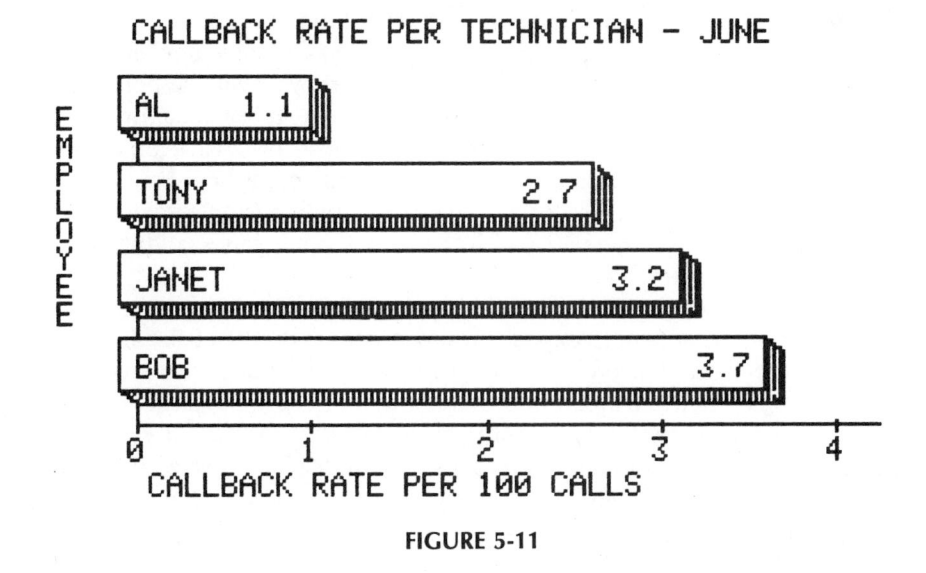

CALLBACK RATE PER TECHNICIAN - JUNE

EMPLOYEE	Callback Rate
AL	1.1
TONY	2.7
JANET	3.2
BOB	3.7

CALLBACK RATE PER 100 CALLS

FIGURE 5-11

add a trend line to any long-range group of information to see which direction you've been heading and project what you can expect the future to bring. If you create this bar chart comparison each month for your service technicians, you'll soon know who has the best (and worst) callback rate. This particular method of examination doesn't include the dollar cost of these callbacks. Not to ruin the reputation we just gave Al, but his callback problems might be terribly costly, so it's important to look at that, too. The ideal way to examine your warranty costs for your service department is to chart their data jointly—on a dollar basis and callback rate. The dollars tell you just what you've spent, while the callback rate shows you how satisfied your customers are.

Finance Charge Problems

At first glance, the finance charges you add to past due accounts might seem to be a blessing. After all, it's money you didn't really have to go out and earn.

While that sounds fine, we'll bet all those customers who don't complain don't always *pay* the finance charges that you put on their statements. They might pay their bill, but often ignore that $1.57 late charge. If your business is like ours, the finance charges you add to your old accounts are really an extension of your own credit situation: you have to borrow money to carry your customers, so any past due charges they do pay just help offset the interest you have to pay your banker. And in reality, there probably isn't a business owner around who wouldn't prefer to handle everything in cash, both what he or she purchases and for the work he or she sells. It not only simplifies things like accounting and payables and receivables (there won't be *any* of the latter two), but eliminates the cash-flow problem every business faces from time to time.

Probably the worst thing about finance charges is that they simply mean one thing: someone's not paying their bills when they should. When you have *any* finance charges to add to your accounts, it means those accounts are older than they should be. That's a problem for any business, because even as you add those finance charges and watch their total accumulate, invoices are getting old, customers who haven't paid are leaving town, and those customers with available cash are sending it elsewhere. If you were getting paid, you wouldn't have any finance charges to record.

All of this doesn't mean you shouldn't add finance charges to your old accounts. These days people expect it, and it does help offset the interest you have to pay when you borrow money so you can stay in business while you wait for people to pay their bills. A much better way to handle the situation is when you find a customer (preferably before you install or deliver what you sell) who appears to have a cash problem is to consider financing the sale yourself. This gives you a written agreement (that can be legally recorded) that the customer will pay so much every month. This method is much easier to enforce than the "open account with interest if you're late" many of us offer our customers.

Figure 5-12 is a simple line chart that plots the monthly finance charges that were added to old balances over a nine-month period, for last year and this year. It's obvious the monthly finance charge totals are greater this year than they were last year, for every month. Unless we increased the rate at which we calculate our finance charges, it tells us we've got more dollars tied up in those past due accounts receivable. Our collections aren't as successful this year as they were last year.

We can also do a quick calculation to tell us how many dollars were old during each period. For example, let's say we add a 2% interest charge on all accounts over 60 days old. For month 8, our total finance charges last year were about $55. $55 is 2% of $2750 (you calculate this by dividing 55 by 2 and moving the decimal point two places to the right (55/2 = 27.5—when you move the decimal point two places to the right, you end up with 2,750). This year our finance charges during month 8 were $75. When we do the calculations, we know we have $3,750 in accounts that are 60 days old or older.

You can get the same information, of course, with a chart of your monthly accounts receivable totals, if you break down their amounts by age. However, even this rough estimate presents us with a disturbing picture. At a 2% finance charge rate, each additional dollar in monthly late charges is equal to $50 in old

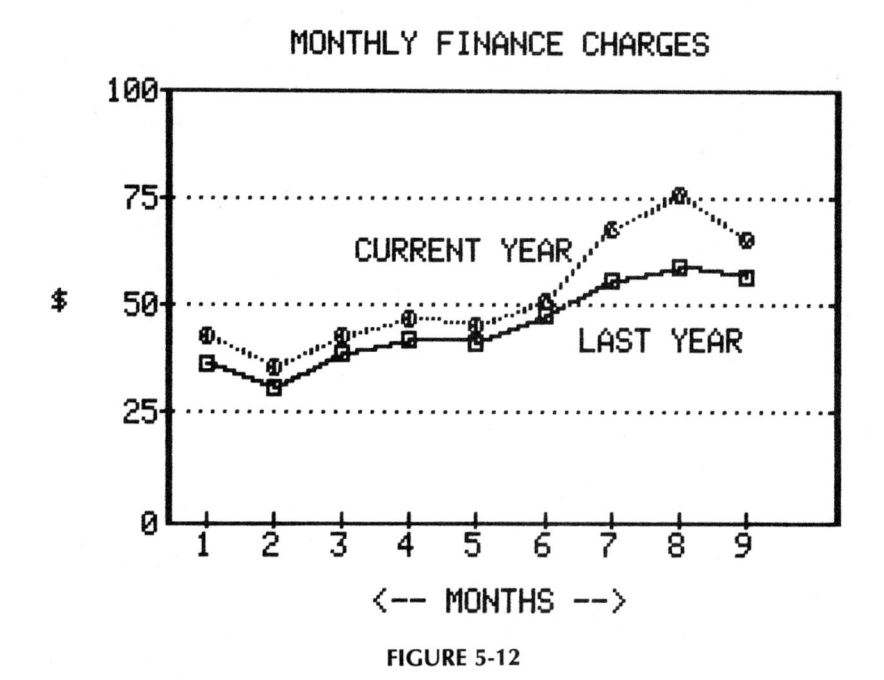

FIGURE 5-12

receivables. As we saw above, an increase of $20 in finance charges (for month 8 from last year to this) means we've got an additional $1,000 in accounts that are 60 days old or older.

More Finance Charges

Another way to examine this same information is to plot it as a percentage of your total accounts receivable. If you do this for your business, you'll usually find it will run within a specific range, and so if you see it leave this area, it's an indication your collection methods have changed and are either better or worse than they've been.

Figure 5-13 presents a 24-month look at our fictional business and plots its finance charges as a percentage of its month-end accounts receivable total. In this case, this percentage stayed in the 1% to 1.5% range until just recently, where it took a sharp jump. It's a warning signal that the total we've got in old accounts is growing (unless we recently raised the rate at which we add finance charges, or changed the terms as to which accounts are charged late charges). In any case, this example warns the business owner of a potential problem and the need to find out why it's happening and take steps to correct it (restrict credit, call more of the old accounts to collect more of that old cash, and so on).

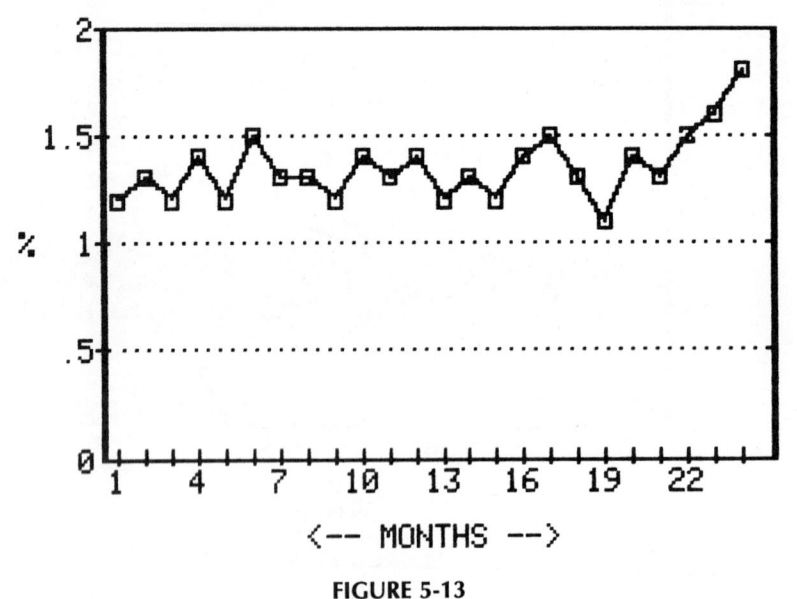

FIGURE 5-13

It's interesting to note that this same picture can tell you a lot about the state of your accounts receivable total. For example, if you assessed a 1.5% late charge and produced a graph like Figure 5-13, you've got a definite problem, as it appears that *all* of your accounts are overdue. In this example, where our (fictional) business charges a 2% late charge to its past-due customers, the business owner has cause for concern, as his or her late charges are approaching 2% of the outstanding accounts receivable balance. If it reaches that 2% level, then *all accounts are overdue*.

A logical extension of this illustration is to carry its data a step further and add a trend line, as shown in Figure 5-14.

For this example, we've eliminated the zero line on the graph, which, while it changes the picture of the information, gives us a better feeling for the rapidity of the rise of the trend line.

The trend line shown here is based on the 24 original months of information and projects for six more months. While we can see the recent breakthrough that jumped over the 1.5% mark, the trend line predicts that we'll *average* more than that, after another six months of doing business as we have been. If we really want to have more old accounts, we simply have to do nothing; they'll most likely grow without any help from us. However, that's the last thing we want to happen, and so these last two examples serve as an effective warning that our

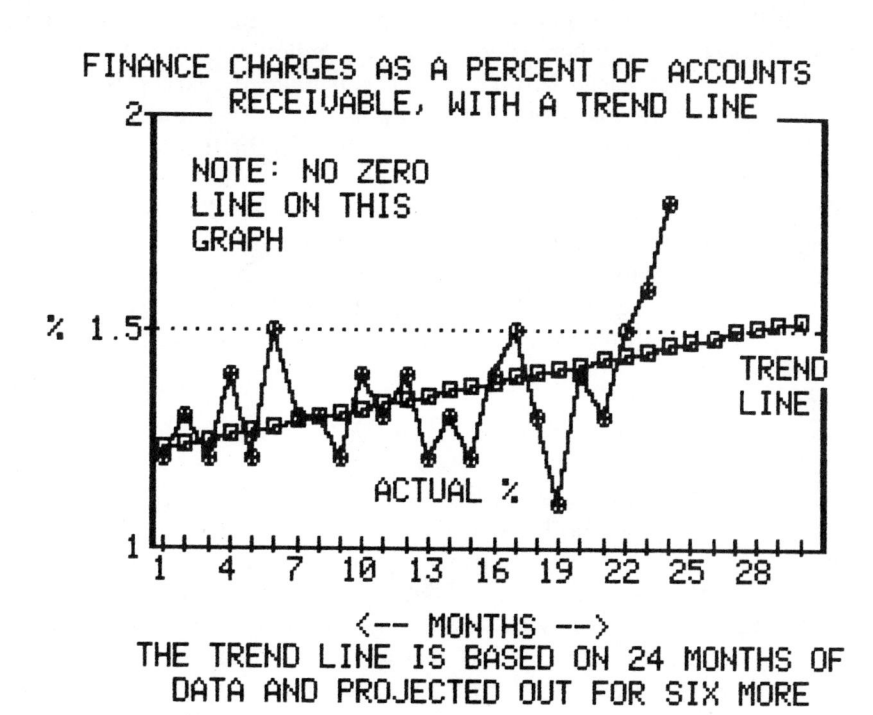

FIGURE 5-14

collection procedures aren't working. We need to change things, to get those old accounts back under control.

It's important to note that the quality of everyone's accounts receivable total decreases as an account gets older. *Quality* in this sense means the probability that the account will be collected in full. The older a balance gets, the less likely it is that you'll collect at all. Associated with this, in Chapter 8 we'll cover accounts receivable from a collection standpoint, to find out how to calculate and graph the collection period for your business.

On the Good Side

Not everything is wrong with the occurrence of finance charges, of course. For many businesses, they provide a substantial source of income. If you carry your own contracts (and have good methods to screen out poor credit risks), you'll make sales to people who otherwise couldn't be your customers. Many businesses can get a higher markup, too, if they have liberal credit terms—people who can't qualify to borrow money (except from you) aren't in a strong position to argue about the price of the merchandise.

The key here is to create some systematic accounting method to track your credit costs so you can compare them to the cash inflow your credit terms bring into your business. It's easier if you consider your finance charges as a separate income account, just as you now track things like labor sales, material sales, and so on. The idea is to separate it and keep track of both the income you get from finance charges and their associated costs.

Your costs must include all of your expenses to handle your credit sales, including the extra postage and paperwork involved, and needs to incorporate the collection costs and bad debt write-offs you incur. Once you do this over a period of time, you'll have a good handle on exactly what effect your credit policies are having on your net profit. You might find even when you add in the cost of your bad debts, the total you collect in finance charges more than makes up the deficiency.

Graphs are an ideal tool to examine this relationship; you can visually see if your credit terms are making or losing money for you.

Figure 5-15 tracks the cumulative finance charges our fictitious business collected for the latest 12 months, along with the actual costs involved in making these collections. It's best to use a cumulative chart for this examination, because when you write off an account as a bad debt, its cost will show up in the month you write it off. That single month, then, will show that you took a beating, but the rest of your monthly comparisons will appear acceptable. The cumulative chart lets you compare your total costs to the total amount you've collected in finance charges over a period of time. This is a more accurate way to look at

```
FINANCE CHARGES: RECEIPTS AND COSTS
              (CUMULATIVE)
```

FIGURE 5-15

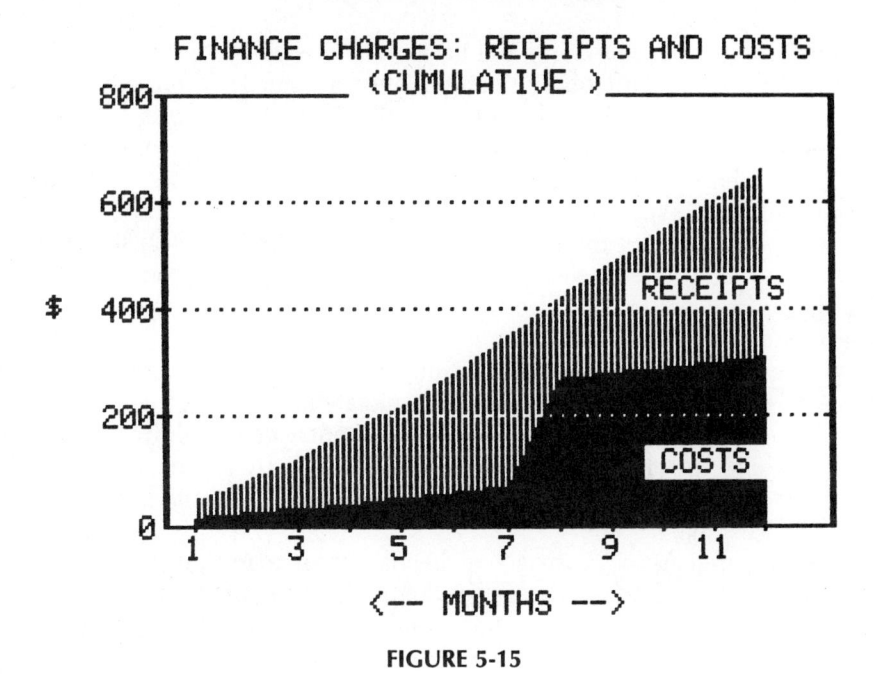

these figures, because what you want to compare are your *total costs,* and the cumulative chart does it for you.

Figure 5-15 shows that our fictitious business made a good profit on its finance charges during the first seven months charted. In month 8, however, the business had a huge expense (in relation to what its costs had been) that it charged against its finance charge *expense account.* The company probably wrote off an account as a bad debt, so the total cost amount really jumped. This indicates (since we're charting the latest 12 months of data) that month 8 was most likely the last month in this company's fiscal year, because that's when accounts that seem hopeless are removed from the accounts receivable total and recorded as a bad debt.

Even with the huge jump in month 8, the business is still showing a good profit for its finance charge account. If it can be sustained, the business is doing the right things in this area.

Summing Up

Although you have all sorts of things in your business that are beneficial to study, this chapter covers three areas of concern for most business owners.

Since many of us work on a bid basis, where we have to provide estimates to potential customers, the quantity and quality of our sales is directly related to the number and potential sales volume of the estimates we present. Because sales volume depends on bid volume, that's an important comparison to make (we do so in Chapter 3). It's often equally valuable to look at the sheer quantity of bids we present, especially in relation to the number of jobs those quotations produce. Are we creating more or fewer bids than we did last year for the same period? How's our sales success? At what rate are we selling our jobs? Is the trend line up or down for this information? In other words, is our selling getting better or worse?

We also need to know the average value of the estimates we present, because the volume of sales we'll create from those quotations will have a direct relationship to it. Is the trend of this information—the potential dollar value of our average estimate—going up or down? Why? Let's look at a trend line based on this information and project what our average volume will be a few months from now. Is it where we'd like it to be?

Warranty repair costs are a real headache for many businesses. If they contribute substantially to your cost of doing business, then it's worthwhile to track them, starting with a look at their total as a percentage of your total sales. Once you know, historically, how much you should spend on warranty repair labor, you'll be able to see immediately when you begin to have a problem in this area. It's also helpful to examine the trend of warranty repair costs, which gives you a feeling for the quality of the equipment you sell.

On the plus side, a good warranty program means happy customers, so you want to strive for a happy medium. You need to make sure you collect for any just claims against the product suppliers you work with, while at the same time making sure your customers are satisfied.

Along the same line, anytime you have labor repair costs, you'll have people problems. Some service technicians are terrific—few callbacks, good profits—while others are just the opposite. Those extremes are easy to spot; it's the marginal ones that are more difficult to discover, but you can do it if you track their service data and graph it.

In this day and age, you're expected to add finance charges to old accounts. While you want to do this, of course, it's not the good thing that many business people sometimes think it is, because *any* finance charges mean you have old accounts—just the thing you neither want or need. There are some helpful ways to examine your finance charge information, including the idea of plotting it as a percentage of your total accounts receivable, both as raw data and with a trend line. Once you have a long-term historical look at your information, you'll know in what range the information should remain and have an immediate warning if it ventures out on its own. You also want to break out and compare the total you receive for finance charges with what it costs you to carry those accounts.

Other Ideas

If you send monthly statements to your customers (where better to add finance charges?), you might find it helpful to plot the number of statements you send out on a this-year versus last-year basis. The average amount on each statement is sometimes a useful figure to know and keep track of.

Is there a relationship between the total accounts receivable you have at the end of a month and the number of statements you send out? Is there a relationship between the number of statements and the total finance charges for a period? How would you track the extra expenses you have when you start to add finance charges? After all, besides the aggravation you get from people who don't pay, you may send them extra statements (just as a nice reminder), notes requesting payment, certified letters to let them know you're serious, and so on (all the way up to legal fees or collection agency costs as you try to collect impossible accounts). It all starts with old accounts, and old accounts provide a red flag of warning by the exact dollar amounts of your monthly finance charges.

On warranty equipment, it's often worthwhile to plot the incidence of warranty repair on a per-brand basis. We looked at things from just a dollar standpoint (what were our costs for each brand we sell, for every $10,000 in sales?). Why not look at this information from a percentage basis (the number of repair calls per 100 units sold)?

Inside the areas of the number and value of the estimates you make, the warranty repairs you get stuck for, and the finance charges you try to collect from your not-so-good customers are any number of areas to examine and chart. Spend a bit of time to determine what's important to you, and you'll quickly have a better handle on your business.

Direct Costs

6

While the words *sales* and *gross* and *net profit* are music to the ears of every businessperson, words like *direct labor* and *material costs* are not. They conjure up images of cash spent, wages paid, dollars going out the door. But since they're something we all have to deal with, we'd better be aware of how they work inside our own businesses and have some insight as to what trends to look for that might cause future problems.

Probably the best thing about direct costs is that there usually aren't many of them to worry about—often, we have just labor and materials, with perhaps a bit of freight or outside services thrown in. But for what they lack in numbers they more than overcome in dollar amounts; in any business, direct costs are the second largest item on your income statement, right after your sales total.

What are Direct Costs?

Simply put, direct costs are the dollar totals you can assign directly to the production, delivery, installation, and warranty service costs of what you sell. You "test" for direct costs by asking if the item *varies* in direct proportion to the number of things produced and sold. The more you sell, the greater the total of your direct cost items. If you don't sell anything, you don't have any direct costs.

Generally, things like material and labor are pretty easy to track. *Your* salary is obviously not a direct cost: you'll (probably) take home a check regardless of how much the business sold this past week. However, if there were no sales, you shouldn't have any direct labor or material costs.

There are also some gray areas in which you and your accountant might have to dig a little bit to put into their proper places. Salespeople who work for you might receive a salary plus a commission bonus of some sort. If they get paid whether they sell anything or not, their salary belongs in the overhead column. If they receive a bonus based on their sales, the standard salary is still an overhead item, but the bonus—since it can be directly tied to sales—is a direct cost amount. Freight on any materials your company buys should show up as a direct cost item; freight on office supplies should not. You can get quite involved here, so most business owners leave the chore of what to put where up to their accountant; the dollar figures you get from your accountant will almost always have things in their correct place.

Where to Start

All direct cost totals are shown on your income statement. Direct labor is usually listed as just that, often with any extra payroll tax items shown separately. The materials you used are derived by taking your beginning inventory, adding any purchases you made during the period the statement is for, and then subtracting your current inventory. The figure you arrive at is the amount of material you used for this period. Other direct cost items will also be listed as part of your cost of sales, and can include things like freight, equipment rent (if it can be charged to specific jobs), outside services, and so on.

The First Picture

Since direct costs should vary in direct proportion to your sales, the first place to look is at a picture of these two items.

Figure 6-1 charts our fictitious business over a 12-month period. It's pretty obvious that both the solid and dashed lines show about the same ups and downs with one apparent oddity: costs seem to lag behind sales about a month. However, this isn't unusual, as often sales are recorded in one month while the invoices for at least some of the materials used aren't received and tallied until the following month.

While the sales line climbs at a faster rate than the cost figures do, that's to be expected. The dollar totals are greater for sales than they are for costs, as sales are recorded on a *retail* basis, while direct costs are totaled, of course, on a *cost* basis. In all, Figure 6-1 is the sort of picture we should expect to see from a comparison of our sales to our direct costs. Any variation—particularly if the two lines head off in opposite directions—might signal a problem.

DIRECT COSTS

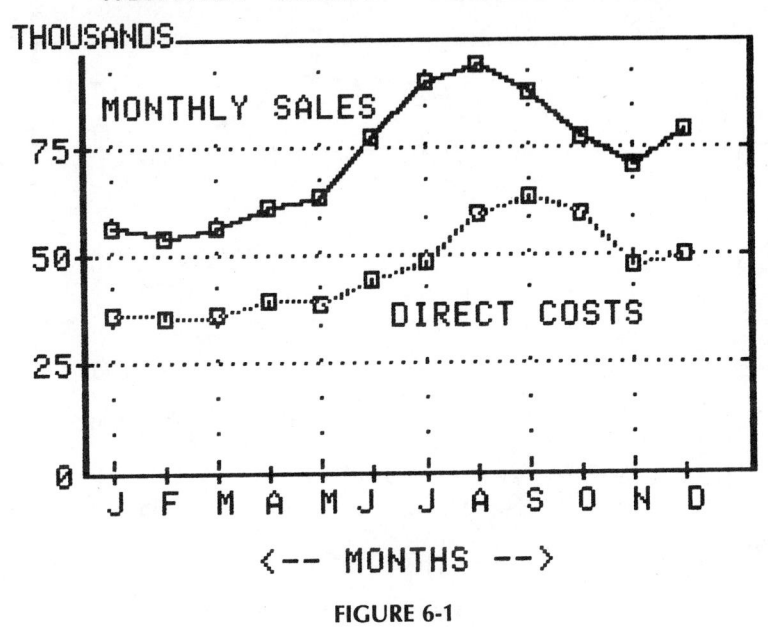

```
        MONTHLY SALES / DIRECT COSTS
THOUSANDS
         MONTHLY SALES
   75

   50                      DIRECT COSTS

   25

    0
       J  F  M  A  M  J  J  A  S  O  N  D

              <-- MONTHS -->
```

FIGURE 6-1

    Things aren't always as they appear, of course. Let's break down the direct cost total into its two biggest areas—labor and materials—and see how they compare to our sales.

    Figure 6-2 shows us how our direct labor rose and fell in comparison with our monthly sales totals. Again, the two lines are similar, but without the lag effect we saw in Figure 6-1. That also makes sense, as payroll checks are written every week (or two), and so our labor costs will generally be incurred during the same month the sales are billed. Again, this business doesn't show any real aberrations.

    In what's almost a replay of Figure 6-2, Figure 6-3 plots that same sales line along with our material costs for the yearly period we're examining. We can see that the lag effect is back, which is to be expected from a chart that includes material costs. That's because the invoices for the materials bought will trail sales much of the time. Probably the most notable thing about this graph is that if we examine it along with Figure 6-2, it's obvious that labor is more volatile than materials are. Material consumption varies with sales, of course, but not to the degree that payroll does.

    This is the case with many businesses and often can be a problem area. While materials can be kept under a pretty tight rein (with a good inventory control program), labor is more difficult to manage. In many industries, materials can be inexpensive in comparison to the total labor it takes to produce a product.

FIGURE 6-2

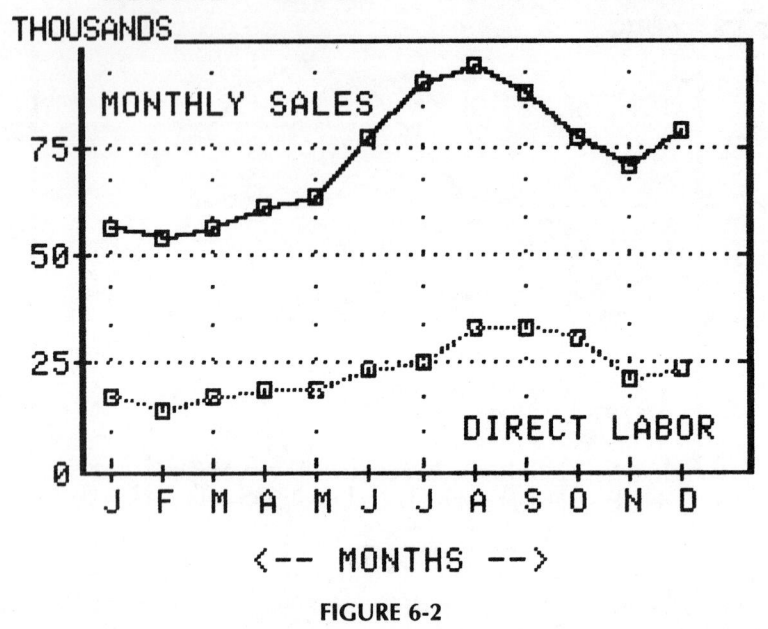

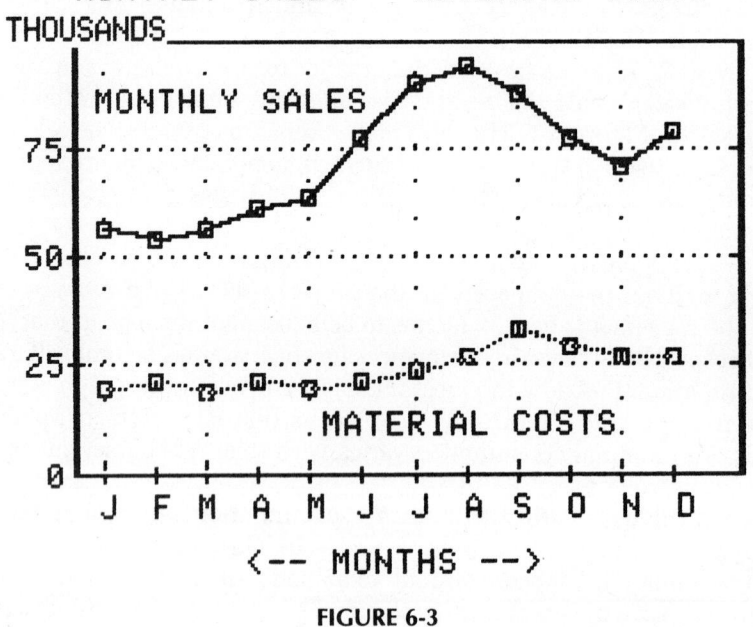

FIGURE 6-3

From just a labor standpoint, a few more coffee breaks or some poor bidding, or just a few problems on the job, and our costs can soar. For many businesses, too, material costs are negligible, while the cash they must spend on labor consumes a huge percentage of their total cost dollar. This series of graphs warns the business owner that *labor* is something to watch closely.

Labor Versus Materials

The next logical thing is to examine direct labor and the cost of materials on the same chart. Each business has its own trends that apply on a historical basis. In many companies, when the cost of direct labor exceeds the cost of the materials used, the business cannot make a profit. For those periods when it spends more on material than it does on labor, the bottom line is black rather than red.

You can find how this relationship works in your own business with an examination of your financial statements. Perhaps you'll end up with figures like these:

YEAR	COST OF MATERIALS	COST OF LABOR	PROFIT (LOSS)
1980	$156,092	$191,092	($11,092)
1981	163,373	151,872	3,003
1982	161,762	147,044	11,098
1983	171,092	151,091	12,404
1984	173,092	179,092	(4,202)
1985	167,020	152,095	17,093
1986	171,009	149,094	27,092

For every year in this fictional example, when the cost for labor exceeded the cost of the materials used, the business lost money. While no percentage will hold true all of the time, based on its recent financial statements, this business can pretty well figure that when labor costs are higher than material costs, it will lose money.

In your own business, a study of this sort might tell you that when your materials cost more than labor, you won't make a profit. Or when labor is 15% higher than materials, you have a profit problem. But the answer is in your figures somewhere, and an examination like the one above will give you the answer to what's true for you.

This generally is correct on a monthly or quarterly basis, too, which gives the business owner who doesn't get a monthly income statement a chance to visually see how he or she is doing.

One of the best ways to chart this sort of data—once you know what holds true for your own business—is with a column chart like Figure 6-4. These figures

```
         DIRECT LABOR / MATERIAL COSTS
   THOUSANDS
      40
      30
      20
      10
       0
         1    2    3    4    5    6    7    8
                  <-- MONTHS -->
         LEFT BAR (SOLID)  = DIRECT LABOR
         RIGHT BAR (DASHED) = MATERIAL COSTS
```

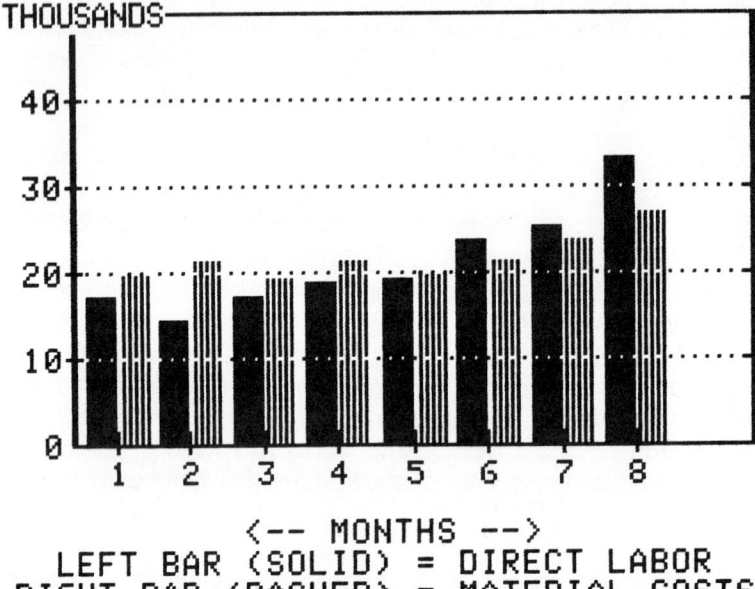

FIGURE 6-4

for materials and labor costs can usually be generated internally, without a formal income statement from your accountant.

In this example, the left bar represents the direct labor costs for the first eight months of the year, while the right bar plots the cost of materials for the same period. For the first five months of the year, material costs exceeded sales. Starting in month 6, the situation reversed itself, and by month 8 there was a significant difference between the two figures.

The business owner whose records indicated he or she showed a profit only when materials exceeded labor costs would immediately see a problem. Even without an income statement that figures the bottom line exactly, Figure 6-4 gives this business owner a picture of his or her condition, a situation that's getting worse by the month.

Obviously, when one month shows a reversal of the comparison your business needs, it might be just a temporary thing, and the graph simply signals that you might want to watch details a little closer. Once you get the same warning for three months in a row, though, it's an indication you have a major problem and that action needs to be taken. Otherwise, the rest of the year might end up the same way—and you'd finish it with a loss.

While the column chart gives the business manager a feel for the dollar values of labor and materials, the same data on a line graph tells him or her the *rate* at which the figures are moving. It's helpful to examine the same data over the same time frame and on the same scale with a line-chart format, as we've done in Figure 6-5.

Figure 6-5 uses the same information we just looked at but tells us a little more about the situation. First of all, we can better see that even early in the year our material costs were slowly decreasing, while labor costs were on the rise. The line chart gives us a better feeling for the *movement* of the data. This in itself might have given the alert owner a bit of a warning that more serious problems were right around the corner.

In May, the totals for labor and materials were about equal, which in effect means this business probably didn't do better than break even for the month. In the May-June period, the lines crossed each other; from a historical basis, we know it probably lost money during June. And while things got a little better during July, by the end of August this business had a major problem. Sadly, there's no reason for it; in this particular example, if the business owner had the charts we've looked at, there was ample warning: he or she could *see* the lines moving each month.

This is especially true when we use the line graph: the line that plots the cost of materials is consistently falling, while the line that represents direct labor rises in all but two of the months. Even in the June-August period, when the cost of materials starts to increase, it doesn't match the *rate* of rise that labor took.

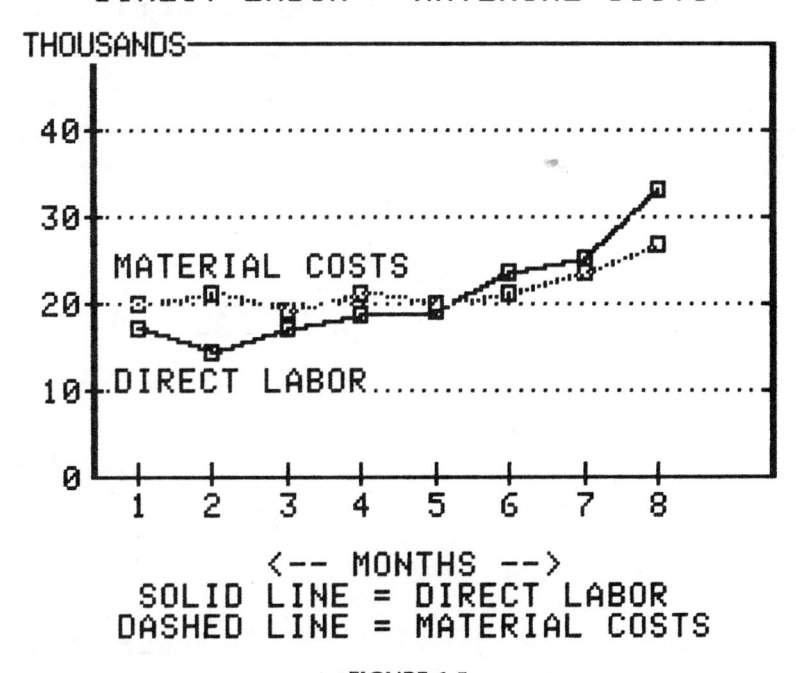

FIGURE 6-5

A Closer Look

It's often helpful to expand just a section of this sort of graph to get a closer look at the rise and fall of the data sets. Figure 6-6 does just that and plots in a line chart the four totals since labor and material costs were equal back in month 5. It's important to note that when we create a chart without a zero line, we get a distorted view of the information. Since it represents a critical period for this business, however, the business owner might gain more understanding of his or her situation with a *closer look* at the data.

While Figure 6-5 gives the user a good feel for the rate of change of materials and labor costs, Figure 6-6 really brings the point home. In this example, while Figure 6-5 uses a scale that ran from zero to 50,000, the scale for Figure 6-6 starts at 15,000 and runs only to 35,000—a much narrower focus. However, when you ask your plotting program to change the scale of a graph, it's important to note that the relationship between the numbers doesn't change.

An expanded closeup view like this often makes the information easier to digest. It also serves to put a scare into business people who know they must keep labor costs lower than materials if they're to make a profit. From that viewpoint, an image like Figure 6-6 will motivate this business owner to do something to correct things.

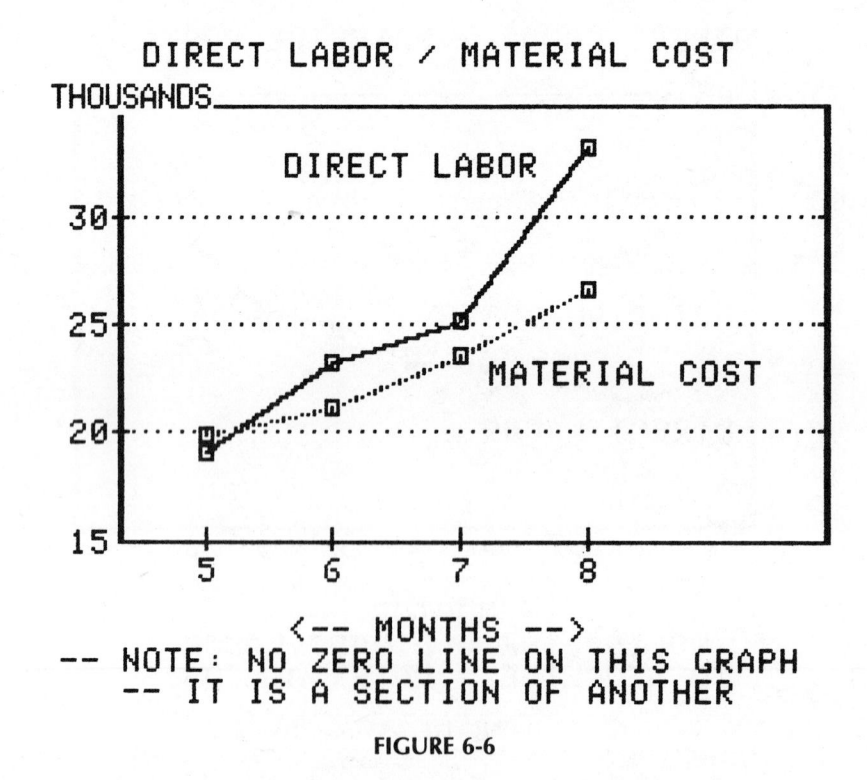

FIGURE 6-6

DIRECT LABOR / MATERIAL COSTS

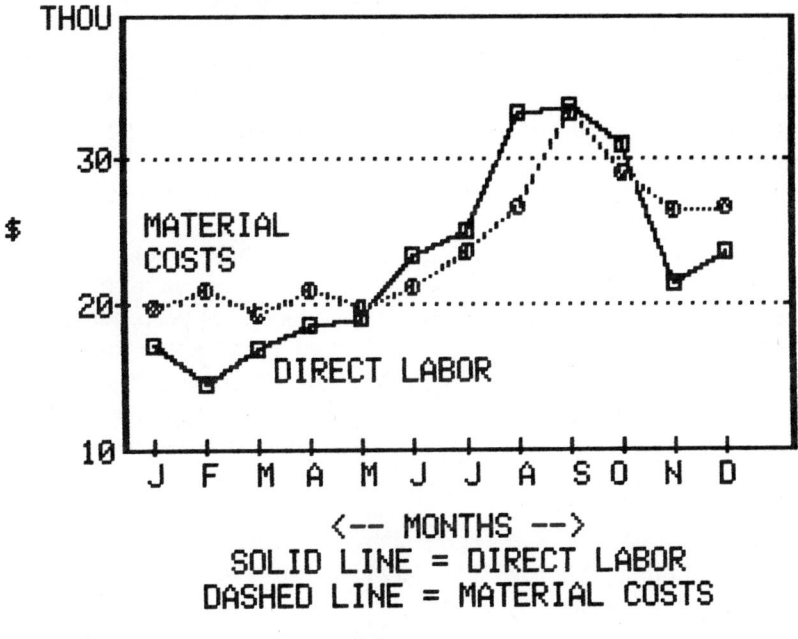

FIGURE 6-7

The Proper Picture

To put things back into the right perspective, Figure 6-7 again looks at the same data we've been poring over, but for the whole year.

We can see how the material and labor lines intersected in May, how labor costs increased faster than materials did, and finally we can see the results of the corrective action the business owner took. By Autumn, the trend had started to reverse itself, and for the last two months of the year, the monthly cost of materials was once more higher than what the business spent for labor. In effect, the business was making money again.

One at a Time

Since direct labor and cost of materials will make up the greatest portion of direct costs (in some cases, all costs), it's worthwhile to examine them in a little more detail.

In our own business, we not only discovered that we had to keep labor costs lower than material costs (as outlined above) to make money, we also found that we could only make a profit when those labor costs were 30% of sales or lower. Since we have a sales figure every month as well as a total for direct labor costs, it's an easy matter to plot this percentage on a monthly basis.

Figure 6-8 charts the direct labor as a percentage of monthly sales for our fictitious business over the first three quarters of the year. If we assume this business works on a similar basis to our own, it probably made a profit during any month where direct labor totals 30% or less of its sales volume. During those months when the labor costs got carried away and rose above that 30% line, the business most likely lost money.

This chart was plotted over a one-month longer basis than the earlier ones were, to show graphically the affect of some corrective action on the part of the business owner. By September, the rise in the labor/sales percentage had been reversed, and the business started to steer toward a profitable course.

This particular chart can also be used for any other comparison(s) you find important to your business. You might find that you only make money when materials are less than 35% of sales, or when labor and materials *together* are less than 67% of your sales total. The percentages are different for every business, of course, but once you get a feel for what they are, you'll find they generally hold true over a period of time. It's also worthwhile every three months to examine these figures on a quarterly basis; the data gives you a different impression than it does when you see it every month.

Figure 6-9 plots a trend line for the direct labor as a percentage of sales for

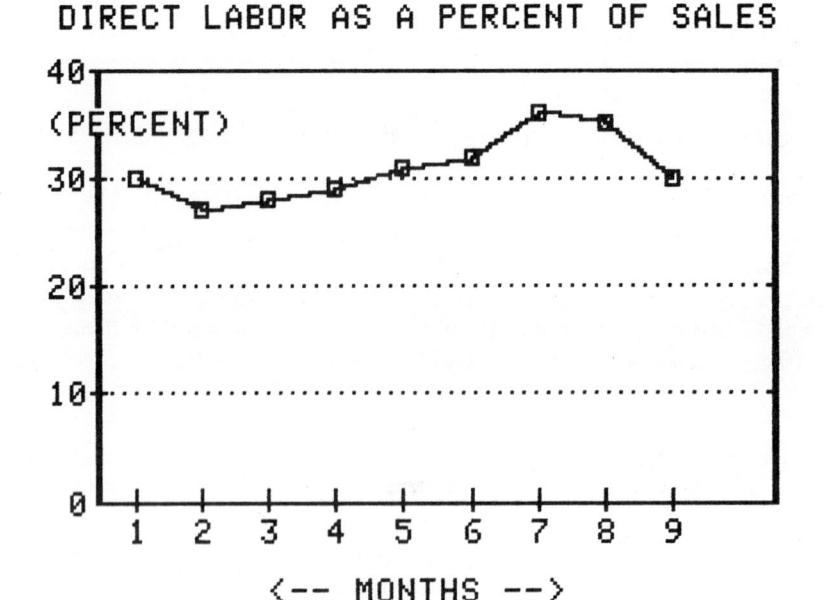

FIGURE 6-8

DIRECT LABOR AS A PERCENT OF SALES

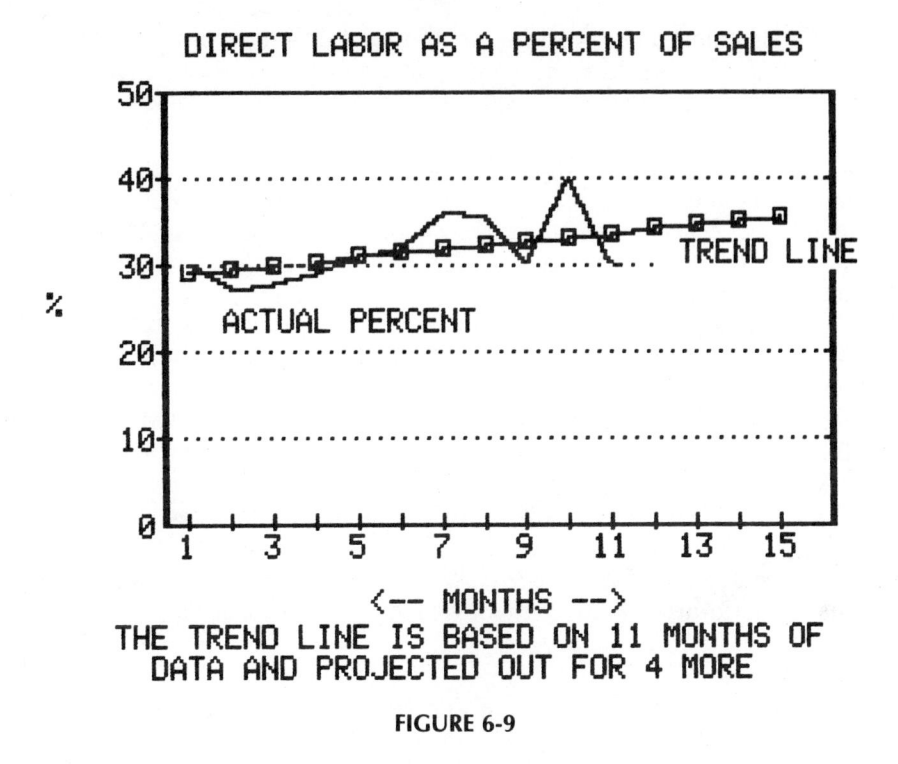

[Graph showing actual percent and trend line fluctuating around 30-40% over months 1-15]

<-- MONTHS -->
THE TREND LINE IS BASED ON 11 MONTHS OF
DATA AND PROJECTED OUT FOR 4 MORE

FIGURE 6-9

our fictional business, with a projection that extends to month 15. The actual data is also plotted. The disturbing thing about this picture is how the rate of the data is growing—it's going in exactly the direction we don't want it to. While we had an idea from Figure 6-8 that our labor, as a percentage of our total sales, was rising, this illustration confirms it and serves warning that we'd better take some corrective action to lower our labor costs (as a percentage of our sales).

Zeroing In

Since direct labor costs for this business are volatile and form such a large part of its costs, it's helpful to examine any *associated* costs. For our fictional example, we've grouped *all* other costs that are directly concerned with labor and called them "payroll taxes."

There are all sorts of things you can classify as payroll taxes, including unemployment taxes at the federal level and that large expense that employers must match what their people contribute, Social Security. In your business, payroll taxes are anything that varies in relationship to your direct labor costs—the more checks you write for payroll, the more these extra taxes add up. Most businesses also have to carry some sort of workmen's compensation insurance, in case an employee gets hurt on the job. Others must pay a state unemployment tax. For this example, we've lumped them all together and called them payroll taxes.

Figure 6-10 plots two widely variant figures, but ones that have a direct relationship. Because payroll taxes (in this example) approximate 10% of the total direct labor costs, it's an easy matter to multiply them by ten. They can then be charted on the same scale as direct labor, and the business owner can get an idea of the *rate* of change between the two lines (if any).

Figure 6-10 plots the direct labor costs for this business for the first five months of the year, along with its payroll taxes multiplied by ten. For the first three months, the amounts varied at about the same rate. From March to April the gap closed a bit. A little change of this sort might be attributed to part of the payroll being recorded in one period, while the business might have been slow to pay part of the taxes that were due.

However, the movement of the two lines made a marked change in the April-May period: the two lines look like they're on a collision course. While payroll costs flattened out a bit, the taxes *rose*. The business owner who spots something like this needs to discover why there's been a change; perhaps compensation

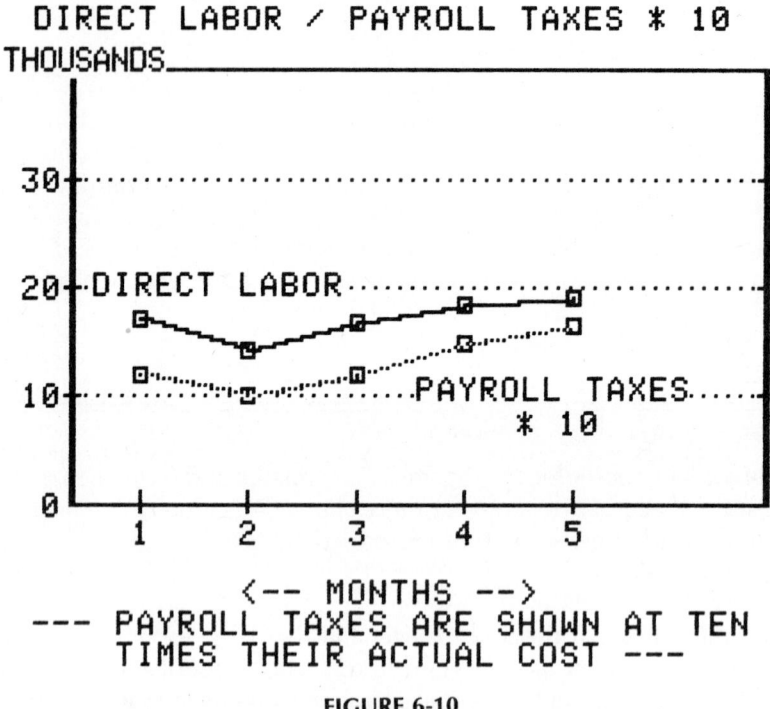

FIGURE 6-10

insurance rates went up and payroll taxes as a percentage of costs increased. As always, these two lines are directly related to each other, and as such, should rise and fall at the same rate. If they don't, we need to find out the reason.

Total Costs

Once you add together all your direct costs, it's helpful to compare their total from last year to this. However, since your sales will be more or less than last year's (and so will the dollar value of your direct costs), it's usually more useful to examine the figures as a *percentage* of sales. If you look at them on a percentage basis, it doesn't matter if sales rise or fall; direct costs as a percentage of sales should be about the same. You know what this percentage was last year and if you made money or not during that time. So, you should have some feeling as to how you're doing if direct costs are a higher or lower percentage than they were last year.

Figure 6-11 plots the direct cost percentages over the first four months of the year. We can see an obvious rise in the figures for the current year.

For some reason, the business this year is spending more of its dollars for direct costs, on a percentage basis, than it did last year. Have wholesale prices

FIGURE 6-11

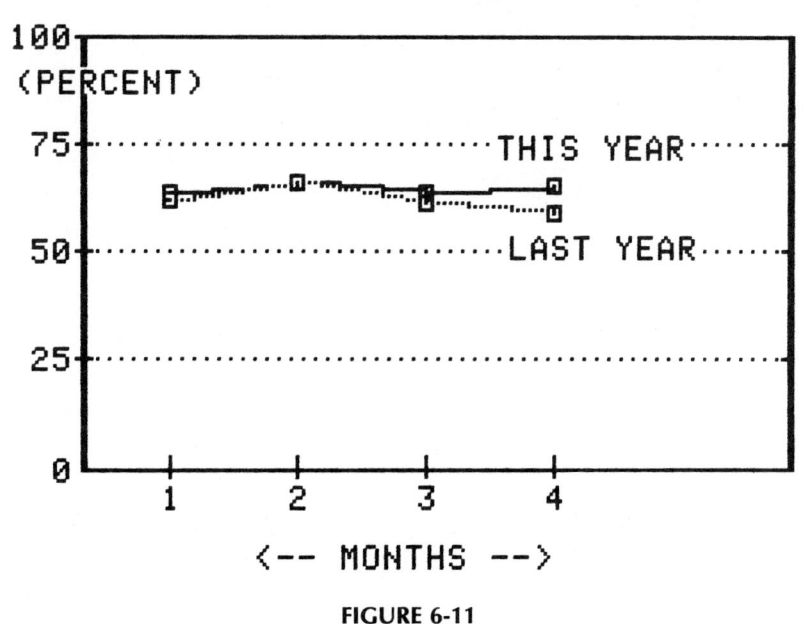

gone up without a corresponding increase at the retail level? Have the employees slowed down? Did the business put a major labor raise into effect, without incorporating it into its pricing structure? Has some component of direct costs (like freight) taken a big jump?

To get a better idea of the seriousness of this sort of increase, it's a good idea to again expand the graph to get a clearer picture of what the figures are doing. Figure 6-12 eliminates the zero line (as is noted on the graph), and because it's plotted over a narrower scale we can get a better idea of the *rate of change* of the data.

While January's figures looked about the same on Figure 6-11, the expanded graph shows that this year's totals were definitely higher than last year's totals. We can also see that during the February-April period last year, our direct costs as a percentage of sales decreased, while the opposite is true for this year's work. In fact, both Figures 6-11 and 6-12 show the two lines heading off in opposing directions.

This is precisely where business graphics can help us. Once business owners see that they have a discrepancy in two similar data sets, they need to examine their information to determine its cause. When something as critical as direct costs increase on a percentage of sales basis, any business faces a serious problem.

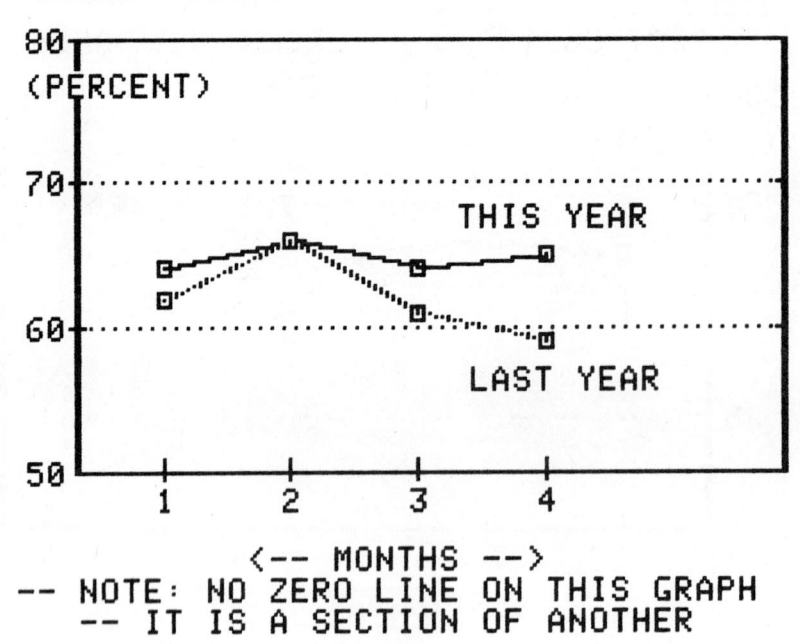

FIGURE 6-12

Another Way to Look

While they're not useful for everyone's applications, a *stacked bar chart* presents a unique picture and is particularly suited to manufacturing businesses. In effect, this graph lets you combine two or more data sets into one column of information. For our purposes here, where we're examining direct costs, they have their own helpful niche when it comes to taking a look at our costs on a per item basis.

While each business that fabricates things in quantity has a method to track all of the costs that go into their products, it's often difficult to picture where those costs are changing (if they do) over a period of time. Although Figure 6-13 illustrates only two broad categories of expenses, the basic concept is what's important: the use of a stacked bar chart gives us a feel for what's happening to the costs for our fictional business.

As with our other graphs, this one is designed so the grid lines assist us when it comes to understanding the information. Since both labor and materials—the two categories this graph plots—each consume about $15 of cost per item produced, the logical grid line to use scales at $15 increments.

There's a definite limitation to this type of graph, in that if *both* data sets

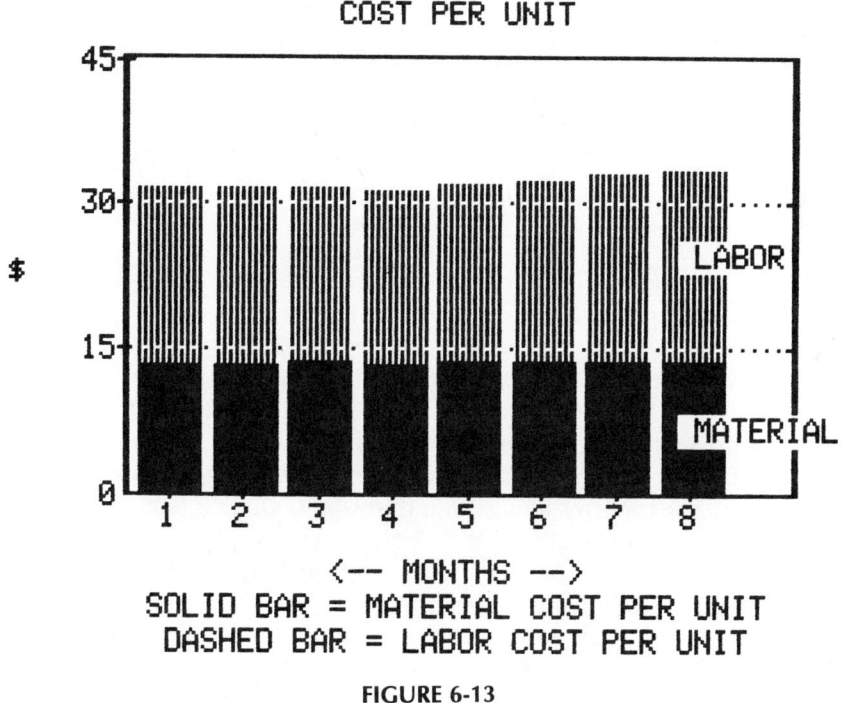

FIGURE 6-13

jump around a lot in terms of their dollar amounts, you can get a good reading for your total costs, but it's impossible to understand each individually. If that's the case, you're better off to graph each component of your product cost on a separate chart. Figure 6-13, however, finds our fictional business with a pretty steady cost of material line. With the help of the grid line located at $15, we can see that our material costs remained pretty steady for the eight months charted.

Since the total cost per unit is creeping up, albeit slowly, we know the problem is in our labor area. And in fact, if we kind of let our eyes believe that the $15 grid line is the bottom of the *labor* part of this picture, we can really see the monthly variations in the cost of our labor, on a per unit basis.

While the stacked bar chart is useful only in certain areas, it's very helpful to the manufacturer who needs to examine not only the total cost of each product the business produces but also needs to know how each component part is changing.

Summing Up

Direct costs are also called *variable costs* because they vary in direct relation to what you sell. In most businesses, you can chart sales and direct costs and they'll rise and fall at the same rate.

Since the largest part of any business costs are direct costs, a small rise in that area produces a big change in its bottom line. A simplified example might find a business operating with these percentages:

> 30% for its material cost
> 30% for its labor cost
> 30% for its overhead costs
> <u>10%</u> for profit before taxes
> 100% total sales volume

If the business had a sales volume of $100,000 for a particular period of time, it's easy to convert these percentages into dollar figures—material costs would come to $30,000, labor costs would be the same, and so on.

What these figures mean is that a 5% increase in direct costs will result in a reduction in net profit of almost one-third: $3,000. The total direct costs for this business come to $60,000. If they increase by 5%, that removes the $3,000 (5% of $60,000) from the profit column. Even a slight increase in direct costs has a truly negative effect on the bottom line.

In the fictional example we plotted, we found that labor costs were a little more volatile than material costs, that they varied a bit more in relation to sales than materials did.

We not only focused our attention on direct labor, but found if we looked at part of the year with both a column-chart and line-chart comparison of materials and labor, we understood more about our business. The column chart gave us a feeling for the amounts and let us see exactly when the two amounts reversed their historical trend, when labor costs started to exceed those of the materials our business used.

The same information in a line chart told us even more about the *trend* of this data. We saw that even early in the year the business's labor costs were on the rise, while material costs were going down. Once the lines converged and then started to head off in opposite directions, it was obvious this business had a problem. The line graph, though, gave us a look into the future; we could *see* the direction our costs were moving. While we always need to mark, right on the graph itself, when it doesn't have a zero line, we found if we expanded just a section of our labor/materials graph, we could see the *rate* of change well enough to perhaps motivate us to do something about it.

Another key to any examination of direct costs is to look at its various components in relationship to sales. For this fictitious example, we concentrated on direct labor and learned that when this business incurred labor costs higher than 30% of its sales, it lost money. It's fairly easy, then, to plot the labor as a *percentage* of sales, with (in this case) 30% marked as a grid line. When the graph shows the percentage higher than the 30% line, the business probably isn't making any money. If the company can hold it *below* that level, though, it'll probably show a profit at the end of each month.

This should be taken a step further, of course. The knowledgeable businessperson will also plot material costs as a percentage of sales. He or she will also look at any major component of direct costs in relation to the sales total, and also as a percentage of direct costs themselves. Put a profit line on the image, to track its movement in relation to the other data. We've only looked at labor as a percentage of sales, but there are any number of alternate approaches that could be just as valid. We examined labor because it is more important in this specific example; your own business might be different. However, once you know the two or three comparisons that are meaningful for you, you only have to chart them.

Since labor was our focus for this study, we also found it instructive to examine it in relation to its associated costs. To simplify things, we lumped all the taxes, etc., together and multiplied the total by ten. That let us put this data on the same chart as direct labor. As always, these two lines should rise and fall at the same rate; any aberration is a cause for more investigation.

Finally, we looked at total direct costs as a percentage of sales. As our sales volume goes up or down, so do our direct cost dollars. Direct costs should remain about the same *as a percentage* of sales from year to year. If this percentage goes up, it's a signal to look closer. If we can decrease direct costs as a percentage of sales, we'll add dollars directly into the profit column. Here, too, an expanded chart can be of help, as we can focus on the *rate* of change between the two data sets. In certain instances, particularly if our work involves two major cost items, a stacked bar chart gives us helpful information.

Other Ideas

Since direct costs form such a huge portion of any business's dollar outlay, it's well worthwhile for the business owner to look at his or her own figures to determine what's important and valid for his or her particular line of work. If your business uses 800 items and very little labor, you'll naturally want to pay more attention to your cost of materials than you do to your labor expense. If freight is a major expense every month, then it pays to chart it, always with an eye to somehow reducing this particular expense.

While we plotted payroll taxes in comparison to direct labor, it's often useful to get a year-to-year picture by charting this year's payroll taxes compared to last year's or a historical long-range look at payroll taxes as a *percentage* of direct labor.

If you're in a manufacturing business, it's a terrific help to plot labor against the number of units you produce each month. Along the same line, chart your material cost along with the units total. You might have to multiply one of these figures (as always, by 10 or 100) to get them both on the same graph, but they should go right along the same line, shouldn't they?

If gasoline or delivery costs are a major expense, break them out of your direct cost total and plot them compared to last year. Chart them in relation to sales—as you do more sales volume, you can expect your gasoline/delivery costs to increase. But they *should* move right along with sales and if they don't, you'd want to look closer to find out why. You can expand this to total vehicle costs and compare it to your sales volume.

If you run a lot of trucks, plot their costs on a column chart on an individual basis. Chart them individually in relation to the sales/deliveries/pickups each vehicle made. If truck "A" costs you $15 per stop and truck "B" costs $25, you've got to ask *why*. Learn the significant ratios and comparisons for your own business and plot them on a regular basis. If you do, you'll reduce your costs.

Overhead

7

The worst thing about overhead is that it's always there. Whether we sell anything or not, overhead goes on and on and often seems to grow with a life of its own. There are a lot of different things that make up our overhead total, often a number of small items that by themselves are insignificant but together add up to a lot of dollars.

It's important to note, though, that while overhead is usually considered something of an independent item (we have to pay its costs even if sales are poor), it's still related to the sales our business makes. How do you measure and talk about your overhead? As a *percentage* of sales. As our sales increase, we can expect our overhead to take something of a jump at the same time. To create those sales, our overhead will rise as its total grows from its many pieces: advertising, paper and office supplies, phone calls, rent. So while much of our overhead must be paid regardless of our sales picture, it's vital to understand that there's still a relationship between sales and overhead.

Any examination of overhead should concern itself with (1) ways to reduce the overhead amounts, and thus its total, and (2) a look at the direction the various things that make up our overhead costs happen to be moving up or down at a particular point in time.

Wrong Images

It's important to know in advance that we're never going to get a perfectly accurate overhead picture. For example, telephone costs are commonly included as an overhead item; our business will (probably) have a phone whether it sells anything during a specific period or not. However, as our sales increase, so will the cost of our long-distance calls. This same line of reasoning lists our utility costs as an overhead expense. In actual practice we may find that our gas (or oil) and electricity costs increase as we do more business, for we might stay open longer, work on Saturdays, and so on.

In truth, too, many small businesses simply charge their entire phone bill to "telephone expenses," without removing the cost for advertising in the yellow pages and charging that to their "advertising expense" column. Freight is often lumped together and posted into one account, without regard to whether a particular freight charge was for delivery of a new desk (overhead) or for delivery of the products we sell (direct cost).

The Choice

While none of this matters a whole lot to the bottom line, it has a tendency to distort some of the pictures we see. Often, too, when we start a detailed examination of a specific area of our business, we'll discover that our expenses aren't being broken down as they should, so we have to make a choice. We need to decide whether we want to *change* the way costs are distributed, to be more accurate, or whether we should leave them the same so we can compare them to other periods. Once we change things, we can no longer make valid comparisons (either numerically or graphically), as the data is based on different criteria.

For instance, for years we've lumped all of our truck costs into a category called "auto." Once gas prices started to jump, we wanted to know how much of that auto expense was for gasoline alone. We could also break it down into the money spent on repairs, the cash spent for tires, for maintenance, and so on. In another area, we put all our office expenses into a category called "office." These days, it would be nice to know exactly what our postage costs are, without all the other amounts for legal pads, pens, scotch tape, and so on.

Probably the best solution to this problem is that when you find an area of your own business that isn't broken down the way you feel it should be, leave the old breakdown as a general heading and create new, more detailed areas to track. For example, you might have a file where you store information for your vehicle costs. Once you start examining it in detail and with graphs, you might find this study will cause you to want more information on your vehicle repair costs. This amount may not be broken out of your "total vehicle" account, so you'd have to go back through old invoices or checks to find its total. An examination of this information might make you want to search further, perhaps to look at your repair costs on a per truck or per mile basis. This doesn't mean you should stop tracking the original vehicle cost account, but rather use your *new* ideas as an adjunct to the main file.

Overhead Details

Our examination of overhead in this chapter will focus on the general, overall picture of this expense as a whole, and then we'll break things down into a few smaller parts and see how they look. Since there are so many different areas that add to the total overhead amount a business reports, we cannot touch on them all. However, the same approach and methods of examination and types of graphs will work for each section of your own overhead. The idea is to examine overhead as a total cost, and then you'll have to determine which areas of your total overhead are important for you to take a closer look at.

While it's helpful to look at a graph that compares overhead to total sales, and perhaps equally as useful to examine a chart that shows this year's overhead compared to last year's, let's take things a little further and see what a picture of six months of overhead along with a trend line shows us.

Figure 7-1 is a column chart for the first nine months of a year, for our fictional business's monthly overhead. Overhead includes office salaries, postage, rent, accounting fees, and so on—anything that doesn't directly relate to the creation of sales. It also uses the capability of our plotting program to create a

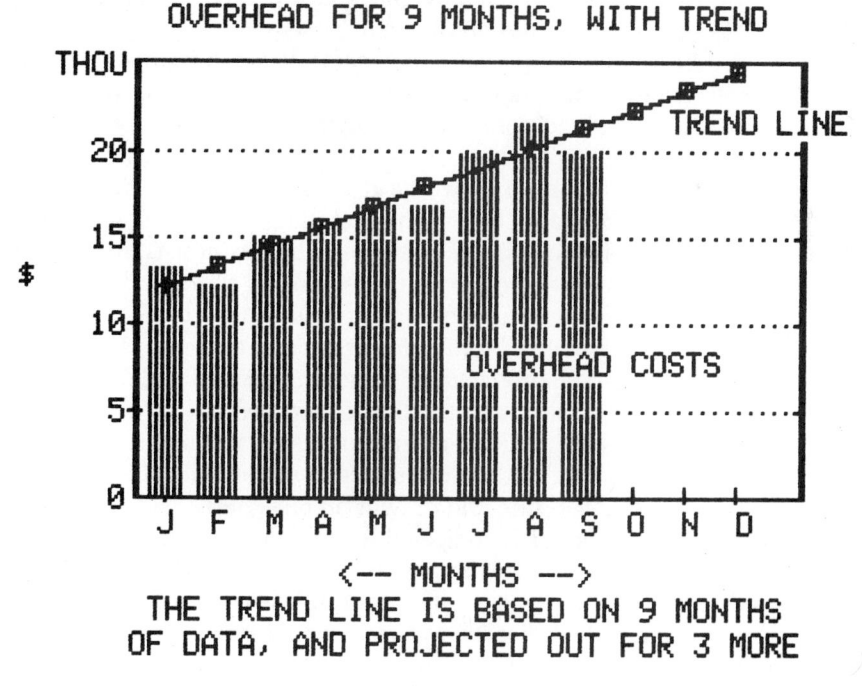

FIGURE 7-1

trend line, based on the six periods of data. This line shows the *trend* of our numbers and projects what the total will be for the next three months.

At first glance, we see a disturbing picture. None of us like to see our costs increase, and that's especially true in the case of overhead. Anything we can save and not spend on overhead goes directly into the profit column.

While overhead exists whether our business does any business or not, this overhead figure is rising. Why? Unless we've recently increased our office staff or advertising or some other expense, overhead should remain pretty stable. This picture tells us this one isn't, but it's something of a false reading in that it shows raw overhead data but tells us nothing about sales during the same time.

Overhead and Sales

If our sales dropped during this six-month period, this business has a definite problem, especially since the overhead trend is up. But once we see a picture like this one, it's important to link the overhead amount to sales, to get a better idea of exactly what's happening inside our business.

A more accurate way to gauge how our overhead is doing is to make a comparison of it to our sales, and plot overhead as a percentage of sales. Figure 7-2 does so, this time over a nine-month span.

Let's say that this business—over the years—has determined that it must allow 24% of its sales dollar to cover its overhead expenses, and this could be called its "maximum overhead percentage." Anything higher than this seems to put the business into the red. A lower figure, of course, is a worthwhile goal. In any case, this company must keep its overhead at 24% or below or it'll lose money. This figure is noted on the graph. One of the best things about this sort of picture is that the business owner can instantly *see* where the business is making money and where some adjustments need to be made. During the first few months of the year, its overhead as a percentage of sales rose to where the business was probably in the red every month; something was done to correct this situation, and the line showed a marked drop in the 5-6 month period. Since then, although it's been rising slowly, it's still under the break-even point.

It's also helpful to scale a graph of this sort as we've done here. The scale from 0 to 32 might seem odd, but since it scales in increments of eight, it allows us to plot the 24% breakeven line and draw it on our chart.

Any important line should be indicated with a side-scale mark and grid line. To do this, you often must instruct your plotting program to scale things according to the range that will be of the most help to you. In the example above, once our fictional business determined that its overhead should stay at 24% or below as a percentage of its sales, a grid line on any graph that tracks the overhead percentage immediately shows any rise or fall in the data. You can do much the same when your data generally runs within a specific range of figures. If your

OVERHEAD AS A PERCENT OF SALES

```
32
         ┌──────────────────────────────┐
         │      □─□                      │
      24 │□─□      □─□                   │
         │   ANYTHING     □              │
         │   MORE THAN 24%   □─□─□       │
    % 16 │.....IS TOO HIGH..............│
         │                               │
         │                               │
       8 │...............................│
         │                               │
         │                               │
       0 └──┼──┼──┼──┼──┼──┼──┼──┼──┼────┘
            1  2  3  4  5  6  7  8  9
                  <-- MONTHS -->
```

WHEN THE OVERHEAD FOR THIS BUSINESS RUNS
MORE THAN 24% OF ITS SALES, IT LOSES MONEY

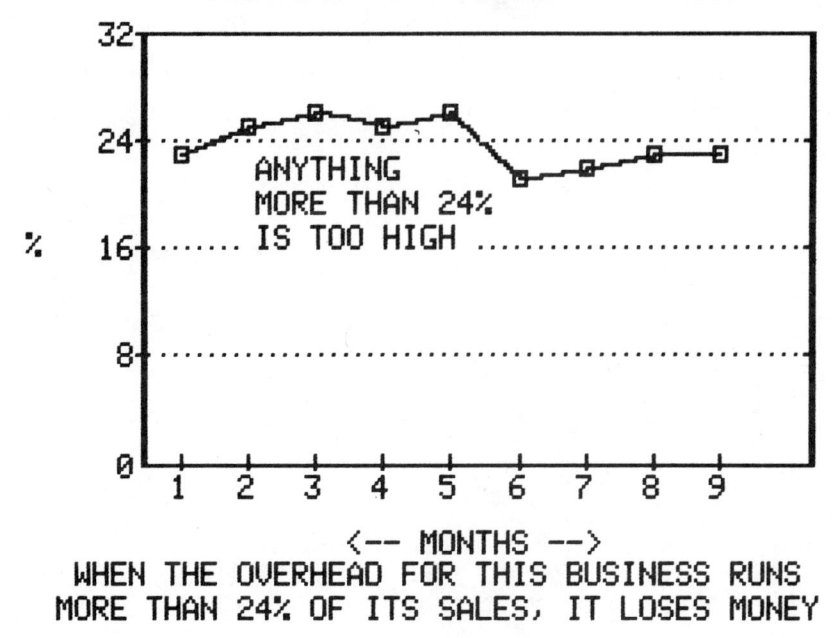

FIGURE 7-2

overhead, as a dollar total, runs between $3,000 and $3,500 per month and you're plotting it, ask your graph to scale in increments of $500. The grid lines will *outline* the average range of your information and make it easier to spot any deviation.

A Closer Look

Figure 7-3 examines the same information that Figure 7-2 plotted, with the addition of a trend line based on that data. The maximum overhead (24%) for this business to have and still show a profit is noted on the graph. The scale marks are the same, but note that there is no zero line plotted. While the graph is physically the same size as Figure 7-2, it covers only the data points between 16% and 32%—a much narrower scale. This gives us a different picture, as the data points will rise and fall at a much more severe angle because the scale is expanded.

We eliminated the zero line to make it easier to see the trend line for our data. What's important about Figure 7-3 is that the *trend* of our overhead as a percentage of sales is dropping. Remember that this graph only covers half as

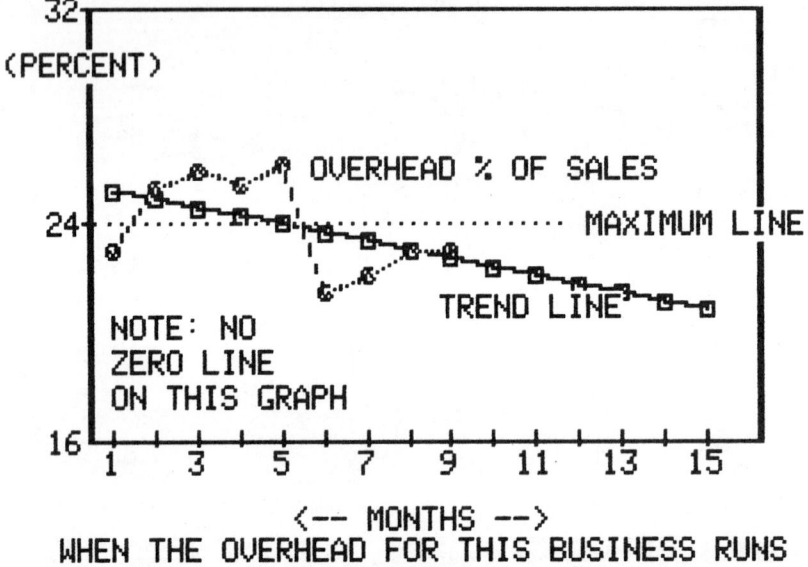

```
       OVERHEAD & ITS TREND AS A % OF SALES
   32
     (PERCENT)

                    OVERHEAD % OF SALES
   24                                   ......  MAXIMUM LINE

                                 TREND LINE
          NOTE: NO
          ZERO LINE
          ON THIS GRAPH
   16
      1    3    5    7    9   11   13   15
                <-- MONTHS -->
      WHEN THE OVERHEAD FOR THIS BUSINESS RUNS
      MORE THAN 24% OF ITS SALES, IT LOSES MONEY
```

FIGURE 7-3

much in scale measurements as Figure 7-2 did, so the gains and losses in the lines are much sharper.

What can we figure out about this business so far? For the first nine months of the year under study, its overhead rose in terms of raw figures. It also rose as a percentage of sales for five months, then took a drastic plunge, to back below the breakeven point. The last few months see the overhead as a percentage of sales rising slowly. However, the overall trend is downward. In effect, this means that sales are rising at a faster rate than overhead is, and when we project our overhead percentage a few months down the road, it's well below what this business can stand and still produce a profit.

Specifics

Once you have a feel for what total overhead looks like, you need to go inside your business and see where your overhead dollars move. We're going to take a close look at utility costs (at electricity in particular) and office salaries. These same concepts and methods of examination are valid for almost any overhead item. *You* might want to look at phone costs, or office expenses, or what you spend on fuel oil every month. Most overhead costs can be viewed the same way, first with an examination of the general area (auto costs, insurance, and so on) and then a move to a more specific section *within* a general area.

Utility Costs

Certainly it's valid to create graphs that compare our utility expenses this year with what we spent last year; that at least tells us how we're doing in terms of any cost-cutting measures we've adopted. Once we're a few months into a year, another way to examine our monthly utility bills is to plot their total costs along with a trend line. Often, because the actual amounts rise and fall from period to period, it's hard to discern the trend of the data until we plot a trend line.

Figure 7-4 is a column chart (to give us a good feel for the actual dollars we're spending on costs) for the first six months of the year for our major utility expenses. If we looked at this data alone, it would be pretty obvious that it's a growing expense. Once we add a trend line, we can project that this part of our

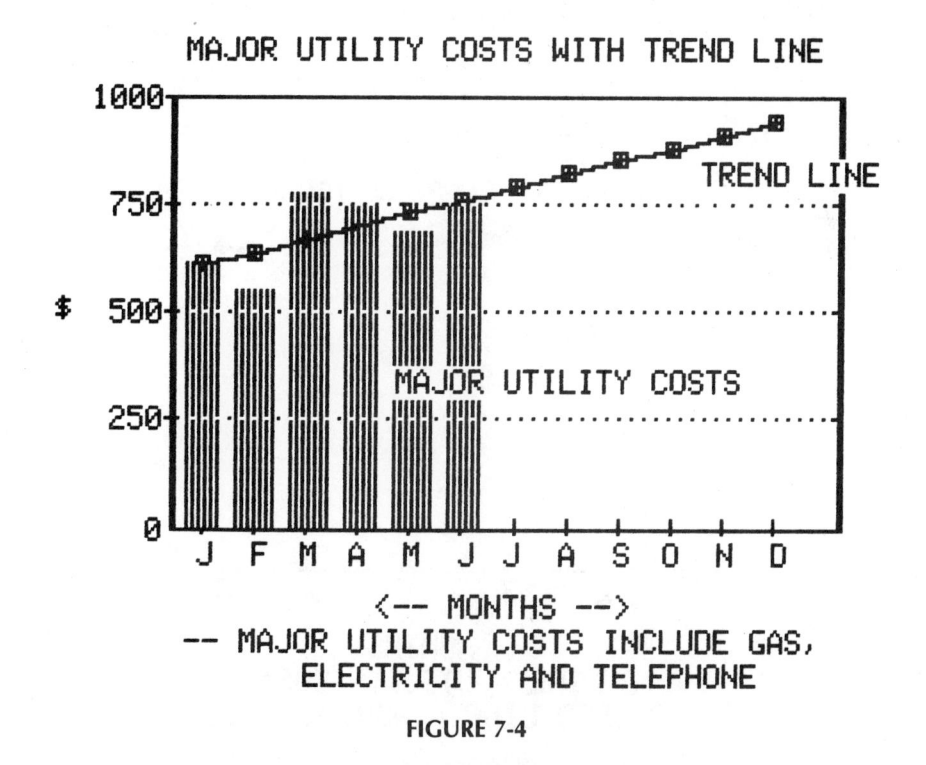

FIGURE 7-4

total overhead is growing at a very rapid rate. Unless sales are growing, too, at about this same speed, we need to do something about our utility costs. This should include an attempt to discover which part of their total is growing (or are all our utility bills?) in an effort to determine *why* as well as *where* the dollars went.

Utilities and Sales

Probably the first place to look is to see if the rise in utility costs matches a similar increase in sales. Since utility costs aren't anywhere near as large as our sales total, we can multiply them by a factor of 10 (10,100, etc.) so we can plot both data sets on the same chart.

Figure 7-5 plots our monthly sales figures for the first six months of the year, along with our total utility bills multiplied by 100, so they're on the same scale. We can see that while they matched each other in their movements for the first two months of the year, we had a huge jump in utility costs over the next two months. Why? Did we use more gas or electricity or incur more telephone charges? In effect, Figure 7-5 tells us that *sales* were not the cause for the jump in utility bills.

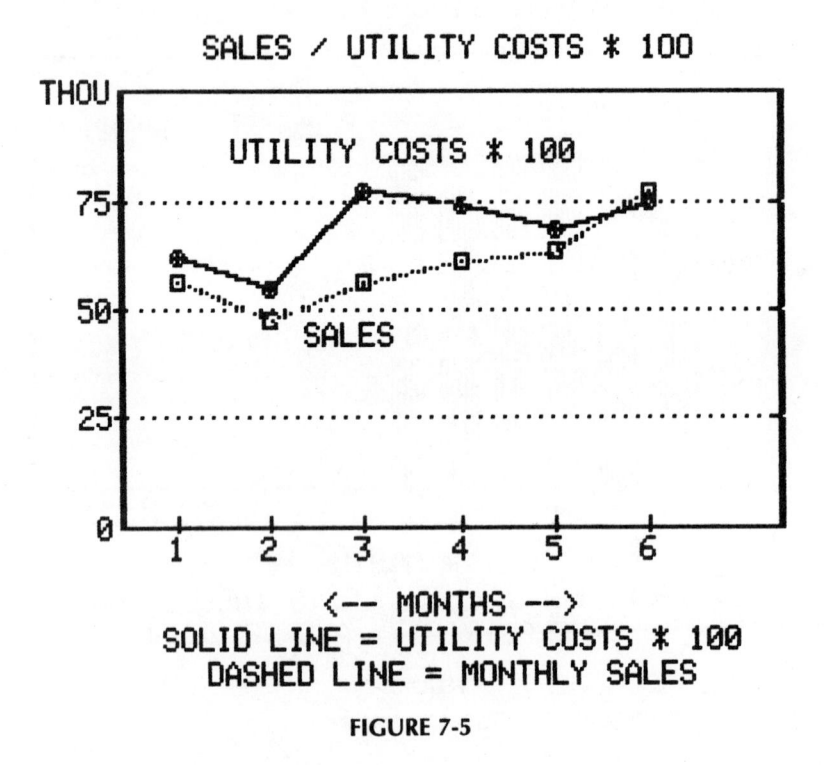

FIGURE 7-5

A Closer Look

While you might want to examine each amount that makes up your utility expenses, we're going to examine electricity—its use and cost. This may or may not be the area that caused the huge jump in utility costs, or might be part of a larger problem. The important thing here is to remember that you can look at any similar area in much the same manner, examine it with the same graphs and ideas.

Figure 7-6 charts the cost of our electricity as a percentage of our total overhead. For the first four months of the half-year period shown, our relative cost for electricity remained about the same—about 20% of our total overhead. It took a significant jump in May. Have we started to use air conditioning? Was there a rate increase? Were we able to reduce our total overhead while our electric bill remained stable (which would, of course, cause it to rise as a percentage of overhead)? If this were your business, you'd probably know the reason.

If we plot these same figures on a column chart on the same scale, we can get a better idea of their growth rate. Figure 7-7 does this, and adds a trend line to the chart.

While we've extended the projection for a longer distance than we should (we can hardly predict six-months' worth of a trend from only six-months' worth of information), Figure 7-7 makes its point: electricity cost as a percentage of our total overhead is rising, and growing fast.

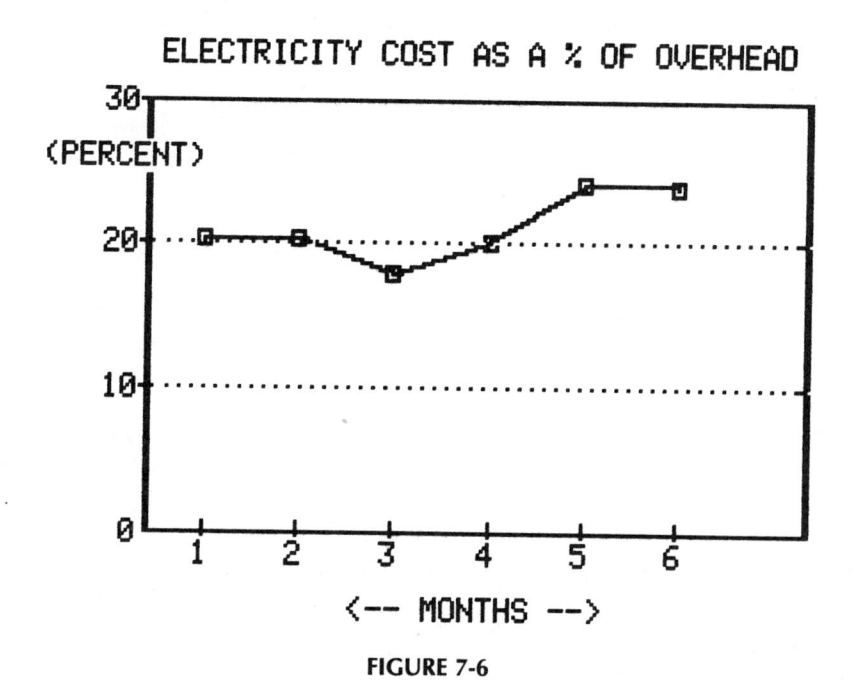

FIGURE 7-6

BUSINESS GRAPHICS

ELECTRICITY AS A % OF TOTAL OVERHEAD

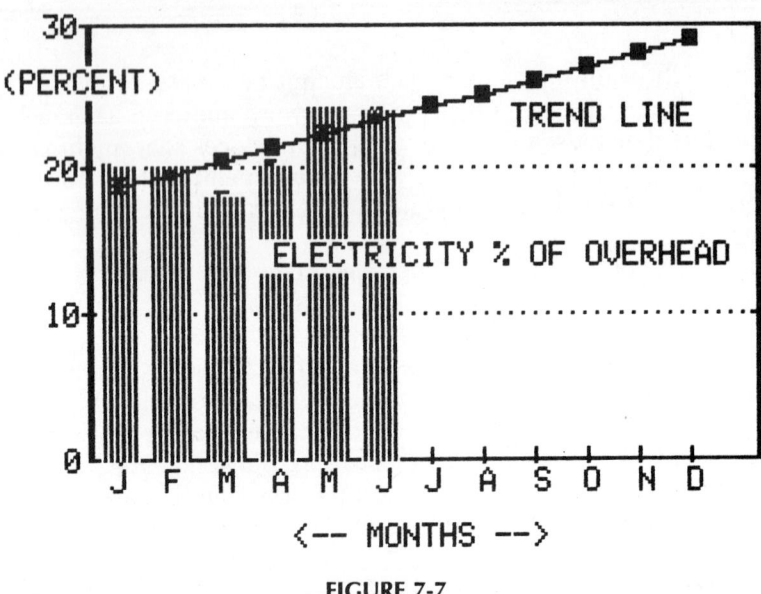

FIGURE 7-7

This doesn't tell us that our monthly electricity bill is the cause for the total rise in our utility expenses, but points a finger at our local utility and/or our own use of this product. Let's look at our usage.

One of the best ways to examine the usage for anything our business consumes, whether it's gallons of gasoline or therms of natural gas, is a historical line graph over a two- or three-year period. Figure 7-8 charts the average number of kilowatt-hours we've used on a *daily* basis, for two full years plus part of 1986. This is calculated by taking your total kilowatt-hour usage figure (for example, 3,300) and dividing it by the days in the month (say, 30). This example means your business used 110 kilowatt-hours per day, on the average, for the month under study. This particular example is an excellent one to use if you have any tenants for whom you pay utility costs—it's often hard to appreciate total costs (since they only rent a part of your building), but easy to see the total used as a daily average.

Both 1984 and 1985 show a similar picture—a mid-year rise (air conditioning in use?) with a drop in the fall, to a yearly low around January. 1986 started out much the same, but for some reason our usage really took a spurt and reached a new historical high in April. Sadly, it remained at that point for the next two months. It seems obvious from a historical vantage point that something drastically changed for our business in terms of our actual kilowatt-hours of *use*.

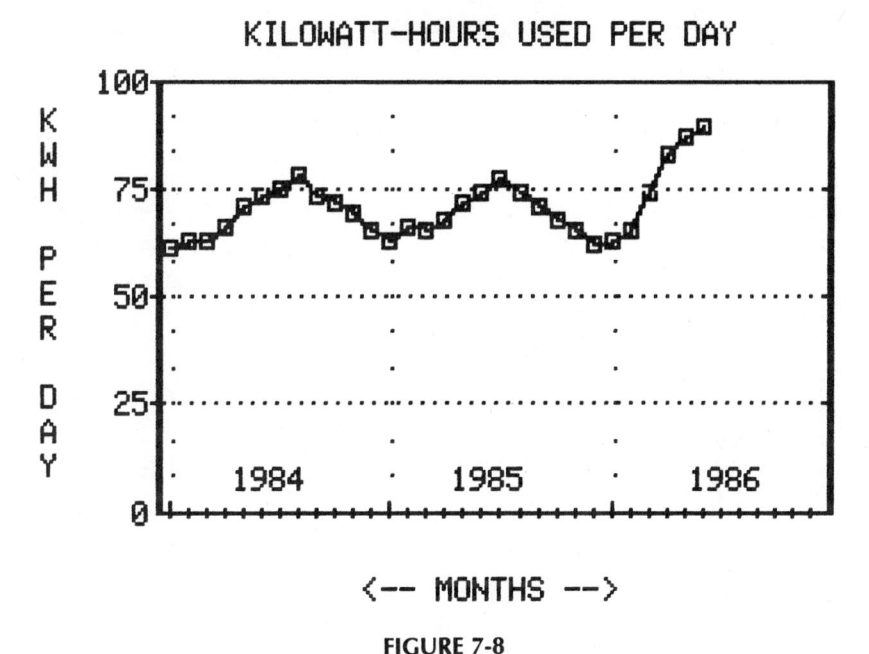

```
             KILOWATT-HOURS USED PER DAY
       100
    K
    W
    H    75
    P
    E    50
    R
    D    25
    A
    Y        ·    1984    ·    1985    ·    1986
         0

              <-- MONTHS -->
              FIGURE 7-8
```

The Historical Trend

The next logical step is to examine how we've used electricity over this same long period of time by adding a trend line to our picture. Figure 7-9 does this, and simplifies our look at the actual use totals by plotting them as a thin line, rather than (as Figure 7-8 did) charting them with blocks—they would "block out" our trend line.

This particular example shows a six-month projection of a trend line, based on 30-months worth of information—long enough to tell us where our business is heading. While no scale numbers are listed on the right side of the graph (and the horizontal grid lines were left off to make the plotted lines easier to see), it's obvious that we started back in January of 1984 with a use of about 60 kilowatt-hours per day, and by the end of the time the trend line forecasted our daily use at 76 kilowatt-hours per day. This 16 kilowatt-hour difference is a 26% rise (16/60) in daily use; if our electricity costs .07 cents per kilowatt-hour, it will raise our monthly bill by about $34.00.

Perhaps the worst thing about the trend line we see in Figure 7-9 is that the increase has been constant; we should have seen and done something about it before we found ourselves in the middle of 1986 with a growing and harder-to-solve problem on our hands.

```
               DAILY KILOWATT-HOURS USED W/TREND
         125┬
             │
  K    100┼
  W        │
  H     75┼                                    ....·  TREND
             │     ...                ...    ..
  U          │   ..   ...         ...    ...       LINE
  S          │            KWH USED
  E     50┼
  D          │
          25┼
             │     1984         1985         1986
           0└┴─────────────┴─────────────┴─────────────
```

<-- MONTHS -->

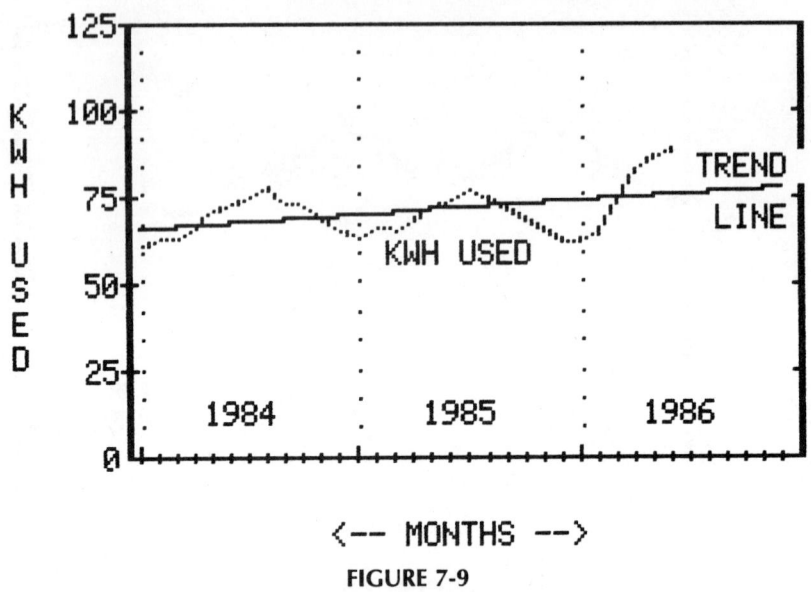

FIGURE 7-9

This example is a good one to show the *seasonality* of certain costs. Just like what we sell (and how much we sell) varies by the time of the year, our costs often do the same. If you have higher electricity costs during the summer (perhaps because of air conditioning), they'll show quickly in a graph. Likewise, you'll be able to spot any change from your historical trend.

Office Salaries

A major part of anyone's overhead total is that of office salaries. Even if you are your only employee, your salary probably contributes a huge share to your total overhead cost. A logical thing to track plots both your monthly overhead figures and your monthly office salary total. Figure 7-10 charts these two items over a 12-month period. As we know, these 12 months represent the *last* 12 months, not necessarily the latest calendar or fiscal year.

What Figure 7-10 tells us is that our overhead rises and falls at a greater rate than office salaries, although when our overhead total increases, it does so at least in part because we expended more cash in the office salaries area. This is shown by the little bumps in the data for months July and August.

While this sort of comparison is helpful, it's often of more use to have the spreadsheet we use take our data and do the math to compute what our office salaries are as a percentage of our overhead figure.

Figure 7-11 tells us that over the past 12 months, our business has made

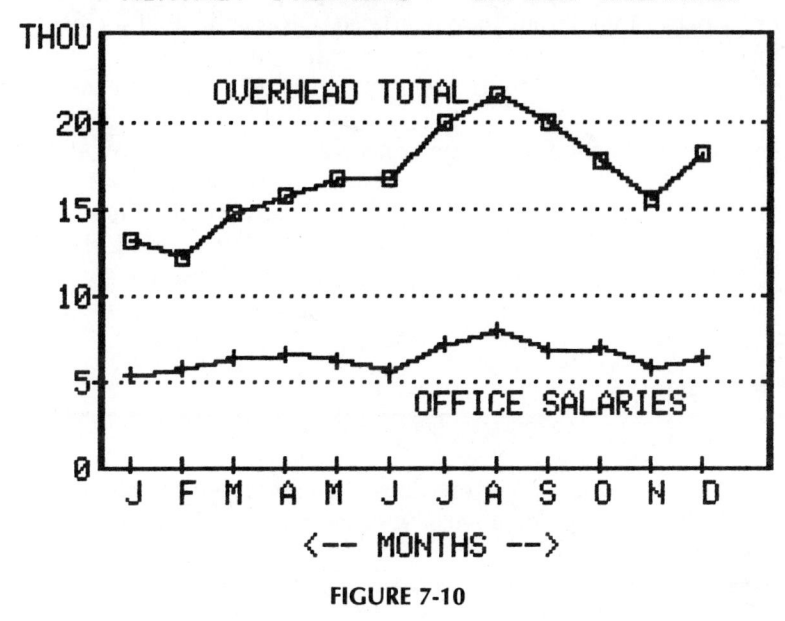

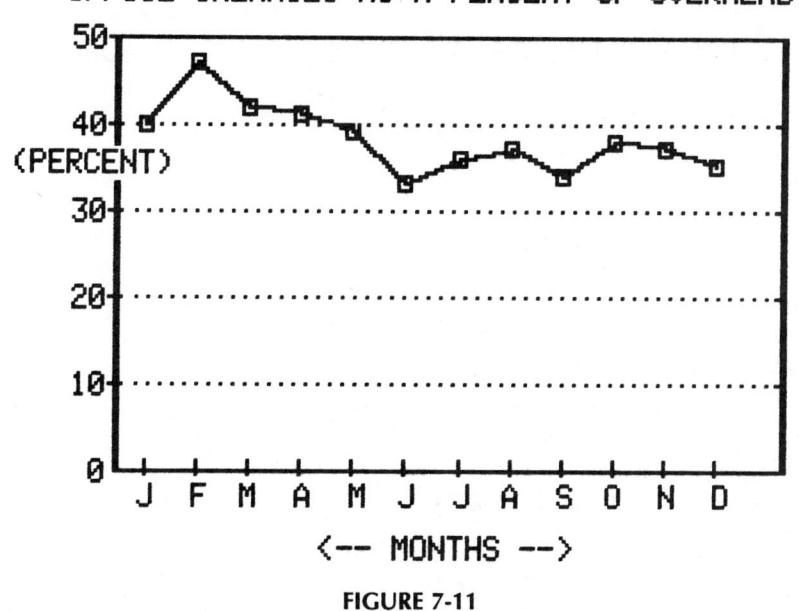

FIGURE 7-10

FIGURE 7-11

some significant improvement in what we spent for office salaries, at least in terms of its percentage of our total overhead. Obviously, if all the *other* areas of our overhead took a big jump, this percentage will go down, so the alert businessperson has to look at his or her total overhead, too, as well as this percentage figure.

Once you're satisfied that your overhead isn't out of control and its growth causing your office salaries to drop in relation to the total amount, you could be generally satisfied with what Figure 7-11 tells you. While office salaries were high on a percentage basis during the early part of this period, they have been brought down and since May have been in the 30-40% range.

Who's Best?

For a business with more than one location and/or department, it's helpful to chart office salaries as a percentage of your total overhead figure on a department or location basis.

Figure 7-12 shows us the overhead information broken down on a percentage of overhead basis for each of the five locations of our fictional business for the month of June.

A bar chart gives us a good feeling for the relationship of each store's

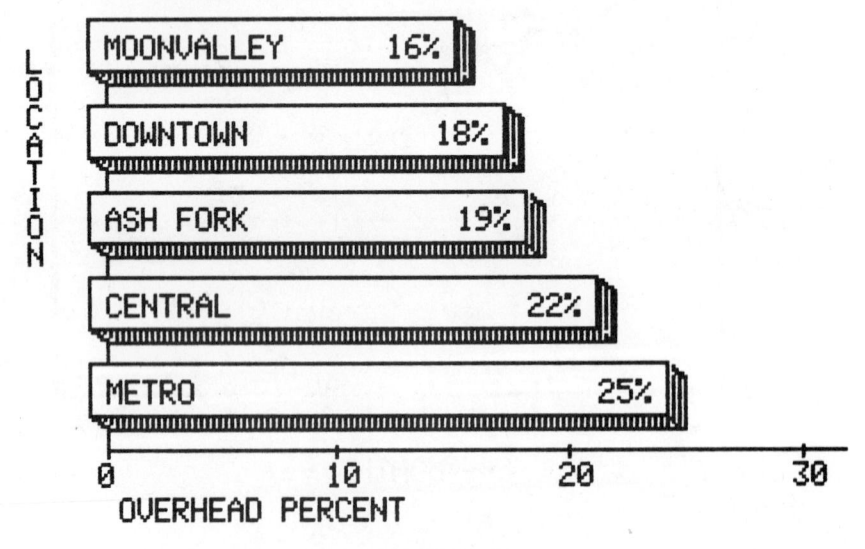

FIGURE 7-12

overhead in relationship to its peers. The figures illustrated in Figure 7-12 show a discrepancy in overhead percentages for each of our locations. The Metro store is considerably higher than any of the others: why? The Moonvalley store has the lowest overhead percent: why?

One way to help discover the answers to these questions is to break things down a bit, to examine a major part of anyone's overhead—office salaries.

If we use a bar chart for this sort of display (see Figure 7-13), it's easy to transmit the information to our office managers. While each store is shown in how it relates to its peers, no one *individual* is singled out, so our people as a group will accept this sort of data. Those who work in Moonvalley should be pleased with their performance for June, while the Central and Metro locations are running way out of line compared to the three others. Why?

One month's comparison of this sort isn't a long enough time period on which to base any management decisions, of course, but if you create this sort of chart every month (or every quarter), you'll soon *know* which locations or departments spend more of their overhead than they should.

Payroll Pie

It's also a useful tool if every quarter you create a pie chart to display your salary data, but base it on a different criteria. While the bar chart of Figure 7-13 shows

OFFICE SALARIES AS A % OF OVERHEAD

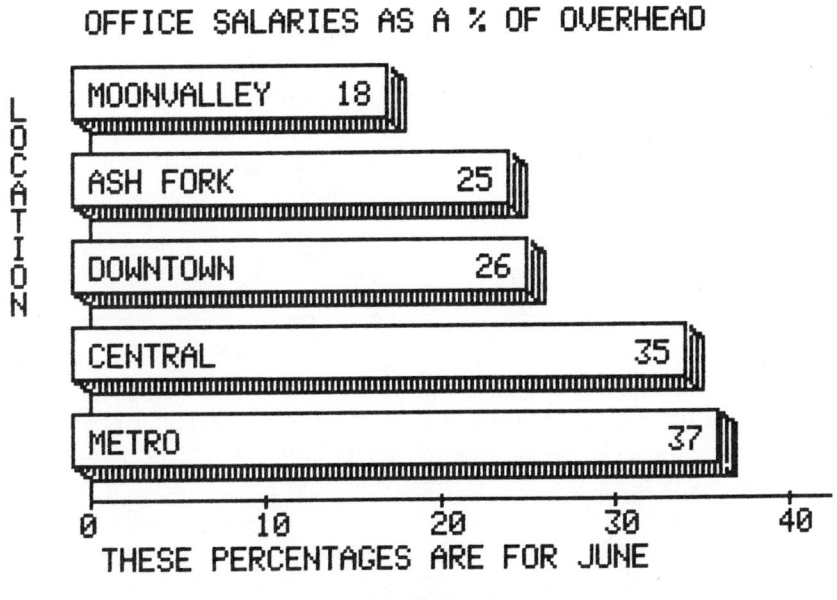

LOCATION	%
MOONVALLEY	18
ASH FORK	25
DOWNTOWN	26
CENTRAL	35
METRO	37

THESE PERCENTAGES ARE FOR JUNE

FIGURE 7-13

OFFICE SALARIES — FIRST SIX MONTHS

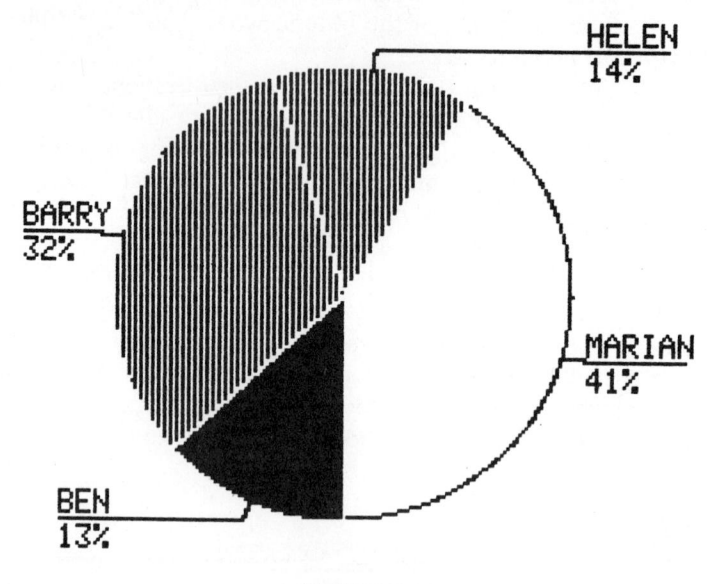

HELEN 14%
MARIAN 41%
BEN 13%
BARRY 32%

FIGURE 7-14

the relationships among the data, a pie chart like Figure 7-14 shows how each item relates to your total office salary expense as a *whole,* on a per-person basis.

This example gives the business owner a feel for who in the office is getting what share of the salary pie, in this case, over the first six months of the year. Do you see any of your people who are making more than they contribute? Less? The point is, with this sort of breakdown the manager can understand the figures more effectively. This sort of example probably isn't one you'd want to show your employees.

Advertising and Sales

The only reason to spend any money on advertising is to create more sales. A lot depends, obviously, on the business you own as to what sort of advertising makes sense. If you get a lot of work over the telephone, the Yellow Pages might be vital to your success. Perhaps just some institutional advertising in your local paper is all you need. A lot of businesses run weekly or monthly specials and/or coupons to promote sales of one product or another.

If advertising does create sales for your business, it seems logical that you ought to be able to plot that relationship, all with an eye to determining *when* your advertising is effective as well as *what type* of advertising works for you.

In most cases, the advertising you do today won't bring people into your store tomorrow. There's almost always a time lag between when an ad appears and when you feel its effect on your business. This period varies by the type of advertisement as well as where you place the ad. This book isn't the place to discuss what sort of advertising is best for any specific purpose; rather, we simply want to give you the tools to help discover what works for you, and in what time frame you might expect some response to the ads you do run.

Because of the time lag involved between when a prospect sees your ad and when they respond to it, in order to chart the effectiveness of your ad budget, you almost always have to *move* your advertising information forward into the future just a little. Then, for example, you can plot March's advertising at the same point as April's sales. That gives you a one-month lag time. You might also want to move your advertising two (or even more) months ahead in time; your business is different from others in terms of how long it takes your prospects to respond to your advertising.

Once you find a correlation, though, you can measure future advertising against this norm, which in turn lets you know how your current advertising is working. If you find that historically your business increases its sales roughly two months after advertising appears, but your business decreases in volume after a major ad campaign, you'll know the first place to look is at the ads you ran two months ago. Weren't they effective? Where did they run? Did you change your ads or the media or the general approach? Since you expected those ads that appeared 60 days ago to create sales during the current month, if your sales decrease, you probably can blame it on the ads and/or where they ran. Most graphics packages include the capability to move data forward or backward in time. This means you simply have to enter the dollars you spent for your advertising and then use the statistical functions of your graphics program to find out what lead/lag period applies to your work.

Converting the Numbers

Because your sales dollars are much higher than those you spend on advertising, an adjustment must be made in the figures so they'll fit on the same chart. As we've done in other cases, you can often multiply the smaller figure by 10 or 100 to get it into the range of the larger amount. There is another way to handle this problem, and one we'll use in this example, just so you'll know what it looks like.

Figure 7-15 is a picture of two graphs that were created with two separate *windows* that our software drew on our screen. It broke our screen display into

MONTHLY SALES

ADVERTISING, LAGGED ONE MONTH

<-- MONTHS -->

FIGURE 7-15

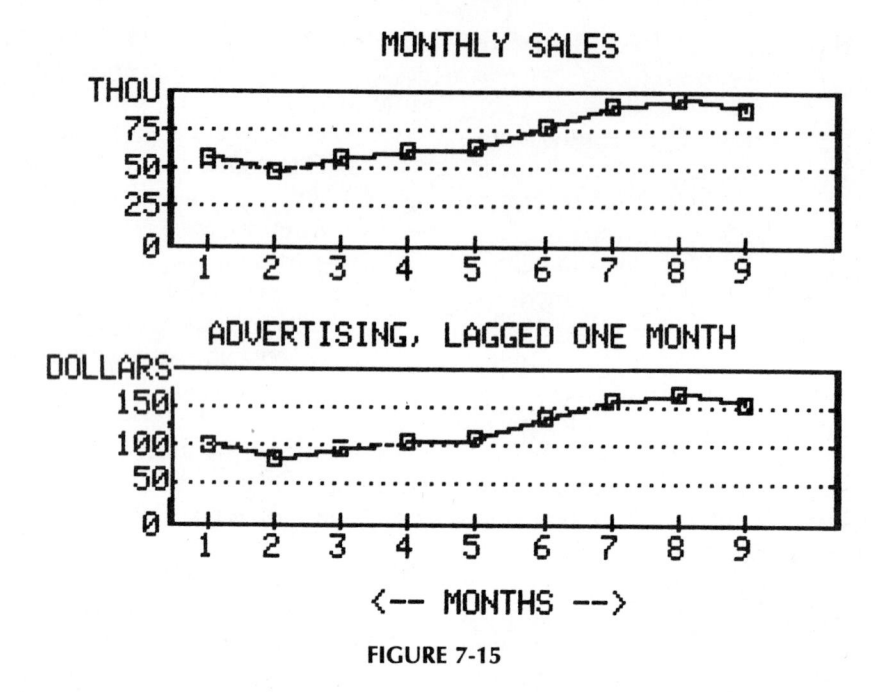

two sections, and created a graph in each. In this case, our fictitious monthly sales are shown as raw figures, in the top window. The range covers a nine-month period. Since we've broken our screen display in half, so to speak, our up-and-down scale is much narrower than usual. For this example, that doesn't create a problem, and what we want to examine is the rate of rise and fall of the lines in each chart.

The lower picture plots advertising over the same period, but rather than multiplying out the figures, we've kept the exact dollar amounts. So the scales of the top chart and the lower chart are widely different—the sales graph has its data plotted in thousands while the advertising graph's data is plotted in hundreds. However, because of the windows we're using, even though the information isn't plotted on the same graph, we can see the relationship between the two items. The sales line has almost exactly the same configuration as the advertising line. Advertising, as you'll note, has been lagged one month, so we've taken into consideration the time period it takes prospects to respond to the ads.

The basic relationships between the numbers in each chart are the same in terms of the directions they move on the chart itself. For this example, it appears there's a direct relationship between the advertising done one month and the sales volume the following month—both lines rise and fall at about the same rate, at roughly the same times.

A Warning

One thing needs to be kept in mind with any discussion of advertising and its associated sales. You don't want to get the idea that each time you increase your ad budget you'll gain a corresponding jump in sales. While that's what we all hope for, the real world just doesn't work that way. Not all ads are effective; not every promotion comes through with greater sales. It's pretty easy to look at graphs like these and think that we can increase advertising by 20% and thus cause a 20% rise in sales. Much more study on a lot more data is called for before we can draw such a conclusion.

The sort of picture and feeling we get from Figure 7-15 does tell us our advertising is working, that it does affect our sales volume. That's good and valuable information, but if you use advertising in your business, you need to look into things a bit deeper.

Advertising Pie

Any business should be able to measure—in some way—the success of its advertising. Large corporations have an advantage along this line, as they can afford major marketing studies and reliable testing. The small businessperson doesn't have the cash to fund such complex operations, but still has perhaps the best method of all: a simple question to each customer.

You wouldn't be offended if the salesperson you bought your last car from asked you why you came into his place of business, would you? Or if the plumber you called to fix that leak asked why you called his company. You can do the same thing, and if you don't want to ask on a person-to-person basis, you can simply print up some postcards and send them along with your invoices. Let your customers tell you why they called you.

Figure 7-16 details the advertising expenses for our business for the first six months of the year. A pie chart is ideal to plot this sort of thing, as it gives us a feeling for where our dollars went in relation to all the money we spent on advertising. We can quickly see we spent our ad dollar in three major areas, while radio and direct mail together equal about a quarter of the total.

There's no way to know if this particular ad "mix" is right or wrong without some associated data. That's why you need to take your customer survey, to find out as best you can which ads are working and which aren't pulling their weight.

Figure 7-17 shows the results of a mini-survey, and when it's examined at the same time as Figure 7-16 is, tells us exactly what's effective (and what's not) for our advertising. Note this graph is called "sales by media," and means just

ADVERTISING BY MEDIA – 1ST SIX MONTHS

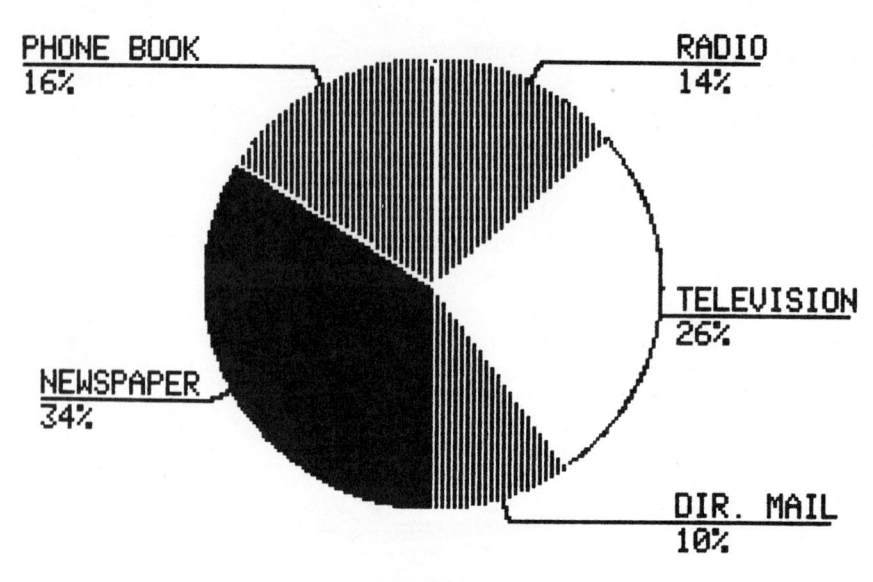

- PHONE BOOK 16%
- RADIO 14%
- TELEVISION 26%
- DIR. MAIL 10%
- NEWSPAPER 34%

FIGURE 7-16

that—it's the sales volume we tallied up, based on what our customers reported to us. Again, we use a pie chart to get a feeling for how each individual total relates to the whole picture.

We can visually see that our newspaper ads produce more on a percentage basis than we spent on the ads themselves. The yellow pages didn't do so well during this period, and the dollars we spent on radio provided about the same (percentage-wise) as the percentage of our advertising budget we spent there. Television is the big surprise—we spent 26% of our advertising dollar for television ads, but it produced 34% of our sales. Direct mail didn't work.

What conclusions can we draw from this? While we don't want to eliminate the poor performers out of hand, we need to examine them in more detail. For instance, perhaps direct mail did so poorly because of the advertising literature we sent. Or because of the mailing list we pulled prospective names from. Perhaps television did so well because of the *times* the ads ran, or because of the quality and focus of the ads themselves.

There are obviously all sorts of variables, and it might seem impossible to make a decision based on this set of data. That's true. However, it's a starting point, a place that gives you something of a benchmark for the future. It also motivates you to *change* the direct mail distribution list or whatever advertising information you're sending out. When you run the same sort of test six months from now and produce the same set of graphs, what if they tell you exactly the

SALES BY MEDIA PER CUSTOMER SURVEY

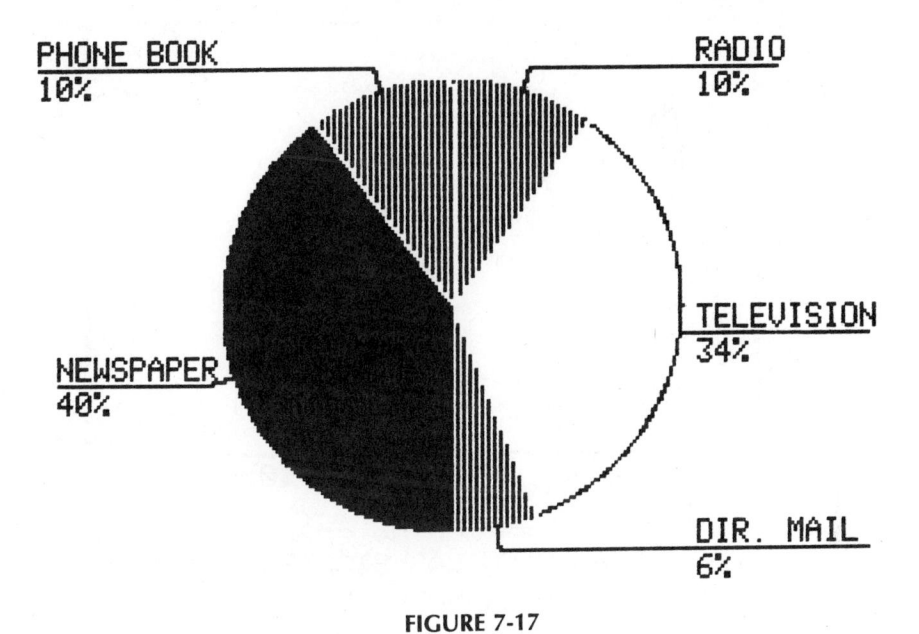

- PHONE BOOK 10%
- RADIO 10%
- TELEVISION 34%
- DIR. MAIL 6%
- NEWSPAPER 40%

FIGURE 7-17

same thing? *Then* it's probably time to eliminate direct mail and put the money you were spending there into television. The whole idea of all this, of course, is to put your advertising dollars where they're the most productive. Business graphics can help you see exactly where that is.

Inside Percentages

While it's valuable to examine some overhead item like advertising as the percentage we spend in this area or that versus the percentage of sales each advertising media produces, it's useful to take things a step further.

Figure 7-18 shows how we used the statistical functions of the microcomputer's graphics program to manipulate the raw data for our advertising costs along with the totals for the sales we recorded. It pushed the ad dollars a month behind the sales figures and then converted each into a percentage of change, over a 12-month period. What we see, then, is how each figure changed on a percentage basis, from one month to the next. Figure 7-18 is a truly fascinating look at advertising and sales for our fictional business, as it tells the business owner that when advertising is increased on a percentage basis, sales will rise at roughly the same rate, one month later.

```
          % OF CHANGE FOR ADVERTISING & SALES
     30
     20
     10
      0
    -10
    -20
    -30
        2    4    6    8    10   12
              <-- MONTHS -->
     -- ADVERTISING WAS STARTED A MONTH
             AFTER SALES WERE
```

FIGURE 7-18

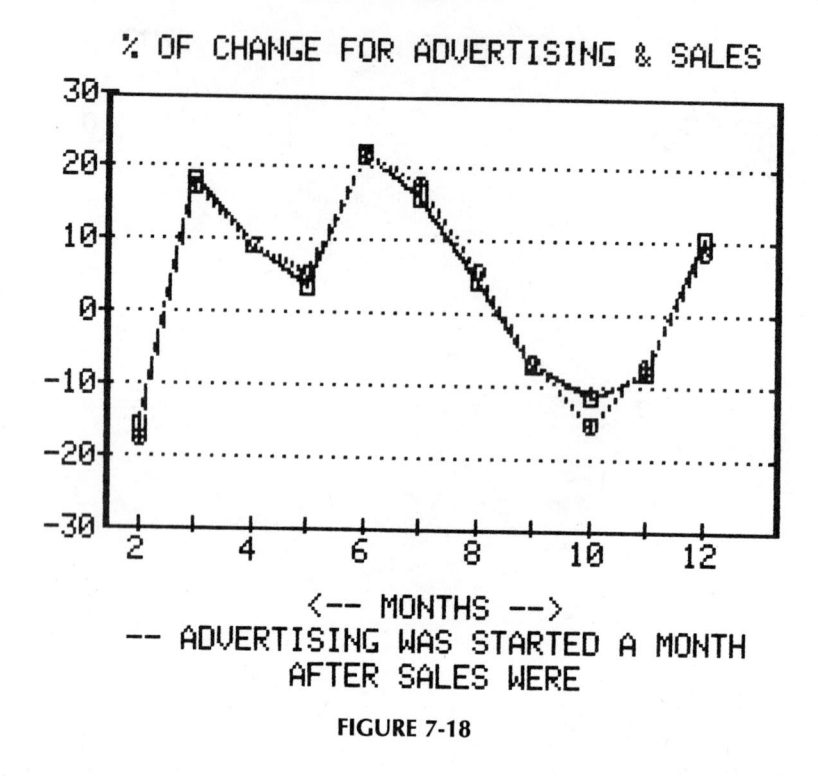

At first glance, this might look like an awful graph—you can't tell one line from another. In fact, it's just the opposite, and it is presented here to make a point. We must always keep in mind the data we're examining and the picture we might get from it. In this case, we're plotting the percentage change in our sales, along with the percentage change in our advertising, moved back a month before the sales were recorded. In effect—since the lines move at seemingly the same rates and in the same directions—this tells us that a 5% increase in advertising will cause a 5% rise in sales. An 8% drop in advertising precipitates an 8% drop in sales. Isn't this the cause/effect relationship between the two that we'd want to see?

In actual practice, it would be rare for two plotting lines to end up this closely as they move over time. But Figure 7-18 is shown here to give you an idea of what you'd hope to see: a precise correlation between the percentage changes in your advertising expenses and the sales they produce.

Both lines rise and fall at about the same rate, during the same time periods, and since they're both on a *percentage* basis, we can plot them on the same chart. This particular set of information shows a definite correlation between the data sets and confirms—just for this data, of course—that when advertising is increased, sales will jump at about the same rate. It's also interesting to note that this seems to hold true over a wide range of percentages, from a drop in advertising of nearly 20% (twice) as well as an increase in the ad budget of almost 20% (again, twice). This lends validity to the data and seems to be a recommendation to try to push things a bit to see exactly how much we can spend on advertising, how much sales will rise along with it, before we reach the point where sales will no longer flow with our advertising dollar.

That point certainly exists for every business, but doesn't it make sense to try to locate it? Once you do, you'll know that you cannot spend more than X dollars on advertising—anymore than that doesn't bring in worthwhile results.

Sales and Overhead

We're going to end the discussion with overhead right where we started—with a note on how overhead relates to sales. Did you ever wonder why the more successful you are, the harder it seems to make money? The more you cut costs and lower your overhead, the more difficult it seems to be to stay in the black? There's a paradox in business that involves both our sales and our overhead totals.

Most of the time when we think about sales and overhead, we automatically divide the overhead total by the sales amount, and so get a percentage figure. $400,000 in sales with $100,000 in overhead means we perform this equation: 100,000/400,000, which gives us a 25% figure—overhead is 25% of our total sales. But the same line of thinking runs both ways. If we divide our sales volume by our overhead figure, (400,000/100,000), we come out with $4.00. This is the amount of sales we have to make to justify a $1.00 increase in our overhead total, if we want to keep our overhead as a percentage of sales at its new, lower level.

If we want to give someone a raise of $10,000 per year, we'd have to increase sales by $40,000 *just to break even*. This is because of the 4-1 ratio this business has now (an overhead of 25% means the overhead dollars will divide into the sales total four times). To keep its overhead at the current level, this business must sell $4 for every $1 it adds to its overhead total. If we want to buy a new truck that really won't increase our operating efficiency, and this year's share of the payments will run $5,000, we'll have to sell *four times* that amount—$20,000—just to break even.

All of this assumes that same 4-1 ratio, based on sales of $400,000 and overhead of $100,000. But let's say you really work at reducing your overhead, and drop it from $100,000 to $80,000. Your overhead as a percentage of sales goes from 25% to 20%, a drop any businessperson would be pleased with. But the reverse figure moves from 4-1 to 5-1 (now you divide your sales of $400,000 by your new overhead of $80,000). Now to justify a $1.00 increase in overhead, you have to somehow raise sales by $5.00.

Therein lines the paradox: the more successful you are at reducing overhead also makes the basic problem a bit tougher to cope with. It's something not enough businesspeople are aware of and can be a crucial factor when we have to decide

```
             SALES DIVIDED BY OVERHEAD
    5.00
            LAST           CURRENT
    4.75
            YEAR           YEAR
    4.50
    4.25
$   4.00
    3.75
    3.50
    3.25
    3.00
        1     2     3     4     5     6
            <-- QUARTERS -->
```

FIGURE 7-19

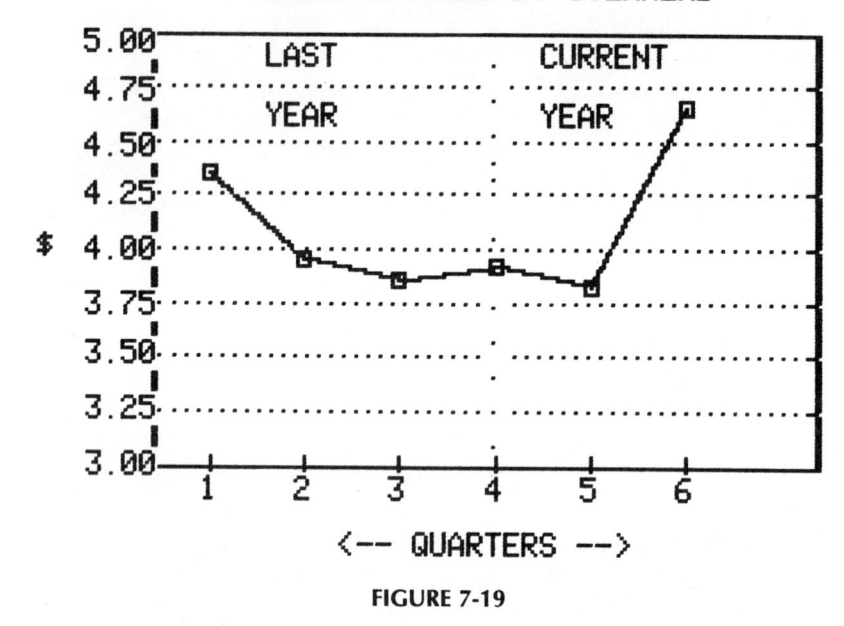

whether to buy this or that, approve a raise for one employee or another, and so on.

Figure 7-19 covers one year plus the first two quarters of the following year. From most of last year and the first quarter of the current year, our "reverse overhead" figure ran in the $3.75-$4.00 range. We knew that if we wanted to buy something, we'd have to raise sales by $4.00 just to maintain our current profit percentage. Naturally, if what we bought increased our productivity and sales jumped *more* than this amount, it would be a good investment.

The latest quarter, however, finds us with a lowering overhead and/or rising sales figure, which causes a major jump in our reverse overhead amount. Now, we see that any increase in overhead will require a 4.75-1 rise in sales; each dollar we raise overhead must have a corresponding $4.75 increase in sales, or we'll head toward the red end of the profit picture.

There's obviously nothing wrong with trying to reduce overhead; in fact, it's a major goal of any business. But it's equally important to know that as we're successful in lowering our overhead total, we also make it more difficult for our business to stay profitable. Any *increase* in overhead must be matched with a higher rise in sales, if we want to stay at the lower overhead percentage. It's a paradox we have to deal with, and if we plot it on a regular basis, we'll be able to see the exact figure as well as the trend of our numbers. We'll be able to make more reliable decisions.

Summing Up

Overhead exists in every business, and while much of its costs are fixed, others vary at least in some respects as to sales. As our sales increase, we can expect overhead to also take a jump. There are ways to examine different overhead areas and at the same time take a concentrated look at overhead as it relates to sales. We not only need to know what our overhead percentage is, but also what its trend line tells us. We need to look hard at utility costs (and at any part of it that contributes to the total cost). Other expenses of this sort can be examined in much the same way. We want to examine things like this on the basis of their historical trend and a forecast based on their long-term performance.

Office salaries often form a major part of anyone's expenses, so must be examined from the inside out, including making charts of our people individually, to gauge if someone is overpaid or underpaid. Office salaries—since they are much of any business's overhead—also can be examined on the basis of department and/or location. Often, we'll find that the store with the highest overhead percentage can blame much of that on having the highest salaries for its people. There's a graphic way to explain this sort of thing to our people, without pointing at any one person in particular.

Advertising is another expense most of us have, and we need to take a close look at it. Where is our advertising working? Where are we spending cash for little return? Should we spend more on advertising? How can we find out? These are all areas where business graphics can help.

Finally, the relationship between sales and overhead cuts both ways, and we can gain knowledge about what's happening inside our business by dividing one into the other from both directions. There's a paradox few businesspeople understand, yet it's one that holds true for all businesses: the more successful we are, the more difficult it is to make money—all because we lowered our overhead. We need not only to discover, but to chart exactly how much we have to increase sales for every dollar we raise our overhead figure.

Other Ideas

There are all sorts of ideas associated with overhead, because it forms such a huge part of anyone's business. There are all sorts of little entries that may or may not be important to you and your work, so we simply want to suggest a few you might examine.

Office supplies are a major expense (as is postage) for many businesses. How do yours compare this year to last? As a percentage of your total overhead?

Phone costs are an expense that's always there, yet rises and falls with our sales volume. How can you cut your phone bill? What are your phone charges as a percentage of overhead? Are they better or worse than last year's?

While we looked at advertising only as it related to sales, it also can be compared to what we spent last year on advertising. How about a five-year graph that charts sales and advertising, with the ad dollars placed behind the sales totals, so they'll plot on the same month? Are there other ways to chart the effectiveness of your advertising?

Since there are many things that make up your total overhead totals, it's often worthwhile to examine them as a percentage of that overhead and plot it over time. The more you can dig back into past data and plot this information over a long time period, the more helpful it will be.

Financial Statement Items

8

The *best* thing about an examination of your financial statement data is that you work with ratios, measures of comparison most business people are familiar with and can easily find out more about. Unfortunately, the *worst* thing about a look at this information is also that you work with ratios, for several reasons.

For some reason, business people are expected to know about ratios for their business. When their banker or accountant mentions the *quick ratio* or the *acid test,* they assume we know what they're talking about. Sadly, even if we're one of the lucky ones who went through business school, a real understanding of ratios often escapes us, perhaps because the only real basis of comparison is the facts and figures we can gather from industry-wide sources. Although that data is helpful, it still is related to our business only because those people are in the same line of work that we are. But their market is different. Their product lines are different. The ways they do business, handle their customers, work with money, pay their bills—they're all different than the way we do things. We share the common bond of a particular industry with many of the same problems, to be sure, but the most accurate things we can compare our business to are its own ratios, based on a history of the business itself.

National statistics—as the people you get them from are the first to admit—are sometimes based on incomplete data. It isn't that the information is incorrect, but rather that it's (sometimes) drawn from too small a sample to get a statistically correct picture. When you combine that with the fact that your local business conditions are widely different than those of a business even in a neighboring town, it's obvious that if you can extract and track the proper financial information from inside your own company, and examine it in the right ways, it will be more valuable to you than entire books of national averages.

This isn't to say that you should ignore those industry figures. On the contrary, your banker will have a copy of them and probably will compare their averages to your own figures when you ask for a loan. How extensively they make their comparison varies by how much they know about you (and probably by the amount of the loan you request). The vital thing is that you're aware of the fact that your banker will use industry-wide figures, and since he or she is concerned with them, you must be, too. If one ratio varies significantly from what appears to be the norm for your industry, your banker will probably ask you to explain why. There can be all sorts of good reasons why your business heads away from what the national average is, of course. If you have your own internally generated information, you'll be able to provide a logical explanation, (hopefully) in a manner that will convince your banker that there's nothing wrong with this specific variation.

Ideally, then, financial ratios should be examined from two points of view: (1) how they're performing from a historical perspective, based on information generated from inside your business, and (2) how they compare to national averages for other businesses like yours. The first examination—based on your own past history—will be more useful to you, while the latter—when you compare your figures to industry averages—will be helpful when you talk to your banker.

A Look at Reports

There are all kinds of reports your accountant might create for you, all with information gathered from your business records. The problem is in its presentation. Not that it will be incorrect (your accountant will make sure everything balances), but rather in that all the data you might find important to keep track of may not be easily available.

In our own business, for instance, we have an account that tracks how much we spend on office supplies. The data that flows into this area includes everything from paper for the copying machine to postage to cash register tapes to making up the cash when the pop machine comes up short. There are times, though, when it would be helpful to look inside this area and find out exactly what we spend on postage during a particular time. While all the information is there, it's not broken down separately. For us to figure it out, we have to go back through our cash disbursements journal and manually find and add up every check we wrote for stamps and postage. In other words, while the information is inside our accounting system, it's not always available in the breakdown and/or formats we need. Some digging is often required to extract the data that we want to track.

There's also the problem of the sheer volume of information we have available on our financial statements. We always look at the bottom line to see how we did profit-wise, but once we know that, we find all kinds of other data there. What's important? What should we pay attention to? What should we graph? Why? While businesses vary, you'll almost always get a period-end and year-end balance sheet that shows your financial position at that particular moment in time, and an income statement that explains how you did from a profit standpoint over the period of time covered. This distinction is important, because the balance sheet captures a day in time, while the income statement covers your performance over a period of time. There are other associated reports, including a flow of funds statement, that indicates where your cash came from during the period under study, as well as where you spent it all.

Because there's a lot of information, it might seem overwhelming to attempt to study it. If you try to cover it all, it can become an impossible task, so the secret is to determine what areas are important for you to understand in terms of running your own business and to follow them closely. One way that helps you know which areas are vital and which are not is business graphics; a few charts can help you determine what's important, and what's not, for you, personally. Your accounting people are a terrific help here, too, as they can suggest places for you to start; since they know your business from a financial viewpoint, they'll have a good idea of what's important to its proper operation and can make suggestions on which areas to examine.

Assets

This book is not the right place to explain how you value your assets (what you own or can turn into cash) or how to evaluate your liabilities (what you've got to pay, someday). Likewise, we're not going to cover how you'd set about gathering the information for your income statement, where your overhead comes from, or suggest you use a certain type of inventory valuation. Those subjects are more properly served in accounting books. We will look at their relationships, how one sometimes affects the other, and so on, but for a basic knowledge, here are two suggestions. The first is to ask your accountant. That might seem obvious, but even though we pay his or her bill, we often feel that we should know enough (somehow) to understand all those pages of information they give us. They wouldn't spend the time to figure out all those things and type them up if we didn't understand all of it, right? If there's something you can't figure out, swallow a bit of pride and ask; your accountant won't mind and probably will be pleased that you had enough interest to want to know. The other area is to pick up a good accounting book or two and take a look at those areas that you're not quite clear on. One recent good one is *How Accounting Works: a Guide for the Per-*

plexed, by James Don Edwards, Roger H. Hermanson, R. F. Salmonson, and Peter R. Kensiki. It's published by Dow Jones-Irwin (Homewood, Illinois 60430). The book is well written and explains things clearly.

While it's important that you understand how things work inside your business before you attempt to chart its information, that doesn't mean you need to know how this or that operates as well as your accountant does. After all, that's his or her business. In many cases, the graphs we'll use as example illustrations will also serve as a guide to how one part of your business relates to other areas, how one thing affects another, and so on.

For example, while each business that allows its customers to charge their purchases has accounts receivable, and every business owner is concerned with how well his or her cash arrives, we often don't track our average collection period—how long it takes us to convert those sales into cash. We'll cover both the calculations and the best way to graph the data, and once we do, you'll be able to estimate the cash you'll have available a month from today.

You'll find out how efficiently you're using the cash you have invested in your business, on a basis that you may not have thought of. While you may calculate how your profits are as a percentage of your sales, you might not figure out how they are in relation to the investment you have in your business. Would you be better off with that cash in the bank than you are with it invested in your own business?

Since you've got money invested in your company, it's important to know who else does, too. If you're the sole owner, you might think that you've made the total investment, but that's (sadly) not correct. Those folks to whom you owe money have an interest in your business, too, and if you don't believe it, don't pay them and see how they remove their share. There's a definite relationship between what you've got invested in your business and what others should have; you'll find out how to figure that out and graph it.

The important thing is not to be afraid of financial ratios and their associated data; like anything else, they're simply a tool to help us be better at what we do—business.

The Bottom Line: Profits

Probably the logical spot to start any examination of your financial statement information is right at the place where everyone's eyes go: the profit line. While there may be more valuable places to look—in terms of information to tell you how you're managing your business—that bottom line is still all-important.

Figure 8-1 shows us the picture of a business in trouble. It's a line graph that plots 24 months of information, and even without a trend line, it's obvious

PROFIT AFTER TAXES PERCENT

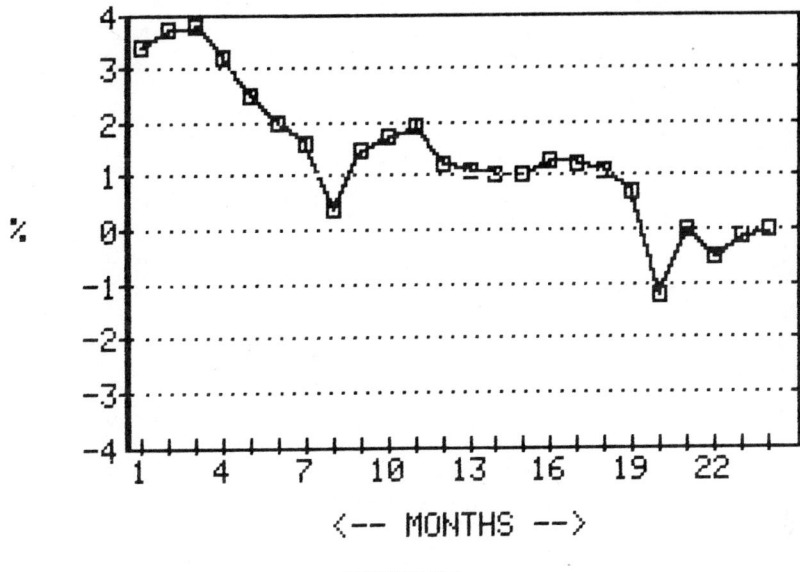

FIGURE 8-1

this business has a problem. At the start of this particular period of time, the business had a net after-tax profit that amounted to 3% to 4% of its total sales volume. That's nothing to shout about, to be sure, but it's still a profit, and one many businesses would be glad to make.

During the next few months, the profit line went steadily downward, until by month 8 the business was doing little better than breaking even. A small recovery took place, followed by a long period of profit in the 1% range. Again, nothing to be particularly proud of, but at least the business was still in the black. A trend line done during this period would most likely have shown a downward trend. By months 19 and 20, the profit line plunged again, to where the business was losing money. By the end of the 24-month period (which, as we know, can represent either the last 24 months or a two-year period on a calendar basis, whatever's the most helpful to us) the business had somehow managed to climb out of the red, but was producing a zero profit.

In all, this isn't a particularly good picture, and indicates that the business has serious problems of one kind or another. It doesn't tell us where those problems might be, of course, but if this were your business, you should be disturbed by this graph. Probably the worst thing about it is that things are seemingly getting worse almost monthly.

However, a business owner who saw this graph at the end of the charted period is still *in business* and so has the chance to pull the company out of the difficulty it's in. More sales, a better effort to cut costs in all areas, a strong drive to reduce overhead to its lowest possible level, a close look at employees and how they're doing—all are methods the business owner must use to change the condition of his or her profit level.

To bring things into the right perspective, Figure 8-2 shows you the result you'd hope for, if this were your business. It plots the same information you just looked at, along with another 12 months of data. In effect, it shows you the position the business found itself in after another year had gone by. Something was done (again, the graph doesn't tell us *what*, but rather shows us the result of the action) to change things. Perhaps more sales were created, overhead was lowered, employees were motivated to be more efficient, costs were cut, but whatever it was, the business turned its profit situation around.

This is a good picture, because it shows you how the business climbed out of its depressed condition and restored its former profit level. The end of the three-year period finds this business at close to its original profit percentages. Further, the rate of profit seems to be improving: early in the graph, the trend was obviously downward, while the current trend is rising.

A Long-Range Trend

It appears that business is on the upswing for this company, but as with most things, it's worthwhile to take a closer look at the data. Figure 8-3 plots a trend line, based on the 36 months of information you've been examining, and projects it for six more months. Because of the long time frame (36 periods of data), you can expect the trend line to give you an accurate picture, and when you couple it with the short (6-month) projection period, you can feel safe that the projected data will be accurate, too.

The original information is also plotted on Figure 8-3, as just a background line to the trend line. While that trend line appears to be pretty straight (a closer look on a narrower scale would confirm this observation), even with this wide scale you can see a slight downward jog at about month 29. In effect, while the data fell to a level where the business lost money and then pulled itself back up close to its original condition, the trend line indicates a slight drop in the overall picture. This means that even with the current rise in profits, the business still needs to do more to bring its profits up. Ideally, the trend line for net profit will rise, and this one shows a small fall late in the data. It tells you that the overall *drop* of the data was greater than the total gain it made. To get things on an even keel (and, hopefully, to get that trend line heading upward), the profit picture needs to improve even more.

FIGURE 8-2

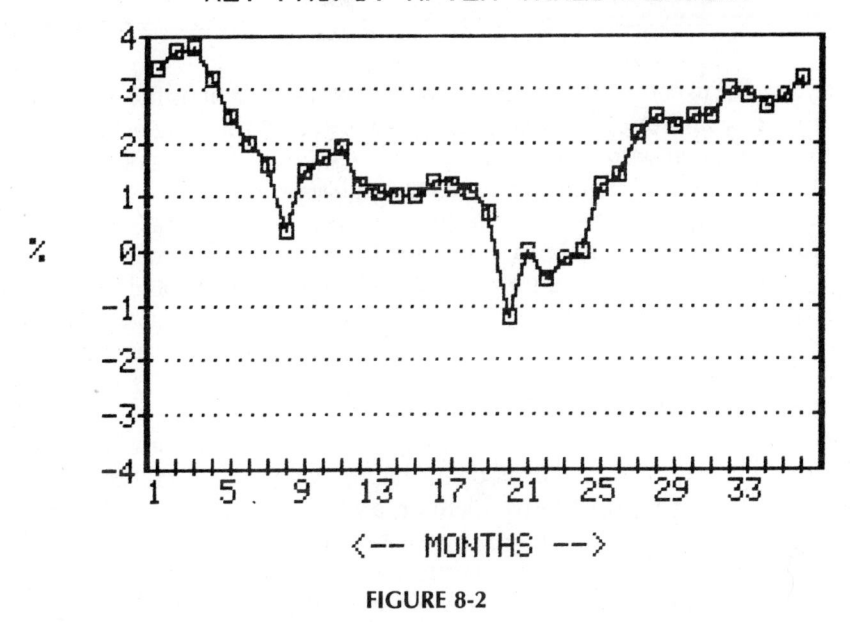

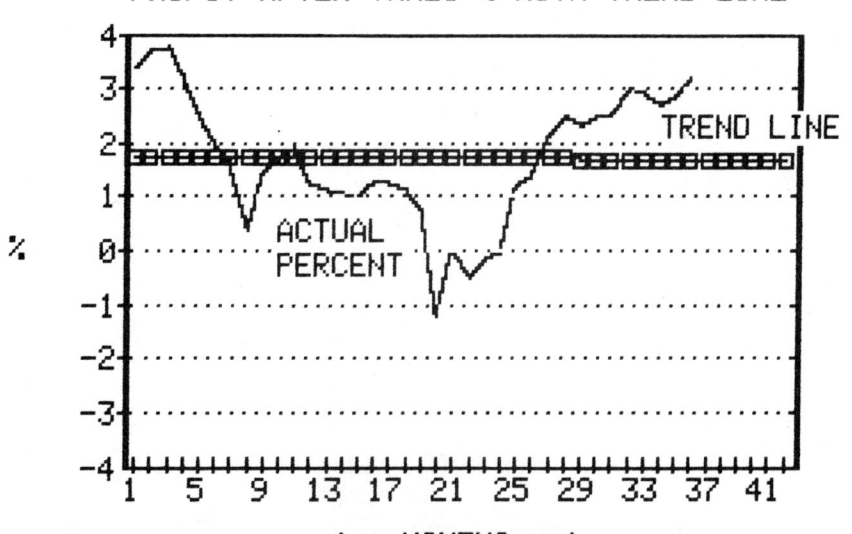

FIGURE 8-3

Profits and Assets

While you need to compare your profits to your total sales (this is the most common way to look at profits), it's equally useful to examine the relationship between the profits your company makes and the total assets of your business. This gives you a feel for how effectively you're managing those assets.

Assets in this example are the total assets a business has at a particular time—cash, inventory, buildings, equipment, vehicles, and so on.

Figure 8-4 plots ten quarters of information for a fictional business and shows the net profit the business produced divided by its total assets, at the end of each quarterly period. The net result—a percentage figure—is a measure of how well the business is using its assets.

Remember that assets in this sense are what a business owns (including financed items), so in essence, these assets are what the enterprise has available to do business. If the manager is doing his or her job properly, the assets are being used in their most effective manner, and this line will rise. Conversely, if the manager isn't handling assets well (poor scheduling, sending people and equipment out to a job when it's too late in the day to accomplish anything, keeping too many dollars invested in slow-moving inventory and not enough to pay current bills), this line will fall. Even without the benefit of a trend line, this

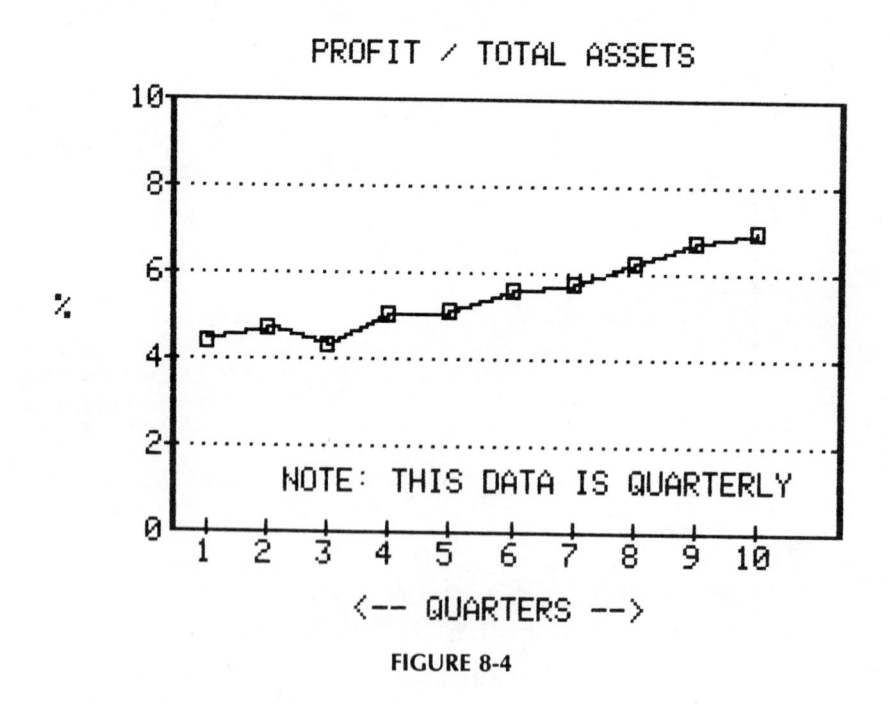

FIGURE 8-4

data seems to be rising. In effect, this tells us the business is doing something right, because it's producing a profit that is growing, in relation to the dollars the business owners have in assets. There are averages for any industry, of course, as to where this line should be, but in general, it should run between 5% and 15%.

Since this ratio compares the net profit a business makes in relation to everything a business owns, including both owner-invested capital and borrowed money, it is probably the most accurate way to find out how a business is managing its money. Not just cash, but the use of all assets are taken into account, so in effect the focus is on how effectively you, as the business owner, are controlling the assets you have.

There's an additional note on this graph to let the user know the data is quarterly. Since most of the information we've looked at here is plotted on a monthly basis, it's important to note any variation to make it easier for someone who looks at a graph to understand it.

Profits and Net Worth

Another way to look at profits is to examine them in relation to the net worth a business has, over a specific period of time. Assets—what we just compared profits to—include all that a business owns. Net worth, on the other hand, is what the business is worth, once you subtract any liabilities (what the business owes) from its assets. As such, net worth is a smaller figure than assets (unless the business doesn't owe anything to anyone), so we should expect the profit percentage in relation to net worth to be higher. Net worth is, in theory, the amount the business owner would receive if he or she sold the company: it is, as the term implies, the *worth*, the *value* of the enterprise. Again, each industry has an average; this line generally should be higher than the cost of borrowed money, and a well-managed business should be able to earn 25% on its invested capital.

The reverse of this would ask the business owner(s) what kind of a return they'd expect on their investment, if they sold the business and had its net worth in the form of cash, ready to invest. What would you consider to be the minimum rate of return you should receive? Whatever it is in your own mind, that's the least you should expect your business to produce for you. If it's not, it's not being managed as well as it should be.

Figure 8-5 is an example of the picture you want to see when you examine your business. This particular illustration covers ten quarters of information. While the business was doing poorly at the start of the period under study (in about the 12% range), from quarter 5 on it's been producing profits in relation to its net worth at a greater than 20% rate. Since it's unlikely the business owner could take that cash out of his or her business and invest it at a higher rate, he

NET PROFIT / NET WORTH

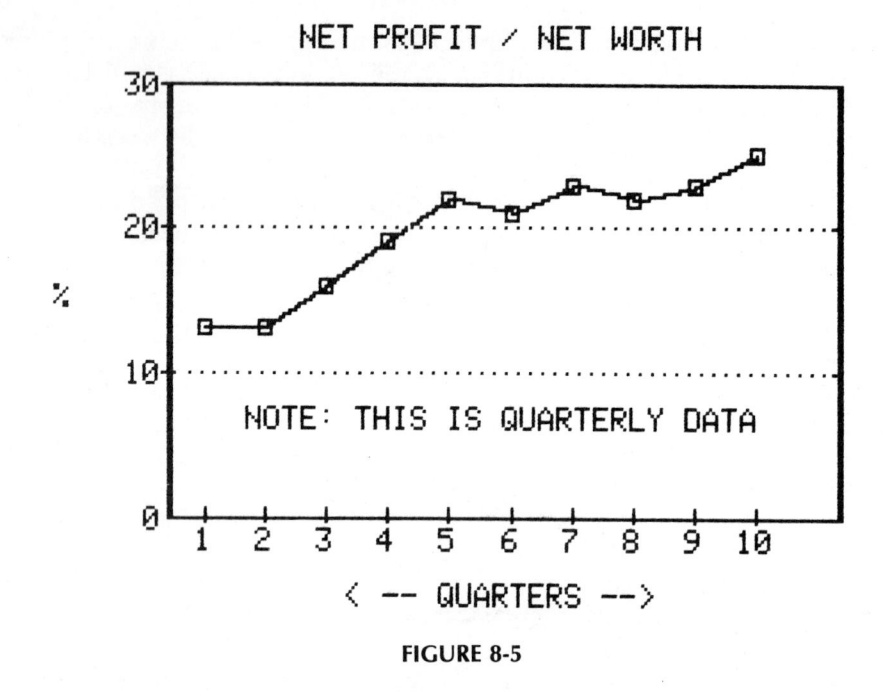

FIGURE 8-5

or she should be pleased both with the progress this business has made since the first plot on this graph, and also with the current level of return on his or her investment.

Even without a trend line, this two and one-half year's worth of information is obviously heading upward, and lately the business is making about a 25% profit on the investment the business owner(s) have in their company.

Assets and Liabilities

One ratio your banker will want to examine as soon as he or she gets your financial information is one we've all heard about—the *current ratio,* the ratio between current assets and current liabilities. Current assets are described as cash or things that you can reasonably expect to convert into cash during one operating cycle or within one year. An operating cycle is the time it takes for you to put stock into your inventory, sell and/or deliver it, and ultimately, convert the sale into a payment from your customer.

As such, the most common things you'll find in your current asset figure are cash, inventories, prepaid expenses, temporary investments, and accounts receivable totals. There are some fine lines here; your accountant is the final guide as to what should be included in current assets. For instance, you might have an old piece of machinery that you want to sell. While you fully intend to sell it during the current period, unless you have a sales contract with a purchaser for the equipment, it really isn't a *current* asset, as you might not be able to convert its value into cash during the current operating cycle or one-year period. Likewise, an investment in the stock market might be considered current, as you simply have to phone your broker to convert it into cash. However, if the market value for this particular stock is severely depressed, you probably won't sell it during the current cycle. It, then, shouldn't be included in your current asset total.

Current liabilities are considerably simpler to understand: they are the bills you must pay during the next year. Current liabilities include accounts payable, any notes due during the year, any taxes due and payable, and the current portion of your long-term debt. As such, you'll most likely pay them from the funds you receive from current assets; thus the relationship between the two amounts.

Current assets compared to current liabilities are a direct measure of your capability to pay your bills. The general rule of thumb says you should have twice as much dollar value in current assets as you have in current liabilities. Short-term lenders consider this to be an important guideline to the health of your business, because they expect to be paid from the cash you collect from current operations.

On the flip side, you also don't want to have *too high* a ratio, especially if it's caused by slow-paying customers or nonmoving inventory. For instance, you might have (at the end of one period) $30,000 in accounts receivable plus $30,000 in other current assets—a total of $60,000 in current assets. At the same time, you might have a total of $30,000 in current liabilities. Your ratio, then, is 2-1 ($60,000 to $30,000).

At the end of the next period, let's say you were hit with a slew of slow-paying customers and poor collection procedures; your accounts receivable total $60,000, while other current assets come to $30,000—a total of $90,000 in current assets. If your liabilities stayed the same, you find yourself with a 3-1 ratio ($90,000 to $30,000). In this case a higher ratio is not better; it simply means you've got a lot of customers who aren't paying their bills.

Any study, then, of the current ratio calls for you to watch for a variance from what your established pattern has been. If your business has been doing fine with a 1.8 to 1 ratio, then you want to examine things more closely whenever that ratio varies in *either* direction.

There's an associated ratio called the *acid test* or *quick ratio* that examines much of this same information, but looks more at what can be called "instant liquidity." It's a more uncompromising test than the *current ratio* because it compares cash or what can be quickly converted into cash (and doesn't include inventory, because you might not sell it right away) to your current liabilities. In effect, then, it gives you a picture of your business at a moment in time with its liquid assets compared to the obligations you have to meet during the next year. As such, it's like comparing the cash in your wallet to your total expenses over the next week, so it's a harsher look at your bill-paying capability. Since the *acid test* ratio is directly concerned just with cash, you'll find more detail on it in Chapter 4 on cash flow. Usually, a value here of less than 1-1 indicates that you must sell something from your inventory to meet your current obligations.

It's also necessary to note that the 2-1 figure most people want their *current ratio* to have isn't correct for all businesses. This is especially true when a large part of your current assets are made up of inventory, because this is an area that—depending on your industry—is hard to evaluate. Some businesses, like ones in the food industry, move their inventory almost daily. Others, perhaps in an industry like machine tool parts, might have stock sitting around on their shelves for months at a time. The important thing is that if you have a large percentage of your current assets tied up in inventory, the 2-1 ratio figure probably won't apply to your work. As always, it's necessary to discover the right level for your own business and base any corrective action you take on that figure.

Figure 8-6 is a long-term look at the current ratio for our fictional business. It plots the information over a 36-month period (either the latest 36 months, or the last three years on a calendar basis—whatever is the most helpful to us at this time). This isn't a particularly good picture, if we assume this business needs to maintain the *average* current ratio, a 2-1 breakdown. This graph, since it's designed like the others we've shown, is scaled to help the user understand it. In this case, the scale is set to indicate the 2-1 ratio level. Early on, during the

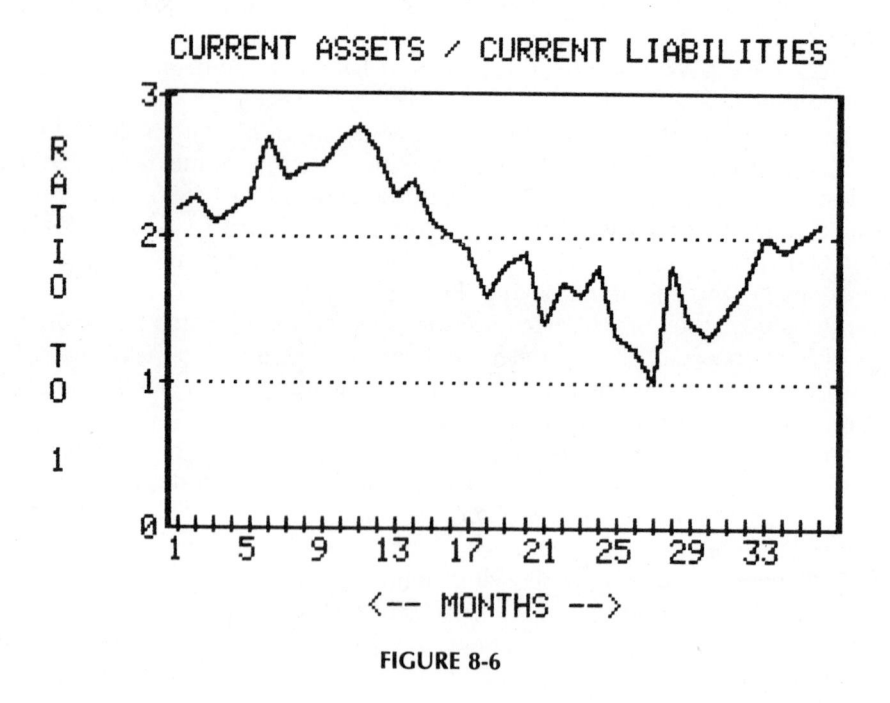

FIGURE 8-6

FINANCIAL STATEMENT ITEMS

first 12 months, the business kept its current ratio above the 2-1 mark, but from month 16 until just lately, the current ratio fell below 2-1. At one point it got all the way down to an even mark: 1-1.

The whole idea of this ratio is to measure a business's capability to pay its bills on time. The ratio of 2-1 is a generally accepted basis that allows a margin of error and takes into account that all current bills don't get collected during the current period. Current assets include things such as inventory, which may not be converted into cash for some time to come. Current liabilities include payments due within a year from when the ratio is calculated. When this ratio approaches the 1-1 figure, though, there's no margin of safety for the business. If this were a purely liquid asset measurement (the cash you have compared to the cash you owe), this low ratio might be acceptable. In this case, because you don't know *when* your inventory will turn into cash or *if* everyone who owes you money will pay, you need a safety margin.

One of the major limitations of the current ratio is that it only indicates the position of the business in respect to paying current liabilities through the liquidation of current assets. While we can estimate some future performance with a trend line analysis of the ratio data, it is *not* as accurate when it comes to predicting future performance, as, for example, a study of cash flow can be. It's

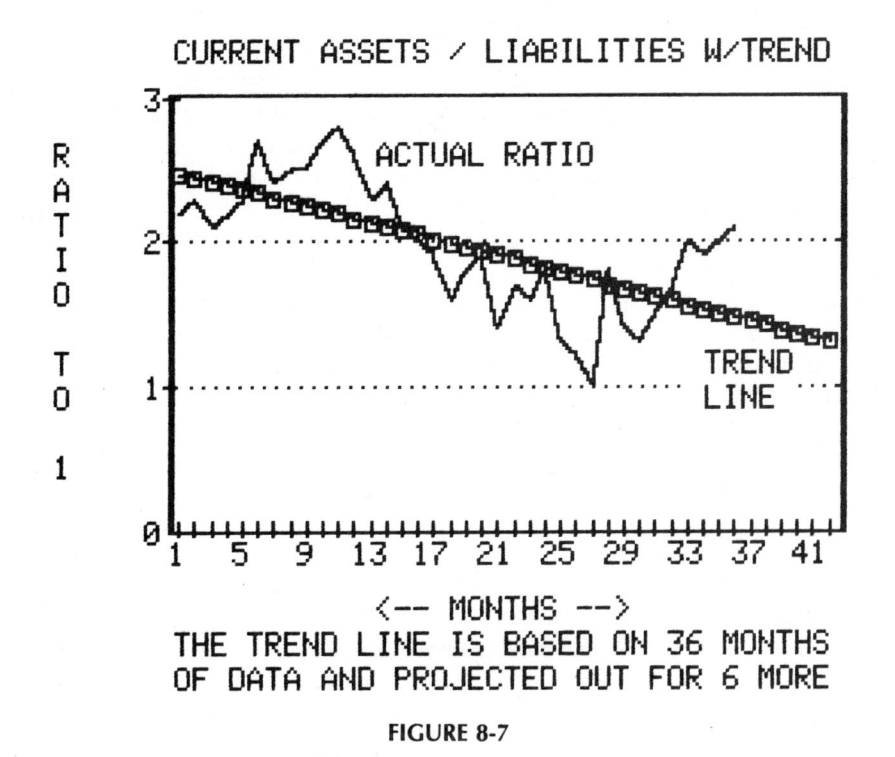

CURRENT ASSETS / LIABILITIES W/TREND

<-- MONTHS -->
THE TREND LINE IS BASED ON 36 MONTHS
OF DATA AND PROJECTED OUT FOR 6 MORE

FIGURE 8-7

important to understand the built-in limitations this ratio has, but it is equally necessary to track it, because of its widespread use, particularly among the bankers you'll do business with.

Figure 8-7 plots the trend line of the current ratio for our fictitious business, based on 36 months of data, and projects that line for six more months. Since it's based on a long series of data, we can expect that it's pretty accurate and that this ratio concentrates on current information only (which—judging it only by its name of "current assets"—we should expect it to do).

This chart only adds to our feeling that our fictional business has a problem with its current ratio and confirms what our first impression was: the current ratio is getting worse by the month. Even the recent rise in the ratio isn't enough to change the momentum the trend line has built up. If we keep in mind the limitations that are built into any study of the current ratio, we still find an image like the one we see in Figure 8-7 to be disturbing, and (hopefully) it will motivate us to change conditions, to correct the direction our current ratio seems to want to go.

Liabilities as Assets

It's also interesting to note that liabilities can be *sources* of assets—a seemingly odd relationship that we often don't understand. The asset and liability accounts in your business aren't to be confused with *net worth*, the value of your business that grows or shrinks based on your profit performance and investment total. Assets and liabilities *offset* one another; when you increase your assets (through the *use* of a liability) one cancels out the other, while your net worth position remains the same.

For example, your business might borrow $5,000 on an open line of credit with the payment due in 90 days. You've created a liability (the $5,000 loan repayment), but at the same time you've increased the total of your current assets. Likewise, when you purchase items for your inventory, you increase the asset value of that inventory total; at the same time, of course, you increase your current liabilities. In either case, the net worth amount remains the same.

The pair—assets and liabilities—compose a unique duo that, when you work one against the other in the proper manner, can add to your cash flow when you need them to.

Asset Pie

At the end of a year (or any specific period that's helpful to you), it's a good idea to plot your assets as they each individually contribute to your total asset base.

FINANCIAL STATEMENT ITEMS 189

Figure 8-8 is a pie chart created at the end of a yearly period that illustrates how the four breakdowns our fictional business keeps track of each look in relation to our total assets. Without other supporting information we can't, of course, draw any conclusions from this one chart, so we'd want to make this graph at the completion of every quarter or every year. We don't know if the inventory total of 19% of assets is where it should be, or if fixed assets (23% of the total) are larger than they should be or not. Only a long-range study of this information will tell us that, and a pie chart doesn't lend itself to an examination of time series data. It does, however, give us a guide to each asset's contribution to the total asset base at this time, which is useful information.

Since all the data is shown on a percentage basis, and those percentages are listed on the graph, the business owner can both see and read how each asset contributes to his or her total. Since the manager will know what the dollar amounts of the assets are, it's usually easy to convert the percentage figures listed into a dollar value. Cash, for instance, amounts to 7% of the business' total assets. If those assets totaled $100,000, the owner would know that—at this particular moment in time—he or she had about $7,000 in cash or cash equivalents.

One thing we can see from this picture is the large percentage of our business's assets that accounts receivable total. Since they amount to slightly more than half of all the assets this business claims, they'd better be *good* accounts, dollars the business must be able to collect. If a study at the same time

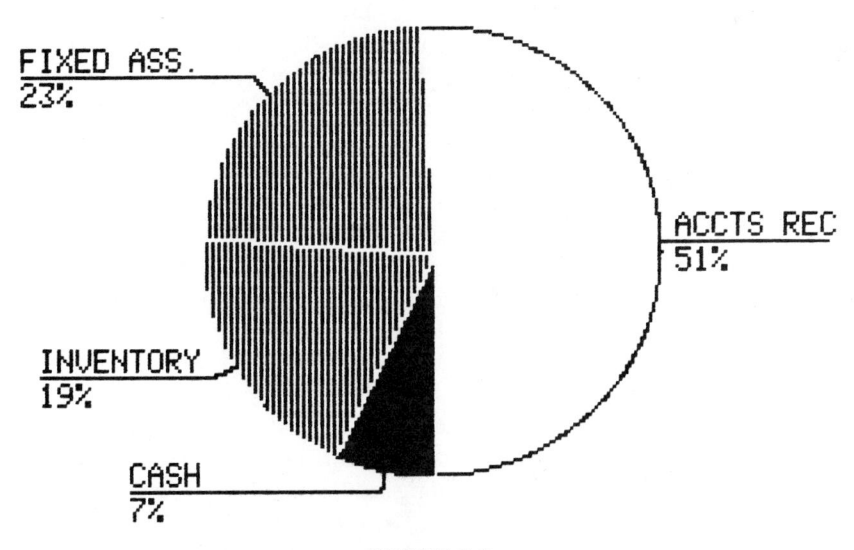

FIGURE 8-8

indicates this company had, say, 20% of its accounts older than 90 days, this business has a real problem.

The conversion process can be taken a step further, of course, in that once you know what percentage of your accounts receivable are in what "age" bracket, you can calculate pretty easily (or have your spreadsheet do it) what percentage of your total assets are tied up in receivables that grow older by the day. Again, this information can motivate the business owner to do something to correct a bad situation.

Fixed Assets

One problem many business people have is a tendency to invest too many dollars in what are called *fixed assets:* trucks and machinery and equipment that never gets sold but rather is purchased to make the business more productive. Your microcomputer is an investment in a fixed asset—termed that not because it's *fixed* in place but rather that it represents a fixed obligation that must be paid over a period of time and/or a dollar investment that took a fixed sum of cash (a liquid asset) and converted it into machinery or equipment when you wrote the check.

Along with most fixed assets comes *depreciation,* which in effect adds cash back to your business and, most often, interest costs that must be paid (anytime the purchase of an asset is financed). A problem arises if sales slip a bit and cash flow is impeded. Suddenly, the business owner finds she or he doesn't have enough cash to cover the payments contracted for when all those trucks and expensive equipment were purchased. But how much of an investment in fixed assets is too much? A balance must be found, as always, since without enough fixed assets (and their associated costs), the business won't be able to do business.

Figure 8-9 plots a two and one-half year period (ten quarters) of the percentage relationship between fixed assets and the net worth of our fictional business.

Even without a trend line, we can see that our fixed assets as a percentage of our total net worth is increasing. In effect, this means either we've been putting more dollars into fixed assets, or our net worth is decreasing for some reason, or we have a combination of the two conditions. While each business is different, a rule of thumb is that a business shouldn't have more than 75% of its net worth in fixed assets, as it begins to get top-heavy with the machinery to produce sales, but without the cash—the liquid assets—and inventory to sustain those sales.

If this were your business, you might want to put a trend line on the data illustrated in Figure 8-9 just to give you a better idea of how serious a problem you have. You'd also want to take a long and hard look at what you've been purchasing in the way of fixed assets and whether they're really improving your sales and/or production efficiency. Perhaps the high ratio won't hurt your busi-

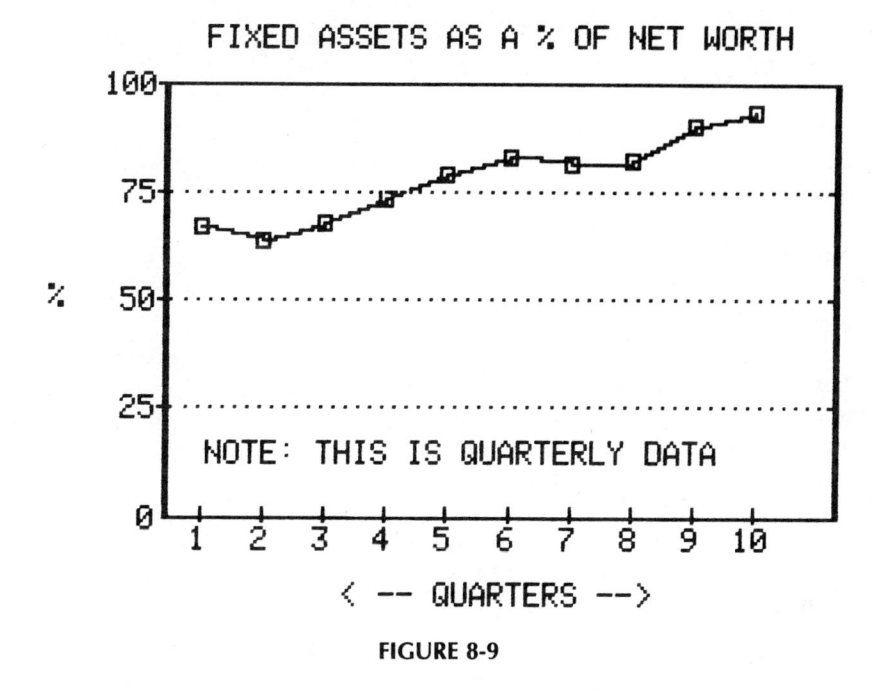

```
          FIXED ASSETS AS A % OF NET WORTH
     100┬
        │
        │
      75┼ ......................□──□..............................□──□
        │         □──□──□────□──┘                           □──□──┘
        │      □──┘
   %  50┼ ..............................................................
        │
        │
      25┼ ..............................................................
        │        NOTE: THIS IS QUARTERLY DATA
       0└──┼──┼──┼──┼──┼──┼──┼──┼──┼──┼
           1  2  3  4  5  6  7  8  9  10
              < -- QUARTERS -->
```

FIGURE 8-9

ness. In any case, a graph like Figure 8-9 sends a warning to the business owner that perhaps she or he is spending cash where it shouldn't be spent.

Measuring Efficiency

While we all strive for more efficiency and are constantly looking at our people to see how they're doing, you need to turn the examination around and see how you're doing, in your role of business manager. How efficient are you?

In a sense, when you break things down inside your business, you have in effect a number of assets and are asked to do business with them. You have a certain sum of cash, a specific dollar amount in inventory, an amount that customers owe you, trucks and equipment, perhaps a building, and so on—a quantity of assets. While you can change the mix of these (take some cash and buy a new copy machine), you only add to your assets when your business creates a profit or you increase your investment (or, if you operate another business form, like a corporation), when others increase their investment in the business. Likewise, your assets decrease when you cause an operating loss or when you remove assets from the business (a dividend payment, the purchase of a personal vehicle).

That might seem elementary, but in essence at this particular point in time, your business has a combination of assets that together are listed on your financial statement along with their specific dollar value. The way you use your assets has a direct bearing on whether you show a profit or a loss. If you handle things right and keep the proper dollar amount in inventory (so you have the right stock on hand at the right time); have the proper equipment (so your people can be efficient in their work); handle your accounts receivables correctly (so you get paid when you should); and so on, your business will show a profit. Since your assets have to be manipulated properly for your business to be successful, you can gauge your performance not only by using the profit amount as a yardstick (as we saw earlier), but also with the movement of your assets—what's called the *asset turnover rate*.

Turnover of assets simply means the number of times your operating assets can be divided into your sales during a particular accounting period. Operating assets are those you use to create sales in the usual operation of your business (as contrasted to, say, a building you own but rent to someone—that doesn't affect your business operation).

Figure 8-10 plots the asset turnover rate for our fictional enterprise over a 36-month period. Just as we examine our inventory turnover to see how it moves through our business, this illustration plots the same type of image and tells us how often our assets *turn* during the normal course of operations. Unless our inventory is turning, being sold, we won't make a profit. Unless we're using our assets effectively, the bottom line will be red, too.

Lately, our business has been improving and has made quite a comeback from where assets weren't turning even once a month. What's the proper asset

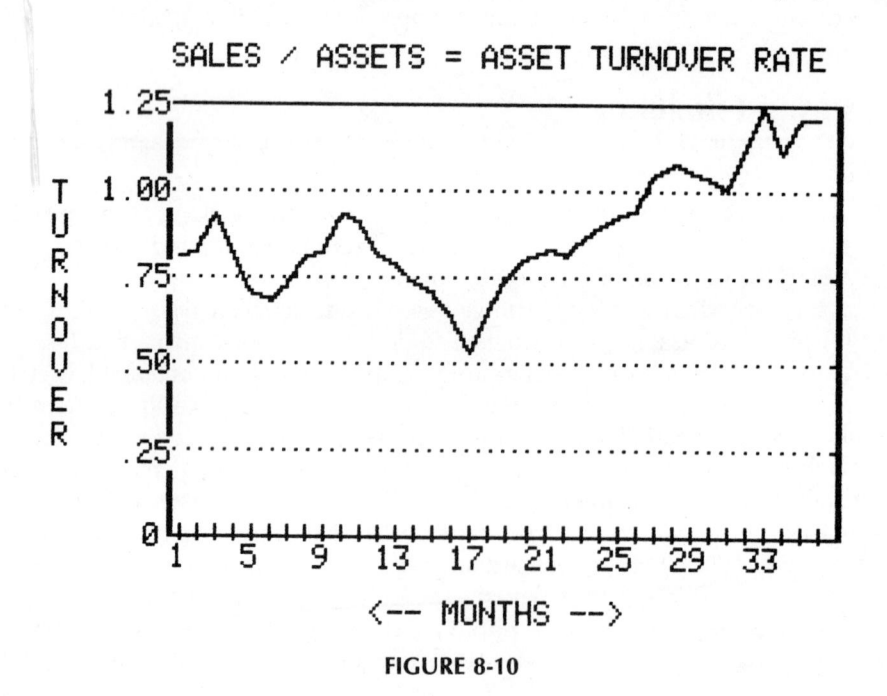

FIGURE 8-10

turnover rate? Only through a long-term examination of your information will you know what's right for you. Asset turnover charts are usually done on a yearly basis, while Figure 8-10 covers things from a monthly standpoint. Turning over your operating assets only once or twice a year would probably not be a particularly good performance, while turning them over at that rate on a monthly basis, as this example shows, is a completely different picture and probably means the business owner is doing the job well. The higher the ratio, the better the performance.

You can carry this approach a step further and create an *earnings power* ratio, a comparison that puts an exact figure on your efficiency as a manager. You multiply the rate of profit your business made (in comparison to its sales) by the asset turnover rate. The more a business can sell and the more it's capable of earning on each sales dollar in relation to each dollar it has invested in operating assets, the higher will be the return on each invested dollar. This figure shows how effectively you, as a manager, are using the assets you have available.

Liabilities and Net Worth

Just as we looked at fixed assets in relationship to the net worth of your business, it's useful to make the same comparison between the liabilities you have and what your net worth is. You can examine your total liabilities or your current liabilities in relation to your net worth; we'll use current obligations. This look at net worth won't insure you'll have the *cash* to pay your bills, but gives you a good idea of the health of your business.

Figure 8-11 illustrates the value of our current liabilities as a percentage of the total net worth of our business, over a 36-month period. As often is the case, even without a trend line we can see this business is heading toward difficult times, as its ratio of current obligations to its net value is constantly rising. Simply put, this is a comparison of what is owed on a current basis to the net worth of the business. As a rule of thumb, anything over about 75% is probably too high (you can determine what's right for you through long-range charting).

Let's add a trend line to give the bad news a bit more force. Figure 8-12 plots the same data we just examined, with the addition of a trend line that shows its average direction and projects where the business will be six months from now. Since the trend line is based on three years worth of information and only projects for six months, we can expect this to be an accurate picture, if business conditions and our way of doing business stay about the same.

Unfortunately, the trend line predicts that our current liabilities will soon approach 100% of our net worth, so in effect we'd owe the same amount as what the business is worth. And the liabilities for this example are *current* obligations—part of what we have financed over a long period of time isn't shown as a current liability. So, our condition is even worse than what we'd expect from these pic-

FIGURE 8-11

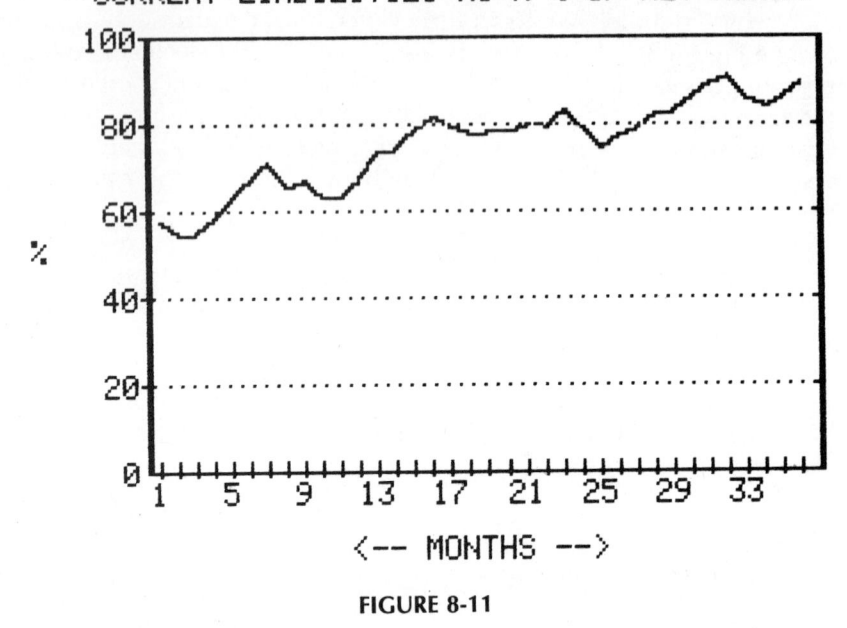

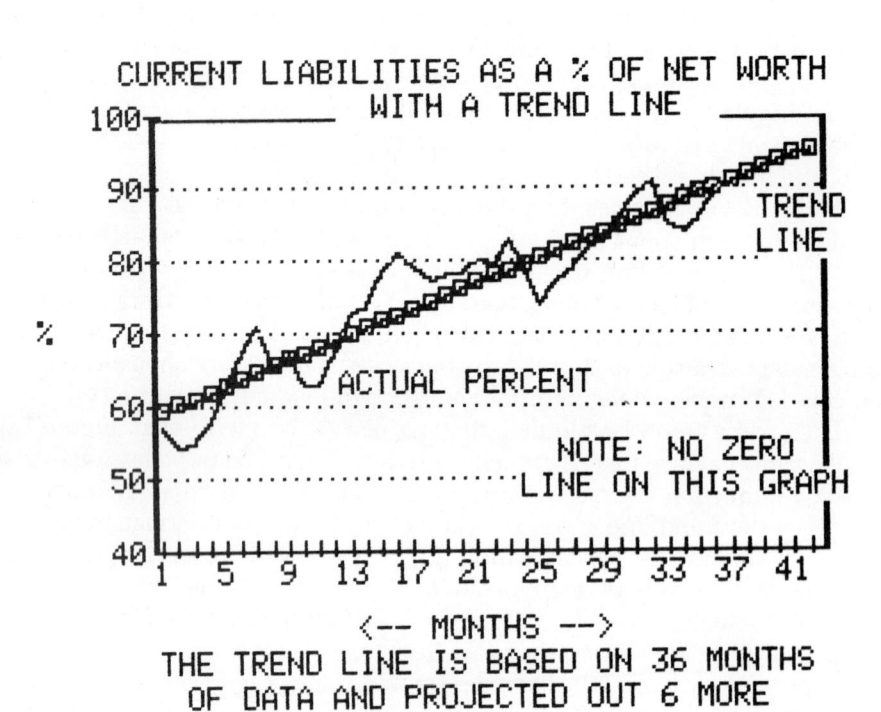

FIGURE 8-12

TOTAL LIABILITIES / NET WORTH

FIGURE 8-13

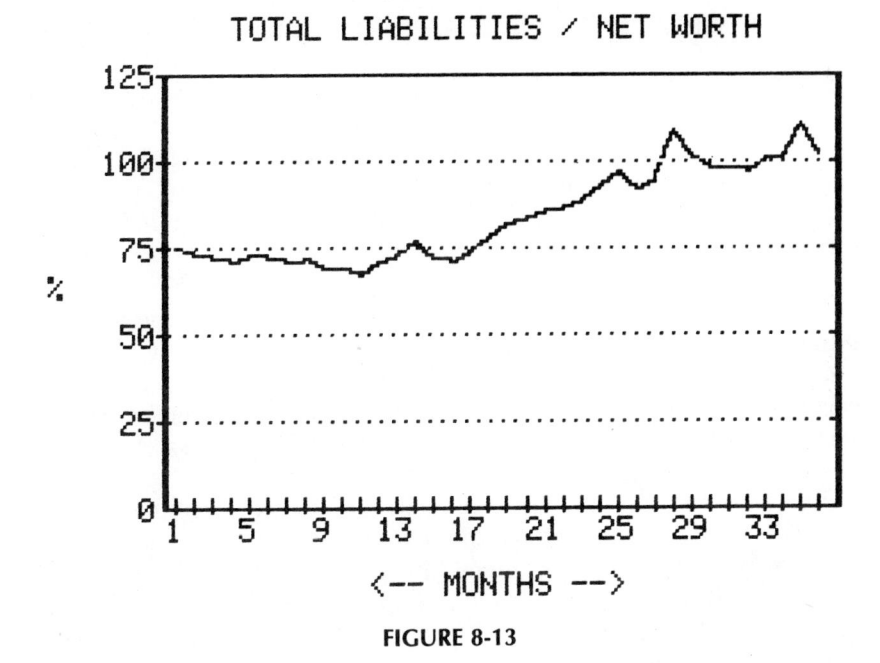

tures, and we might even be in a position where outside creditors own more of our business—through the obligations we have to them—than we do.

A Worse Look

Let's add in those long-term liabilities and see how bad the picture really is. In Figure 8-13 we can see the relationship between everything we owe (total liabilities) to what we own (net worth), and it's a discomforting look. Lately, in fact, we have reached that stage where our creditors own more of the enterprise than we do, and if we were to liquidate at this particular time, we may not be able to pay all the outstanding obligations of our company. A business in this position often finds itself with severely restricted credit (who wants to loan money to a business that owes more than it's worth?), and it will have truly difficult cash problems if sales slow down even a little.

More Interest Problems

If the business owner with the company that has all the poor financial information we've been examining can turn things around and finds a bank who'll consider a loan, he or she might find their banker requesting an unusual figure: the business's *times interest earned* data.

In effect, the ratio is simpler than it sounds. If your business made $15,000 in profits last year and had total interest expenses of $1500, it can be said to have *earned* its interest costs ten times. This is calculated by dividing the net profit (usually after taxes) by the total interest expense for the period under study.

Anyone who might loan you money is a candidate for this information. Since they'll expect repayment out of the operating funds your business produces, a primary concern for any lender is to consider how safe the loan is. If you can display the capability to earn many times over the amount of the interest you'll have to pay, your loan will be a better gamble.

A normal guideline calls for this figure to be at least 10-1, although the higher it is, the more likely you'll get any loan you might request. The obvious danger is, of course, that if a business has a low ratio, if it's not earning enough profit to cover the interest, the loan is in danger of not being repaid at all.

Figure 8-14 is another look at a business with an upcoming problem. For the first four quarters under study, the ratio was at least 10-1, but since quarter 5 it has been steadily dropping. Since this is something of a long-range look at things (two year's worth of information), this is a picture that should disturb any business owner. It *will* bother a banker who examines it, so it's important for us to understand and track.

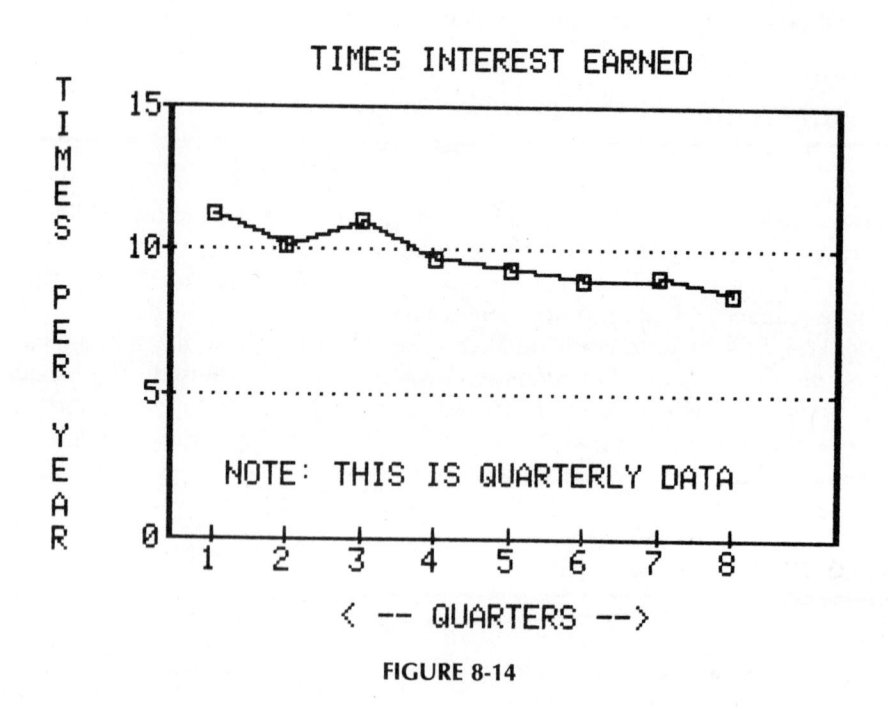

FIGURE 8-14

Collecting Cash

Anyone with accounts receivable dollars owed them automatically gets a bit of extra baggage with the receivable process. While one class of customer always pays, there's another that never does. In between those two extremes are the people who you figure will pay, but you just don't know when they might get around to it. Unfortunately, the customer whose account ends up as a bad debt or as a candidate for the collection services *passes through* this middle ground, and we don't have any accurate way to determine who's going to pay (eventually) and who we'll have to turn over for collection.

Two things you can do is to track how your finance charges are going (as we did in Chapter 5) and to study the average collection period your business has. All of these calculations, of course, are ideal candidates for your spreadsheet program.

The most accurate and helpful way to examine this information is to calculate and chart it on a monthly basis. In essence, this describes the time period you need to convert your in-stock inventory into cash, and includes the time it takes you to get the material, deliver and/or install it, send the bill, and to collect for the job.

The first stage is to compute your daily credit sales. It's important to note that you want to work with only *credit sales*, those sales you charge to your customers through your accounts receivable system. To calculate your average daily credit sales, you divide your net credit sales for the month by the number of days during the month. These are in contrast to, say, *cash sales*, where you collect for the purchase at the same time you sell it.

For example, you might have sales of $45,000 that you charged to your customers during one monthly period. If there were 30 days in this particular month, when you divide 45,000 by 30, you find your average credit sales, per day, were $1,500.

Your accounting system will also give you your starting period and ending period accounts receivable figures. You'd total them and divide by two, to arrive at an average. For example, if at the end of last month your accounts receivable came to $50,000, and at the end of the current month they total $60,000, you'd add these two figures together (they total $110,000) and divide by 2, for an average accounts receivable balance of $55,000. You divide this by the average amount of credit sales you made each day ($1,500), and the resulting figure (37) tells you the number of days it took your business, on the average, to collect its accounts receivable. The figure, the turnover rate, tells you how many times your receivables turned during the period under study. If you normally ask for payment on a 30-day basis, and find that you have a period like this example—a 37-day time frame to collect your cash—you have a minor problem in this area.

This figure can be graphed, and it's very helpful to examine its fluctuations over a period of time. Once you've gathered enough information on your own business, you'll most likely find that your collection period will run within a specific range of days, except for certain times of the year when someone else gets the payments you should be receiving. You might discover, for example, that on the average your collection period is 30 to 35 days. In effect, this means you can expect payment within that period for most invoices you send out. But you might also find that during certain periods of the year, the slow times, your collection rate might move into the 50–60 day range.

Figure 8-15 plots the average collection period for our fictional business over 36 months. The most striking thing about this picture is that for a long time, our collections ran in the 30- to 40-day area. With a *net 30* payment schedule (common for many businesses), that's probably the range we should expect to see. Then, about in the middle of the third year, our collection period took a drastic jump. While it has been brought back into its normal range, there had to be some reason for the increase in slow collections, and we need to take steps to see that such a rise doesn't hit us again. Were a lot of our customers during this period those we should have spotted as slow-pay, by using better credit-checking procedures? Were we lax in calling old accounts to ask for payment? Whatever the reason, it would be helpful to know what happened, and why.

While, as always, the most helpful comparison you can make is to compare your current collection period with your own past history, a rule of thumb is that the average collection period shouldn't exceed what you request as payment terms

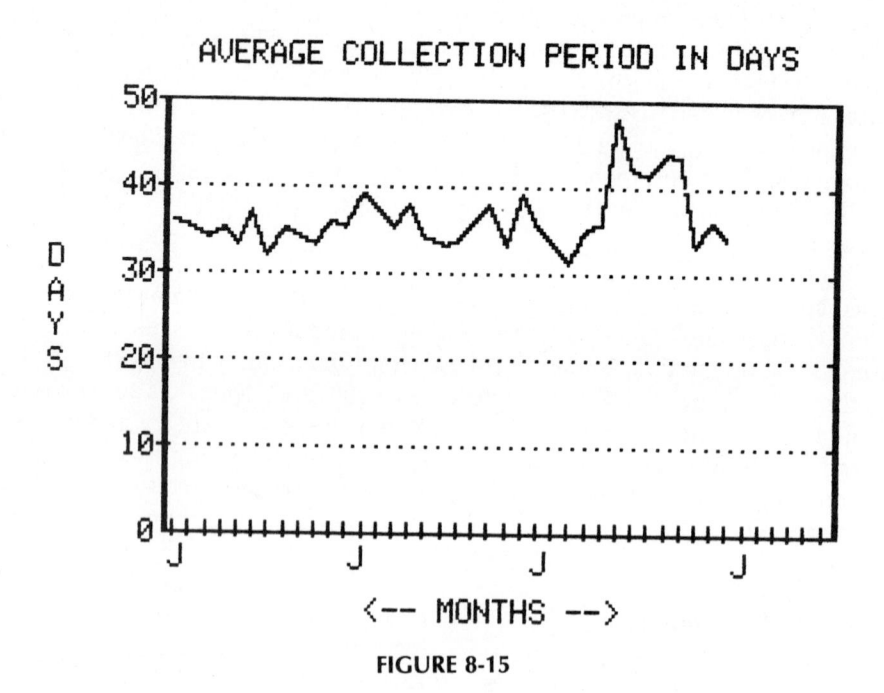

FIGURE 8-15

FINANCIAL STATEMENT ITEMS

by more than 30%. If you normally ask your customers to pay on a net 10-day basis, your collection period shouldn't be longer than about 13 days. If you ask for payment within 30 days, your average collection period shouldn't be longer than 39 days.

Along with any discussion of the average number of days it takes your business to collect its receivables, it's important to note that there are other considerations to keep in mind. If you feel, when you talk to a potential customer, that she or he is someone who'll pay their bill, it might be worthwhile to extend credit to them, even if their probable collection period will run considerably longer than what your average is. The point is, you don't want to reduce your sales volume simply to enforce an arbitrary collection period. There's a happy medium for your business that you need to find and work from.

A logical extension of Figure 8-15 would be to take the same information and ask our plotting program to create a trend line of the data. Once we see it (in Figure 8-16), it seems obvious that we should have done this sooner, because the trend line projects the unhappy picture that we'll have close to a 40-day collection period if things stay as they are, six months from now.

As often is the case, we really can't tell from the data itself that the trend is rising. Even the big jump came back down to what appears to be our normal

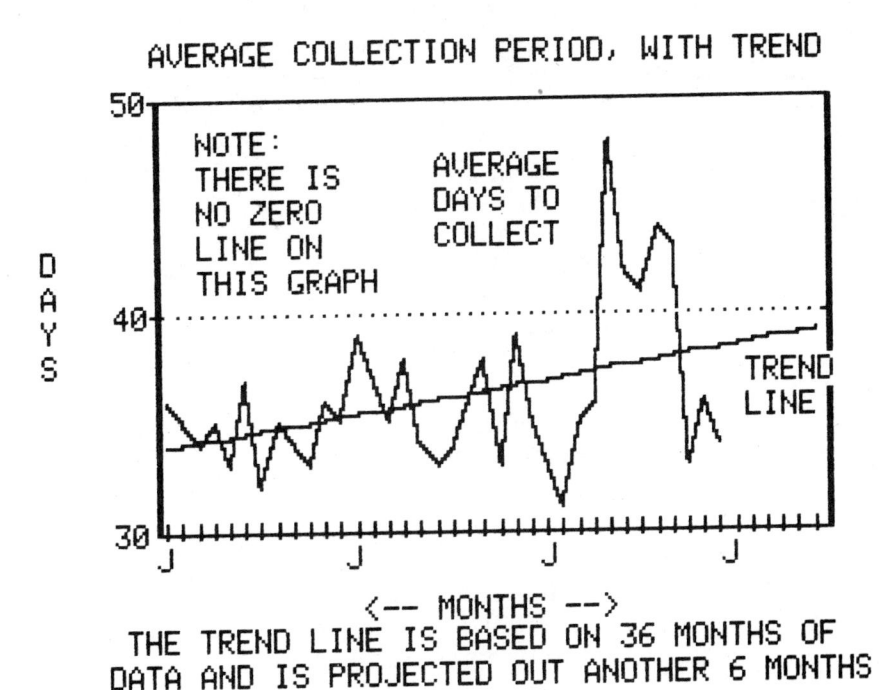

FIGURE 8-16

operating range, but the overall trend is still upward. As noted on the graph, there's no zero line, so the data lines rise and fall much more sharply than they did in the earlier graph. But this close-up brings home a good point: we have a problem with the overall *trend* of our collection period, and we need to do something to reverse the situation, or we can expect significant cash flow problems in the near future. Perhaps we can screen our credit customers more effectively. Maybe we need to turn down work where there appears to be a credit problem. It might be worthwhile (and almost always is) to get on the phone and call customers, just to make sure our work was satisfactory and to mention, "by the way, we haven't received your check." Our suppliers don't hesitate to call us if we get a little slow in paying their bill, and we must do the same with our customers. It might be something as simple as letting each customer know, when you allow them to charge, exactly what your credit terms are, and what will happen if they get behind.

Summing Up

There are probably a hundred ratios you could track and graph that will be helpful to you. We've tried to suggest some of the more obvious, along with a number of unusual ones, as they often give you another useful way to examine your information besides the *acid test* and *quick ratio* and other things you're so accustomed to.

Ratios for balance sheet and income statement items are only tools, and while they can be compared and graphed and examined, they remain just that: a method to help you understand where your business has been, and (perhaps) in which direction it's going. You need to be aware of industry averages for each ratio, mainly because the financial people you deal with must use them as a judge to gauge the quality of your business. After all, they're not around to see the daily operation of things and can only estimate your capability to repay a loan based on your past performance and any financial information to which they have access.

Three sources that can be of help for information about your own industry and what ratios should be examined and what they should look like are:

1. Your own accountant. She or he has the knowledge and often the information on what to look for and how to examine it.
2. Robert Morris Associates (Research Department, Philadelphia National Bank Building, Philadelphia, PA 19107). This firm gathers and summarizes industry averages, which you can use as a basis of comparison for your own business.
3. Dun & Bradstreet, Inc. (99 Church Street, New York, NY 10007). Get to know your local D&B people; they have all sorts of financial information you'll find helpful.

Ideally, you'll have access to past information from your company that you can go back through and find data for a long-range look at your personal financial picture. This is the best comparison you can make, of course, and once you chart the information you'll be able to see exactly when there's any deviation from past trends.

The logical place to start any examination of financial information is with your profit line. It's useful to compare profits to sales (that's the standard comparison we all make) and also to assets, as that gives you a measure of how you're managing the assets you have available.

Profit also can be compared to the net worth an enterprise has, to give you a feel for how well your investment in the business is doing, as an investment.

One comparison any banker will make when he or she examines your financial information is to look at your *current ratio*, a guide to whether or not you can pay your current obligations from the resources you have available now. You need to know, then, what current assets and current liabilities are, as well as the historical trend of this ratio for your own business. Although it's worthwhile to compare its performance to industry averages (which your banker will certainly do), if you know what your long-range current ratio shows, you can better explain any deviation from what appears to be the norm. It's vital to know what your own current ratio has been in the past, as either too high *or* too low a ratio is a sign that there may be a problem.

It's also helpful to remember that liabilities can be sources of assets; when cash flow becomes a problem, you might be able to help things out by creating a liability (a loan of $10,000 means you have to pay it back, with interest, but also gives you the $10,000 to use in the meantime).

Since assets are the total of what your business owns, it's helpful to take a look at their distribution—*where* do you have your cash invested? Are accounts receivable a major portion of your total assets? If so, it's vital that the business owner makes sure those receivables are collectable. You may also want to track individual asset groups over time, to see if their value, as a percentage of your total asset base, rises or falls.

No examination of assets is complete without tracking and taking a hard look at the fixed assets your business has. Since many businesspeople have a tendency to put too many of their dollars into fixed assets (thus locking up cash that perhaps should be used elsewhere), this is an area that needs constant vigilance.

While we looked earlier at assets in relation to liabilities and as part of their own pie, it's also useful to examine them from another direction to see how rapidly they *turn* inside our sales. This comparison measures the efficiency at which the business owner manages his or her assets—the more use you can make of your assets, the more successful your business will be.

It's also necessary to look at the other side of the balance sheet, at the liabilities your business has. One good way to examine what you owe is in relation to the net worth, the *equity* you have in your company. While we chose as an example a look at current liabilities to the net worth value, it's equally useful to examine your total liabilities in relation to this figure. This ratio tells the business owner how much outsiders—in the form of creditors—have invested in the business.

Anyone who loans you money has one major concern: whether you'll repay the loan on time. One way they gauge your capability for this is to see if your business is earning enough cash to support its operations and make enough profit to pay the interest on the loan amount. This is often done with something called the *times interest earned* ratio, which simply divides the total interest obligations of a business into its net profit, usually over a one-year period.

Finally, since accounts receivable probably form a major part of your current assets (and are perhaps a big share of your total assets), it's important to take a look at their movement, how they *turn*. Just as the business owner must keep his or her inventory turning in order to create sales (and thus profits), you also must keep your receivables moving, to keep your cash coming in. If your receivables stop their movement, your cash stream stops *flowing,* and your business ceases to function. One excellent way to look at your accounts receivable is through the use of your average collection period, the time it takes your business, on the average, to convert its credit sales into cash. You might find there are times of the year when your collection period gets slower because of seasonal variations in your sales. Outside factors might influence the cash you collect—at income tax time, do people send checks to their Uncle in Washington, D.C. instead of you? A trend line based on a long-range look at your historical data is also useful to see the overall direction of your credit sales collections.

Other Ideas

Within the whole area of your financial statement information are all kinds of things you might find it helpful to examine, and we've just scratched the surface in this chapter. Some of the ratios that could logically go here have been extracted and are covered in the chapters on specific areas. Here are some additional ideas.

You may want to compare your net worth (owner's equity) to just the long-term debt your business has, and plot it over a period of time. This gives you another view of how much you have invested in your business as a comparison to what other people have, on a long-range basis.

One thing many business owners take a hard look at is their gross profit margin (gross profit as a percentage of total sales). Since your overhead and net profit must come from your gross profit, it's an important thing to track and chart over a period of time.

Within the profit area itself, you may find it useful to break down your profit and look at it from a couple of directions. Examine your operating profit before taxes as a percentage of sales; profit after taxes as it relates to sales. Chart profit (either before or after taxes) over a length of time, on a this-period compared to last-period basis.

You might want to examine your accounts receivable as a percentage of your total sales, and/or to find out what percentage they are of just the credit sales you make. All this with an eye to determining if you have too much in your total accounts receivable (poor collection procedures, easy credit) or too little (too stringent credit policies). As always, you need to strive for the balance that's right for your business.

While we looked at fixed assets in relation to the other assets our fictional business carries on its books, it's often useful to examine fixed assets in relation to total sales, as those sales are what you produce through the use of the fixed assets you have available. How about a look at other assets in relation to sales? Is there any correlation?

The *equity ratio* examines how much of the total value of a business is owned by the people who "own" the company. You calculate this by dividing the total assets into the owner's equity amount. Since assets include the value of everything a business owns (including financed items), this gives you a measure of the proportion of the total assets you—the owner—have invested in the business at any given time. When this percentage is subtracted from 100%, you're left with the percentage that others have invested in your business, either through loans or (accounts payable) payments you owe them. From the viewpoint of someone you ask for a loan, the more you have invested in your business, the safer they'll feel. However, if you, as the business owner, can effectively use borrowed funds to create profits above the cost of those funds (the interest you must pay), then you may want to do so.

We haven't touched on corporations, where any number of people might have cash (or other assets) invested in a company, but if you operate this form of business and have outside investors, you may want to keep track of their return on investment (per share of stock), dividend payments, the price-earnings ratio per share of stock, and so on.

Probably the most important thing about all this ratio analysis is to simply look around and examine each area until you can determine what's most important to your business and its successful operation. Don't be afraid to ask your accountant, to buy and read accounting books, to send away for more information. Track the data you find most useful over a period of time, put trend lines on it to get some idea of where you're headed, and you'll find that a study in this area—financial statement information—will produce real results in terms of real profit dollars.

Payroll

9

Odd as it may seem, you can pick up almost any accounting book and not find even a reference to *payroll*. Things like cash flow and balance sheet items and net profit are covered, but for some reason, that bane of the businessperson that comes along every Friday is often ignored.

But *you* know about payroll, don't you? Probably more than the experts, at that, who may never have had to meet a payroll. Whether you sell anything this week or not, whether you collect any cash today or not, whether your bank account on payday morning shows $10 or $10,000, your employees still must be paid, and it's difficult for someone *not* in the position of a business owner to appreciate this fact.

Payday Problems

Associated with payroll are any number of problems. The most obvious is the collection of enough cash to cover our payroll checks, but along with this difficulty comes the payroll function itself (keeping track of every penny, creating correct checks) as well as a confusing array of government tax forms to fill out and send money along with.

Thankfully, your microcomputer can help with just about everything, including making a suggestion or two on better cash management so you will have the cash available when you need it (see Chapter 4 on cash flow). But payroll often appears to be a dead end from an analysis viewpoint. After all, it must be paid (as must all its associated taxes); there's really no way to *analyze* payroll, other than to track its total; payroll amounts are difficult to relate to other parts of the business; and it's most often done on a weekly basis while other costs are computed monthly, which makes comparison difficult.

Payroll Comparisons

While payroll certainly doesn't have all the implications and variations the businessperson can find in his or her balance sheet or overhead statement, it does have its own niche and unique ways it can be examined, with an eye to making the act of paying as painless as possible.

Since all cash ultimately comes from sales (even if you borrow or invest money, it still must be repaid with sales revenues), that's the logical place to start your examination of payroll. Generally, your payroll total should rise and fall in proportion to your sales or production volume. This won't be the case if you compare your total payroll to gross sales, because total payroll includes office and perhaps sales salaries. Your overhead wages must be paid whether there are any sales or not.

So while you'll want to track your total labor figure, to get an accurate estimate of how labor relates to sales requires you to remove any overhead salaries from its total. It also means you need to compute and *add in* any fringe benefits that apply to this direct labor. Only then will you get an exact summary of your labor costs as they relate to sales. When you've calculated this figure (usually on a monthly basis), it can serve as a means to make a number of helpful comparisons.

Sales and Labor

Once you know your actual labor costs, a graph like Figure 9-1 can tell you a bit about your payroll situation. It's a simple line chart for the first six months of the year that plots gross monthly sales along with the net payroll total. While the first three months of the year saw sales drop, the payroll for this fictitious business remained about the same. Management may have kept some people working when sales decreased a bit, so those employees would be available later on when they were really needed.

When sales started to spurt a little, starting in April, the payroll cost also increased. This tells the business owner two things. First, when the business grows in sales, it will also incur more labor costs (which is logical). Second, at least at this point in time, labor costs aren't rising as rapidly as the sales growth. That's a good sign that management has some control on what their people are doing. Even with widely varying data sets (sales all over $50,000 a month and

SALES THIS YEAR / PAYROLL THIS YEAR

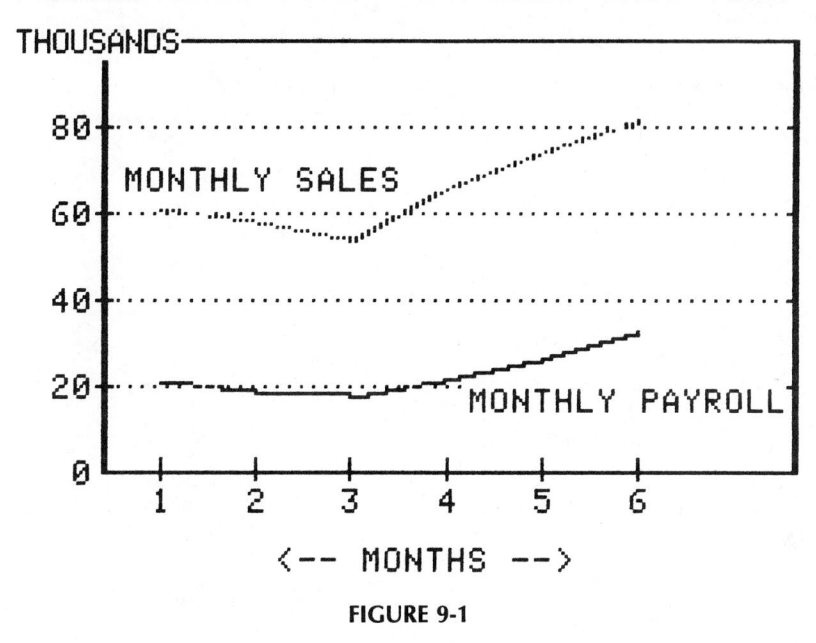

FIGURE 9-1

labor around $25,000 a month) a line graph like this lets the business owner see a picture of two important variables—sales and labor.

A Problem Picture

The opposite image would show the two lines at variance—sales would decrease while labor rose, or sales would remain stable while labor increased, or if sales did show a gain, the labor line would show a more *rapid* rate of climb. The line graph is ideal to display all of these conditions, because what's important to this particular analysis is the rate of change. What we want the graph to tell us is *how fast* one line is moving in relation to the other. As we'll see in a moment, there are other graphs that give us a picture of how labor should relate to sales in terms of a proper percentage, but the first thing to look at is to see if labor is rising the same or at a faster rate than sales.

The Historical Picture

While the truly vital thing any business manager wants to be aware of is what's happening right now, a picture of the past can also be helpful to see how things are at the present. Here's a list of the direct labor costs for the fictitious business we're examining, without any fringe benefits figured in. The list is done in this manner because if you want to use this technique yourself, you'll easily be able to compute the current cost of any fringe benefits you pay your people, but it might be impossible to go back a year or two and extract the same information.

MONTHLY PAYROLL TOTALS
(EXCLUDING FRINGE BENEFITS)

	1986	1985	1984
JAN	18,365	19,305	21,316
FEB	16,207	18,317	17,309
MAR	15,317	16,204	16,307
APR	18,902	21,317	22,065
MAY	23,761	26,024	27,392
JUN	28,605	27,319	28,066
JUL	33,806	31,065	34,651
AUG	39,417	36,021	35,092
SEP	32,804	29,804	30,652
OCT	29,613	27,613	28,017
NOV	28,416	23,019	28,312
DEC	26,302	22,046	21,065

As often is the case with so many figures, it's impossible to get much information from them in their present form.

One good use for this sort of historical data is to put it into a long-term frame of reference. If we graph it all chronologically, we can see a running image of three year's worth of payroll information. Figure 9-2 does just that. Its data starts with the payroll total for January of 1984, runs for 36 consecutive months, and ends with December of 1986.

Any Problems Here?

What would you say if this business belonged to you, and in January of 1987 you were examining your last three years of payroll information? Would you be pleased with the picture Figure 9-2 gives you?

Obviously, you'd need more information, and the logical step is to look again at current sales. This long-term picture shows that your payroll (at least during 1984 and 1985) went down early in the year, had a tremendous rise during the summer months, and went down to below $20,000 per month as one year ended and the next began. 1986 started out much the same, with a greater rise to its peak. We'd expect that would be due to an increase in sales. However, when the autumn drop took place for 1986, it was neither as long nor as precipitous as the fall during the two prior years.

```
       MONTHLY PAYROLL, LAST THREE YEARS
    THOUSANDS
    40
    30
    20
    10
     0
       84          85          86
              <-- YEARS -->
```

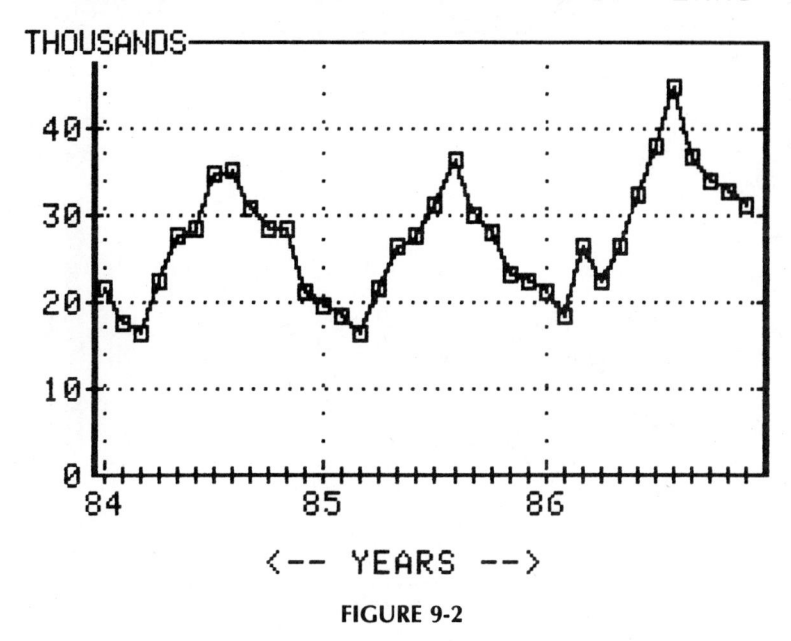

FIGURE 9-2

If your *sales* total followed a similar pattern, the change in the way your direct labor "moves" probably means it's adjusting to the changes in sales. However, if your sales for 1986 approximated those of the two prior years, then there's some other reason why labor costs are higher this year, and why their late-year decrease isn't as severe as it has been.

Figure 9-2, then, doesn't give you definitive information as to what might cause 1986's aberration, but because of the variation in the data, the alert businessperson will ask questions to find out *why* they happened as they did.

Direct Payroll Comparisons

While Figure 9-2 didn't compare payroll figures directly, it's often useful to do just that. Just like we find it helpful to see a picture of how our sales this year compare to the sales we tallied last year, an examination of payroll on the same basis is also helpful. Figure 9-3 is a column chart for 1985's direct labor, along with all of 1986.

The first thing you'll notice is that the monthly totals for 1986 started to greatly exceed those of 1985 in the month of June. If your *sales* justified this increase, that's fine. If not, the alert manager should have started to take corrective action no later than August. The one uptick in June might not mean much, and

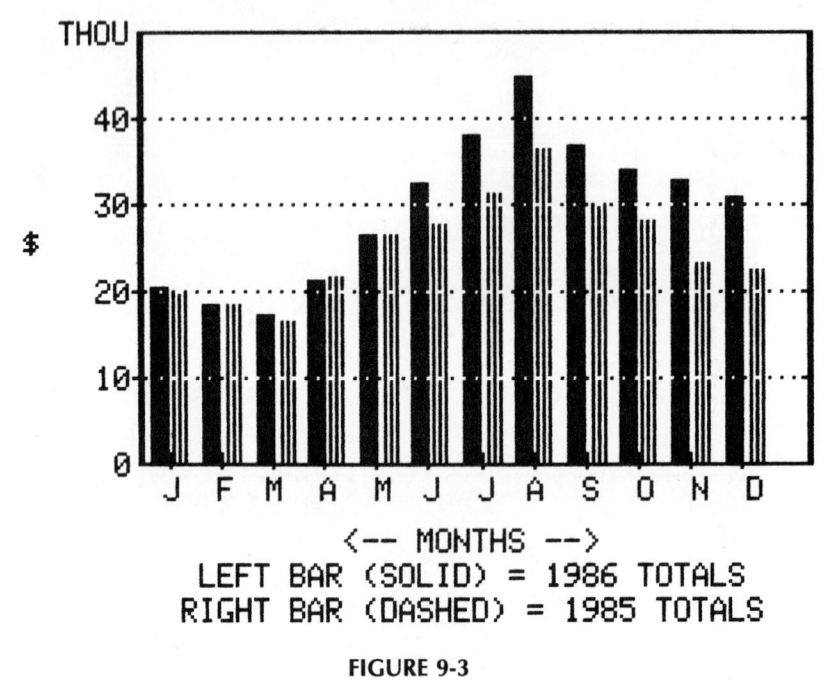

```
              MONTHLY PAYROLL 1985 / 1986
      THOU
       40

       30
    $
       20

       10

        0
          J   F   M   A   M   J   J   A   S   O   N   D
                      <-- MONTHS -->
              LEFT BAR (SOLID) = 1986 TOTALS
              RIGHT BAR (DASHED) = 1985 TOTALS
```

FIGURE 9-3

a jump in July might not, either, but when August's figures were in and plotted and you showed three straight months with higher payroll this year than last, it's time for immediate action.

One of the best things about comparing two similar data sets with a column chart like the one in Figure 9-3 is that the design of the graph itself helps us get a feeling for the quantity of the numbers, the total amount of payroll for which we wrote checks.

Payroll Details

Once we determine to work only with payroll cost, we can start to compare it to the production our employees create—how many jobs they install, products they build, service calls they make. While the most obvious thing to graph is the number of units produced per dollar of payroll, unless you manufacture something, you may not be able to break down your figures in this manner. Each business is different, of course, and often a direct comparison is impossible because of a wide variation in what you do. In the average retail appliance store, you and your people might sell a number of products (washers, refrigerators, etc.) as well as service them. You might also have delivery time and counter time and perhaps even a bit of time where there's not much to do but clean up the place.

If it seems impossible to break down your time and your people's time into one basic function, then create a graph similar to Figure 9-4. This graph compares direct labor to hours worked. While this might seem to be an easy comparison to make, in reality it isn't, because of the wide spread in the numbers themselves. Since payroll is a high figure and hours worked is always much smaller (in terms of raw numbers), we must *adjust* either one or the other so we can plot them on the same chart.

It's important when you divide one figure to lower it or multiply a figure to raise it so it approximates another, to multiply or divide by 10, 100, 1000, and so on. It's necessary to raise numbers by adding zeroes to them, which we do by multiplying by 10 or 100 or 1000 or even 100,000. This is because what we want the graph to show us is the relationship between the numbers; the *picture* is what's important, not the raw information itself.

When we multiply all of a data set by 100, for example, we keep the relationships the same: 5 is to 3 exactly the same as 500 is to 300. If we divide by 10, the relationships stay the same. 1776 is the same to 986 as 177.6 is to 98.6. All we want to do when we compare widely differing data sets is to adjust their figures so they'll fit on the same picture, so we can get a feeling for what their

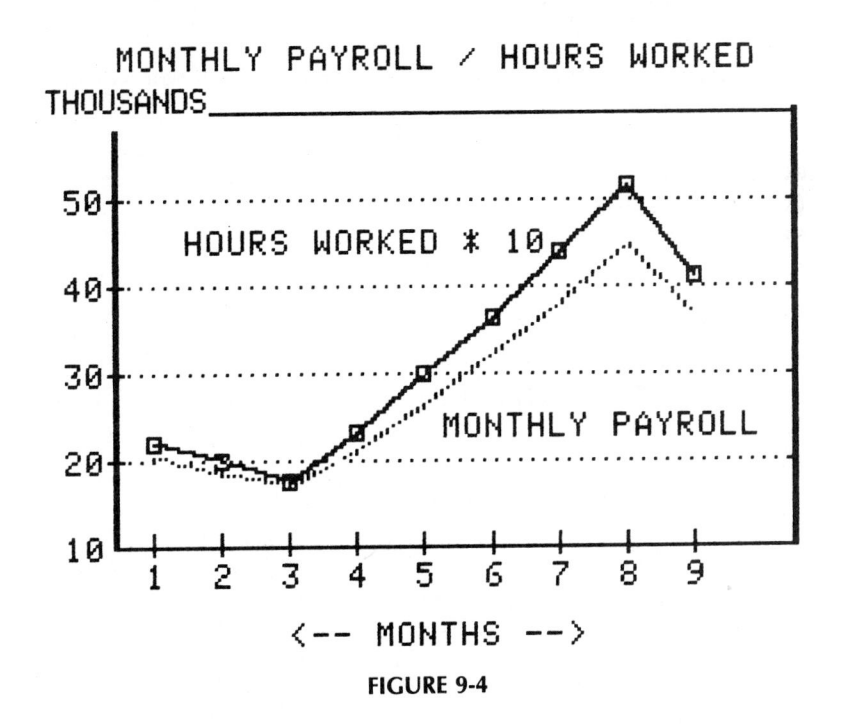

FIGURE 9-4

relationships are. If we multiply by 10, we simply add a zero to each figure. A multiplication by 100 adds two zeroes, and so on. The relationships between the figures remain the same.

Figure 9-4 plots direct labor in its raw form (all the figures are in the thousands) along with hours worked *times ten*. Direct payroll for the first plot shows on the graph as about $21,000; hours worked *times ten* shows as roughly 21,500. If we then *divide* this by ten, we get back to the actual hours worked of 2,150. By multiplying the hours-worked figure by 10, we can put both payroll and the hours-worked data on the same graph.

What does Figure 9-4 tell us? For the first three months, the rate both lines went down was about the same—as payroll decreased, so did the number of hours people put in on the job. That's as it should be. However, the last six months of Figure 9-4 tell us a different story. Now we discover that our payroll is rising at a slightly slower rate than hours worked. Why? Have we changed our basic labor factor? Is our average hourly wage lower than it has been? The gap grows wider, too, as the months go by, through August, although it gets a bit narrower when we examine September's data. Something is happening to our labor, and we need to find out what it is.

A stronger danger sign would be any wide variance—a payroll line running up or down at one rate and an hourly line heading off wildly in its own direction. A number of things can cause a large variation in the rate the numbers move, including a simple slow-down of production time. One extra 15-minute coffee break a day for those 20 employees adds up to five hours per day of lost productivity. This type of change in your operation will show up quickly in a graph of this sort, as it's obvious that a payroll line and an hours-worked line should increase/decrease at the same rate.

Individual Payrolls

In any business with more than one department, it's helpful to break down things by those areas, to determine who's selling, who's making a profit, and so on. While this has long been done on a sales basis, often all payroll is handled at a central location, and so all payroll data is lumped together. If you can get into that information and extract individual amounts for each division or department, you can create two useful graphs.

Figure 9-5 is a column chart for June of 1986. The left (solid) bar totals the sales volume for each individual department of our fictitious business, while the right bar indicates its direct labor costs. Even a cursory examination tells the business owner that the department with the highest sales (building supply) spends more payroll *per sales dollar* than, say, the sheet metal department.

```
        SALES / PAYROLL FOR JUNE, 1986
```

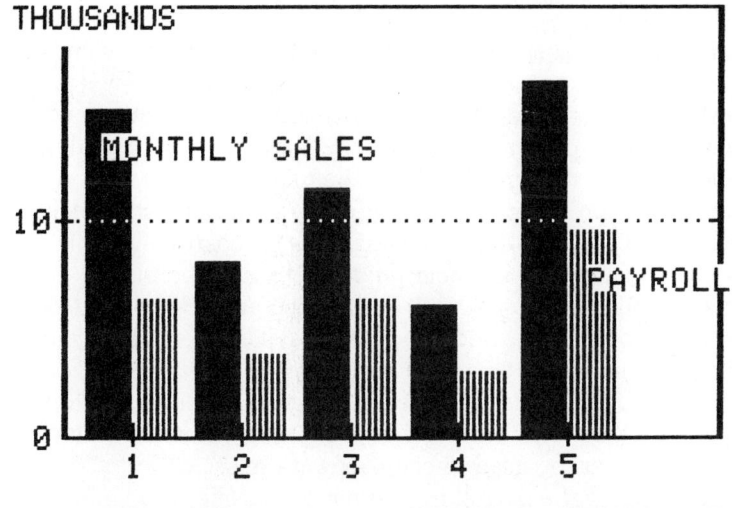

FIGURE 9-5

There could be a good reason for this, of course. The building supply department might require a great deal of labor for each sales dollar it produces. Likewise, the sheet metal department may have a huge product cost involved in what it does, compared to a small labor cost amount.

A similar chart that registers total costs and profit would tell you where the profits were. But the purpose of Figure 9-5 is to compare direct labor and sales, to give the manager a visual picture of how much labor it takes for each department to produce its sales.

As such, a column chart is ideal. Each department's records are broken clearly into two lines, so it's easy to compare one with the other. The individual ratios between labor and sales will vary with each business (and for that matter, with each department within a business). The low labor/high sales of sheet metal or the high labor/low sales of service *might* be exactly right for this particular company. With things broken down in this way, the manager can *see* what the situation is. The general, overall view of total sales and labor costs is just an added benefit from this column chart.

Payroll Pie

Once you have the departmental totals, the first thing most businesspeople will do is to create a sales and profit breakdown so they can see where their profits come from. A pie chart is ideal to display this. While this chapter is on payroll, we can get a helpful comparison if we use the pie chart breakdown of profits alongside a pie chart of payroll costs for the different divisions.

Figure 9-6 is a profit picture for June of 1986, for each individual department. The percentages listed represent the share each department contributed to the total profit the business as a whole produced. If that profit was $10,000, then Sheet Metal provided 23%, or $2,300, of the total profit. While this picture is one every business should create and tells a story all its own, it's even more revealing once you put it next to the payroll picture.

Even though pie charts aren't really designed to compare things, when you have two similar pies (two data sets representing the same branch or type of information), they can be used to compare data sets.

Figure 9-7 takes the payroll figures for this business and breaks them down into its five departments, by percent. Again this chart can stand alone and tell its own story. Wholesale, as you might expect, gets the smallest share of the

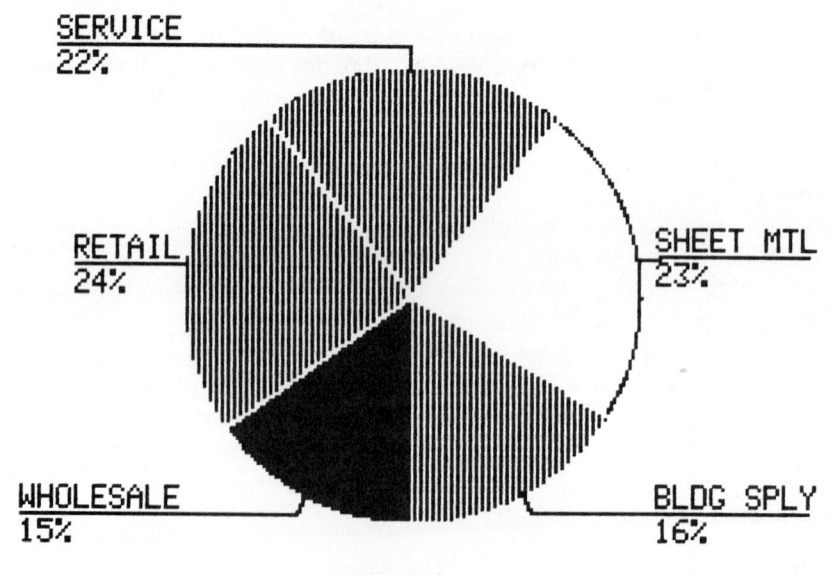

FIGURE 9-6

PAYROLL BY DEPARTMENT FOR JUNE 1986

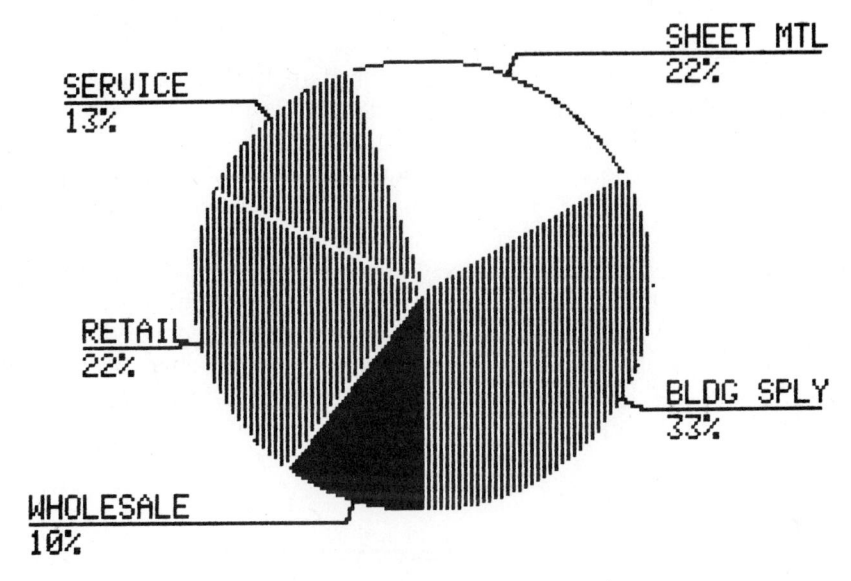

SHEET MTL 22%
SERVICE 13%
RETAIL 22%
WHOLESALE 10%
BLDG SPLY 33%

FIGURE 9-7

PAYROLL & PROFIT AS A % OF THEIR TOTALS

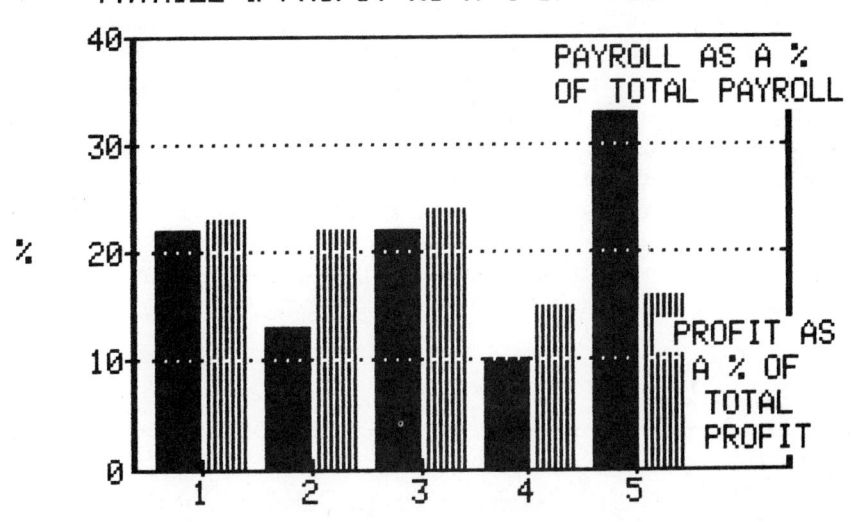

PAYROLL AS A % OF TOTAL PAYROLL

PROFIT AS A % OF TOTAL PROFIT

1= SHEET METAL   2= SERVICE DEPARTMENT
3= RETAIL   4= WHOLESALE
5= BUILDING SUPPLY

FIGURE 9-8

payroll dollar. Building supply, which produced the highest dollar volume, also ate up the largest amount of the payroll pie. Again, you'd expect that.

What turns out to be a surprise is that four of the departments produced a profit percentage in excess of the payroll percentage they drained from the business. Each of the four did better than its payroll share. Building supplies, though, while it still produced a profit (which after all, is better than a loss) took 33% of the labor dollar but only provided 16% of the net profit.

While each of those pie charts can stand on their own and still give us a comparison, we can combine their information in a column chart as was done in Figure 9-8.

Now we can see a direct comparison on a percentage basis of our payroll costs to the profit produced for each department for this particular business. Four of the five parts of our enterprise are making a profit percentage that's *higher* than its percentage of labor costs. This combined column chart makes things even clearer and easier to understand. Unless the figures are normal, there's a definite problem in building supply.

Where to Look

What this sort of comparison gives you is an indication that something might be wrong out there in building supply. Perhaps it's not; some areas of any business will not produce the profit they should. This sort of breakdown might be perfectly proper for this particular department. It might even be a loss leader of sorts—a necessary area to have available for your customers, who you hope will come in to shop in building supply but buy from another department.

However, this same graph might show the business owner something he or she didn't know before now—a problem in the building supply department.

The point is, of course, that without this sort of visual communication, the business owner might not be aware of the situation in building supply and continue along with one major area of his or her business that doesn't make anywhere near what those invested dollars could be producing.

Inside Payroll

With any payroll the businessperson inherits a number of things; one of the most significant are those lumped together and called *fringe benefits*. These can include anything from vacation pay to insurance to letting someone take home a company vehicle at night. In all cases, they add up to dollars that too often aren't considered when payroll is examined. One of the purposes of any sort of analysis is to get the business owner to consider areas that perhaps haven't been as fully explored as they should be, and your fringe benefit amount is one such cost.

We're no different than anyone else. When we get our paycheck, we look at the take-home pay, the bottom line. Sure, we know all the deductions are listed on the check stub, but who pays much attention to them? It's the same with any fringe benefits you provide to your people. Too soon, they not only don't think of them as a part of their pay, but *expect* to receive this or that and create all sorts of problems when the business tries to cut expenses by eliminating a benefit or two.

Our Sad Story

A few years ago, for example, we allowed each employee to drive a truck home at night. Our thought was that it would eliminate vandalism to the vehicles and provide a good fringe benefit at the same time. We initially calculated that it would cost us about fifty cents per employee per night, considering gas and wear-and-tear, and so on. We took things a step further and let each employee know that this fringe benefit in effect added "X" amount to their pay per hour.

Then along came the oil embargo, and a decision by Uncle Sam that he should control and allocate gasoline. The price per gallon skyrocketed, and with it, our monthly gasoline bill. The condition was aggravated when two of our people moved about 20 miles out of town. But, you can't tell an employee where to live, so we didn't think too much about it. By then the practice of taking a truck home at night was expected. The wife got the car and the husband drove the company truck.

The situation rocked along for some time before we created a graph that showed us our monthly gasoline bills in relation to the prior year's amounts. The difference was astonishing! Our monthly cost for gas had just about doubled, and we really didn't realize it. Well, the trucks were soon back on our lot (vandalism or not) and you can imagine the picture our graph of gasoline usage showed then: *it dropped*.

Charting Fringes

The point of all this is to make you aware that fringe benefits have a way of not only entrenching themselves in our everyday work, but of growing while we don't see their increased cost. Part of the problem is that often—in dollar amounts—fringe benefits are considerably smaller than the payroll figures we work with, and so have a tendency to be forgotten. As we know, this holds true for both management and labor; graphs that chart fringe benefit costs let both parties know what's going on.

We can use the same method we learned earlier—to multiply the fringe benefit cost by 10 or 100 or whatever to get it in the same general area as payroll. After all, what we want to examine is the *rate* of change and any differences between the two lines. They should go hand-in-hand; as payroll increases, so should our fringe benefit cost total. If they don't follow one another, it's an indication of a possible problem.

The first way to examine the relationship between payroll and your fringe benefits is with a column chart like Figure 9-9. This shows the direct payroll amounts as the right bar and the fringe benefit amounts multiplied by 10 as the left bar. Probably the most significant thing this particular graph tells us is that payroll generally is about 10 times greater than this business's cost for fringe benefits, at least during the six-month period examined. Put another way, this business spends 10% over and above its net labor dollar for fringe benefits, dollars its employees might not even realize they're receiving. There are some minor variations in the monthly totals, probably because the fringe benefits aren't always paid during the same month the payroll is for.

In this example, for some reason fringe benefit costs took a jump in June to where there's a marked difference between the two columns.

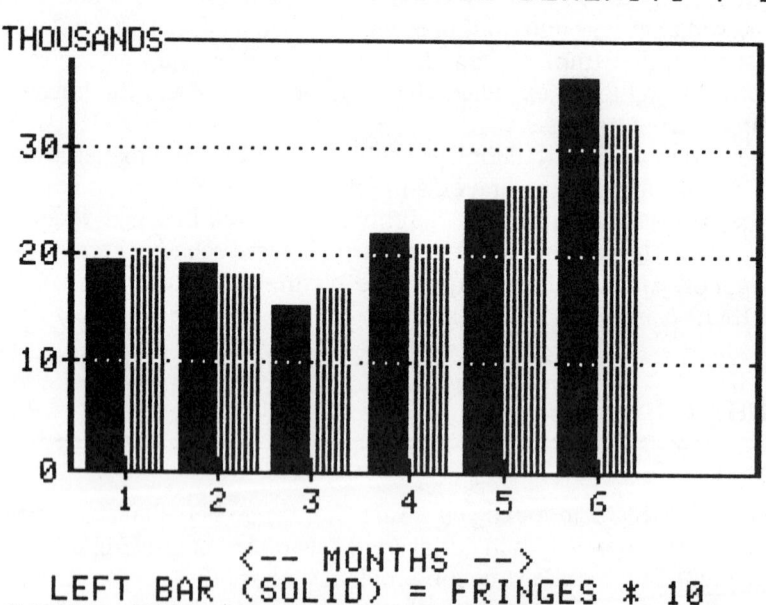

FIGURE 9-9

The business owner would look at this chart and wonder why the lines were about the same for five months and then made a significant change. Did everyone start to take their trucks home? Were some people given an extra vacation day or two during this period? Did a big raise go into effect? While the raise itself won't directly add to the cost of fringe benefits, many of us have agreements that affect this fringe or that based on the pay rate. If these benefits are on a percentage basis, a jump in pay might cause a significant difference in your fringe benefit cost. The alert manager will note the change in the monthly figures and set out to discover why it happened.

A Step Further

While the businessperson who looked at Figure 9-9 saw only a half-year's totals (and thus is at a disadvantage), let's suppose you had the yearly amounts calculated and held Figure 9-10 in front of you. This is another look at payroll compared to fringe benefits multiplied by ten. The line chart, as we know, gives us more of a moving picture of the image and is a useful adjunct to the same data on a column graph.

You can immediately see the jump in fringe benefit costs that started in

FIGURE 9-10

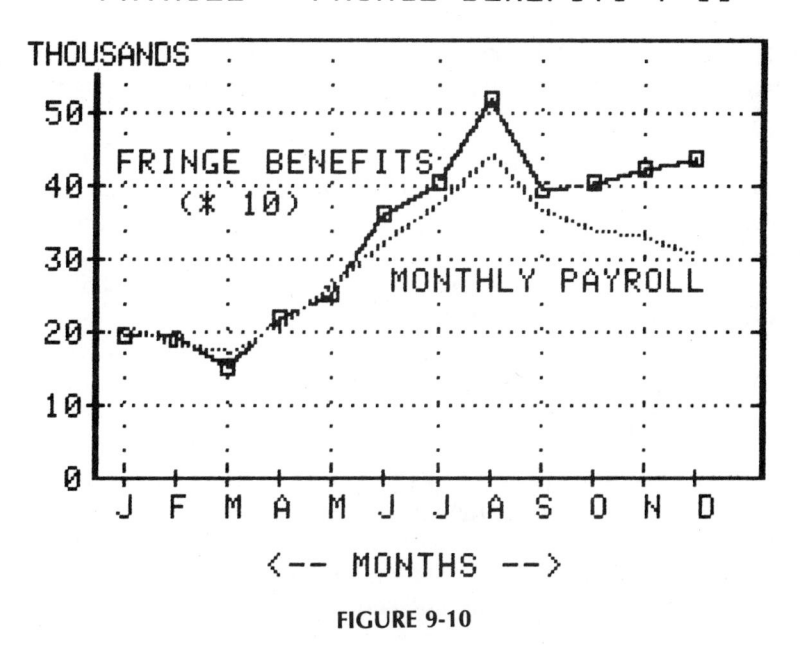

May and probably have a good idea why it happened. The lines are parallel for some time, but then in October they made another split. This one is more significant and dangerous than the last, as the former leveled off while this one takes us to the end of the year with our payroll and fringe benefit lines moving in opposite directions. Our payroll shows a reduction, but the fringe benefit line has on its own started increasing at what appears to be the same rate as payroll is decreasing.

This situation is completely untenable. No later than October, the manager should have started to search for the reason why the two lines were heading apart. By November, where the situation has gotten worse, she or he should have found the solution and implemented whatever steps were required to reverse it. Now, December's come and gone and the situation is worse and deteriorating rapidly.

Why are fringe benefits out of control? Are the figures right? Was there some *deferred* payroll—an amount we'll pay an employee at some future date—that wasn't included in the payroll amount but whose fringe costs were added into fringe benefit totals? Did something in the union contract trigger an increased layout? Did insurance rates double? There obviously can be any number of reasons for the shift, and it's vital the business owner discover the reason and, to the best extent possible, change policies so the amounts start to get back on the same line.

At the very least, assuming the figures are right, it's necessary to inform the employees of their new-found gains, to make them aware of the raise they perhaps didn't expect and probably don't see or appreciate.

Payroll's Relation to Profit

Payroll has, of course, a definite affect on the bottom line. If we can somehow cut our total payroll, we'll make more money. If our people slow down and payroll costs increase, we'll find less money in the till come the end of the year. Every business has a historical figure for payroll—if labor's percentage stays below "X" amount, the business will make money. If not, if the payroll total is above "X" percent, the business will end up in the red.

While it's helpful to compare payroll and labor to other amounts, one of the best comparisons is to the sales figure itself. If you go back through your records, you'll find that for those periods where your labor was less than 25% of sales you made money, and where it ran over 25% of the monthly sales volume, you lost money. The actual percentage will vary, of course, with every business, but in most cases you'll find it's a surprisingly correct number to use.

Once you know that, it's an easy matter to create a line chart like Figure 9-11, which shows payroll as a percentage of gross sales, on a monthly basis.

Figure 9-11 tells the businessperson a number of things. First, for some

PAYROLL AS A PERCENT OF SALES

FIGURE 9-11

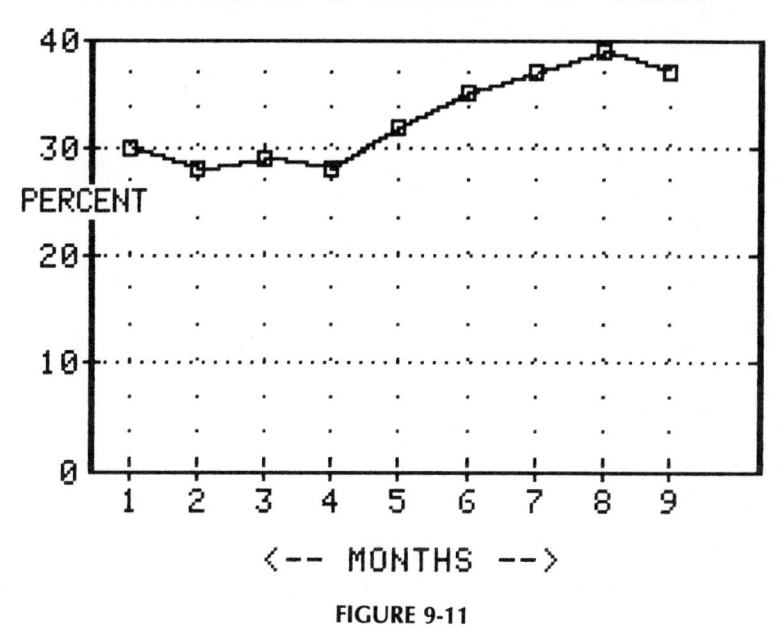

reason the payroll as a percentage of sales took a big jump in May. While it started coming down in September, there was a four-month period where it was considerably higher than it had been earlier in the year. The sign that it's coming down in September can be viewed as a positive one, perhaps as the direct result of management's efforts to reduce it to a lower percentage.

Now if this business's historical average indicated that it made money whenever its payroll averaged less than 40% of gross sales, the business owner would feel pretty comfortable. While the percentage started to rise in May and almost got to the breakeven point in August, the drop in September is an encouraging sign.

What if this business only made money when its payroll percentage was 30% or below? Early in the year it flirted right on the edge of major problems and jumped off when May arrived, as its payroll as a percentage of sales took a huge jump. Even with the slight drop in September, this business has a real problem as its direct labor percentage is still up around 38%. Even the bit of profit it made during the first quarter of the year cannot compensate for the money it has lost since.

It appears that whoever managed this business missed a significant warning back in May and ignored it ever since. But perhaps that's too harsh a judgement; the owner might not have *known* the relationship between sales and payroll, and sadly, just didn't realize what was happening to the business. Again, that's why

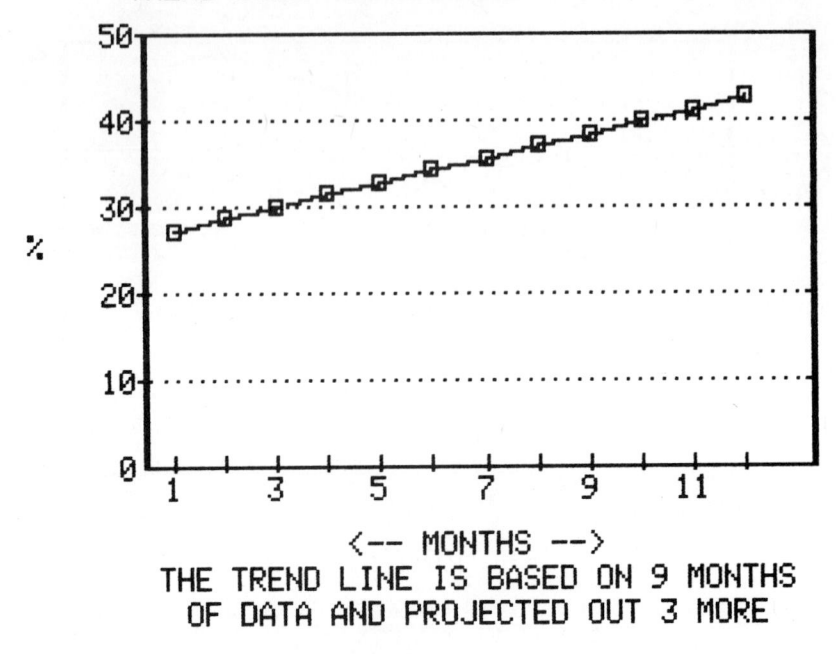

```
           TREND LINE FOR PAYROLL AS A % OF SALES
       50
       40
    %  30
       20
       10
        0
           1     3     5     7     9     11
                   <-- MONTHS -->
           THE TREND LINE IS BASED ON 9 MONTHS
           OF DATA AND PROJECTED OUT 3 MORE
```

FIGURE 9-12

we spend the time to dig out the information and chart it—it can act as an early sign of approaching danger.

An obvious way to improve the warning these figures might give you is to let your plotting program calculate a trend line, based on your own figures. This will give you a sense of which direction those amounts are heading.

Figure 9-12 charts a trend line based on the latest nine months of figures and projects them for another three months. While this is too short a time span on which to base any major decisions, it at least is a starting point, and tells you that payroll, as a percentage of your total sales, is going in the wrong direction. Since it's based on recent data, it has the benefit of being current, and the short (three month) projection on this graph should be reasonably accurate.

Payroll and Cash Problems

As anyone who's had to meet a payroll knows, you must have the cash in hand on payday. With most other bills, a delay of a few days might cost you some interest and a black mark in your credit file, but little else. With payroll, though, your employees expect their checks, and the business must be able to cover them.

Because of this, there's a distinct relationship between cash flow and your payroll requirements.

In the chapter on cash flow we saw the results of a situation that happens to many small businesses, and often they're not aware of it. They'll get a terrific spurt in sales, but since the customer payments for those sales *lags* a bit behind the sales themselves, the business owner is put into a cash-poor situation. Payment must often be made before the cash is collected for the work.

This same thing exists for payroll, but on a more definite basis. While material suppliers can often be put off for a time until your anticipated cash arrives, your employees expect their checks on payday. So every week or every two weeks (whenever you pay), the cash in your bank account must cover the cash outgo for payroll and its associated taxes.

The next illustration assumes a few things about some of the amounts we've used as examples. In this case, it's based on the assumption that the costs for this business average half material and half labor. It follows, then, that one-half of its *net cash* will go for payroll. The term *net cash* can be defined as the cash you have left once your overhead amount has been removed.

This is, of course, exactly backwards from the way most business owners look at cash—they think once they've received "X" amount of dollars, if they pay their material and labor costs, what's left is for overhead and profit. But in real life, the overhead amounts *must* be paid along with materials and labor. The phone company won't wait for its money with any more patience than your material suppliers will.

In effect, this means you need to go through the following simple calculations to determine how much cash you'll have available for payroll, and then with a graph you can quickly see if it'll be enough.

You start with the cash you expect to collect (or did collect) for the period you're working with. In this case, we're doing things on a monthly basis. Let's imagine your cash inflow for March is $36,307. Let's also suppose the overhead for your business runs 23% of sales, so you can expect to spend about 23% of your cash (since it's based on sales) on overhead. 23% of $36,397 is $8,351.

If you deduct this amount from your available cash, you have:

total cash	$36,307
− cash for overhead	− 8,351
net available cash	$27,956

Each business varies, of course, in how it distributes its money for labor and materials, but as noted, let's assume this business has about a fifty-fifty breakdown. Half of the total available of $27,956 could pay labor costs and the other half will be used to pay for material used. This means that $13,978 is the total available during March for payroll purposes. If your net payroll is more than this figure, you have a problem.

Figure 9-13 tracks the payroll amounts and the cash available for payroll

```
CASH COLLECTED / NEEDED FOR PAYROLL
THOUSANDS
```

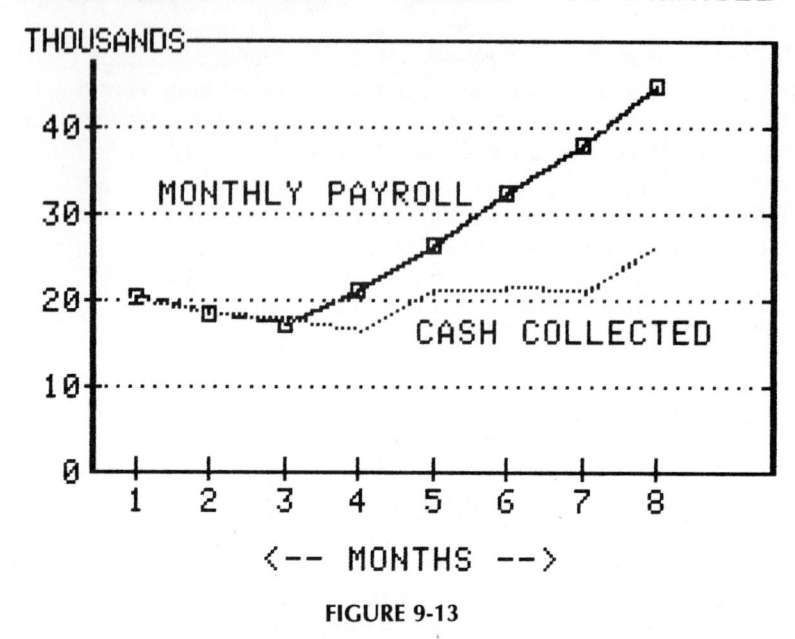

FIGURE 9-13

for the first eight months of the year. The payroll is the actual monthly payroll cost for our fictitious business and cash plotted is what's left when you remove 23% (for overhead) of the total cash collected and then divide by two—this business uses 50% of its cash for labor and 50% for materials.

For the first quarter of the year, there's a bit of a cash surplus in the payroll account. However, when sales start their summer spurt in May, payroll also takes a huge jump. Throughout the summer the situation gets worse as the need for payroll dollars constantly outstrips the available funds.

In effect, since you must make payroll every week, dollars are stolen from other areas of the business (material purchases, overhead, profit) to make up the difference. These other areas suffer, of course, because then there aren't enough dollars to handle their cash requirements.

While this example might appear exaggerated, even if we split the total cash in half (and assumed we'd pay the overhead out of leftover funds), this business will *still* be cash-poor from May on.

When the situation reversed itself after the first quarter, the smart businessperson would take some steps to increase the cash available for payroll. Perhaps you can ask for a partial payment when the contract is signed, or work on a "draw" basis where you can collect something every month based on the percentage of completion. This isn't a *total* cash problem—it will eventually catch up—but a *cash flow* problem. The point is, when you see something coming along (as shown in Figure 9-13) in April and May, and especially when the lines

```
            SALES AND PAYROLL TREND LINES
     THOU
      80+
      60+
   $
      40+
      20+
       0
         1   3   5   7   9   11  13  15
              <-- MONTHS -->
         THESE TREND LINES ARE BASED ON 12
       MONTHS OF DATA AND PROJECT OUT 3 MORE
```

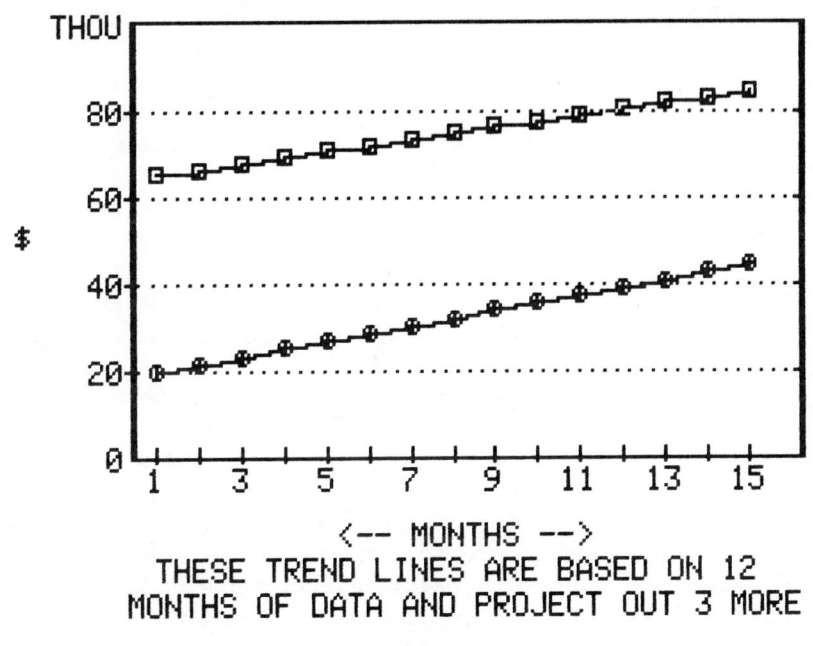

FIGURE 9-14

really start to spread out as they do in June, you have a major problem that's getting worse by the day, and something must be done to correct it.

One other approach is to compare the trend lines of two data sets, rather than just plot a trend line along with the information it's associated with.

Figure 9-14 charts two trend lines—for sales and for payroll—with each based on 12 months of data, and projected for three more months. Both figures show about the same amount of rise, so this is the image we'd want, as it indicates that our labor costs are rising at about the same rate as our total sales.

Summing Up

Even though payroll forms a little niche all of its own, the businessperson can use a microcomputer to examine it in detail, to find out exactly where the payroll dollars go.

There's usually a direct relationship between the sales we make and our payroll cost. Naturally, if we can somehow produce more sales with the same amount of labor, that's terrific—but unusual. More often an increase in sales volume means we have to hire more help or have our people work longer hours.

The first graph to create to examine payroll is a line chart that plots sales and direct labor payroll costs. If either line has decided to head off in its own direction for one reason or another, we'll be able to see it and note its rate of change. A minor shift or two probably means little; a major variance between the lines might signal an upcoming major problem.

Another useful thing that helps us understand where all of those payroll dollars have gone is a historical line chart over a three- to five-year period. Since this sort of thing really pushes the data together, we get an image of the *flow* of the information, where it rises and where it falls during each year. If there's an aberration somewhere in our current data, we usually can spot it.

Anyone in a manufacturing business has a bit of an advantage in that they usually can measure their exact output in relationship to payroll. Each dollar of payroll produces "X" number of items, and it's easy to chart and see any variations. The average retail store lumps everything together (both for sales and for payroll), and so it's a bit more difficult to evaluate how its workers are doing.

One way is to compare the number of hours worked to the net payroll—both of these totals should be easy to collect. While these figures will often be wide apart in terms of raw numbers, we can adjust one or the other by multiplying or dividing by something that will add or subtract zeroes from the end (by 10, 100, and so on). That way, we can plot them on the same graph, with the same scale. Generally these lines should increase and decrease at the same rate, unless there's a marked change in the hourly rates of pay.

If your business includes separate divisions or departments, it's helpful to break out the individual information for their payrolls, and equally useful to examine the payroll data compared to the sales each department produces. Does the labor for one division or department far outstrip the profits it contributes? Should it? Could it do better? While a column chart is the ideal way to look at these sorts of figures, you can also use two pie charts next to each other to get a feeling for profits compared to labor costs per department.

We also need to take things a bit further inside of our payroll and look at fringe benefits—those dollars our people might not even realize they're receiving. Often, too, fringe benefits have a way of becoming invisible to the business owner, and a study of payroll will perhaps bring things to our attention that we haven't considered in some time. What percentage of the labor total do fringe benefits amount to? Is it high or low? Growing or shrinking? While fringe benefit amounts *should* rise and fall with labor costs, do they?

Payroll can also serve as a profit indicator. There's a specific historical percentage of sales figure that each business's labor should be *less than* for those periods when the business earns a profit. If you check your past history you can usually get a good idea as to what this percentage is for your own business. Once you know it, you can chart the monthly percentage figure that labor is to sales and have a good idea whether you made money during the period the data is for.

Finally, since your employees expect their paychecks on payday, payroll has a distinct relationship to cash flow. In some businesses, particularly those that are highly seasonal, there are certain times of the year when sales boom—and with the growth in sales comes a huge increase in costs, including payroll. While we have to cover the paychecks we write *on payday,* often we don't get paid for the work our people do until a month or two later. This can create a real problem with our cash, as we're often forced to rob dollars from payments that should go to our material suppliers and/or for overhead items, to make payroll.

We can plot our cash and payroll information so we have something of a moving line—it changes every month—to get a feeling for where the two data sets are heading. If we can spot this cash deficiency in advance, we have the chance to do something to correct it.

Other Ideas

While we've suggested a number of specific graphs to use to examine payroll, often there are other areas you can look at to gain some insight into where your payroll dollars are going.

For instance, it might be useful to plot what your average dollar per hour payroll cost is this year, compared to last.

It also is a good idea to plot your fringe benefit costs for this year and last, to get a feeling for how they're moving, if they're growing faster than perhaps they should.

There are a number of associated taxes involved with payroll that, like fringe benefits, often aren't considered as part of your total cost. But they are, as usually they're collected as a *percentage* of your payroll total; as your payroll increases, so do these taxes. It's helpful to plot them on a monthly basis from year to year, just to see that something's not being figured incorrectly. It's also useful to look at the taxes in a pie chart format—again, to see where our dollars are being spent.

Inventory

10

Any business owner fights a constant battle with inventory: you worry over what to order and when to order it, have to work to get it delivered on time, wonder if it will sell once it's in stock, have to care for and insure it until it's sold, and then you worry if you'll get paid once the items are gone. While it's a truism for any business that without inventory you'll soon be out of business, it's equally true that without the *right products* to sell, at the *right price,* your business will be on the ropes just as fast.

Often, a business owner whose retail sales are minimal assumes that a lot of things about inventory don't apply to his or her work. The feeling is that only *retailers* have inventory problems. But oddly, it's often the company that doesn't have racks filled with product that needs the most help in understanding inventory control. Even a real estate company (that markets something hard to define—customer service) still must have the right product available for each prospect, at the right price. They must have the right "inventory" in terms of the listings they carry, the best financing contacts (to help prospects "buy"), the proper people to create and present contracts, and so on. The insurance company (who sells more of an intangible than an insurance business?) must have the right "inventory" for its prospects, plans and ideas that people are interested in and will buy *today,* the right prices, good merchandising and so on, or it, like the retailer, will soon be out of business.

Someone on the wholesale level faces many of the same inventory problems the retail store owner does, with one added difficulty: the quantities a wholesaler works with (and thus the costs) are often huge. Order dates sometimes must be months in advance of when you feel you'll need the products, because of the quantity of merchandise involved. While the wholesaler has little customer *shop-*

ping, cost is often more of a factor than in the retail world—and so, then, is the price at which the wholesaler buys merchandise. An extra percentage spent at the time of purchase may mean thousands of dollars in lost sales because buyers in the wholesale market are so price-conscious.

The Nonretailer

Often, too, the company that relies on major equipment sales for much of its sales volume finds itself with inventory problems. Not in the sense that they don't have the right equipment on hand, as customers often expect that their purchase (car, air conditioning system, custom-made bookcases) will have to be ordered or produced, but since they don't see day-to-day operations in the same light that retailers do, they have problems looking at inventory the right way. Since "we have to order that, you know" is the byword, they feel they don't have any inventory difficulties.

The retailer watches as customers come into his or her store, notices how they examine this or that piece of merchandise, note how they weigh its price against a value picture they have in their mind, and make a buying decision. If the customer walks out and leaves the item still on the retailer's shelf, the business owner knows (1) the product was wrong for this customer, (2) the price was too high for this customer, or perhaps, (3) this customer was just shopping. Whatever the case, the sale was not made and the businessperson knows it instantly. Once they see a particular item examined and not purchased time after time, it's clear the price is incorrect according to what the prospects feel it should be and/or the people who do consider the item aren't really prospects for it.

But the business owner who must *order* most of what he or she sells just doesn't see this daily interaction between merchandise and potential customer. If your business operates on a "per order" basis, it's vital to understand that the same relationship exists between your products and your prospects as exists between the retail store and its customers. Even though you don't have everything on hand—it has to be ordered or produced to order—you still must have access to the right merchandise, the right inventory, at the right price.

In our heating and air conditioning business, for instance, it's impossible (from a financial standpoint) to keep every size of every furnace and/or air conditioning unit on hand. They have to be ordered, and our customers usually don't have a problem with this process. These days, one major concern of anyone who's considering this sort of purchase is *energy efficiency.* "How much will it cost to operate?" is a question we get every day, from nearly every prospect we talk to. They want to know what the most efficient unit is, why it'll cost less than another brand or system, and focus on that during the buying/selling process. Even though we don't have these units in stock, we *must* be able to talk intelligently about what's available, show a prospect why she or he should purchase this or that system, and so on. While we don't have a warehouse filled with merchandise of all assorted shapes, sizes, and efficiencies, we still have to have it available, know about it, be able to price it right, and so on—exactly like the retailer.

Sales and Inventory

While it's obvious when you think about it, one of the primary functions of management is to make sure there's enough of whatever you sell *on hand* to supply the needs and wants of your customers. Surprisingly, many businesspeople tend to ignore this part of their operation, and turn over the control and management of whatever inventory system is in use to someone not qualified in any manner to determine what to buy, where to purchase it, and when to place the order. Too often the duties of inventory control fall to the person who puts away the stock: that employee is left to record what came in and went out, to fill out purchase orders, and so on. Or the business owner simply orders what he or she feels necessary, just because a salesperson took him or her out to lunch today. The end result is the business doesn't have the right product to sell at the right time, and/or at the correct price.

It's a funny thing, but have you ever gone into any of the nationally franchised fast-food chains and found them out of something? Sure, they might have an equipment breakdown and so might not be able to make that milk shake you ordered, but have they ever been out of hamburgers? Buns? French fries? Why not? Well, you think, *that's their business,* and you're right. But isn't the same true in your own line of work? Enough said.

Inside Inventory

Business graphics are probably not the best way to examine the product quantities you should have on hand (there are mathematical formulas to tell you that), and perhaps not even a really helpful way to determine when one item or another should be ordered. Instead, graphics lend themselves to a detailed look at specific aspects of the inventory process, details that might escape a casual glance at the procedure.

As with sales, we're not going to chart the obvious—total inventory this year versus last is the one that most people automatically track. It's one you may want to follow, of course, on a monthly basis, as it gives you a feel for one year compared to the other. Since you know how you did financially last year, you'll gain an idea of how things are going this year.

Because everything in any business starts with sales, we'll begin at the same point with inventory. There's always a connection between the sales we produce and the inventory we control. This doesn't necessarily mean that more inventory will mean more sales (it might, though—will it for *your* business?).

Figure 10-1 is a simple line graph that plots the month-end sales for our fictitious business, along with month-end inventory totals, over a 12-month period. As we know, this sort of graph can cover a calendar year period or the latest 12 months, whichever the business owner finds most helpful at a particular time.

This is the picture you should get when you compare sales and inventory—as your sales increase, your inventory total will rise to support it—or is it vice versa? It seems to be a question of what comes first (like the chicken or the egg)—does more inventory produce more in sales, or does an increase in sales volume *force* a growth in the stock on hand? While each business is different, it's obvious that you won't have any sales unless you have something to sell, so it stands to reason that inventory is the starting point for all that follows. The sales line will go up and down more sharply than the inventory line, as your sales data are plotted on a retail basis, while your inventory totals are recorded at their wholesale cost.

It's more of a help to take this same information and use a spreadsheet program to divide your inventory figures by your total monthly sales, to see what percentage your inventory is of your total sales. Figure 10-2 illustrates this.

Again, this is the picture you'd expect to see, as your inventory as a percentage of your total sales remains pretty steady. There was a little blip early in

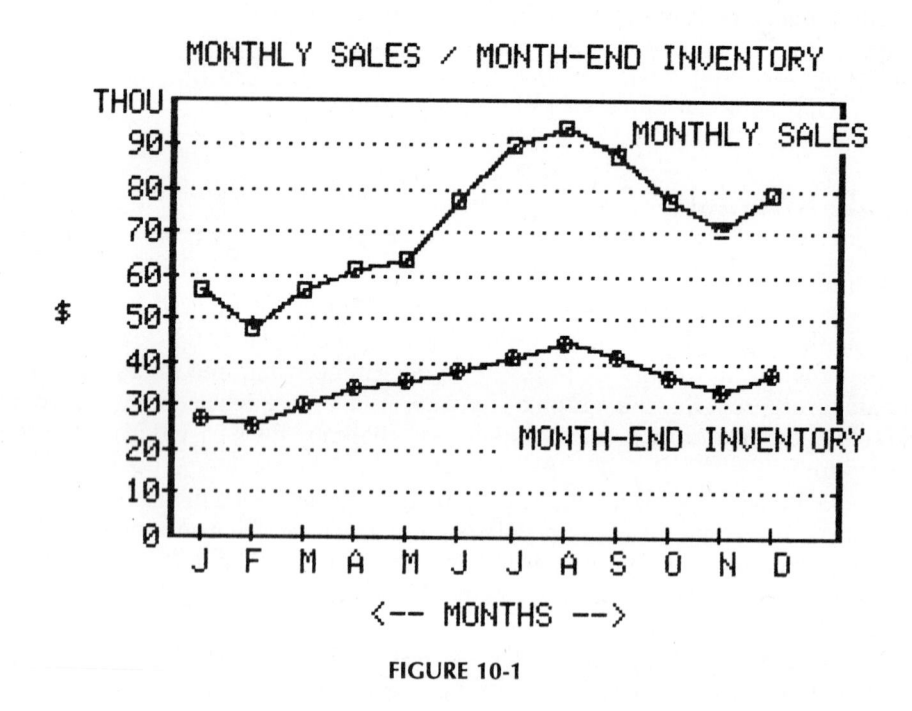

FIGURE 10-1

INVENTORY AS A PERCENT OF SALES

FIGURE 10-2

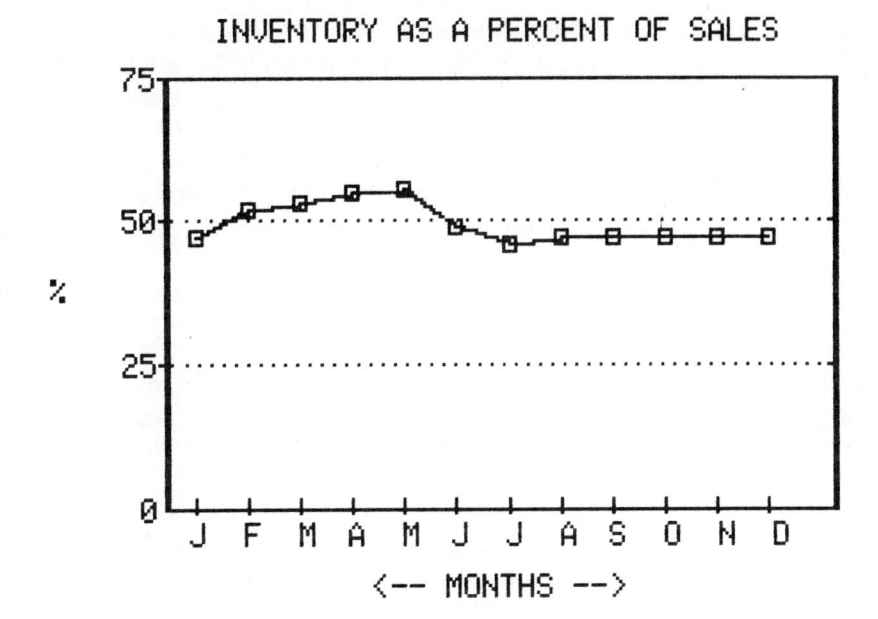

the period where the dollars you had invested in inventory totaled more than half of your sales volume. That might be fine, of course, for some businesses, and not for others. In this particular example, since the rest of the data indicates that the inventory amount is most often less than 50% of the sales figure, when it rose above that mark it should have warned the business owner that there could be a problem with inventory. As your inventory as a percentage of sales starts to increase, it's a sign that what you have in stock simply isn't moving. Since the percentage figure is directly tied to sales, an increase points a worrisome finger right at inventory as a problem area. There are only two reasons for inventory to increase as a percentage of your total sales: if your inventory value increases and/or sales decrease—both of which mean what you have on hand simply isn't selling. Period.

Moving the Stock

Probably the most widely accepted method to examine inventory is to look at its turnover rate—how often you *turn*, or sell, the stock you have on hand. This is most often expressed in the number of days it takes your inventory to be sold and taken out of stock. This figure is computed by taking the cost of goods sold for a particular period and dividing it by the average inventory during the same period. On a yearly basis, you'd calculate your average inventory by adding up the totals for each month-end inventory figure and dividing the result by 12.

If you spent $500,000 for merchandise during one year, and your inventory during this same time averaged out to $50,000, you can say that you *turned* your inventory ten times. You carried an average stock of $50,000 and sold (on a cost basis) $500,000 worth of merchandise—ten times the amount you had on hand, on the average.

If you spent that same $500,000 on merchandise (the *cost of goods sold* figure from your income statement) and maintained an average inventory of $100,000, then you only turned your stock five times.

Generally, the more often you can move your stock, the more profit the business will make, as the whole idea in any business is to *sell* things. In a moment we'll move to a method that ties your inventory directly to sales, but let's examine what a graphed turnover rate looks like.

Figure 10-3 shows how often, in days, our fictional business turned its inventory, on a historical basis. This figure is calculated by dividing 365 (days in a year) by the turnover rate (in the example above, the 10 or 5 times each year the inventory turned). If your inventory turned 10 times over the year, you divide 365 (days) by 10 for a result of 36.5—every 36½ days, you moved your

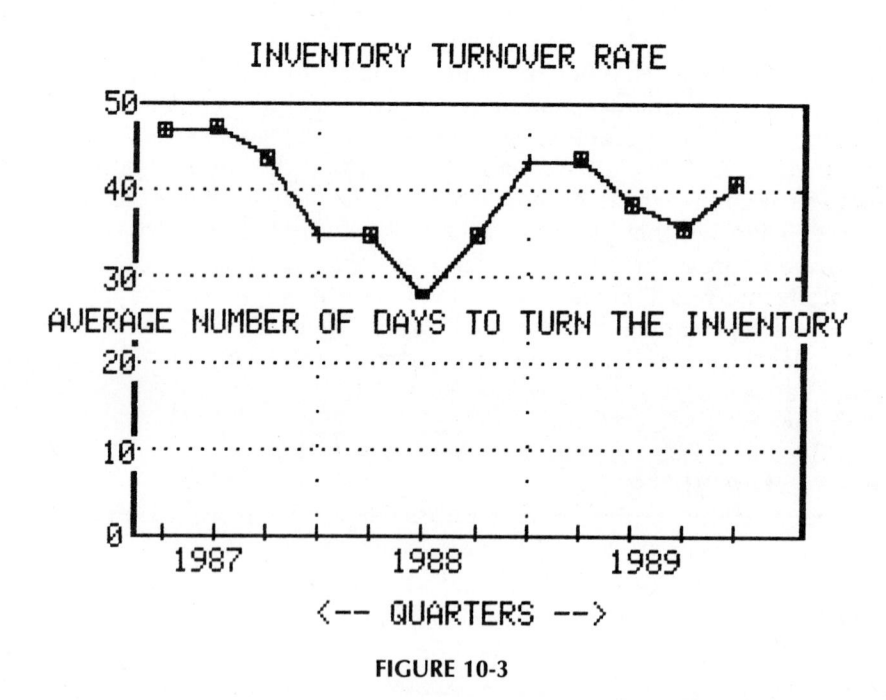

FIGURE 10-3

entire stock of inventory. The second example, where the turnover rate was 5, yields 365/5, or 73—it took you 73 days to turn your stock.

It's obvious that the business that can move more products will be more successful, so the general rule of thumb is to work to lower your turnover rate. The spreadsheet program you use to track your financial information (before you send it to your graphics package) is ideal for doing these calculations for you.

Figure 10-3 plots the average days our fictitious business took to turn its inventory. It's an interesting look at things, as you can almost gauge the profitability of the business once you discover how successful it is at making sales, moving its inventory.

1987 was a good year (at least in the terms we're currently examining). From the first two quarters where the business moved things over about a 48-day period, the end of the year found it with only about a 33-day turnover period. Stock was simply moving much faster. Whatever the business was doing, it was doing it right, as by mid-year 1988, the turnover rate was under 30 days.

Then things took a turn for the worse, and the rate at which this business moved its stock started to rise. By the end of 1989, after showing an improvement along with a few discouraging periods, the business found itself with a 40-day turnover period.

Why were there fluctuations? Since this information ties the cost of the goods you buy and put into stock directly to the sales you make (in terms of inventory cost as it leaves your store), it simply means there were periods when the stock on hand was not selling. *Why not?* is obviously the question you must answer—how would you do so if this were your business?

While general business conditions obviously influence how your sales are, even in bad times some businesses do well. Why? There's no complex answer—they simply sell what they have available for sale. As we know, this covers a lot of ground, and includes not just retail inventory, but merchandise that must be ordered and/or produced to order. What information would you collect and look at to find out why your turnover rate varied so widely?

One good way would be to go back through your past records and examine—closely—what you had on hand during the slow periods, as well as what you had in stock when things were moving rapidly. A comparison of the two lists (and they probably can be pretty general) will give you the answer you need. You most likely won't have to list 100 individual items, but you can concentrate on *areas* of your work, general sections here and there that you had more (or less) inventory for.

Perhaps you'll discover that in the slow periods you had a lot of "X" items laying around, while in the better periods you carried only a few of those, but more of the products your "Y" department sold, and in the best periods you concentrated on "Z" items.

You might also want to examine and study the advertising you did, especially in relation to the items that did move well. Were there special promotions that worked particularly well? Sales for this or that? Did advertising in one media or another lower or raise your turnover rate?

Days of Sales

Any examination of inventory should include a look at a different approach to the relationship between the stock you have on hand and the sales you make with it. For this examination to be accurate, the sales figure you divide your inventory into should be the sales you record that can be traced directly to that inventory stock. Labor and items that have to be ordered should not be totaled in your sales amount, as they did not come from your on-hand inventory.

Since inventory is most often recorded on a cost basis, and your sales are totaled at a retail level, to link the two accurately means you need to adjust one of the amounts; the easiest thing to do is to use inventory—for this purpose—on its retail basis, what you expect to sell it for. For instance, if you normally double the cost of your merchandise to arrive at its selling price, then simply double your inventory cost amount to make the comparisons for this example. If you mark things up by 40%, then divide your inventory cost figures by .60. This is, of course, an ideal task for your spreadsheet package.

For example, if during one month you made sales of $9,000 you can directly trace to your inventory, you can figure that your average daily (from inventory) sale was $300—you just divide 30 days into the $9,000 sales figure. Every day, then, you used up $300 worth of inventory (on a retail basis).

If your inventory at the end of that particular month was $18,000 (again, at the retail price at which you expect to sell the merchandise), you can be said to have 60 days worth of inventory in stock. In other words, you had enough goods on hand to support two month's worth of sales. That's overly obvious with this example, of course, as you could simply divide the monthly sales of $9,000 into the retail inventory total of $18,000 and get the same result: two months. However, the process is exactly the same with odd figures, and again, this is an area where your spreadsheet program can help.

This figure—the days of sales in inventory—can be graphed, just like any other. For most of us, the faster you can turn your stock, the better. Obviously, there has to be a happy medium—if you sell all your inventory too quickly, you're essentially out of business until you can get more into stock. So the smart business owner looks at the days of sales they have available in their inventory from both directions—you don't want too little, or too much, sitting on your shelves.

Figure 10-4 plots the days of sales our fictional business had in its inventory over a 24-month period. Certainly the most significant thing this graph tells us is that this enterprise generally has 40 to 50 days worth of goods on hand at any

DAYS OF SALES IN INVENTORY

FIGURE 10-4

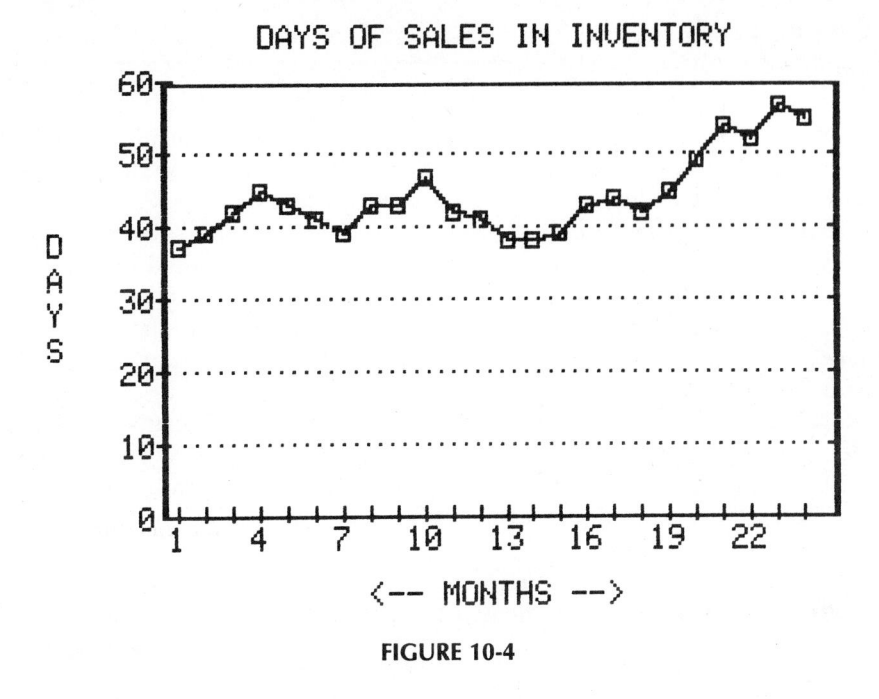

one time. If the business made a profit during this 24-month period, we probably can assume this figure—40 or 50 or so days of sales stored in inventory—is about right. Since this graph was created like our others, we can give some significance to its scale markings; in this case, they were designed to highlight the 40–50 day area.

The break at month 21, then, where the days of sales in inventory rose through the 50-day level (and has remained up there) is a significant change in the way this business is doing its business. Very quickly, the business owner finds he or she is carrying much more inventory than he or she has been, and/or sales have slowed significantly. One of the two has to have happened—since this ratio plots the relationship between sales and inventory, one of the two has changed to create the rise in the plotted line.

The end result of all this means the inventory isn't moving—if it were, sales would be better. This can be the result of poor merchandise selection, incorrect pricing policies, bad service and selling practices, and so on; whatever the reason, the business has a problem with its inventory. For much of the period charted, this business kept around 40 days worth of sales in its on-hand inventory. Now it's got more than 50 days worth of sales stored there—a significant difference in the amount invested in that material. Why isn't it moving?

A Closer Look

When you spot something like the break in what appeared to be a pretty normal operating level (40 to 50 days worth of sales on hand), it's a good idea to take a closer look at things.

Figure 10-5 plots as a light dashed line the same days of sales in inventory figure we just examined. This time though, we've added a trend line based on those 24 months worth of information and asked it to forecast six more months. Of course, the trend line also indicates the general direction our days of sales have been going, which, unfortunately, is up; this is one comparison we'd like to head downward.

The business owner who looks at these last two graphs can see there is a problem and knows where the problem is—in the goods in stock. There *must* be a problem with the inventory, as it's simply not selling. If it were, sales would be up and so the inventory figure would decrease—and with it, the days of sales stored there.

In reality, Figure 10-5 should have been created before the breakthrough at month 21, as it may have indicated the problem before it became a serious

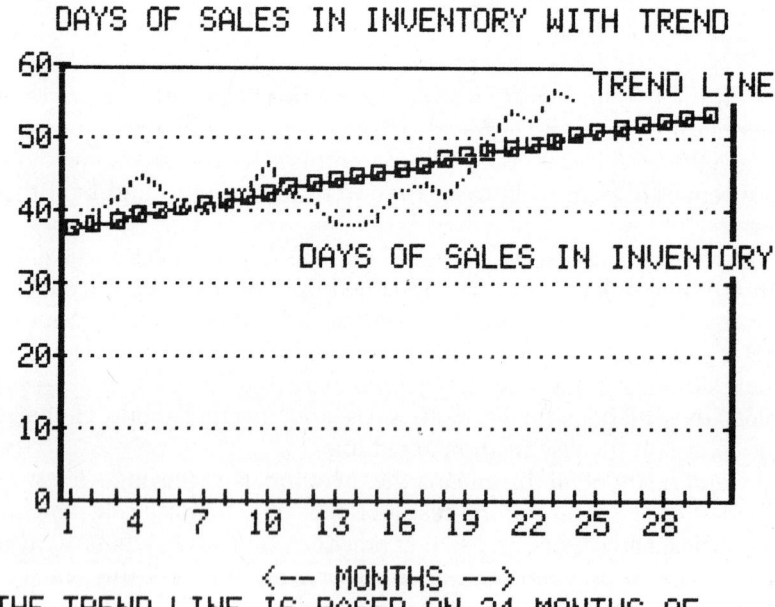

FIGURE 10-5

difficulty. Now the business owner finds there have been four months of high inventory levels, a rising trend and, worst of all, a seemingly poor inventory selection to try to get rid of. It's a difficult thing to correct at this stage, because the stock on hand, if it was right for the market and priced properly, would be selling. Sadly, it isn't.

This particular graph is really useful to the retailer, whose success depends so much on the whims of fancy and fashion. With some historical data to go on, you should be able to see exactly what your days of sales in inventory should be, and if it deviates, you'll see it and know it as a danger signal. Along with the raw data, chart a trend line, as often sales rise and fall in such a way that it's difficult to determine which *direction* they're headed.

You're Out of What?

The bane of having something in inventory is its opposite: you're out of what a customer happens to need. The goal of any inventory control system is to avoid this, of course, but it happens to the best of us. All we can do is try to minimize how often we goof, and so Figure 10-6 is a helpful chart to create monthly, just so we can see if our efforts along this line are working or not.

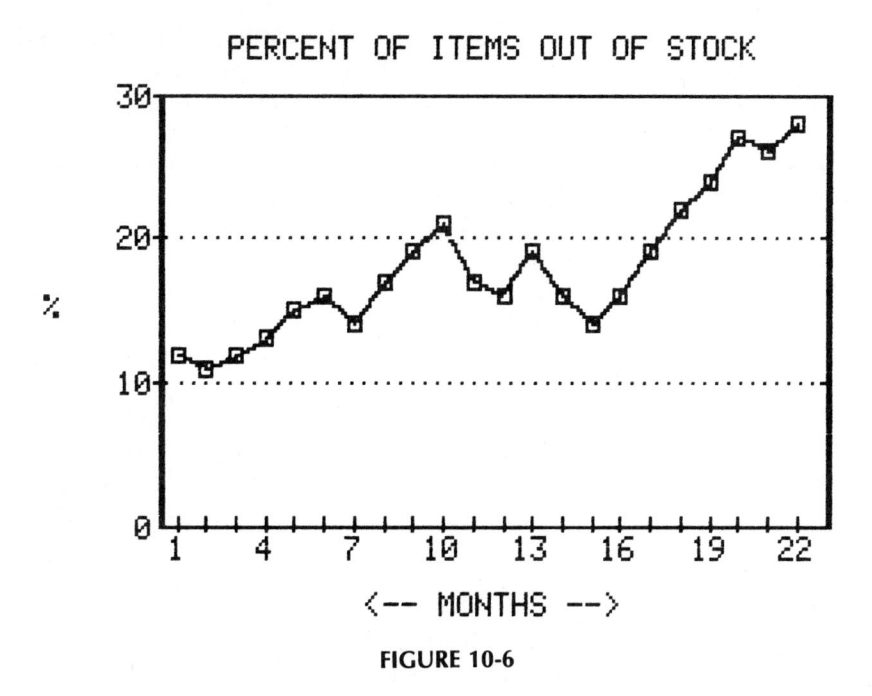

FIGURE 10-6

Figure 10-6 shows us a 22-month picture that's designed to disturb anyone who owns a business. This graph charts the percentage of items our fictional business happens to be out of at the end of each month. For most of the first 18 months of this illustration, we were at least able to keep this figure below the 20% level. This level is unusually high and unacceptable for most businesses; we used it here just for that reason. Too often, what applies to someone else's business does not apply to yours—if your line of work is such that historically you're always out of much of what your customers need, then the 20% figure isn't anywhere near as important as the *trend* of the data. The purpose of using so high a figure here is simply to indicate that the raw numbers are not as important as the moving line of the data is, in terms of understanding your business.

For some reason, for the last five months our out of stock percentage has gone through the roof, and the obvious question is *why?* Aren't we ordering when we should? Has our inventory control system broken down? Aren't people telling us what they took out of stock? Have shipments from a major supplier been slow?

Figure 10-6 might be way out of line for your business—perhaps you work at only a 2% or 3% out of stock level. The only way you'll know what your own figure should be is, of course, to track it over a period of time. You'll quickly discover what's right for you, and so you'll spot any variations in the total. As noted, this figure must be examined in light of your own historical data, and not compared to what someone else figures it should be.

Whatever the cause, Figure 10-6 is reason for alarm. Even without a trend line, it's obvious our record on out of stock items is getting worse by the month, probably by the day, and more and more prospects walk out of our store empty-handed.

Since we have such an obvious problem, it might not seem necessary to make a trend line to show us how fast our record is getting worse, but it's actually a good thing to do for a couple of reasons. It'll show us where we can expect our data to be at the end of a few months, if we continue to do things as we have been. It also gives us a better feel for the *rise* in the information itself; the raw data, even though obviously heading up, still fluctuates. Finally, perhaps it will scare us enough to motivate us to action. After all, if we don't have it, we're not going to sell it. Without something to sell, our business won't be in business.

Figure 10-7 plots the 22 months of information we just examined, along with a trend line based on that data, to project it for another six months. The sad part is that the percentage of things we showed out of stock was only about 10% back at the start of this graph. The trend line ends up at almost 30%, so in the space of two years, this business has gone from a decent out of stock level (for it) to one totally unacceptable. That 30%, viewed another way, means that nearly one-third of its customers will leave the store without buying anything.

The ideal rate at which you should be "out of stock" would be zero—you'd always have everything every customer asked for. In the real world, this is rarely

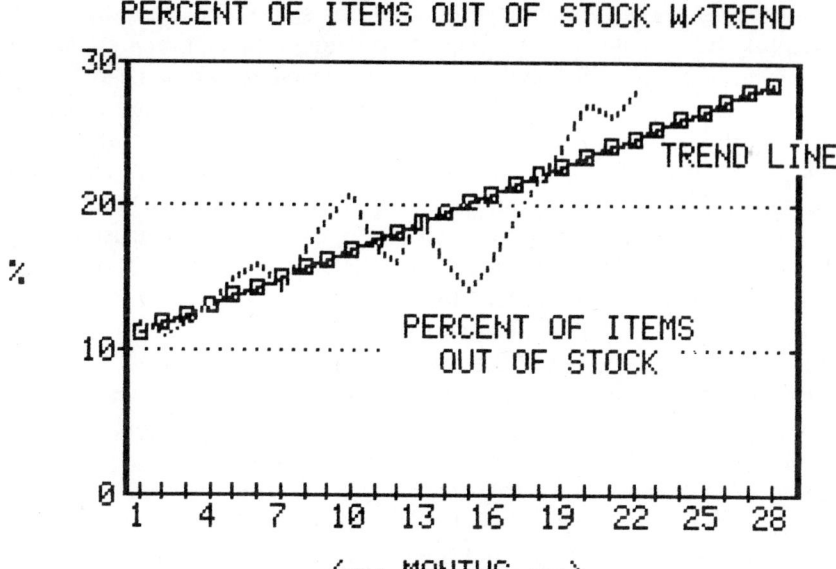

```
          PERCENT OF ITEMS OUT OF STOCK W/TREND
      30


                                                     TREND LINE
      20

  %
                           PERCENT OF ITEMS
                            OUT OF STOCK
      10


       0
        1    4    7   10   13   16   19   22   25   28
                        <-- MONTHS -->
     THE TREND LINE IS BASED ON 22 MONTHS OF DATA,
     WITH A SIX MONTH PROJECTION
```

FIGURE 10-7

achievable, but is certainly a goal worth working toward. By plotting it as we've done here, you get a look at not only where you've been, where the general movement of your information has gone, but with the addition of a trend line, where you'll probably be in a few months. Is it where you want to be? If so, keep working the same way; if not, then it's an indication that something in your method of operation needs to be changed.

Sales/Inventory per Square Foot

Another way to gauge how a store or division performs is to examine the relationship between sales and inventory on a per square foot basis. If one of your locations has 2,000 square feet and keeps $20,000 worth of merchandise on hand, it has $10 worth of goods for every square foot of store space it uses. You calculate this by dividing the inventory ($20,000) by square feet (2,000): 20,000/2,000 = 10. If that same location did $40,000 worth of business during a specific period, you can say it produced $20 of sales for every square foot it has available. You calculate this by dividing the total sales ($40,000) by the square feet in the store (2,000): 40,000/2,000 = 20.

Figure 10-8 plots this data for each of our stores, for the month of June. The column chart format is used because it lends itself to a dual comparison—the left (solid) column is the amount of inventory each store carried during the month, on a square foot basis. It's important to note the inventory figure is at *wholesale*—our cost, not what we expect to sell the merchandise for. This is the manner in which we normally talk about inventory, and the way we'll find the figures inside our accounting system. The right column (dashed) represents the sales each location did for the same month, on a per square foot basis.

An examination of this data tells us that two locations—Metro and Ash Fork—both carried *more* inventory than they produced in sales volume. Our downtown store's inventory and sales were about the same. The other two locations created more sales than the total value in their inventory.

While one month of data is insufficient on which to base any decisions, let's assume for a moment that what we've seen in Figure 10-8 holds true over a length of time. This means, in effect, since the dollar totals are as close as they are for the amounts illustrated, that Figure 10-8 tells the business owner that he or she must keep in stock roughly the same dollar figure he or she expects to sell. Put another way, if one of your stores has wholesale value in inventory of $15,000, that's about what it can expect to sell during the next month. Certainly more study is needed, over a longer period of time, but the basic concept is

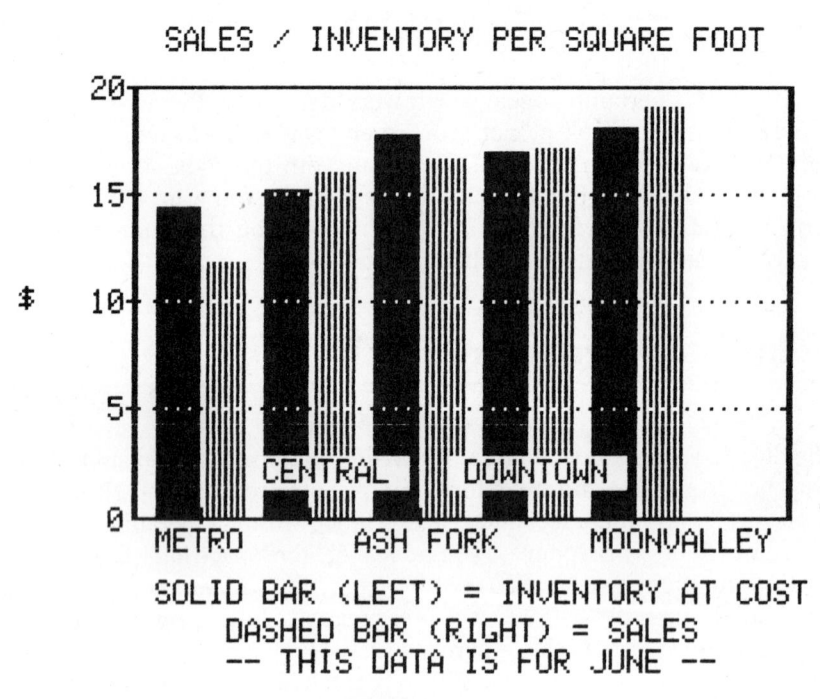

FIGURE 10-8

accurate: once you determine the relationship between what you have on hand (on a wholesale basis) and your gross sales (on a retail level), you'll have a good feel for not only what dollar total you'll need on hand to produce the sales you want to, but also for whether a selective increase in inventory will bring a like rise in sales. Isn't that the whole idea of inventory control and analysis?

Someone who has the stores we've been examining also has the chance to experiment a bit. Why not increase the inventory at one store by 20% and see if sales follow it? Since (based on our assumption that Figure 10-8's story holds true for a long period of time) our sales seem to approximate our inventory cost, on a per square foot basis, might not it follow that if we increase our inventory from $10 per to $12 for each square foot of area, that sales might not also go up by 20%? Would it be worth a try?

Summing Up

At the basis of every sale is inventory, but to sell your merchandise, you not only have to have it on hand (or quickly available), but you must price it right, handle the selling process properly, and so on. People who deal on the retail level have an advantage (from an inventory standpoint) over all other merchandisers, as they see the daily interaction between the items in stock and the people who examine them. But it's important to note that every business shares the same basic types of inventory difficulties. If you order most of what you sell, you still must know what's available, price it right, speak about it in an intelligent manner to your prospects, and so on. The wholesaler perhaps must be more price-conscious than other businesspeople, and has inventory hardships imposed by the nature of this end of things—most notably, the large amounts of cash required to start and stay in wholesaling.

Since inventory control is so important, we must handle it as something vital. Surely, no businessperson would turn over control of his or her checkbook to someone hired just yesterday, yet businesspeople do it all the time when it comes to inventory. The *stockperson* is expected not only to put away the merchandise, but also to reorder when it's necessary, determine who to buy from, and so on. Sadly, the smallest business—which needs tight inventory control for every dollar it spends—gets the worst of things here, as it often doesn't have the cash to pay (or, at least believes it can't afford) someone to handle the inventory in the way it should be taken care of.

Since inventory must come before any sales are consummated, it's logical to plot monthly sales along with monthly inventory totals, to see how one compares to the other. Because everything depends on the inventory you have on hand (or can get), an increase in sales will often follow a rise in your inventory level. How much can you increase it before you reach the point of diminishing returns? Graphics can tell you.

As with most financial information, once you make a study of the raw data, it's helpful to see how things look on a percentage basis, to examine (in this case) what inventory is as a percentage of your total sales. Since your sales depend directly on your inventory, this figure should remain pretty stable. If it does not, it's a reflection of a problem with the stock on hand—it simply is not selling.

Associated with inventory control is how fast things are sold—the *turnover rate* your business has. This needs to be examined both as raw information as well as with a trend line, to see where it's headed. Generally, the faster you can move items from your shelves and out the door the better, so long as the rapidity of this movement doesn't cause out of stock conditions that are unacceptable. The most common way to look at your turnover rate is in terms of the number of days it takes you to move your stock.

It's also useful to change your inventory total from a cost figure to a retail level and compare it to sales; this tells you how many days of sales you'd have left, if you stopped buying right now. It's another indication of how well what you have in stock is moving. Again, a trend line is helpful to give you an idea of how your business will look down the road a month or two.

All of the comparisions with sales and inventory tell the business owner how good his or her merchandise selection is (or, conversely, how poor the product line is). If you have a rapid product turnover, a normal level in terms of the days of sales you have available in inventory, you have a good product mix. If the trend lines of these comparisions is rising, it means products are starting to sit in your stock longer than they should, and you have a problem.

With any inventory comes its Achilles' Heel: you're bound to be out of this item or that, one time or another. Every business has its own percentage that's right; too low a percentage might mean you have things in stock that no one will ever ask for, while too high a rate means too many prospects leave your business without making a purchase. While industry averages are fine as a general guide, it's more important to extract and study this data for your business over a period of time, to find out what's right for you.

Finally, it's helpful to break sales and inventory down on a square foot basis, and plot them as a column chart. This gives the business owner a feel for the level of sales that a certain amount of inventory will produce. If you have more than one location or department, plot them the same way. In general, does a larger inventory mean more sales? For only certain areas of your business, or for them all? Would it be wise to raise your inventory investment here or there to see what happens? *Which* store or division would you increase inventory for? *Why?*

Other Ideas

Inside your own inventory, you probably can find all sorts of examinations it might be helpful to plot. For example, would you like to see visually how many items you're selling per month? While it's not as accurate in terms of financial data as dollar amounts, it's a useful thing to do once in a while, just to get some feel for the number of individual items you and your people handle. Doing this on a historical basis gives you an idea of whether your inventory base is growing or shrinking; you may discover that your sales are up dollar-wise, but you're only handling 40% of the number of items you did at the same time last year. Or that last year your business sold 750 different things, and this year it's working with only 400—is your market shrinking because of what you handle, rather than for competitive and/or economic reasons?

This is a special danger when times are good—we concentrate only on the most profitable areas of our business and (subconsciously, perhaps) start to eliminate those things that don't make as much money, or have a low per-unit volume, or just aren't as interesting as some other things we do. We don't ignore them on purpose, but since the other areas of our work are more important (in our mind), they kind of get pushed to one side. Parts don't get ordered. Jobs don't get scheduled. Work tickets are lost. When the buisness cycle changes, and it always does, we find ourselves with a contracted base of operations. Where once our business performed, say, 20 distinct services, it now might only handle 12. If business slows down, will those be enough to support the level of sales we need?

It's also a good idea to break your inventory down to a low level and chart its course on a per salesperson basis, or per hour of operation basis—anything to get a feel for the way things are headed. You can tie in a trend line, of course, with all of these comparisons, to forecast where you'll be down the road a bit.

A pie chart examination of the different areas inside your inventory—by product group or category—is helpful, as it displays where your dollars are invested. If you can break sales and profits down in the same manner, you might be surprised that a large and costly stock of one product or another simply doesn't pull its own weight, sales and/or profit-wise. Another, seemingly insignificant area of your business might produce profits far in excess of the investment you have there—wouldn't this be a likely candidate for an increased inventory total?

Internal Measurements

11

Whatever type of business you're in, perhaps the hardest area to understand and change (if it's required) is the one that concerns the internal workings of your company.

When you sell something, you have obvious costs: "X" amount of materials were used, "Y" dollars of labor were spent to complete the sale. When you add in an overhead percentage, you'll have a pretty good idea of how well you did on each particular sale. Everything is there in black and white—your materials and payroll and fringe benefits and insurance—everything you spent last month.

Inside any business, though, it's more difficult to understand what's going on. Just as we looked at sales in relationship to its associated cost totals, we need to examine some parts of our business we often don't give much thought to.

Sales and Hours

While an obvious and easy comparison is to look at sales compared to total payroll or to direct labor, it's often more useful to graph sales compared to the number of hours your people work. You can turn this around—as we'll do in a moment—to determine the *sales value* for each hour worked, but let's start with Figure 11-1, which charts the sales and hours worked for our fictitious business. Since the hourly total is much lower in terms of raw numbers than our sales information, we need to multiply the hours-worked figure by ten (for this example) so we can plot them both on the same scale.

In this particular case, Figure 11-1 shows us just about what we'd expect.

```
            SALES / HOURS WORKED * 10
   THOU
     ┤
     │        MONTHLY SALES
   75┤
     │
     │
   50┤
     │
     │              HOURS WORKED
   25┤               TIMES TEN
     │
    0┼─┬─┬─┬─┬─┬─┬─┬─┬─┬─┬─┬─┬
       J F M A M J J A S O N D
           <-- MONTHS -->
```

FIGURE 11-1

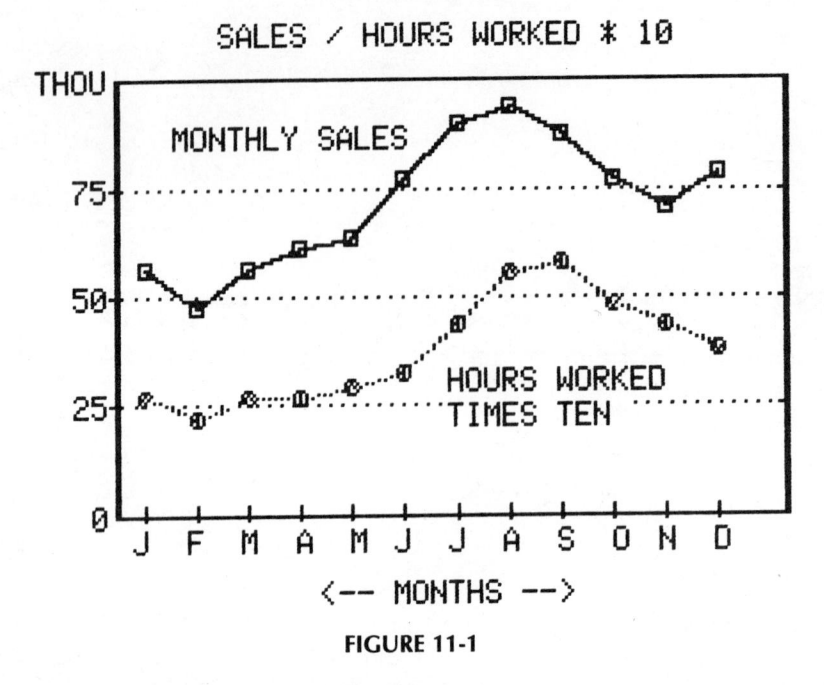

Labor hours and sales rose and fell at roughly the same time. The *trend* of both appears to be increasing at about the same rate of climb—which is as it should be. You could create the same picture with a *window* chart, which means you wouldn't have to multiply the hours worked times ten so it would fit on the same scale.

While this general overview of things is helpful to some degree, it's much more valuable to break these raw totals down a bit and to convert all those hours into a figure everyone can understand and chart.

Inside Finances

Most large corporations publish a financial statement, which puts all their associated data on public display. The average small business, though, often prefers to keep this sort of information confidential. Many small and medium businesses don't even release their financial statements to business information services (like Dun & Bradstreet) but consider it to be only for their own use. One thing not done often enough is to communicate the financial condition of the business to its employees. While they certainly have a stake in how the business is doing—and each business's condition is directly dependent on its people—it's difficult to come up with a method to handle this properly. It's naive to think we can let our people know that we made a $32,000 profit last year without some expectation that they might ask for some of it back in the way of wages and/or profit sharing. Likewise, it's next to impossible to tell our people we *lost* $15,000 last year; they may not even believe us.

Would it be helpful to your business to have some method to let your employees know exactly how your company is doing financially and how they as a group are performing, but without disclosing any precise profit and loss data? You can do it with your computer in two easy steps.

The first is to divide your monthly sales totals by the number of hours your employees worked during that month. If your sales were $50,000 and your people put in 1,000 hours, they produced $50 in sales for every hour on the job. If your employees spent 2,000 hours on the job, they're producing at the rate of $25 per hour.

If you collect your sales and hours-worked figures for a year or so, you'll have a good idea of what the average dollars per hour figure is for your business. If you spend a little more time and list the figures for two or three years, you'll know about what figure you need in order to make money. You'll find that your people will produce a specific figure in sales for each hour they work during those periods when your business is profitable, and a *lower* figure when you're in the red. Each business is different, of course. We've found in our own business that we need $31 dollars of gross sales per hour worked in order to show a profit.

Walt's Secret Formula

Walt Webb is an astute businessperson who makes exquisite glass cases for things like Hummel figurines and Indian kachina dolls. He's a typical small business owner, and he took this concept a step further. While it's helpful to let your employees know what the dollars per hour figure should be, too often—like any other amount—if you post it or put it in a letter, it somehow seems to go over their heads. While business managers are used to working with figures, our employees are more often concerned with the installation or delivery or the service for what we sell. They're not comfortable with our financial data. So Walt *plots* the dollars per hour figure every month and puts the graphs out for all to see.

Figure 11-2 is a close-up look at this data for our fictional business, over a nine-month period. In this particular chart, we have two lines—one for this year's monthly figure, and another for the same months from last year.

For the first seven months of both years, the monthly figure for this business ran in the low twenties; each hour its employees worked, they produced $21 or $22 in sales. While it doesn't tell us if the business was profitable during these periods, it does give the owner a basis of comparison. During the first few months of this year, the employees weren't quite as effective as they were the prior year. The period from month 5 through month 7 showed the lines on an almost identical basis, perhaps as the result of some corrections the owner made in the operation.

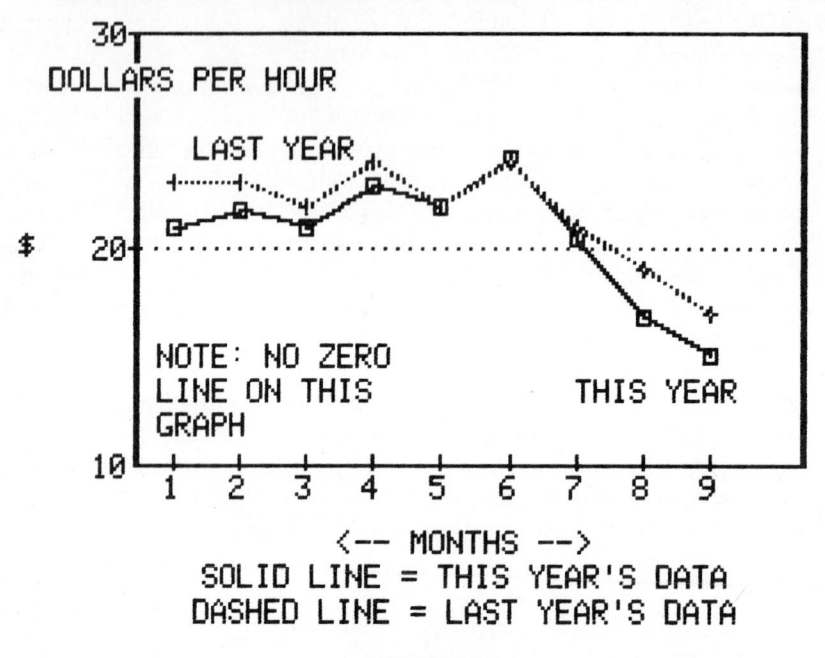

```
DOLLARS PER PERSON PER HOUR THIS YEAR / LAST
  30
  DOLLARS PER HOUR

         LAST YEAR

$   20

         NOTE: NO ZERO
         LINE ON THIS              THIS YEAR
         GRAPH
  10
     1   2   3   4   5   6   7   8   9
              <-- MONTHS -->
         SOLID LINE = THIS YEAR'S DATA
         DASHED LINE = LAST YEAR'S DATA
```

FIGURE 11-2

The three-month period from month 7 to month 9 showed a sharp drop in the figure for both years. If the business made a profit last year, the owner wouldn't be too concerned about the drop. Perhaps it's due to a seasonal fluctuation in the product mix the business sold during this period.

It's important to consider the factor of *seasonal change,* as what you sell can distort your dollars per hour figure. For example, you might charge out one of your employees at $35 per hour. If she or he works for eight hours and sells nothing but labor, your total gross for this employee would be 8 hours × $35, or $280. It's obvious this person created $35 in sales for each hour worked.

However, if this same employee installed a major appliance on that particular day, you'd have to add its value to the sales total. Perhaps a water-softening unit was sold and connected, for a price (including labor) of $480. If we divide this amount by the eight hours worked, the employee comes out with a $60 sales figure, on a per-hour basis.

This tells us two things. First, we often cannot study this sort of data over a short period like a day or even a week, as the fluctuations will be too great. Even on a monthly basis, you'll show a lot of ups and downs. In the case of Figure 11-2, though, since you're comparing the same months for two consecutive years, you probably will get a valid picture. What you sold last July will most likely be close to what you'll sell this July, in terms of how it will add to your dollars-per-

INTERNAL MEASUREMENTS

person-per-hour figure. Second, the important thing about Figure 11-2 is that it's a *comparison* of two similar periods, and as such, seasonal variations are taken into consideration. This business seems to have an obvious problem, though, with its huge drop *both years* from June to September. That doesn't mean that it can't be profitable but that the owner needs to be aware of what happens inside the business from a seasonal standpoint.

Individual Totals

In a case where you want to examine just your service technicians who, let's assume, sell nothing but their labor, you can make a direct comparison from person to person. Since labor is the only thing involved, different periods of the year should produce about the same results. If you can isolate the sales for each individual service technician, you can divide their sales by the hours they worked and arrive at a sales figure per person, per hour.

Figure 11-3 is a bar chart (a column chart would be equally as effective) for the month of January for our fictitious business. Sales produced per hour by each of the four service technicians are displayed, running from the worst to the best. Obviously, one month's look at this sort of thing shouldn't make you want to let Ray go, or to give Tony a raise. That sort of decision depends on a lot more information. This kind of examination, though, is helpful as it gives you an instant

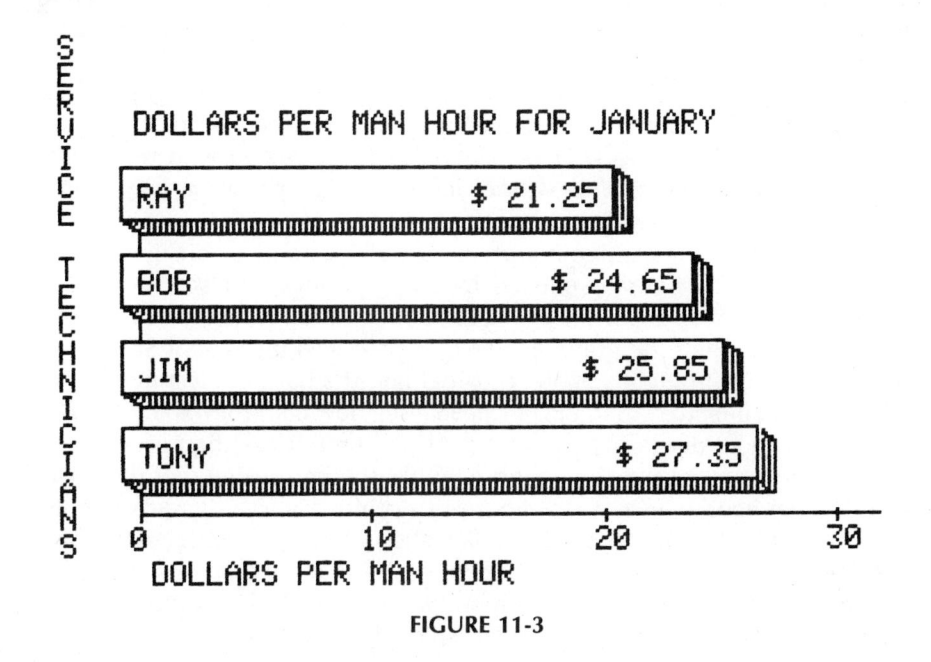

```
DOLLARS PER MAN HOUR FOR JANUARY

RAY      $ 21.25
BOB      $ 24.65
JIM      $ 25.85
TONY     $ 27.35

0        10       20       30
DOLLARS PER MAN HOUR
```

FIGURE 11-3

picture of how your people did for this specific month. Why is one better than another? Did he or she work harder? Smarter?

Certainly another consideration is the *job mix* each employee happened to get during the month under study. For any sort of service work, you'll get a wide variety of work. A service call that should take a half-hour drags out into a half-day. A repair job that could have eaten up six hours goes smoothly and is done in two. One month's worth of information isn't enough to make any sort of determination and should only be used as a general guide to give you something of an impression of how your people are doing. Of course, if *every* month Ray shows up at the bottom of your graph, you know you have a problem with him.

Certainly it's worthwhile to compare each employee using, for example, a line graph over a period of time. However, one of the limitations of a line chart is that once you get over three lines on it—especially if those lines are close to each other—it becomes impossible to read the thing, much less understand its information. In this particular case, our fictional business employs four people in its service department—too many to chart effectively over time.

Break-even Dollars

A much more helpful graph to plot is your people as a group over a period of time, with what you determine is your break-even point shown on the chart. Once you do some study in the area of dollars per person per hour, you'll know about what each employee (as part of the "employee group") needs to produce if you're to make a profit.

This lets you take the concept to your people and post the graph, or even give each one a copy along with their paycheck. Since no one individual or department is singled out, your people will be comfortable with receiving this information. But they *as a whole* will be able to see exactly how they're performing, and when "their" business is profitable.

Figure 11-4 shows a nine-month picture of our fictitious business, charting the dollar per hour figure produced by all employees. It also notes that this business needs $21 per person per hour to break even. It should be obvious to our people that when the graph shows they produced more than $21 per hour, the business was profitable. When they did not, the business lost money. Thus, we have a visual picture that lets our people see how both they and the business are doing, without disclosing any exact sales or profit (loss) figures.

Anyone who looks at this graph who has the knowledge that the business needs $21 per hour to break even can see this company has a significant problem. What's worse is that the *trend* of the data shows a steep drop that dates back to June. Even the fact that we found in Figure 11-2 that the drop this year parallels last year's decrease over these same months doesn't make it any more acceptable and in fact simply means the manager isn't doing a proper job.

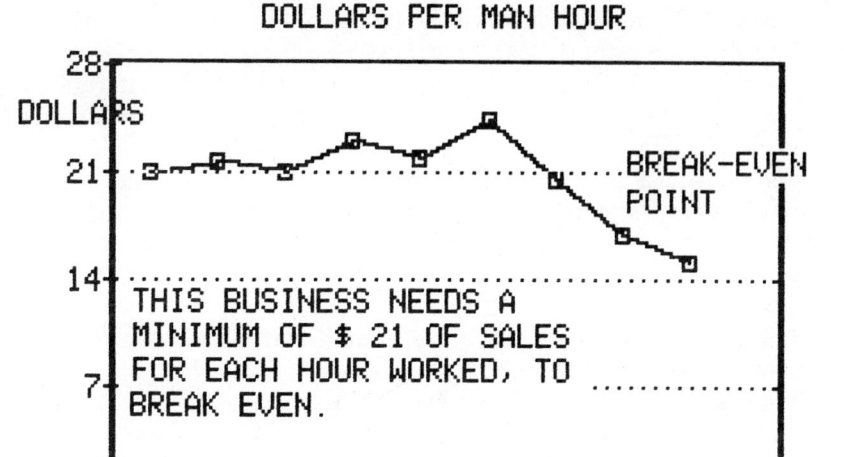

```
              DOLLARS PER MAN HOUR
    28┐
DOLLARS
    21┤ ·□···□──□───□───╱╲──□───╱╲······BREAK-EVEN
                              ╲    ╲        POINT
                                    □
    14┤ ·····································□····
       │ THIS BUSINESS NEEDS A
       │ MINIMUM OF $ 21 OF SALES
     7┤ FOR EACH HOUR WORKED, TO
       │ BREAK EVEN.
       │
     0 └─┼──┼──┼──┼──┼──┼──┼──┼──┼─
         1  2  3  4  5  6  7  8  9
              <-- MONTHS -->
```

FIGURE 11-4

Debt and Equity

The investment the owners of a business have in that enterprise is called *equity*. If you're the sole owner of your business, you've made all the investment into the enterprise. Large corporations have stockholders who collectively invest cash into the business. Equity also comes from any *retained earnings* the owner(s) leave in the business.

In many small companies, the owner(s) don't have enough cash invested to cover the required purchases of major equipment and/or buildings, things necessary (in the eyes of management) for the business to properly do its business. So the business owner finds him or herself with some long-term debt—long-range financing to cover these major purchases.

While it seems obvious there should be some relationship between the *equity* the owner(s) of a business have invested in the company to the *long-term debt* that business determines it can service without a cash flow problem, we often don't consider the connection between the two when a possibly profitable venture comes along. Perhaps we'd like to expand to another area of our city or county and have the opportunity to buy a building there. A used piece of major equipment might become available. Often these opportunities seem to arrive when our cash position is at its worst, so while we make a good investment, we add to our long-term debt at the same time.

Figure 11-5 charts the amount the owner(s) have invested in the business along with the long-term debt the business has, for the first six months of the year. While the owner's equity has remained fairly stable (which it would, barring the infusion of more capital and/or some large profits that can add to the retained earnings figure), the long-term debt total grew rapidly in the March to April period. The business took on a major obligation during this time; let's say that it bought a major new piece of equipment. The graph shows us visually that with this particular purchase, suddenly this business finds itself in a position where outside creditors essentially have nearly as much invested in the company as do its owners.

This isn't necessarily a bad thing, of course, and some businesspeople strive for just this sort of leverage. *Leverage* in this context allows the business owner to expand his or her own financial base with the investments and/or loans of others. But it's important to note that there are certain dangers associated with this position, not the least of which is the fact that almost certainly there's another (possibly large) monthly payment to be made now, to service the new debt.

From a working capital standpoint, the company now will find itself with less cash to use for business operations. Naturally, it would expect the new equipment to start to pay its own way (and thus end up as a good investment), but in real life this often takes time. What do you suppose might happen to this business if it experienced a sudden, sharp drop in sales revenue? Those monthly payments for its long-term obligations would still be there, but perhaps the *cash*

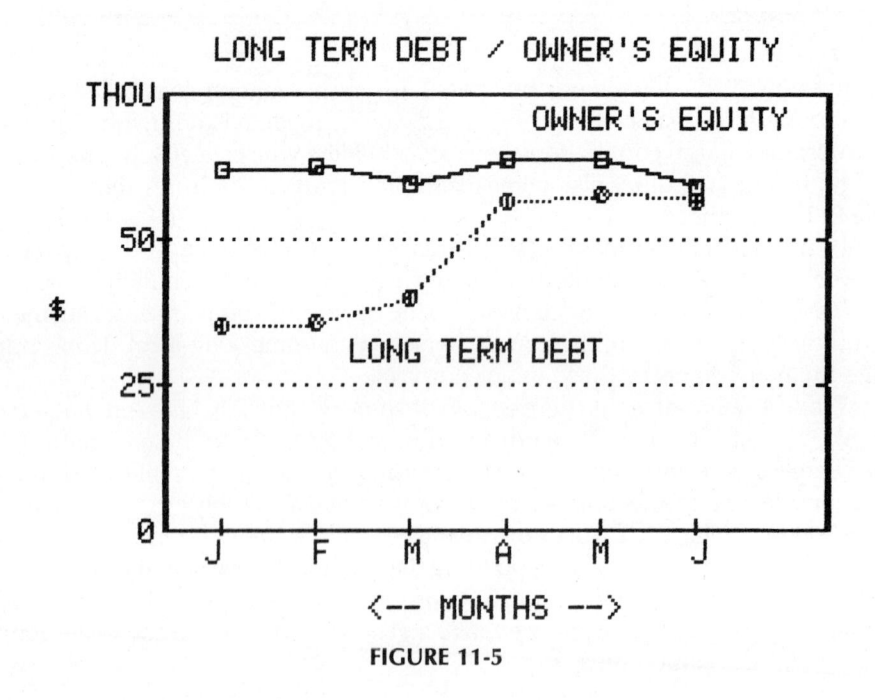

FIGURE 11-5

to make the payments would not. This is one major danger that confronts you if your business invests more than it should through long-range financing.

Figure 11-5 should also disturb the business owner during the early months of the year. Generally, unless a major investment in plant and/or machinery is made, the total dollar value of a business's long-term debt should decline, even if only slightly, every month. Most things are handled these days on a monthly payment basis, and so the debt total should have decreased (at least a bit) during the time before the major equipment purchase was made. Instead, it rose slightly, which might indicate that for some reason, this company wasn't making its payments on time. If that's the case, the intelligent manager should be aware of it, and this fact might even be a good reason to *postpone* the purchase of the major obligation this business took on during the March to April period.

Figure 11-6 shows us the same basic information we've just looked at, but with the long-term debt translated into its percentage of owner's equity. Unfortunately, we can see the percentage rising during the first quarter of the year, just as the dollar total increased. Even *after* the business made the investment in new equipment, its long-term debt as a percentage of equity continued to increase—a possibly hazardous condition. This is especially true as the percentage of long term debt to owner's equity gets close to that 100% mark, as in effect that means others own more of your business than you do. This severely restricts your ability to borrow money, cash that might be needed to get through one of those short-term sales slumps we all have.

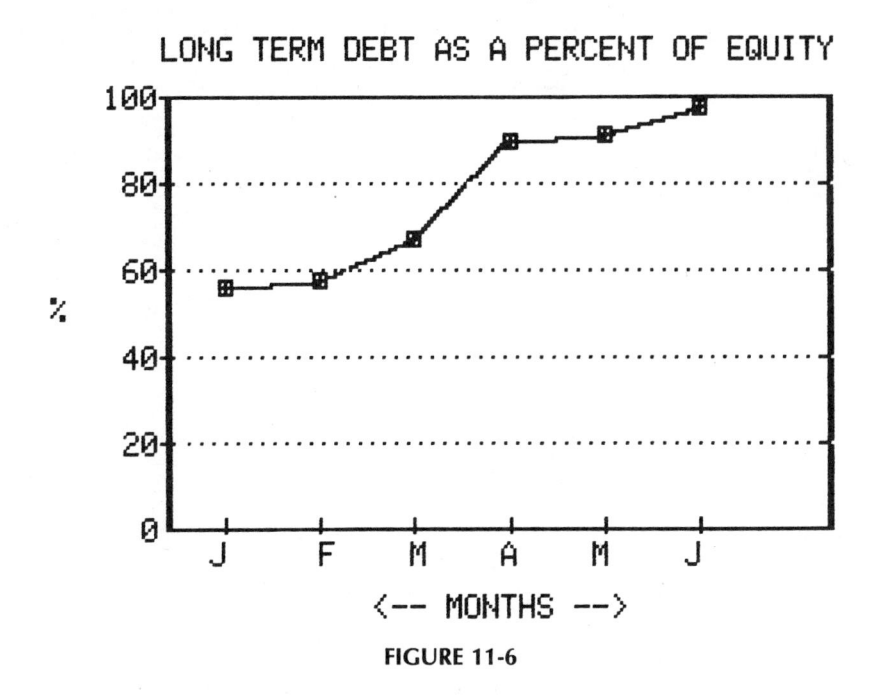

FIGURE 11-6

Investment and Depreciation

Associated with any examination of long-term debt and its relationship to cash outflow is a connection between the total amount invested in equipment and/or physical plant with the depreciation we can take on this investment. Because the gross value of our physical plant and equipment is so much larger than the depreciation amount(s), it's difficult to create a graph that shows both items so we can understand their relationship. The easiest way to look at this is with a line graph that displays our depreciation as a percentage of the total value we have for our operating plant and associated equipment.

Since depreciation can often be a major expense in terms of what we see on our balance sheet (and will eventually require some cash or financing to replace the depreciated items), a good way to examine it is as a percentage of the total value of our plant and equipment, as shown in Figure 11-7. And in truth, depreciation does affect our year-end cash position, as with less depreciation we'll have more income taxes to pay—*in cash.*

Figure 11-7 shows the percentage that the current depreciation amounted to, compared to the total value of our physical plant and equipment. The business owner who looks at Figure 11-7 can visually see the percentage jump for the third quarter because of the equipment purchase she or he made. A machine will be depreciated over a shorter period than a building would be, and thus a

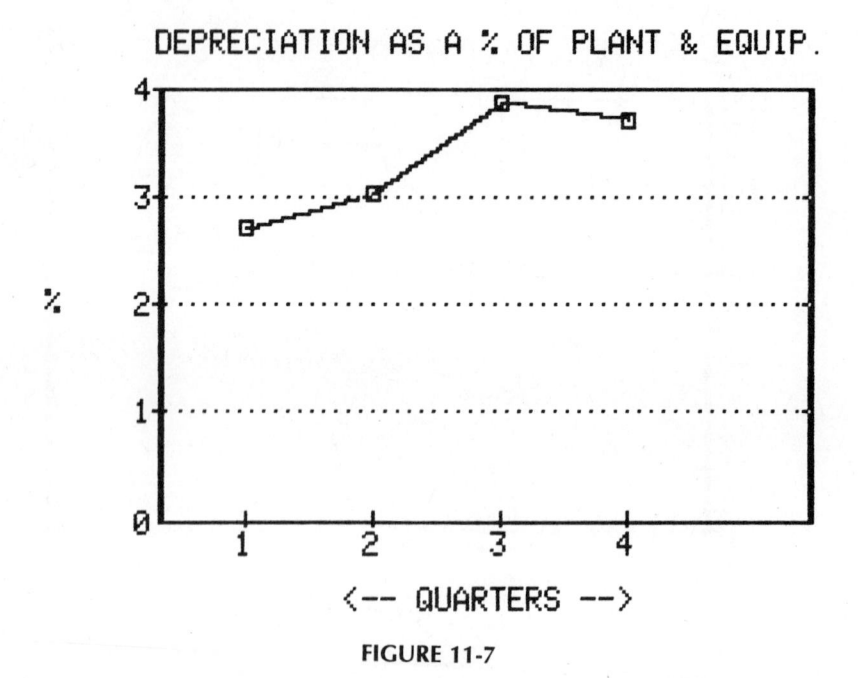

FIGURE 11-7

INTERNAL MEASUREMENTS

purchase like the one our fictitious business made could cause this rise in depreciation as a percentage of the value of equipment and physical plant.

The Bottom Line

To tie this all together, we also need to examine an entire year's graph for long-term debt as a percentage of the equity invested in the business. The drop we just saw in depreciation as a percentage of plant/equipment won't always be matched in terms of the rate of fall with a drop in debt as a percentage of equity; that will depend on exactly what the business owner does to reverse the trend. Let's look again at the long-term debt as a percentage of equity for our fictional business.

Figure 11-8 stretches out the same data we looked at earlier in Figure 11-6 and displays what a graph *should* look like, assuming the owner(s) took the correct steps to change the situation. We can see the rise in long-term debt as a percentage of owner's equity during the first half of the year, when (perhaps) both late payments and a major investment caused a sharp jump. From July on, the owner(s) of this business turned the situation around—they found a dangerous condition back in the early summer and took steps to reverse it. Perhaps more cash was invested into the business. Maybe a location with a negative effect on

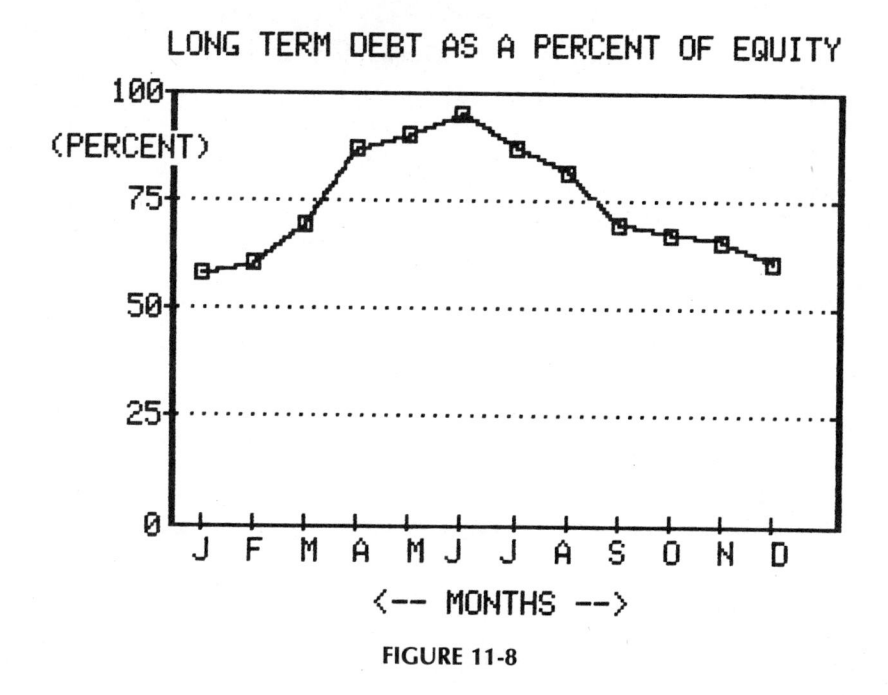

FIGURE 11-8

this ratio was sold. Perhaps the company restructured its payment schedule for its long-term debts. The important thing is, *something* was done to reverse the situation, to lower the ratio of the owner's equity to long-term debt. This business gained some breathing room and has protected itself against a sudden drop in sales.

Working Capital as a Form of Control

As another way to examine how things are inside our business, a look at working capital is often helpful. *Working capital* is defined as the excess of current assets over current liabilities and in effect is the amount of cash your business has available to do business with. A line graph like Figure 11-9 charts the first six months of the year for both the sales and the working capital for our fictitious business.

As always, any aberration in the figures is a sign to look at things a bit closer. In this case, while working capital remained stable for the first quarter of the year, its total dropped during the second quarterly period. Sales, meanwhile, rose.

This may not indicate anything significant, of course—perhaps the sales we

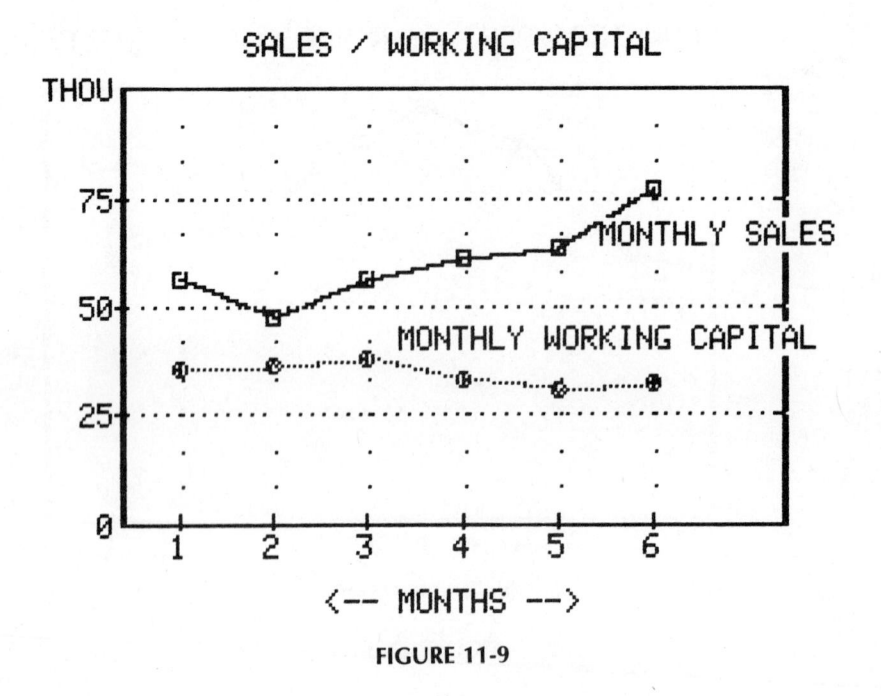

FIGURE 11-9

INTERNAL MEASUREMENTS

made during the last three months were those that required we put out a lot of capital to finance them. If that's the case, this cash will be returned to us in the form of revenue. It's equally possible, though, that we've lost money during this period, and the cash that's disappeared from our graph is really gone. The alert manager will spend some more time to find out why working capital is decreasing. Is it because the rise in sales is using it or because there are problems with the sort of sales we're making?

Figure 11-10 paints the picture as even more of a problem than what Figure 11-9 intimated. Here we see our working capital as a percentage of sales. This gives us a good feeling for the *trend* of our working capital, whether the sales revenue we're creating adds to or subtracts from it; here, it's been heading lower since February.

It's important to note that working capital isn't an end-all; we might be making all sorts of profits and putting that cash into another area of our business. Perhaps we used it to reduce some of those long-term debts. The purpose of Figure 11-10 is to tell the business owner that working capital is *shrinking*. A sharp decrease in working capital may mean the business could have a future problem doing business.

As always, the *amount* and *percentage of sales* of working capital vary by business. If the majority of yours are cash-only transactions, you don't require as much working capital as the business that lets its customers charge everything they buy and allows them liberal payment terms. This latter business might gain

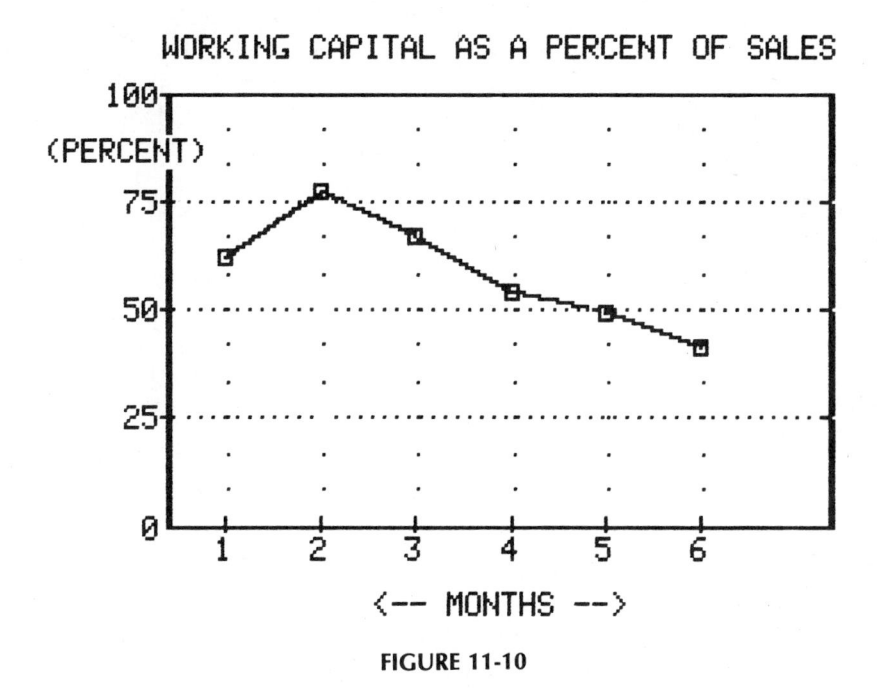

FIGURE 11-10

```
      DAYS OF PURCHASES IN ACCOUNTS PAYABLE
   100
   (DAYS)
   75
   50
   25
    0
       1   2   3   4   5   6
         <-- MONTHS -->
```

FIGURE 11-11

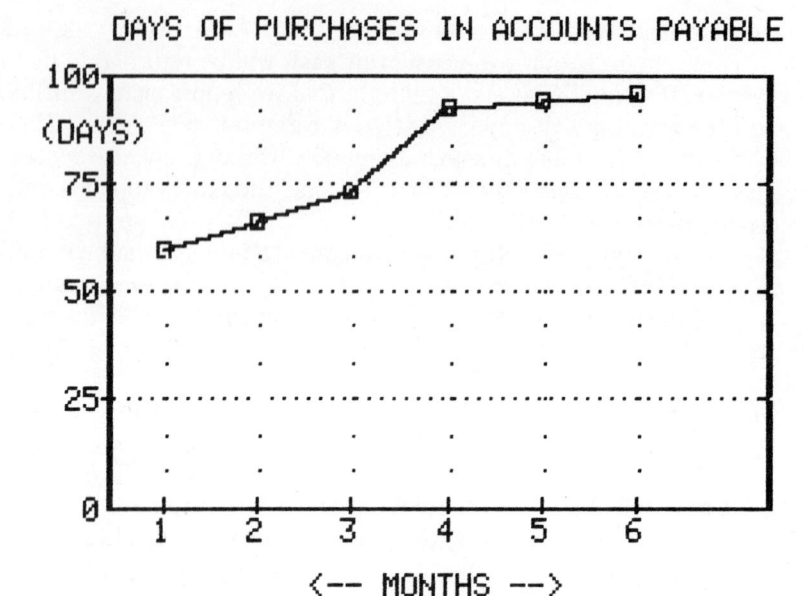

something in the finance charges it tacks onto late bills, but in the meantime it needs more cash just to operate.

Figure 11-10 shows our fictional business going from a high percentage of working capital in relationship to sales back in February (about 75%) to a low in June of around 40%. No business should have this sort of variance, and that's the real point of this example. Your business does things a certain way. You handle your customers in a specific manner. Unless you change the way you do business, your working capital as a percentage of sales should remain pretty stable. If you find something inside your business that causes something like we've seen here—a 35% change in working capital as a percentage of sales within a four-month period—you need to find out why.

Another way to examine this same thing is to plot working capital on a basis of its *percentage* increase or decrease, month to month or every quarter. It really brings home whether your cash position is getting better or worse—and by how much.

Old Bills

In almost every business, certain items are charged and carried in the form of an obligation as accounts payable. While we all make comparisons between accounts payable this year versus last, and receivables compared to payables, and even sales compared to accounts payable, there's another helpful relationship that involves payables that we often don't consider.

Assume that we purchased $9,000 worth of materials in January. If we divide this by 30 days (to keep things simple, we'll assume each month contains 30 days), this means we averaged $300 worth of material purchases per day. If we have $3,000 in accounts payable as of January 31, we can say that we have ten days worth of purchases in our accounts payable total. We calculate this by dividing our accounts payable ($3,000 in this example) by our average daily material purchases ($300): 3000/300 = 10. This means we have ten days' worth of purchases in our accounts payable total. Likewise, if we owe $6,000 worth of payables at the end of January, we could say that we have 20 days worth of purchases in that payables total.

The significance of this figure is simply that it gives us an exact indication of how well we're paying our bills (or how poorly we're doing so). While we'll age our accounts receivable totals, we often don't do the same with what we owe (we'd much rather concentrate on the monies owed us, rather than vice versa). It serves as a good method of internal control as it tells us precisely how we stand; if we chart it, we can see how our bill-paying habits look.

Figure 11-11 graphs the number of days worth of purchases we have in accounts payable for the first six months of the year. For this particular example, the total rises from about 60 days worth of purchases back in January to almost 100 days worth for each month during the April-June period. For one reason or another, our payables total is getting progressively worse. The business owner

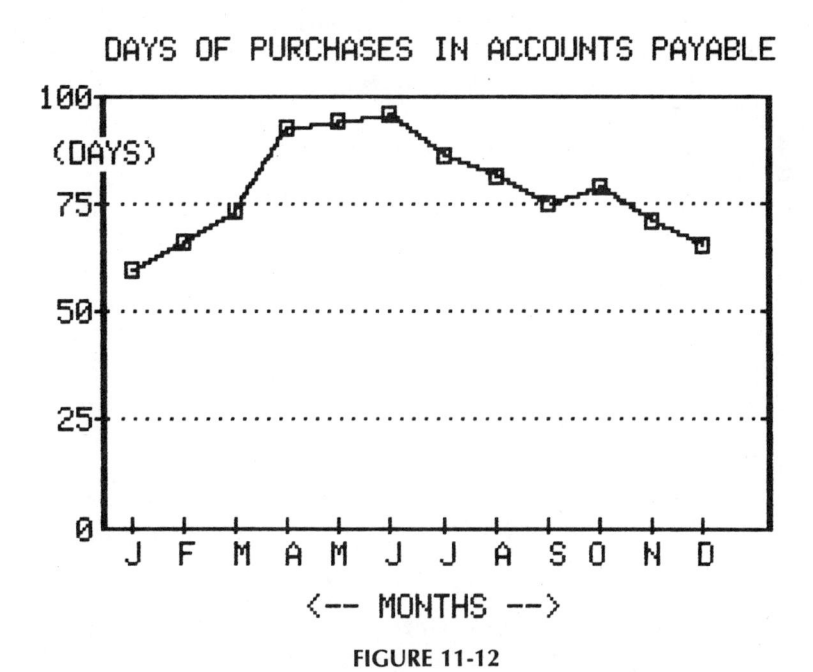

FIGURE 11-12

should have noticed the trend during the first three months, and once he or she spotted the large jump in the March-April period, should have taken immediate steps to correct it.

This is the sort of condition that is only remedied one way: we have to somehow come up with some cash to cover our accounts payable. Figure 11-11 shows we have more than 90 days worth of purchases in our accounts payable total—a time frame that starts to cause phone calls and demands for payment from anxious suppliers.

To help put things into their proper perspective, Figure 11-12 charts the same data we've been examining, but over a whole year. Steps were taken after those terrible first six months to reduce our accounts payable, and at least at the end of the year their total wasn't much more than it was at the start of the year. However, even Figure 11-12 doesn't present a promising picture, in that we still show about 60 days worth of purchases in our accounts payable total. This can create credit problems, raise the possibility that someone will close our open account and might start to put black marks into our credit file. A good goal would be to reduce the total purchases in our accounts payable down to less than a 30-day level (or whatever is normal for your business).

Summing Up

Any study of internal controls—some way to see exactly what's happening inside our business—must start with sales, and a good way to examine it is in relationship to the hours worked by our people. The more hours they work, the more our sales should be. If these two lines don't move in line with one another, we might have a problem.

This same approach should be carried further to determine the sales volume each employee produces for every hour worked. Unless you have a specific group of people who don't sell parts or supplies or equipment, you almost have to examine this figure for all of your people as a group. However, if you have a class of employees you can look at on an individual basis, it's worthwhile to do so.

Once you determine how your people perform in relationship to sales volume, you have an exact figure you can graph and present to them as an indication of how well they're doing their job. You can compare their sales dollars per hour this year to last year. Another way to show the same information is to put a break-even line on the graph; employees can instantly *see* if their work is making money for the business or not.

Another helpful relationship to watch is that between the owner's equity (what the owner(s) have invested in their business) and the long-term debt (what others have "invested" on a long-range basis). As the two figures move closer together—and especially if their *trend* shows them starting to meet—the business can face future difficulties if sales happen to decrease. Those huge monthly payments will still be there, but the cash to pay them might not.

Depreciation is an expense that doesn't consume cash at the time it's recorded. In any business with a major investment in plant/or equipment, it's necessary to watch depreciation both in terms of raw data and on a percentage basis. What is a healthy depreciation percentage for your business? Is the *trend* of your depreciation rising or falling? Why?

As sales increase, working capital often is used up (at least over the short term) to make the purchases to support the sales. However, sales should eventually *add* to the total working capital, as profit is produced and accumulated. Working capital as a percentage of sales is a comparison we need to make monthly, with an eye to its trend, its movement.

Finally, accounts payable form a significant part of the debt of many businesses, and one way to gauge our payables position is to examine it in view of the number of days of purchases we have *stored up* in our accounts payable total.

Other Ideas

Since the investment a business has varies widely with the nature of the business itself, your company might have a major interest in property, buildings, and equipment while another may not. As a general rule, the *net value* of your plant and equipment should exceed your long-term debt. As long as its figure is higher than the dollars you owe and must pay back over a long period of time, this end of things is acceptable. When the ratio exceeds 1:1, however, it's an indication that you're using long-term money to finance immediate cash flow problems, that you're borrowing on a long-range basis to come up with payroll money. That's a danger sign, as a working business must be able to generate its own operating cash as it does business.

Another helpful idea for many businesses is to examine their assets and liabilities in the form of a pie chart, perhaps on a quarterly basis. This gives the business owner a feel for the condition of things as they relate to one another, an idea of how each specific asset or liability category grows and/or shrinks, as represented by the slices of the pie. It's a useful visual picture of the information.

Graphs as a Sales Tool

12

You may not think about it, but you probably already use graphs as a sales tool. A lot of consumer literature includes charts to make a point, to compare one brand against another, to promote the product through the use of graphed data.

Obviously, any use of graphs as something to help you sell more effectively depends on what your business happens to handle. It takes some creative thinking to come up with an idea or two that make sense and will present your product and/or service to your prospects in a manner that encourages them to want to buy from you.

One of the best things about using graphs to help your sales is that they complement each other: both selling and graphics are basically a form of communication. When you make your sales presentation to a potential customer, you want to tell your story, to make the prospect understand that you're the right person to buy from, that you'll have the best service and warranty, that the customer will want to buy from you over and over. To do an effective job, you must have the prospect's time and interest.

Because business graphs lend themselves to the basic process of communication, they can help in a number of ways. It's because of the sales presentation that salespeople have a reputation for talking fast: they want to get as much of their presentation said before the prospect says "No." Pictures can help hold a prospect's interest during an extended presentation. Graphs drive home a point. They can illustrate some things better than pages of facts and figures. With your microcomputer, you can personalize your graphs to make them seem like they're specifically designed for each prospect, an advantage your competition may not be able to duplicate. You wouldn't present a quotation to a major prospect that didn't have the prospect's name filled in on it, would you? Instead of handing the person you're talking to a piece of factory literature, why not present a graph personalized with his or her name?

Where to Start

The place to begin your search on how business graphs can help your sales is to look at what you sell in relation to the selling process itself. You need to list how things happen for your business and then go over your list to see where graphs might be able to help. Once you have a prospect (either because they contacted you or vice versa), what happens? Do you go to their home or do they come to see you at your place of business? What sort of sales presentation do you make? Is there a chance to sit down with your prospect and show him or her a graph or two, to explain why he or she should buy from you? Almost anytime you have a situation where literature is involved—where you give your prospect something to look at and examine—you can find a way to use a graph to help get your message across.

You also must focus on your own products and/or services and ask yourself why a prospect should buy from you. What makes you better than the store down the street? Better prices? Do you have higher quality products for sale? Why are your products better than anyone elses? Do you sell more than one grade of equipment? Why is one better than another? And the bottom line: how can you demonstrate this to your prospect, so she or he will be convinced that you're the one to buy from?

You want to examine your entire selling process, with an eye to finding out when and where graphs might be of value to you.

Most things (if not all) are purchased to solve a problem. This extends all the way from the basics (food, shelter, transportation) to the extras we all want. What problems do you solve for your prospects? A heating and air conditioning business helps with indoor comfort problems; a clothing store helps people not only look good but succeed in their work; a hardware store lets its customers fix things without expensive service labor. Make a list of the problems your business solves for people, constantly searching as to how graphics can make you more effective in explaining how you'll do it.

Get out the consumer literature you have available and examine it. What's on there that could be converted into graphs for a specific customer? A comparison of operating costs? One brand of equipment against another? Often, you can recreate graphs from pieces of sales literature and personalize them with your micro, to make them a more effective sales tool.

It's not an easy task, and you won't be able to translate every idea you come up with into a way to use a graph. The important thing, though, is to have just one or two charts you can call on for each sales presentation. It's interesting that (perhaps) these can be the same basic graph, with only the names changed. After all, what you tell one prospect is probably true for the next person you speak to, so why not use the same picture for each one?

Savings

These days, much of what's talked about during the selling process involves energy costs. Most things you buy today—from a copy machine to a dishwasher to the car you drive—use some form of energy to operate. Given a choice of two (or more) seemingly equal items, it makes sense to choose the one that's going to cost the least to operate over its expected lifespan. As energy bills continue to rise, the operating cost of a product becomes even more important, at least in the minds of your prospects.

There's a danger, here, though, when you get into the area of comparing one product against another, in terms of its operating costs. The tendency is to list or graph the expected expenses over time, to let your prospect know that one brand will cost, say, $2400 to run for five years, while another might only cost $1300 to operate during the same period. The problem is that the focus is on *costs,* rather than on *savings.* The natural tendency for a prospect to say is something like, "You mean, it'll cost me *that much* to run this thing?" Once that happens, you might have lost the sale. The focus instead should be on the cost savings your proposal will give the prospect, as shown in Figure 12-1.

Figure 12-1 is one variation that you might use when you speak about any energy savings that [whatever you sell] provides your customers. The focus is on the savings aspect—brand "A" will save more than brand "B" will. While the graph doesn't spell it out, the comparisons are obviously made to the customer's current brand of equipment. The chart also is personalized with a particular prospect's name, which indicates it was prepared especially for the person you happen to be making your sales presentation to. It's impressive. The area chart format is used because you're working with cumulative data here, the accumulated savings over the three-year period shown. An area chart is ideal to show how the dollars grow with each passing year.

One warning on this type of example: it's easy when you talk about cost savings to show the maximum, and sometimes you might want to extend a graph out for a long period of time. It's difficult for people to see much further than three or four years down the road, so an illustration like Figure 12-1 is probably more helpful than a graph that plots potential utility savings over a ten-year period. That's simply too long a time to relate to. If you find it necessary to look over that long a time frame, use it in combination with a graph like Figure 12-1, so your prospects can see what they'll save over the near term, as well as over a long period of years.

You'll note there are no yearly dates listed on this example, which means it can be used at any time during the year, for any prospect who's considering

CUMULATIVE SAVINGS, UTILITY BILLS

FIGURE 12-1

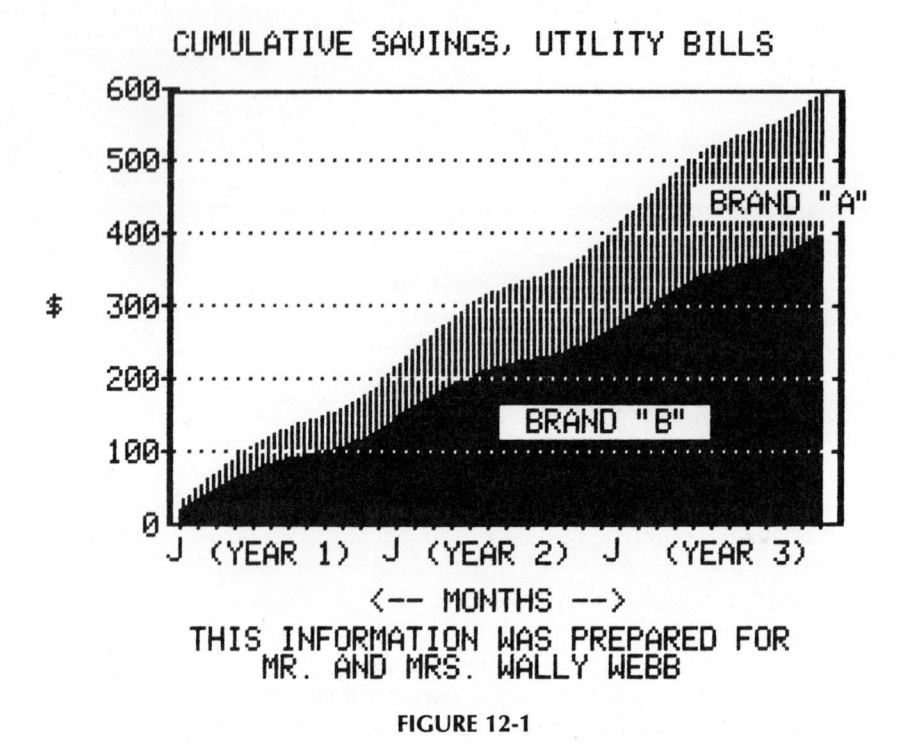

these two brands of equipment. All you have to do is change the prospect's name and reprint the graph to make it personalized. You don't need to redo all the data and redraw the graph before you print it out for your current prospect.

A Trend Line

It's often worthwhile, once you're talking to your prospect about potential energy savings, to have your plotting program create trend lines for your data and plot just them.

The process to accomplish this requires you to enter the initial information, use the statistical part of your graphing program to create cumulative totals, and then ask the analysis part of the package to create trend lines based on the cumulative information. Figure 12-2 shows your prospect the projected *trends* of the two brands under consideration in terms of their cost savings. In some ways, it's a better way to look at things than Figure 12-1. This is because it tells the prospect a long-range story, what his or her savings will amount to over a long period of time, but since the trend lines climb so rapidly even during the early years, a prospect can still relate to the information.

```
           TREND LINES FOR OPERATING COST SAVINGS
      THOU
       10 ┼·······································▢·
                                              ▢
                                           ▢     BRAND "A"
        8 ┼························▢·········
                                ▢
                             ▢
        6 ┼··················▢···················+·
     $                    ▢                   +
                       ▢                   +    BRAND "B"
        4 ┼·········▢·············+·············
                 ▢            +
              ▢         +
        2 ┼·····▢····+·······························
              +
           ▢+
        0 ┼──┼──┼──┼──┼──┼──┼──┼──┼
           1   3   5   7   9  11  13  15
             < -- YEARS -->
        THE TREND LINES ARE BASED ON 12 YEARS
        OF DATA AND PROJECTED OUT FOR 3 MORE
```

FIGURE 12-2

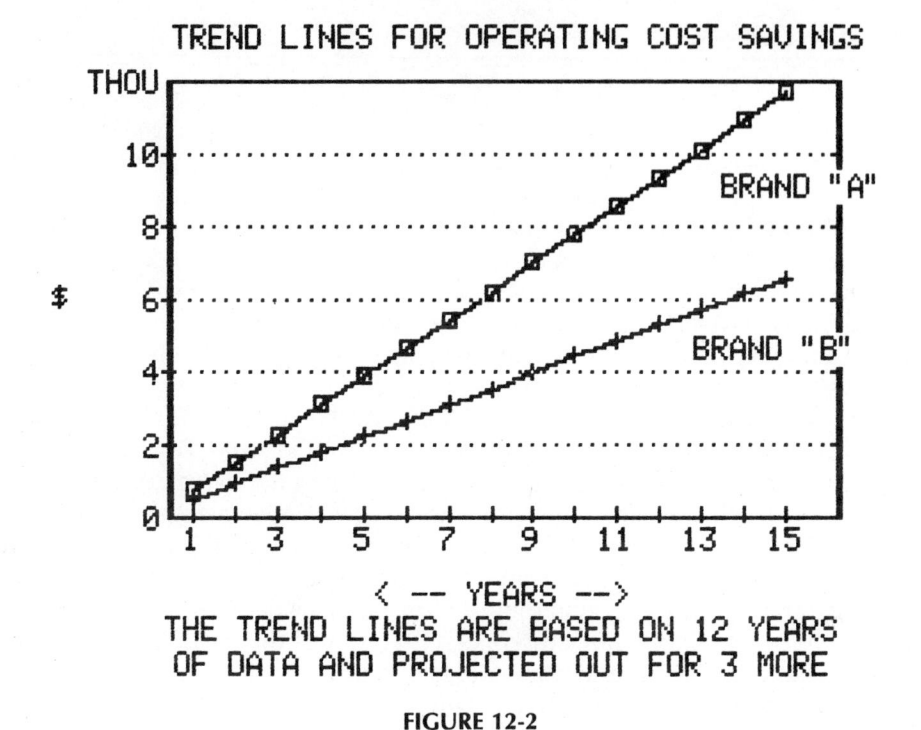

You'll notice that this graph is based on completely different data than Figure 12-1, and could be—because of the large dollar amounts involved—for a commercial application. This sort of look can cover anything from a new cooling system for a large hotel to a computerized energy management program for a hospital. It makes it easy for your prospects to see what cost picture they'll look at over the next few years.

These graphs—a study of the cost savings someone might expect if they buy what you suggest—are also valuable for another reason. In selling, there's something called *buyer's remorse,* and we've all run into it. It's when, after a prospect has signed a contract, he or she begins to have second thoughts. The problem most often comes along when the prospect gets home. His or her spouse or neighbor is often more than willing to volunteer "You didn't buy one of those, did you? Mary Jane down at work had one once and it gave her nothing but trouble. She finally had to sue the dealer. . . ."

The prospect starts to wonder if he or she made a good decision or bought a lemon, if a better deal could have been made elsewhere, and so on. However, if he or she is armed with your personalized graphs that show what the savings will be over the next few years, the prospect can whip them out and show them to the kind soul who has all the words of wisdom to impart. Graphs like these help eliminate buyer's remorse.

Startup Problems

Every so often, a brand new unit, fresh out of the box, simply won't run. The factory is supposed to check everything, of course, but something happens in shipment that knocks the unit out of whack, and products come through that just won't work. It happens not just to air conditioning units and furnaces, but also to televisions and stereos and automobiles, and yes, even microcomputers.

For any major purchase, a potential customer is concerned about how well something is made. They'll more often than not ask about the warranty a product has, but usually don't even consider that something might not operate the first time it's used. After all, it's brand new.

In our business, we try to check every unit before it goes to a customer's home, to make sure it works properly, runs quietly, and so on. If we don't, every now and then we'll get a unit that we install and then find it won't operate. The problem is that the customer doesn't really want the defective unit repaired: he or she demands a *new* unit. After all, they don't want to buy a lemon, something that's going to give them a problem in a year or two, they want a new, perfect system right out of the box. And they're right—that's what they bought and paid for. Often, equipment manufacturers don't see things the same way, and while they're glad to repair the unit, they refuse to replace it with a new one. So, you have people problems right off the bat when you don't check the equipment you sell before you deliver and/or install it.

This is a helpful selling tool, though—tell your prospects that you check out each unit before you deliver it, just to make sure it's not freight-damaged, that it runs correctly, and so on. Once you explain this to them, they won't object if you unpack the product and will appreciate the extra care. Of course, you want to tell them this *before* they make the purchase, as another reason to buy from you.

Figure 12-3 tells your prospects that things sometimes do happen to new units, that every so often they won't work after they're unpacked and plugged in or installed. Many of us have an aversion to knocking the competition (it's bad selling, anyway), but you don't have to even name the brands your competition sells to make this comparison. Just the fact that you'd produce such a graph, give it to your prospects and explain it to them raises your stature in the eyes of the people you talk to.

Wouldn't you be impressed with, say, a television salesperson who handed this graph to you? "Now, it doesn't happen very often," he or she will say, "but once in a while one of the sets doesn't work after it's unpacked. To make sure none of our customers has a problem, we unpack and check every set before it goes out here on the display floor. And here's the record for these three brands in terms of initial startup problems. It helps explain why this one costs more than that one."

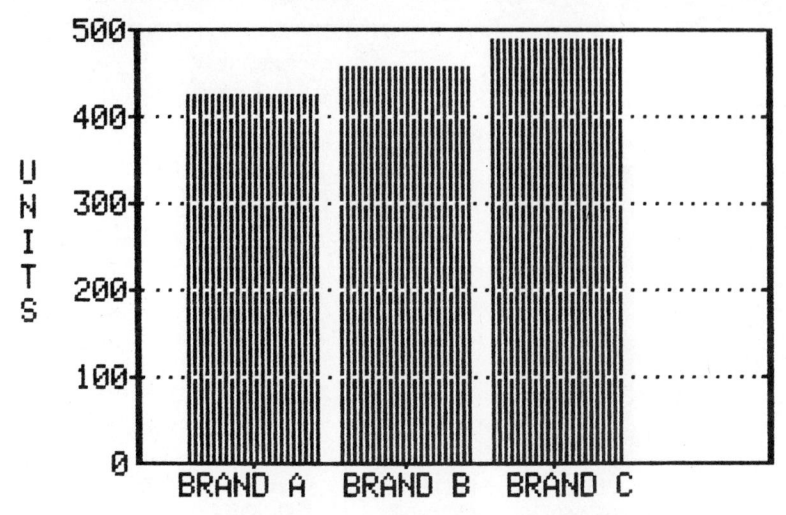

```
           STARTUP PROBLEMS PER 10,000 UNITS SOLD
        500┐
           │      ┌───┐       ┌───┐       ┌───┐
        400┼──────┤▓▓▓├───────┤▓▓▓├───────┤▓▓▓├──────
   U       │      │▓▓▓│       │▓▓▓│       │▓▓▓│
   N       │      │▓▓▓│       │▓▓▓│       │▓▓▓│
   I    300┼──────┤▓▓▓├───────┤▓▓▓├───────┤▓▓▓├──────
   T       │      │▓▓▓│       │▓▓▓│       │▓▓▓│
   S    200┼──────┤▓▓▓├───────┤▓▓▓├───────┤▓▓▓├──────
           │      │▓▓▓│       │▓▓▓│       │▓▓▓│
        100┼──────┤▓▓▓├───────┤▓▓▓├───────┤▓▓▓├──────
           │      │▓▓▓│       │▓▓▓│       │▓▓▓│
          0└──────┴───┴───────┴───┴───────┴───┴──────
                 BRAND A     BRAND B     BRAND C
           THIS CHART PLOTS THE NUMBER OF UNITS
           THAT WON'T OPERATE WHEN FIRST STARTED
             - BASED ON INDUSTRY STATISTICS -
```

FIGURE 12-3

There's not a lot of difference in the plotted data, but it's the point that counts: you took the time and trouble to explain things to your prospect, about how equipment sometimes doesn't work right. He or she will appreciate you for it. If you can't get this data from industry sources, dig it out of your own service records. It doesn't have to be startup problems, of course, but can be things like first year warranty claims or expected lifespan.

How Noisy is That?

In our business, some air conditioning units and furnace systems are quieter than others. Noise level might not apply to your business, but there may be something involved with the *use* of your product that a prospect may be concerned with. It might be the size or speed at which a tree will grow (for someone in the nursery business), the paper quality and longevity (for a book bindery), how fast images will fade (for a custom photo store). Since our business is involved with the operating sound levels of indoor comfort equipment, we'll look at an example of how to talk about it in a selling situation.

SOUND RATINGS IN DECIBELS, BRAND "A" UNITS

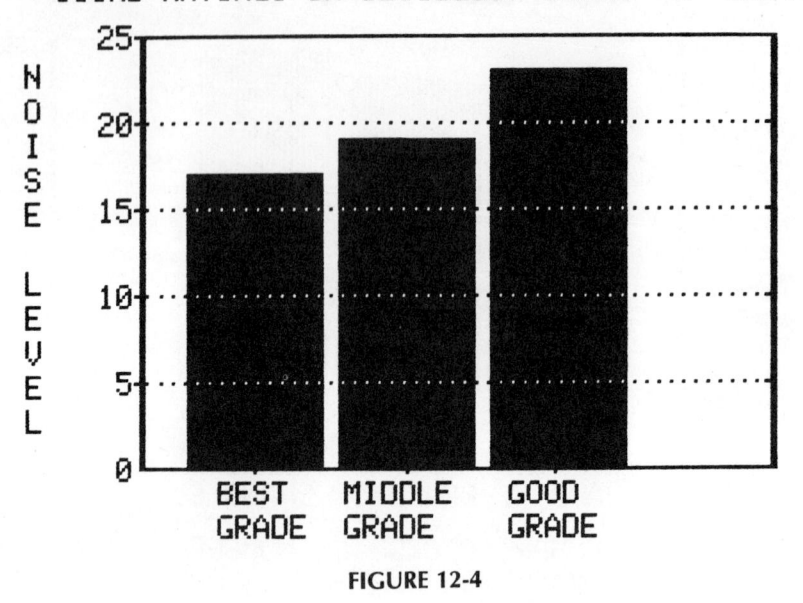

Bar chart — NOISE LEVEL (y-axis, 0 to 25) vs grade:
- BEST GRADE: ~17
- MIDDLE GRADE: ~19
- GOOD GRADE: ~23

FIGURE 12-4

Most equipment manufacturers supply more than one grade of equipment. They'll have their basic model, which is the least expensive but also will be the noisiest, have the fewest self-test and safety features, the greatest number of warranty repair calls, and so on. Many also supply a medium grade of equipment, a cut above the cheapest model, as well as their top-of-the-line equipment. This best item might include things the other grades haven't even thought of in terms of extra safety controls, higher-quality components, lower sound levels, etc. Naturally, your prospect will get what he or she pays for, and it's your job to illustrate why one grade of equipment might in reality be a better buy than another, less expensive one.

Figure 12-4 illustrates the sound levels of three grades of air conditioning units. All are from the same brand, and as you'd expect, the unit with the highest cost makes the least amount of noise. The helpful thing about this example is that it illustrates visually to your prospect that there is a choice, and exactly what one difference is between the available grades of equipment within a given brand. You could carry this out a bit and compare different brands, and even different approaches to the same problem. In our line, that might mean we'd recommend a unit on your roof as the quietest (but most expensive), a second choice as a system in your garage (you might hear it a little, but it costs less than the rooftop unit), and so on. If our prospect wants the quietest system available, he or she will have to spend the extra cash to get it. Something like noise level is difficult to really understand, too, and a graph like this one helps bring the concept home.

More on Costs

While the general focus should be on the potential savings a prospect can realize if he or she buys what you suggest, there are situations where you can use the projected cost figures to your benefit.

Figure 12-5 illustrates the operating costs for [whatever the customer is using], over a five-year period, based on two different levels of insulation a prospect may put into their home. You'll note that you want to stay away from cumulative costs here, as they grow so rapidly that you might get a bad reaction from the prospect. A line graph that shows two cost levels, like Figure 12-5 does, brings home to your prospect the difference in what he or she will spend if either 4" or 8" of insulation is put into their attic.

While this chart is obviously designed for someone selling insulation, the basic concept can be used in many other cases, and is particularly suited to those *options* you have available for sale.

For example, in our own business, we sell clock thermostats, units that automatically lower the temperature inside your home or office at night, when you don't want it as warm. Then, they'll bring the temperature back up to a

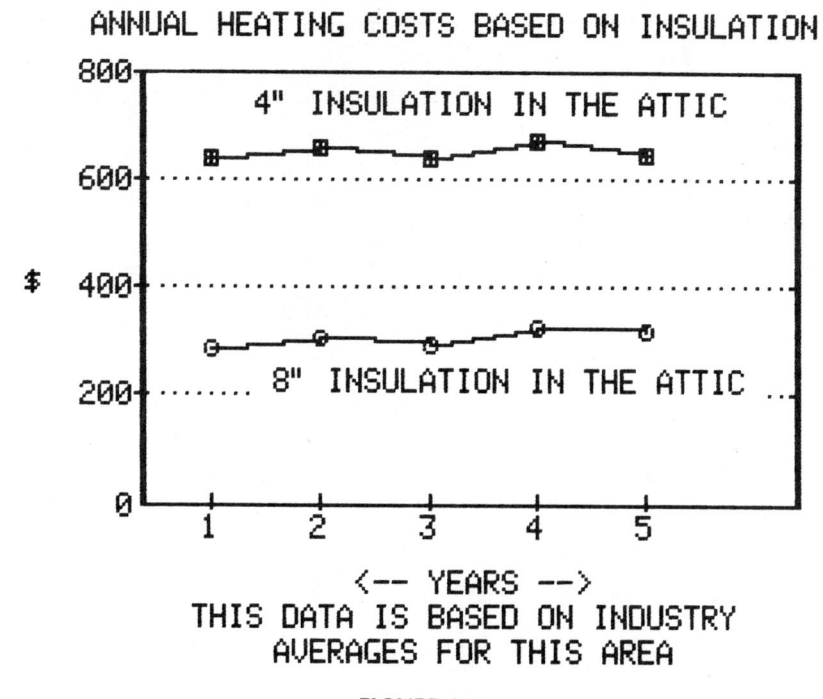

```
    ANNUAL HEATING COSTS BASED ON INSULATION
  800┐
     │  ┌─────────────────────────────────────┐
     │  │    4" INSULATION IN THE ATTIC       │
     │  ■──■─────■─────────■──■               │
  600┤· · · · · · · · · · · · · · · · · · · · │
     │  │                                     │
     │  │                                     │
$ 400┤· · · · · · · · · · · · · · · · · · · · │
     │  │                                     │
     │  o──o─────o─────────o──o               │
     │  │                                     │
  200┤· · · · · 8" INSULATION IN THE ATTIC · ·│
     │  │                                     │
     │  └─────────────────────────────────────┘
    0┼────┼─────┼─────┼─────┼─────┼
         1     2     3     4     5

              <-- YEARS -->
         THIS DATA IS BASED ON INDUSTRY
             AVERAGES FOR THIS AREA
```

FIGURE 12-5

comfortable level before you get up in the morning. If you—through the use of one of these thermostats—lower the nighttime temperature, you can save on your overall operating costs. A graph like Figure 12-5 is ideal to explain the concept to prospects, as they can quickly see (if the chart was designed to show operating costs with and without one of these clock thermostats) exactly what they'd pay to operate their furnace if they spend the extra cash to buy one, and what their costs will be if they use a standard thermostat. The same application works for those things you sell that don't give a prospect a lot of savings, where a cumulative chart wouldn't show a large accumulated savings. Instead, show them the difference in costs through the use of a line chart.

You can take things a step further, too, with a picture like the column chart of Figure 12-6.

On most clock thermostats, there are various *setback* periods. The more you set back the temperature, the more you can save on operating costs. To help get this across to your customers, Figure 12-6 illustrates the savings they can expect for two different setback temperatures—five degrees and ten degrees. This example makes the information easy to understand and *see*. The data is available on the literature from Honeywell.

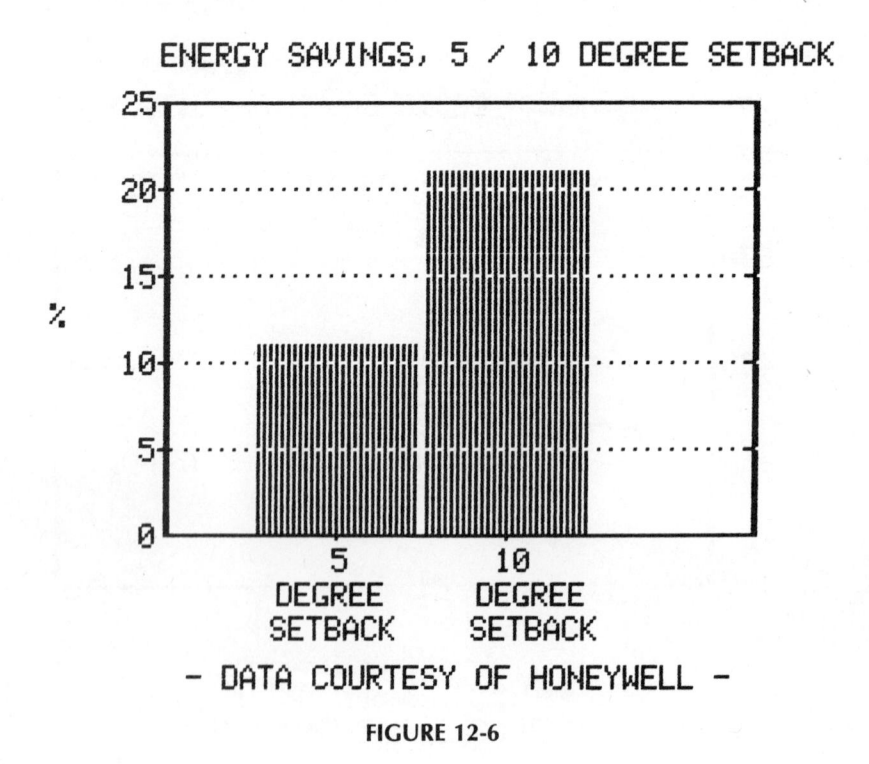

FIGURE 12-6

Payback

In many things, there's a *payback period* that can be calculated to let a prospect know that if they spend a certain amount of money today, they'll save it back (in the form of operating costs or maintenance expenses) over a specific period of time. It gets complex to try to create a computer-generated graph to plot this information, and in reality it's often more effective to use a table of figures to illustrate the point. The idea is a valuable tool, however, and one you should use if the products you sell lend themselves to it.

Another way to illustrate the strength of your product is to thoroughly explain its warranty to your prospect. Unfortunately, a lot of this sort of detail seems to go over people's heads, but you can get around this problem with a graph like Figure 12-7.

If you create a graph like this one and leave it with your prospect, it gives him/her something that really drives home the differences between the warranty periods for the three brands under consideration. Often, when someone hears "this has a 20-year warranty," it doesn't mean much. When seen in this form,

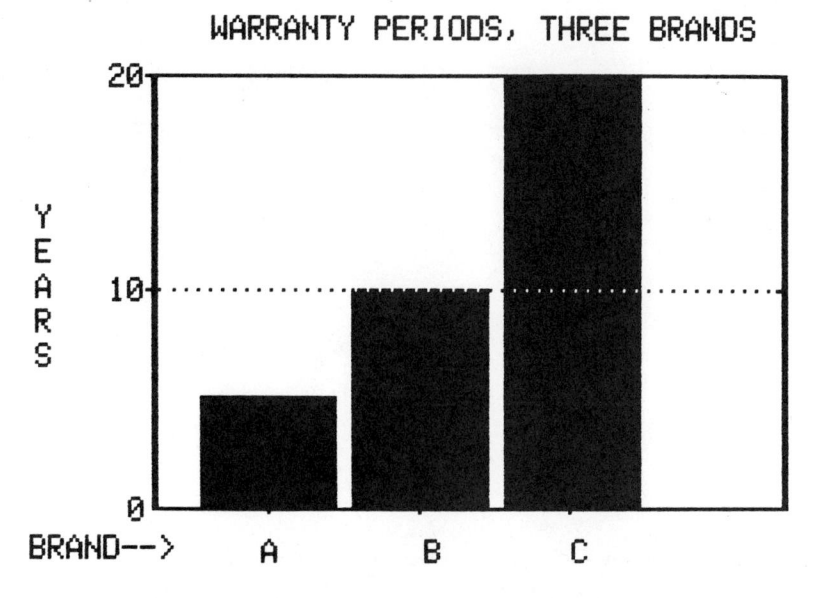

THIS GRAPH SHOWS THE WARRANTY PERIOD FOR
THE MAIN PART OF THE UNIT, FOR THESE 3 BRANDS

FIGURE 12-7

though, it's easy to relate to the differences between brands. You can also use much the same graph in a newspaper ad, to help get the point across that your equipment carries the longest warranty (or is the quietest, the most efficient, and so on).

More on Efficiency

Operating efficiency has more to it than just operating costs. Different things you sell might work better than others, may do a more effective job for a prospect. Or, they might operate better under certain conditions—engineering ideas that are often difficult to explain.

Figure 12-8 illustrates the efficiency rating for an electronic air cleaner, over different air volume levels. An air cleaner is something that takes dust and pollen out of the air and in effect does just what it says: it cleans the air. While it might seem obvious that the more air you move over one of these units, the less efficient it will be, it's sometimes hard to explain this to a prospect.

You'd use this example to show a potential customer that it's best to operate this particular unit at between 1,000 and 1,100 cubic feet of air per minute (CFM).

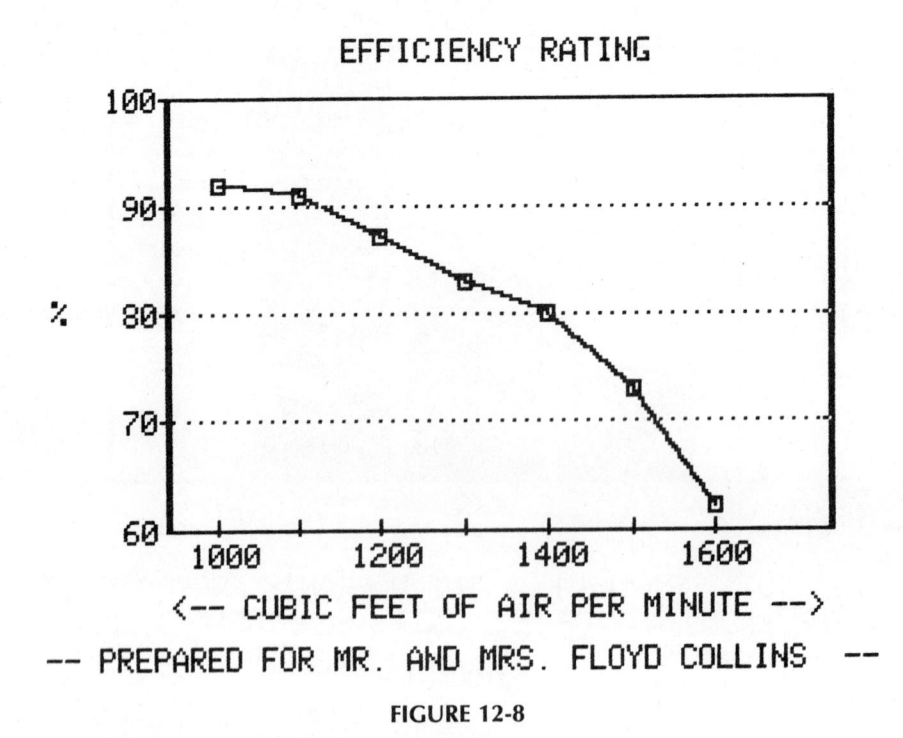

FIGURE 12-8

Once, as shown by the graph, you start to exceed those air volume levels, the efficiency of the unit drops off rapidly. The graph should also be personalized, as this one is, and given to the prospect: it's a good sales tool.

If you're wondering where you might find information like this, examine some of the literature and specification sheets you get from your suppliers. This particular data can be found on literature from Honeywell, which makes the electronic air cleaners we sell. However, while the same chart is available on Honeywell's literature, it's more effective to create a personalized graph for a prospect.

Where the Dollars Go

In any business, one objection we all run into is, "It costs too much." In many cases, this is a valid complaint, but just because this objection is voiced doesn't mean you won't make the sale. On the contrary, it's altogether different than, "We can't afford it," which, sadly, is sometimes the case. But a price objection means simply that the prospect isn't convinced that your product is worth what you're asking for it, that you haven't done an effective selling job.

With most things, it's a question of priorities as to where people put the cash they do have. They obviously need food, shelter, transportation, clothing, and so on—the dollars most likely will be first spent for the necessities of life, or in reality, for what the prospect *perceives* as something he or she must have. While there are all sorts of ways to counter a price objection, one of the easiest is to use a graph to show how the cost of what you want to sell fits in with a larger picture. When we present a proposal for a heating and cooling system for a new home, we sometimes hear that our price is too high, and when we do, the graph shown in Figure 12-9 is useful.

Figure 12-9 shows a prospect a visual representation of the total she or he will spend for their new home, based on six types of subcontractor work. Our end of things, heating, is printed as the darkest area, to highlight it. Once a prospect examines this illustration, he or she often concludes that we really weren't as expensive as originally thought.

If your own line of work doesn't show up as the least expensive based on the other trades you work with, how does it look compared to the whole project? How about on a per square foot or per unit basis? If you weren't competitive within your industry, you wouldn't still be in business, so there's something to your work that will put you in a favorable light when it comes to price. Perhaps it's a price/performance ratio for what you sell compared to what others handle.

A pie chart is very useful for this examination, as it effectively shows comparisons on a percentage basis, without dealing with the dollar figures (which, as you know, is where the objection came from to start with).

CONSTRUCTION COSTS BY SUBCONTRACTOR

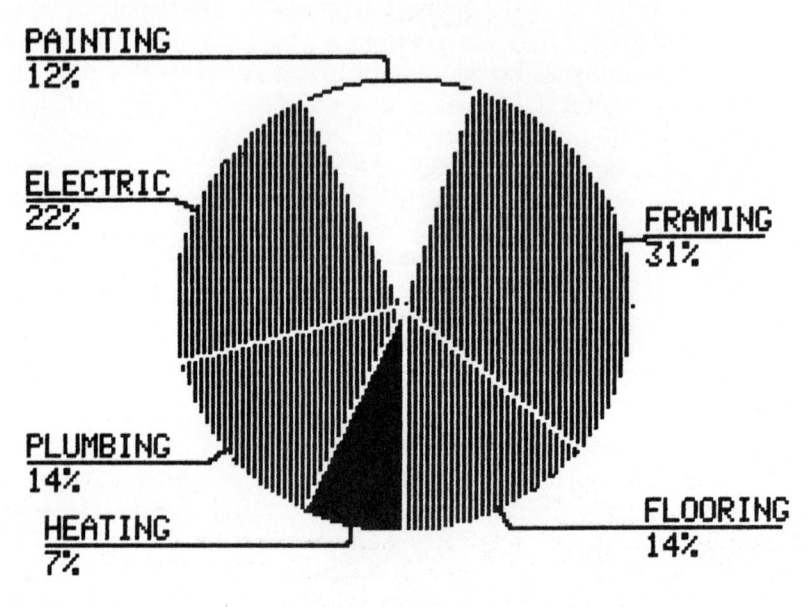

PAINTING 12%
ELECTRIC 22%
FRAMING 31%
PLUMBING 14%
HEATING 7%
FLOORING 14%

FIGURE 12-9

Summing Up

Business graphs can be used in a variety of ways to illustrate what you want and need to tell a prospect; you may be using them now as illustrations on customer literature you hand out. If any of these can be personalized with information about a specific prospect, it makes potential customers feel that since you spent the time and effort to create the graph, you'll probably do a conscientious job for them. So, the first place to start is with your own sales process and the items you sell. Not everything lends itself to a graph that helps sell it; on the contrary, it takes some hard thinking to come up with a few ideas that apply to any business. Think about *why* someone might want to purchase from you; outline the problems your business solves for its customers.

Since many products require energy to operate, a logical place to start is with any savings a customer will enjoy if she or he buys what you propose. A good way to show potential customers the savings they might expect if they buy from you is with an area graph, as it illustrates the cumulative dollars (or kilowatt-hours of electricity used, or therms of gas consumed, and so on) the savings will amount to.

One other advantage of giving a graph (and for that matter, anything that supports a purchase from you) to your prospect is that it will help with the problem of buyer's remorse. Almost everyone experiences this (both from the viewpoint of a buyer and a seller) and anything we can do to support a customer's purchase, the better our chances are that we'll have a satisfied buyer.

You might not want to talk about the unit that won't work fresh out of the box, but every business gets them now and again. You might as well greet the problem at your front door and do something constructive about it. As for graphics, it's useful to talk to your prospect about the ways your company looks after him/her both before and after the sale, and even to use a chart to illustrate why one grade of equipment and/or brand might be the best way to go. If you deal with things that *run,* you may have some units that are quieter than others. Why not create a simple graph to explain this to your prospect?

You can also focus on the add-on items your business handles (again, with the energy-savings approach) and use graphs to illustrate any potential savings a customer will enjoy, if only they spend a little more to start with. Or, does something (as an example from our business, we looked at electronic air cleaners) operate more efficiently under specific conditions?

Finally, if you get price objections, try putting what you sell into perspective, in relation to a larger dollar total. A pie chart can help you do this; it's up to you to find and select and graph the proper things that will put your product in its best light. In our business, for example, we can create an interesting comparison when we compare the cost—as a percentage of the total cost—for air conditioning for your home, as compared to what you spend to put it into your car. In a $100,000 home, a $3,000 refrigeration system represents only 3% of the total. A car air conditioning unit might run $600, which for a new auto that retails for, say $8,000, comes to 7.5%. When you break your price down like this, it seems more reasonable to your prospect.

Other Ideas

Since each business is so different in terms of what it sells and the way it does its selling, perhaps the best suggestion for other ideas is to ask you to concentrate on two things.

First, think about what you want to get across to your prospect. What do you want and need to say to tell your sales story? What's the most important thing about what you sell? What would you say to this prospect if you only could have one minute of his or her time? This thinking forces you to concentrate on the most important areas of your sales presentation, and perhaps you'll list them, which will give you ideas for graphs that can help. Always try to personalize things, too, for each prospect.

Second, try to put yourself in your prospect's shoes and consider what questions he or she would like answers to. What's important to this prospect?

Why? You can often learn the answers to those questions by listening for a few minutes to what the prospect has to say. Once you have some idea of what problem(s) this potential customer wants and needs to solve, then you can figure out the best solution for it. If you think about things from his or her point of view, you'll also come up with some ideas on how graphs can help; if you were this prospect, what sort of chart would convince you to buy from *you*?

A Tutorial Using Lotus 1-2-3™

13

One of the most exciting things about the IBM PC is its capability to work with *integrated* software, systems that send data from one area to another without having to leave one environment and start over with a new program.

While there are other integrated packages available for the PC that give a user more functions than 1-2-3, we've selected it because of its power, excellent documentation, and speed. Perhaps more of an overriding reason is 1-2-3's *popularity*—so many people are using it that it makes sense, if this information is to help the majority of people, to examine the system from a tutorial viewpoint.

What is 1-2-3? It's an integrated package that combines a massive spreadsheet with a number of file management functions, so it can act as a database and search your records according to criteria you specify; to list, for example, all the data that fits specific conditions. The system also has a graphics capability, so you can produce pictures of your information. The same data can be accessed in different ways by each part of the program, so you enter your information only once. You can then use the spreadsheet to manipulate it. You can look through and pull out specific records with the file manager, and you can create graphs based on the data. Perhaps best of all, the command or menu structures of an integrated program are the same for all its functions. Once you learn how to operate one section of the package, you'll most likely find it easier to effectively use each of its parts.

Lotus 1-2-3 is a trademark of Lotus Development Company

Before the integrated concept was available, a user required three or more separate programs to handle the same functions. Often, one couldn't communicate with the other, so data had to be entered in more than one file. That not only took more time, but all information was rarely put everywhere it had to go with complete accuracy.

The problem was partly solved as more software programs started to use the data interchange format (DIF®)—a file structure that allows data to be read by programs other than the system that created it. It's still a multistep process to move information from one program to another, so it's not as easy as integrated packages such as 1-2-3. But even 1-2-3 might not include every function you may need, so it uses the DIF file to communicate with other programs. The definitive book on this process is *The DIF File* by Donald H. Beil (Reston Publishing Company).

Our Pictures

The purpose of this chapter is to present a tutorial for creating a chart, starting with entering data on a 1-2-3 worksheet, to use this program to perform mathematical calculations on the information, and finally, to use the graphics capability of 1-2-3 to create a graph based on the manipulated data. We're going to concentrate on an IBM PC with two disk drives; the instructions are slightly different if you have an XT or an AT, as you'd probably want to install the 1-2-3 program on your hard disk.

Our function here is *not* to teach the operation of 1-2-3; it comes with an excellent manual. There are a number of books available to help you learn the program and one of the best is *Using 1-2-3*, by Geoffrey T. LeBlond and Douglas Ford Cobb (Que Corporation, 7960 Castleway Drive, Indianapolis, Indiana 46250).

Our approach will be similar to what we did in Chapter 1, where we went through the on-screen pictures of a graph. Here, we'll take you step-by-step through the process from initial worksheet creation and data entry with 1-2-3 to the slightly separate part of the package that will draw your graph.

The Main Process

Our general purpose will be to track the sales information on a monthly basis, along with advertising costs for the same period, let 1-2-3 compute our advertising as a percent of our sales, and graph this data. If you're working along with us, boot 1-2-3's System disk in drive A, have a data-ready disk in drive B, and start with the program's blank screen, once you've entered the current date and time.

DIF is a registered trademark of Software Arts Product Corp.

A TUTORIAL USING LOTUS 1-2-3

```
Lotus Access System    V.1A   (C)1983 Lotus Development Corp.          MENU
-----------------------------------------------------------------------
 1-2-3   File-Manager   Disk-Manager   PrintGraph   Translate    Exit
Enter 1-2-3 -- Lotus Spreadsheet/Graphics/Database program
=======================================================================



                              Sun    28-Oct-99
                                     8:34:57am




          Use the arrow keys to highlight command choice and press [Enter]
      Press [Esc] to cancel a choice; Press [F1] for information on command choices
```

FIGURE 13-1

Figure 13-1 is 1-2-3's main menu for its access system, where you select what function you'd like to do. The characters "1-2-3" are highlighted, and since you want to access the worksheet function of the package, just press <ENTER> to get the copyright notice, and then any key to continue.

Figure 13-2 is displayed next—a completely blank worksheet, ready to use. You want to track the months the data are for, and enter the sales, the advertising

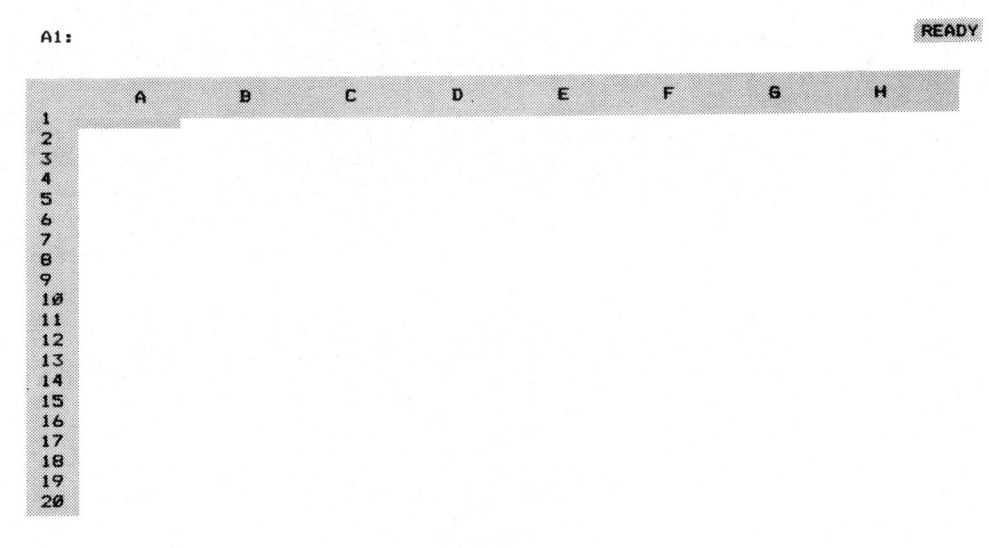

```
A1:                                                                    READY
          A        B        C        D        E        F        G        H
  1
  2
  3
  4
  5
  6
  7
  8
  9
 10
 11
 12
 13
 14
 15
 16
 17
 18
 19
 20
```

FIGURE 13-2

spent during the period, and what that advertising came to as a percent of the sales. Let's put in the first two column headings. To make sure the headings will line up properly, start each with a quotation mark (") to make them right-justify. Enter "Months in cell A1 and "Sales in cell B1.

Cell Sizes

When you arrive at column C1 and enter "Advertising, you can see that the word overflows its cell. When you write something into cell D1, the end of Advertising will be erased. Since 1-2-3 allows you to have individual column widths, let's make column C and D a bit wider so they'll accommodate the headings. A press of '/' displays 1-2-3's worksheet menu, as shown in Figure 13-3.

1-2-3 is always helpful when we see a menu like this; the second line gives one-word explanations of what you can do if you select what the cursor is currently positioned on. In this case, it's on Worksheet, and the system lets you know if you press <ENTER> that Column-Width is one of the things you'll be able to work with. Since you want to change the column-width setting for this column and the next, press <ENTER> to move to the next menu. Once you do, move the cursor so it's over Column-Width. Your screen should look like Figure 13-4.

<ENTER> lets you access the section that will allow you to reset the column widths, as shown in Figure 13-5.

The default, where the word Set is shaded, means you just have to press

```
C1: "Advertising                                                    MENU
Worksheet  Range  Copy  Move  File  Print  Graph  Data  Quit
Global, Insert, Delete, Column-Width, Erase, Titles, Window, Status
      A         B       C       D       E       F       G       H
 1    Months    Sales Advertising
 2
 3
 4
 5
 6
 7
 8
 9
10
11
12
13
14
15
16
17
18
19
20
```

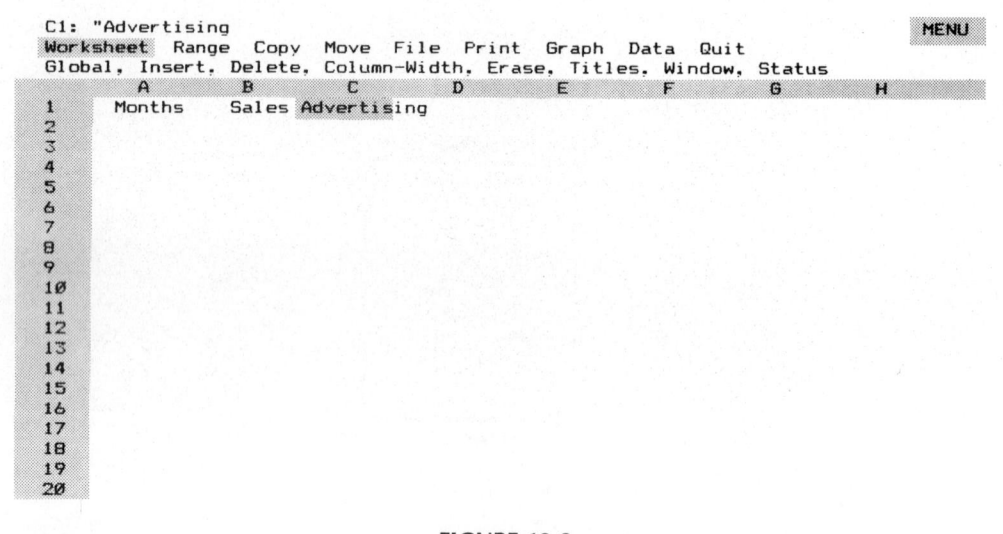

FIGURE 13-3

```
C1: "Advertising                                        MENU
Global  Insert  Delete  Column-Width  Erase  Titles  Window  Status
Set display width of the current column
        A         B         C         D         E         F         G         H
1       Months    Sales Advertising
2
3
4
5
6
7
8
9
10
11
12
13
14
15
16
17
18
19
20
```

FIGURE 13-4

<ENTER> to set the column width. When you do, 1-2-3 asks

Enter column width (1..72): 9

The (1..72) in this line indicates the range of column widths you're allowed, while the '9' is 1-2-3's default setting for its column size. Since we need to make this column wider, answer 15 and press <ENTER>. You'll return to the worksheet, and column C will now be 15 characters wide. While you're thinking of

```
C1: "Advertising                                        MENU
Set  Reset
Set width of current column
        A         B         C         D         E         F         G         H
1       Months    Sales Advertising
2
3
4
5
6
7
8
9
10
11
12
13
14
15
16
17
18
19
20
```

FIGURE 13-5

286   BUSINESS GRAPHICS

```
D1: "Advertising %                                              READY

        A         B          C              D         E        F
 1    Months    Sales    Advertising $  Advertising %
 2
 3
 4
 5
 6
 7
 8
 9
10
11
12
13
14
15
16
17
18
19
20
```

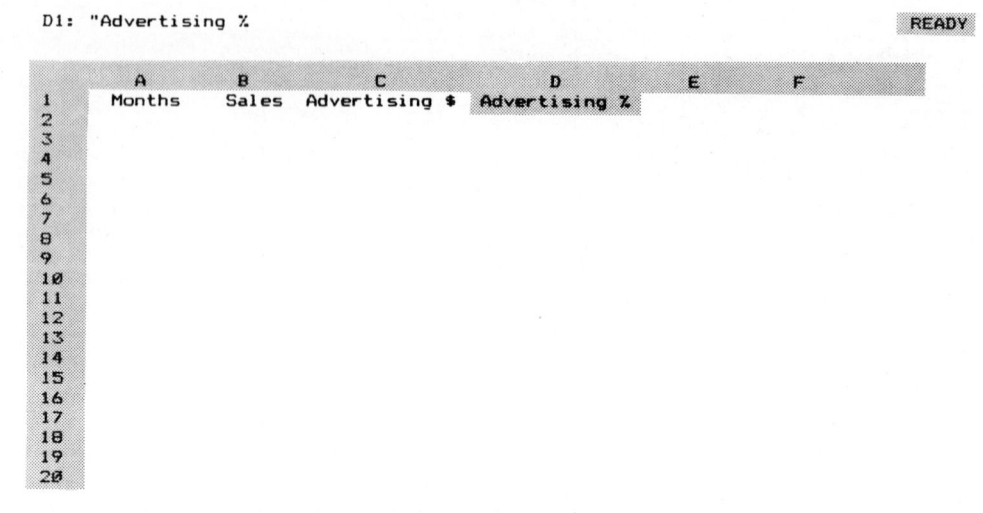

FIGURE 13-6

it, why not move to column D and follow the same procedure, to set its width to 15?

Once you've done that, edit your column heading in cell C1 by adding a dollar sign as "Advertising $ (you'll see it fits fine now), and enter "Advertising % into cell D1. 1-2-3 will now display a screen like Figure 13-6.

Now enter the months in column A, with a quotation mark ("Jan, "Feb,

```
D2:                                                             READY

        A         B          C              D         E        F
 1    Months    Sales    Advertising $  Advertising %
 2     Jan     37883         951
 3     Feb     39983         836
 4     Mar     45545        1010
 5     Apr     54433         998
 6     May     74644        1761
 7     Jun     66525        2165
 8     Jul     37866        1231
 9     Aug     48874        1555
10     Sep
11     Oct
12     Nov
13     Dec
14
15
16
17
18
19
20
```

FIGURE 13-7

etc.) in front of each name, so the columns will line up. When you put the dollar figures for sales in column B, and the advertising totals into column C, they'll automatically right justify, to line up neatly under the headings, as shown in Figure 13-7.

Enter the amounts on your worksheet so it matches Figure 13-7. You need to enter a formula to divide the information in each cell in column C by the sales total in column B. To do this in the best possible way, 1-2-3 gives you some powerful capabilities. The first is its capacity to express things in a percentage format. Since you'll be entering the formula and formatting information into cell D2, and then copying that cell to the locations below it, it's necessary to move the cursor to cell D2.

Automatic Percent

You access the format function with the usual '/,' which displays the command menu. Since you don't want to put *all* the figures on your screen into a percentage format, you need to move the cursor over the word Range and press <ENTER> to let 1-2-3 know you want to affect a specific range of information. Once the cursor is positioned over Range, the default, Format, is shaded, and since that's what you want to do—format a range of numbers—press <ENTER>. Another line lists the options

Fixed Scientific Currency, General +/− Percent Date Text Reset

Move the cursor so it's over Percent and press <ENTER>. 1-2-3 asks

Enter number of decimal places (0..15): 2

The '2' is the default setting, and it's what you want—you need your percentages to be expressed like 2.37% or 4.15%. So, press <ENTER> to accept the default. Since you're not instructing 1-2-3 to format all the numbers on your worksheet in a percentage format, the system will inquire about the range of data you wish to format in this way. It asks

Enter range to format: D2..D2

Since you're working with this one cell (which you'll copy into others in just a moment), simply press <ENTER> to mark your range. The top line on your screen will indicate that the current cell location is formatted to put its numbers into a percentage format with 2 decimal places (P2)

D2: (P2)

The Formula

A logical next step might seem to be to enter a formula to divide advertising expenses by the monthly sales total; for cell D2, this would be expressed as (C2/B2).

However, when 1-2-3 finds no data on which to perform the math functions you request, it displays ERR. In this example, when you copy your formula from cell D2 to cells D3 through D13, cells with no information on which to calculate a result—cells D10 through D13—will display ERR.

There's a way around this, using 1-2-3's built-in @IF function. Essentially what you want to tell 1-2-3 is that if there's no figure in cell B2, then print a zero in cell D2. If there *is* data in cell B2, you can expect there'll be information in the advertising column, too (cell C2), so you can go ahead with the formula you started with: divide the number in cell C2 by that in cell B2, and let 1-2-3 convert and display it as a percentage figure. This is explained in both the Basic Skills section and in the Appendices of your 1-2-3 manual, and perhaps a little more clearly in the chapter on Functions in *Using 1-2-3*. The logic is similar to what you'd find in an IF-THEN *Basic* programming statement:

IF [data A] IS EQUAL TO [data B], THEN [put C in the cell]. BUT, IF [data A] IS NOT EQUAL TO [data B], THEN [put D there].

You'd write the formula like this:

@IF(A = B,C,D)

```
D2:  (P2)  @IF(B2=0,0,C2/B2)                                      READY

           A          B           C              D         E      F
     1    Months     Sales    Advertising $  Advertising %
     2     Jan       37883        951            2.51%
     3     Feb       39983        836
     4     Mar       45545       1010
     5     Apr       54433        998
     6     May       74644       1761
     7     Jun       66525       2165
     8     Jul       37866       1231
     9     Aug       48874       1555
    10     Sep
    11     Oct
    12     Nov
    13     Dec
    14
    15
    16
    17
    18
    19
    20
```

FIGURE 13-8

A TUTORIAL USING LOTUS 1-2-3   289

In essence, this says if A is equal to B, then put C into the cell you're working on. If A is not equal to B, then put D into it.

In the world of mathematics and computers, these letters are known as variables, so once you have the basic logic down, you can substitute real numbers or formulas for the A,B,C, or D figures in the expression. You're writing this formula in cell D2, and once you enter it and press <ENTER>, your command is shown in the first line of Figure 13-8.

The number shown in cell D2 is 2.51—calculated by dividing your advertising total for January ($ 951) by your sales for the same period ($ 37883), and letting 1-2-3 automatically put the result into a percentage format.

Copying

You now need to copy this formula into the other cells in column D. The slash (/) gives you the command menu, so move the cursor over Copy and press <ENTER>. Line two of the control panel shows

   Enter range to copy FROM: D2..D2

Since you're just going to copy a single cell, press <ENTER>. On the right side of line two you'll see

   Enter range to copy TO: D2

```
D13:                                                                    POINT
Enter range to copy FROM: D2...D22      Enter range to copy TO: D3...D13

         A         B          C              D         E       F
  1    Months     Sales    Advertising $  Advertising %
  2    Jan        37883         951          2.51%
  3    Feb        39983         836
  4    Mar        45545        1010
  5    Apr        54433         998
  6    May        74644        1761
  7    Jun        66525        2165
  8    Jul        37866        1231
  9    Aug        48874        1555
 10    Sep
 11    Oct
 12    Nov
 13    Dec
 14
 15
 16
 17
 18
 19
 20
```

FIGURE 13-9

Move the cursor to cell D3 and press a period (.) to tell 1-2-3 that's the first cell you want to copy *into*. Then continue to move the cursor down to cell D13. Your screen will look like Figure 13-9.

The far right-hand side of Figure 13-9 shows your final range locations, where you want to copy *to*: D3 through D13. Also, this entire range of cells is highlighted on your screen, as shown on Figure 13-9. Press <ENTER> now, to complete the copying process.

Figure 13-10 shows you the result, with the original formula you put into cell D2 copied into the next 11 cells below it. Where there is no data on which to base a calculation, 1-2-3 put 0.00%, as a result of your use of its @IF function.

1-2-3 automatically expects your data to be *relative* to its new cell location. That is to say, each time you copy formulas into new cells, their values will change according to their place on the worksheet. You can, if you wish, use an *absolute* address, which means the formula wouldn't change, no matter where you copy it on your worksheet.

In our example here, we want each cell to relate to its new location, as we want the formulas in those cells to operate based on other information in the same row of data. For example, if you scroll through the cells below D2, you'll see that your formula now reflects its new home:

cell D3:	@IF(B3=0,0,(C3/B3))
cell D4:	@IF(B4=0,0,(C4/B4))
cell D5:	@IF(B5=0,0,(C5/B5))
~	~
cell D10:	@IF(B10=0,0,(C10/B10))
cell D11:	@IF(B11=0,0,(C11/B11))

D2: (P2) @IF(B2=0,0,C2/B2)   READY

	A	B	C	D	E	F
1	Months	Sales	Advertising $	Advertising %		
2	Jan	37883	951	2.51%		
3	Feb	39983	836	2.09%		
4	Mar	45545	1010	2.22%		
5	Apr	54433	998	1.83%		
6	May	74644	1761	2.36%		
7	Jun	66525	2165	3.25%		
8	Jul	37866	1231	3.25%		
9	Aug	48874	1555	3.18%		
10	Sep			0.00%		
11	Oct			0.00%		
12	Nov			0.00%		
13	Dec			0.00%		

FIGURE 13-10

Graphics

Once your information is on the worksheet, save it for future reference. The command sequence is /F, which gives you the file menu. Move the cursor to Save and press <ENTER>. You're asked what file name to save the file under; enter a name (perhaps ADVER) and press <ENTER> to complete the save process.

Move the cursor to cell D2, then press /G to put you into the graph-creation section of the main program. Figure 13-11 illustrates the picture you see.

The default for the Type of graph is shaded, so select that by pressing <ENTER>. The second line changes to

Line Bar XY Stacked-Bar Pie

Move the cursor over Bar, to select a bar chart, and press <ENTER>. Your screen will return to the same image as Figure 13-11. The next step is to select the range of information you want to graph. 1-2-3 allows up to six items on each graph; just move the cursor over the A to select it as your first data range. Press <ENTER>. You're prompted

Enter first data range: D2

Since the worksheet cursor already rests on your starting data (you want to create a graph of your advertising as a percent of your sales), you need to press a period (.) to let 1-2-3 know cell D2 is the start of your information. Then, move the

```
D2: (P2) @IF(B2=0,0,C2/B2)                                    MENU
Type  X  A  B  C  D  E  F  Reset  View  Save  Options  Name  Quit
Set graph type
         A         B         C              D           E        F
 1     Months    Sales   Advertising $  Advertising %
 2      Jan      37883         951          2.51%
 3      Feb      39983         836          2.09%
 4      Mar      45545        1010          2.22%
 5      Apr      54433         998          1.83%
 6      May      74644        1761          2.36%
 7      Jun      66525        2165          3.25%
 8      Jul      37866        1231          3.25%
 9      Aug      48874        1555          3.18%
10      Sep                                 0.00%
11      Oct                                 0.00%
12      Nov                                 0.00%
13      Dec                                 0.00%
14
15
16
17
18
19
20
```

FIGURE 13-11

cursor down to cell D9, where your information ends. Your screen will look like Figure 13-12.

The area you selected (D2 through D9) is noted on line 2, and also is shaded in the worksheet area. Press <ENTER> to confirm your selection.

So you can print this basic graph later on, save it onto disk. Move the cursor to cover Save and press <ENTER>. Enter a name for the graph (perhaps MY FIRST GRAPH) and press <ENTER> to save it. If you have a Hercules graphics card, or a color monitor and adaptor, you can ask to view the graph during this process, to see your graph and the changes you make as you enter them.

Since your first graph was so elementary, let's make a few changes to make it more presentable. First, move the cursor to Options and press <ENTER>. Line two will change to

Legend Format Titles Grid Scale Color B&W Data-Labels Quit

To make your simple graph readable, let's use a few of these options to spruce it up a little. Let's first add a title. Move the cursor in line two over Titles and press <ENTER>. Since the First title location, the top of the graph, is the default, press <ENTER> again and enter your title: Advertising as a Percent of Sales. Press <ENTER> *twice,* to save the first title and put you into the title menu once again.

This time, rather than the first title, let's put a title along the X axis that runs along the bottom of the picture. Move the cursor over the X-Axis mark and press <ENTER>. You're asked to enter the X axis title, so enter <--MONTHS--> and press <ENTER>. You can, with the equipment described above, view your graph at any time during this process, to see the results of your changes.

```
D9: (P2) @IF(B9=0,0,C9/B9)                                    POINT
Enter first data range: D2..D9
```

	A	B	C	D	E	F
1	Months	Sales	Advertising $	Advertising %		
2	Jan	37883	951	2.51%		
3	Feb	39983	836	2.09%		
4	Mar	45545	1010	2.22%		
5	Apr	54433	998	1.83%		
6	May	74644	1761	2.36%		
7	Jun	66525	2165	3.25%		
8	Jul	37866	1231	3.25%		
9	Aug	48874	1555	3.18%		
10	Sep			0.00%		
11	Oct			0.00%		
12	Nov			0.00%		
13	Dec			0.00%		
14						
15						
16						
17						
18						
19						
20						

FIGURE 13-12

A TUTORIAL USING LOTUS 1-2-3

```
Lotus Access System    V.1A  (C)1983 Lotus Development Corp.           MENU
-----------------------------------------------------------------------------
1-2-3   File-Manager   Disk-Manager   PrintGraph   Translate   Exit
Enter Lotus Graphics Printing system
=============================================================================




                              Sun   28-Oct-99
                                  8:34:57am






        Use the arrow keys to highlight command choice and press [Enter]
    Press [Esc] to cancel a choice; Press [F1] for information on command choices
```

FIGURE 13-13

To add grid lines, move the cursor over the word Grid and press <ENTER>. Your screen will show

Horizontal Vertical Both Clear

Let's add horizontal grid lines to your picture, and since that's the default selection (the cursor rests over the word Horizontal), press <ENTER>.

Let's now save this graph, by pressing ESC to return to the main menu. There, position the cursor over Save and press <ENTER>, type in a file name (perhaps MY SECOND GRAPH) and press <ENTER>.

Although 1-2-3 is called an integrated package, that doesn't mean you never have to switch disks. In this case, to get a hard copy of your graphs, you need to move to the PrintGraph section of 1-2-3. First, you need to exit 1-2-3's worksheet; the slash (/) sends you to the main command list. Position the cursor over Quit and press <ENTER>. 1-2-3 asks you to confirm that you wish to quit, and once you do, it returns you to its access system menu (Figure 13-13).

Move the cursor over the PrintGraph selection and press <ENTER>. Put the PrintGraph disk into drive A and press <ENTER>.

For now, let's make one change in the default settings—let's have the graph print at half its largest possible size. Move the cursor over Options and press <ENTER>; place it over Size and press <ENTER>. Finally, move the cursor over Half and press <ENTER>. This process looks complex on paper, but once you do it a time or two, it'll go very fast. 1-2-3 allows various *fonts* for the titles you'll put on your graphs. We'll ask 1-2-3 to print the titles for our sample graphs using a font called BLOCK 1, as shown in Figure 13-14.

BUSINESS GRAPHICS

```
Copyright 1982, 1983 Lotus Development Corp.  All Rights Reserved.        MENU
-----------------------------------------------------------------------------
Select  Options  Go  Configure  Align  Page  Quit
Select pictures
=============================================================================
  SELECTED GRAPHS    COLORS              SIZE       HALF      DIRECTORIES

                     Grid:     Black    Left Margin:   .750   Pictures
                     A Range:  Black    Top Margin:    .395   B:\
                     B Range:  Black    Width:        6.500   Fonts
                     C Range:  Black    Height:       4.691   A:\
                     D Range:  Black    Rotation:      .000
                     E Range:  Black                          GRAPHICS DEVICE
                     F Range:  Black    MODES
                                                              Epson FX80/1
                     FONTS              Eject: No             Parallel
                                        Pause: No
                     1: BLOCK1                                PAGE SIZE
                     2: BLOCK1
                                                              Length   11.000
                                                              Width     8.000
```

FIGURE 13-14

Select is the default, so press <ENTER> to select the graph you want to print. 1-2-3 lets you select a number of charts to print in sequence, but for now, just pick one. You'll see a menu of all the graphs stored on the data disk you have in drive B. Move the cursor over MY FIRST GRAPH and press <ENTER>.

Now, press ESC twice to go back to the main menu, and move the cursor to Go and press <ENTER> to tell 1-2-3 to go and get the graph and print it.

The system will then print your picture, although it's not the fastest process in the world. Figure 13-15 is an example of the first graph you did.

Now, using the same process as above, load the second picture you did with

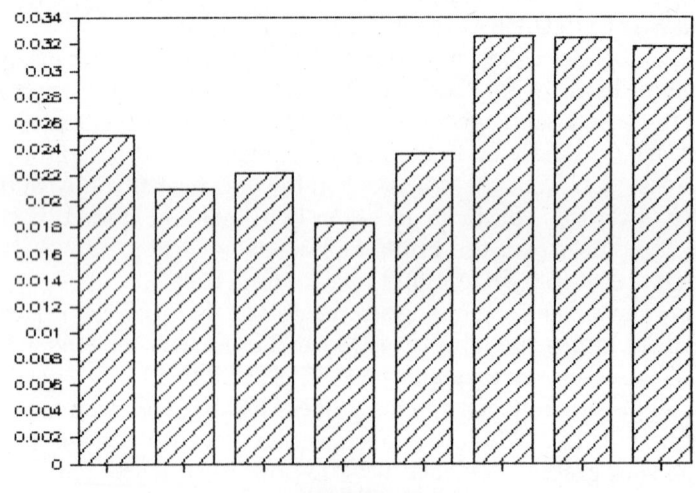

FIGURE 13-15

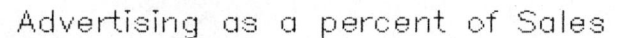

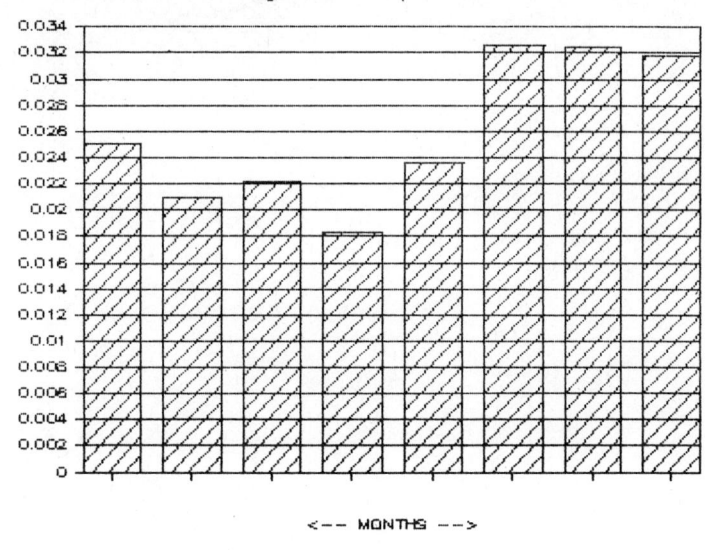

FIGURE 13-16

the title and grid line, and other data, and ask 1-2-3 to print it. It should look like Figure 13-16.

You can then follow the prompts to leave 1-2-3.

Congratulations! You've moved all the way from entering sales and advertising data on a blank 1-2-3 worksheet, to creating a somewhat complex line (the @IF function plus the formula), to printing a hard copy of your information, as a graphics picture. While this basic example is simple, it contains all the main elements you need to create excellent graphs based on your data, using the power of 1-2-3.

Available Software

A

The following list is intended to give you an overall view of the graphics programs available as of this writing. Software never remains stable; in the fast-moving computer world, it seems to change more rapidly than anything else.

A good source of current software information comes from a wide variety of computer-related magazines. Most publications carry software *reviews,* in which the programs are sent along to a (hopefully) knowledgeable person, who'll then test the product and write a critical evaluation of its capabilities, its ease (or difficulty) of use, and so on. While a few readers complain that some reviews are more advertising hype than anything else and sometimes seem to be based solely on the published literature a product has, in actual practice it's rare for someone to review a program without really trying it. Certainly the magazines don't want to lose credibility with their readers by publishing reviews based only on sales literature; the people who write reviews also won't last long in the field if they don't do a thorough job. All in all, magazines are your best source of what will do the job for you, right now.

A more complete source of information is available in the directories that focus on IBM software products. Because of the time it often takes a book to get into print, some of the information you'll find there is out of date when the book is published. However, *most* of the knowledge you'll pick up from these directories is still valid (many programs never change or add features). The key thing to consider when you look at a directory is how the comments were arrived at. The more people who looked at and commented on a software program, the more eyes that examined how the thing works, the better the chances will be that you'll get a realistic and correct picture of things. Also, give some consideration to the basic focus of the directory; if games are your interest, you don't want one devoted to business programs, and vice versa.

The first and obvious place to look is at your local computer store. More often than not, the folks here will be able to offer intelligent help and good advice. The best ones will always let you spend some time with whatever software you're considering, just to try it out. They'll also know how each program they sell operates, and (generally) what its weak and strong points are. If you find a program you think you might want to buy, ask your local store to order it for you, on an "if it will do what its literature promises, I'll keep it" basis.

Available Software Programs

Abstat
Anderson-Bell
P.O. Box 191
Canon City, CO 81212
(303) 275-1661

APC Chart
Aztec, Inc.
23265 South Point Drive, Suite 100
Laguna Hills, CA 92653
(714) 770-8406

APS Graph
Automated Professional Systems, Inc.
270 Madison Avenue
New York, NY 10016
(212) 725-2442

Atlas
Strategic Locations Planning
4030 Moorpark Avenue, Suite 123
San Jose, CA 95117
(408) 985-7400

Automatic Business Graphics
Transaction Systems, Inc.
8708 East 39th Street
Tulsa, OK 74145
(918) 663-3436

Bar Graph Generator
Data Consulting Group
12 Skylark Drive, Suite 18
Larkspur, CA 94939
(415) 927-0990

Basic Business Graphics
Softext Publishing
17 East 45th Street, Suite 605
New York, NY 10017
(212) 986-5985

Benchmark
Metasoft Corp.
6509 West Frye, Suite 12
Casa Grande, AZ 85224
(602) 961-0003

Boardroom Graphics
Analytical Software Inc.
10939 McCree Road
Dallas, TX 75238
(214) 340-2564

BPS Business Graphics
Business and Professional Software
143 Binney Street
Cambridge, MA 02142
(617) 491-3377

AVAILABLE SOFTWARE

btGraf
Bigtrees Software Corporation
P.O. Box D
Arnold, CA 95223
(209) 795-5104

Business Graphics System
Peachtree Software
3445 Peachtree Road
Atlanta, GA 30326
(404) 239-3000

Business Graphics Package
Transaction Systems, Inc.
8708 East 39th Street
Tulsa, OK 74145
(918) 663-3436

Chartman
Graphics Software Inc.
1972 Massachussetts Avenue
Cambridge, MA 02140
(617) 491-2434

Chart Pro
Micro Control Systems, Inc.
143 Tunnel Road
Vernon, CT 06066
(203) 872-0602

Chart-Master
Decision Resources
25 Sylvan Road So
Westport, CT 06880
(203) 222-1974

Chart Star
Micropro International Corp.
33 San Pablo Avenue
San Rafael, CA 94903
(415) 499-1200

ColorWizard
ABM Computer Systems
3 Whatney Drive
Irvine, CA 92714
(714) 859-6531

Condor Graf
Condor Computer Corp.
2051 South State Street
Ann Arbor, MI 48104
(313) 769-3988

Context Management MBA
Context Management Systems
23864 Hawthorne Blvd., Suite 101
Torrance, CA 90505
(213) 378-8277

CP/Graph I
Continental Resources, Inc.
175 Middlesex Tpke.
Bedford, MA 01730
(617) 275-0850

Cue Chart
ISSCO
10505 Sorrento Valley Blvd.
San Diego, CA 92121
(619) 452-0170

Curve Fitter
Interactive Microware, Inc.
P.O. Box 139
State College, PA 16804
(814) 238-8294

Data∗Easy Bar Graph Generator
Data∗Easy Software
877 Bounty Drive, # EE203
Foster City, CA 94404
(415) 927-0990

dGraph
Fox & Geller, Inc.
604 Market Street
Elmwood Park, NJ 07407
(201) 794-8883

DIFmaster
Starside Engineering
P.O. Box 18306
Rochester, NY 14618
(716) 461-1027

Draftsman
Starware
200 K Street, NW
Washington, DC 20006
(202) 331-8833

DR Draw
Digital Research, Inc.
60 Garden Court
Monterey, CA 93942
(408) 649-3896

DR Graph
Digital Research
60 Garden Court
Monterey, CA 93942
(408) 649-3896

Easygraf
Miracle Computing
313 Clayton Court
Lawrence, KS 66044
(913) 843-5863

Energraphics
Enertronics Research, Inc.
150 North Meremac
St. Louis, MO 63100
(314) 725-5566

Enhanced Business Graphics
Strobe, Inc.
897-5A Independence Avenue
Mountain View, CA 94043
(415) 969-5130

Executive Graphics
CR Toren
3700 Gilmore Way
Burnaby, British Columbia, Canada
   U5G 4M1
(604) 437-3521

Fastdraw PDQ
DHD, Inc.
7777 Leesburg Pike
Falls Church, VA 22043
(703) 556-0950

Fast Graphs
Innovative Software, Inc.
9300 West 110th Street, # 380
Overland Park, KS 66210
(913) 383-1089

GDSS
Data Business Vision, Inc.
3510 Dunhill Street, Suite B
San Diego, CA 92121
(619) 450-1557

Giraph Business Graphics
IMRS, Inc.
111 High Ridge Road
Stamford, CT 06905
(203) 359-9655

Golden Software Graphics System
Golden Software
2055 Foothills Road
Golden, CO 80401
(303) 279-1021

Grafcalc
Miracle Computing
313 Clayton Ct.
Lawrence, KS 66044
(913) 843-5863

Graff Hopper
Data Business Vision, Inc.
3510 Dunhill Street, Suite B
San Diego, CA 92121
(619) 450-1557

Grafix Idea
Idea Ware, Inc.
225 Lafayette Street
New York, NY 10012
(212) 334-8043

Grafix Partner
Brightbill-Roberts
120 East Washington, Suite 421
Syracuse, NY 13202
(315) 474-3400

Grafox
Fox & Geller
604 Market Street
Elmwood Park, NJ 07407
(201) 794-8883

GrafTalk
Redding Group, Inc.
109 Danbury Street
Ridgefield, CT 06877
(203) 431-4661

Graphease
Software Solutions, Inc.
305 Bic Drive
Milford, CT 06460
(203) 877-9268

Graphics
Software Products International
10240 Sorrento Valley Road
San Diego, CA 92121
(619) 450-1526

Graphing Assistant
IBM
Old Orchard Road
Ormonk, NY 10504
(914) 765-1900

Graphics Generator
Robert J. Brady
Bowie, Maryland 20715
(301) 262-6300

Graphmaker
Option Ware, Inc.
4 Barnard Lane, Corporate Place
Bloomfield, CT 06002
(203) 243-5554

Graph Magic
International Software Marketing
120 East Washington Street
University Building # 421
Syracuse, NY 13302
(315) 474-3400

Graphit
Miracle Computing
313 Clayton Ct.
Lawrence, KS 66044
(913) 843-5863

Graph 'n' Calc
Desktop Computer Software, Inc.
303 Portrero Street
Santa Cruz, CA 95060
(408) 458-9095

Graphpac
Frontier Technologies Corp.
3510 North Oakland Avenue
Milwaukee, WI 53211
(414) 964-8689

Graph-Pro
Wiley Software
605 Third Avenue
New York, NY 10158
(212) 850-6009

GraphStation
Signiature Information Systems Corp.
8175 Hetz Drive, Suite 300
Cincinnati, OH 45242
(513) 831-8008

GraphPlan
Chang Labs
5300 Stevens Creek Blvd.
San Jose, CA 95129
(408) 246-8020

Graph Power
Ferox Microsystems
1701 North Fort Meyer Drive
Arlington, VA 22209
(703) 841-0800

Graphwriter
Graphic Communications, Inc.
200 Fifth Avenue
Waltham, MA 00254
(617) 890-8778

Gridplot
Grid Systems, Inc.
2535 Garcia Avenue
Mountain View, CA 94043
(415) 961-4800

GSS Chart, GSS Solutions
Graphic Software Systems, Inc.
25117 Southwest Parkway
Wilsonville, OR 97070
(503) 682-1606

HIgraph-III
Houston Instrument
8500 Cameron Road
Austin, TX 78753
(512) 835-0900

Infographics Design Intelligence
Infographics, Inc.
201 Shipyard Way
Newport Beach, CA 92663
(714) 675-4385

KeyChart Business Graphics System
Roland DG
7200 Dominion Circle
Los Angeles, CA 90040
(213) 685-5141

K-Graph
Micro Data Base Systems
P.O. Box 248
Lafayette, IN 47902
(317) 463-2581

Lotus 1-2-3
Lotus Development Corporation
55 Wheeler Street
Cambridge, MA 02138
(617) 492-7171
(800) 343-5414

MetaGraph
Graphicon Systems
399 Sherman Avenue # 10
Palo Alto, CA 94306
(415) 329-1791

Micro-Graf, Print-Graf
Micro-Z Company
P.O. Box 2426
Rolling Hills, CA 90274
(213) 377-1640

Mirrorgraph
Mirror Images
1223 Peoples Avenue
Troy, NY 12180
(518) 274-2335

Peachtree Graphics Language
Peachtree Software
3445 Peachtree Road N.E.
Atlanta, GA 30326
(404) 239-3000

PC Paint
Mouse Systems Corp.
2336 W. Walsh Avenue
Santa Clara, CA 95051
(408) 988-0211

PFS: Graph
Software Publishing Corp.
1901 Landings Drive
Mountain View, CA 94043
(415) 962-8910

Plottrax
Omicron
57 Executive Park, S., Suite 590
Atlanta, GA 30329
(404) 325-0124

PPG
Ganesa Group International, Inc.
1495 Chain Bridge Road, Suite 300
McLean, VA 22101
(703) 442-0442

PC Palette
IBM
Old Orchard Road
Ormonk, NY 10540
(914) 765-1900

PC Slide
Management Graphics, Inc.
2064 Avenue Road
Toronto, Ontario, Canada MSM 4A6
(416) 485-2855

Picture This
Chartpak
1 River Road
Leeds, MA 01053
(413) 584-5446

Presenter PC
Dicomed Corp.
12000 Portland Avenue, P.O. Box 246
Minneapolis, MN 55440
(612) 885-3000

Presentation Master
Digital Research, Inc.
60 Garden Court
Monterey, CA 93942
(408) 649-3896

Pyxel Applications
2917 Mohawk Drive
Richmond, VA 23235
(804) 320-5573

R:Graph
Fox & Geller, Inc.
604 Market Street
Elmwood Park, NJ 07407
(201) 794-8883

AVAILABLE SOFTWARE

Series One Plus—Execu/Plot
Executec Corp.
811 Canyon Creek Sq.
Richardson, TX 75080
(214) 239-8080

Sign-Master
Decision Resources
25 Sylvan Road South
Westport, CT 06880
(203) 222-1974

SlideWrite
Advanced Graphics Software, Inc.
333 West Maude Avenue, Suite 105
Sunnyvale, CA 94086
(408) 749-8620

Statgraphics
STSC, Inc.
2115 East Jefferson Street
Rockville, MD 20852
(800) 592-0050

StretchCalc
Paladin Software
2895 Zanker Road
San Jose, CA 95134
(408) 946-9000

Thoroughbred Color Business Graphics
SMC Software Systems
P.O. Box 600
Basking Ridge, NJ 07920
(201) 647-7000

Tec-Mar
Advanced Systems Consultants
18653 Ventura Blvd., Suite 351
Tarzana, CA 91356
(818) 990-4942

UGraf
Transparent Data Systems, Inc.
P.O. Box 18276
San Jose, CA 95158
(408) 559-0228

UltraFile
Continental Software
11223 South Hindry Avenue
Los Angeles, CA 90045
(213) 417-8031

Video Graph Plus
Windmill Software, Inc.
2209 Leonminister Drive
Burlington, Ontario
L7P 3WB Canada
(416) 336-3353

VisiTrend/Plot
Paladin Software
2895 Zanker Road
San Jose, CA 95134
(408) 946-9000

Zebra Business Graphics
IMRS, Inc.
111 High Ridge Road
Stamford, CT 06905
(203) 359-9655

Book Bibliography

B

Alves, Jeffrey R., Dennis P. Curtin, and Anne K. Briggs. *Planning and Budgeting for Higher Profits*. New York: Van Nostrand Reinhold, 1983, 170 pp., $15.50. This good-sized book focuses on the use of VisiCalc (Apple edition, although other computers can use the information) to create templates designed to help with what the title says.

Anderson, Anker V. "Graphing Financial Information: How Accountants Can Use Graphs to Communicate." New York: The National Association of Accountants, 919 Third Avenue, New York, NY 10022, 1983, 51 pp. A helpful guide to the benefits and pitfalls of business graphics, from an accounting viewpoint, this booklet is well written, with good illustrations.

Angell, Ian O. *A Practical Introduction to Computer Graphics*. New York: Halstead Press/Wiley, 1982, 143 pp., $16.95. A 'how-to' programming book with the emphasis on Fortran programs; the user is expected to have a working knowledge of Fortran; there is a listing of Fortran programs in the book.

Beil, Donald H. *The DIF File*. Reston, VA: Reston Publishing, 1983, 235 pp. This book is *the* guide to the data interchange format, which allows you to move information from one software program to another. There are numerous examples for both the Apple and the IBM PC.

Bernstein, Leopold. *The Analysis of Financial Statements*. Homewood, IL: Dow Jones-Irwin, 1978, 311 pp. An excellent accounting book with the focus on what its title says.

Carey, Omer, and Dean Olson. *Financial Tools for Small Business*. Reston, VA: Reston Publishing, 1983, 269 pp., $12.95. A useful book filled with case examples focused on financial statement data.

Cohen, Neil and Lois Graff. *Financial Analysis with Lotus 1-2-3*. Bowie, MD: Brady Communications, 1984, 317 pp. This helpful book is also available with a disk, so its worksheets are already constructed and ready for use.

Conklin, Dick. *PC Graphics*. New York: John Wiley & Sons, 256 pp., $15.95. 40 Basic programs and instructions on how to form your own graphic images with Basic programs.

Curtin, Dennis P., Jeffrey R. Alves, and Anne K. Briggs. *Controlling Financial Performance for Higher Profits*. New York: Van Nostrand Reinhold, 1983, 170 pp., $15.50. This excellent book uses VisiCalc templates to help with what the title says. Even though it's focused on the Apple, anyone who works with a spreadsheet can easily adapt the techniques here to other computers.

Dixon, Robert L. *The Executive's Accounting Primer*. New York: McGraw-Hill, 1971, 328 pp. This volume is a nuts-and-bolts look at accounting, with numerous real world examples.

Edwards, James Don, et al. *How Accounting Works—A Guide for the Perplexed*. Homewood, IL: Dow Jones-Irwin, 1983, 374 pp., $19.95. An excellent book that not only explains the ins and outs of accounting, but often why things need to be done a certain way. There's also good information on analysis of financial data.

Foley, J. D. *Fundamentals of Interactive Computer Graphics*. New York: Addison/Wesley, 1981, 664 pp., $37.50. Very hardware-oriented and focused on minicomputers.

Fowler, John. *The IBM PC/XT Graphics Book*. Englewood Cliffs: Prentice-Hall, $16.95.

Greenburg, Donald, Aaron Marcus, Allan H. Schmidt, and Vernon Gortner. *The Computer Image: Applications of Computer Graphics*. Reading, MA: Addison-Wesley, 1982, 128 pp., $27.95. A general discussion of the hardware end of computer images, with the central focus on scientific uses, with the emphasis on minicomputer applications. There's an excellent chapter on business graphics.

Grillo, John P., and J. D. Robertson. *Introduction to Graphics for the IBM Personal Computer*. Dubuque, IA: William C. Brown, 1983, 165 pp., paperback. This book is programming-oriented.

Jarrett, Irwin M. *Computer Graphics & Reporting Financial Data*. New York: Ronald Press, 1983, 250 pp., $49.95.

Laric, Michael V. and Ronald Stiff. *Lotus 1-2-3 for Marketing and Sales*. Englewood Cliffs, NJ: Prentice-Hall, 1984, 230 pp., $14.95.

Lefferts, Robert. *How to Prepare Charts and Graphs for Effective Reports*. New York: Harper & Row, 1981. ("Elements of Graphics" was its hardcover title.) This book is focused on the design of charts, starting with grid paper to the size ratio between the height and width of your images.

Lord, Kenniston W. *Graphics with the IBM PC*. Glenview, IL: Scott, Foresman and Company, 1985, 304 pp., $19.95. Author Lord does a good job presenting both details and operating advice on various pieces of hardware and software for the PC.

Lowry, Albert. *How to Become Financially Successful by Owning Your Own Business*. New York: Simon and Schuster, 1981, 407 pp., $14.95. This book (constantly updated) contains a great deal of useful information on the examination of financial data.

MacGregor, A. J. *Graphics Simplified: How to plan and prepare effective charts, graphs, illustrations and other visual aids*. Toronto: University of Toronto Press, 1979, $3.50, paperback. This book helps with what its title implies—how to hand-create graphs.

Osteryoung, Jerome E. and Daniel E. McCarthy. *Analytical Techniques for Financial Management*. New York: John Wiley & Sons, 1985, 282 pp. Although complex in the formulas it presents, this book is filled with useful information that will help anyone understand financial data.

Oystein, Ore. *Graphs & Their Use*. Washington: New Math Library, 1975, $7.50. This book is filled with algorithms and mathematical formulas.

Runyon, Richard P. *How Numbers Lie*. New York: The Lewis Publishing Company, 1981, 182 pp., $7.95. The use and misuse of statistics.

Sandler, Cory. *Desktop Graphics for the IBM PC*. New Jersey: Creative Computing Press, 1984, $14.95.

Schmid, Calvin F. *Statistical Graphics: Design Principles and Practices*. New York: Wiley Interscience, 1983, 224 pp., $24.95. This wide-ranging and excellent book has a lot of good examples of poor charts.

Scott, Joan E. *Introduction to Interactive Computer Graphics*. New York: Wiley, 1982, 225 pp., $17.00. Information on hardware for minicomputer applications; an introduction to the equipment and programming required for minicomputer graphics.

Tracy, John. *How to Read a Financial Report*. New York: John Wiley & Sons, 1980, 156 pp. This book has more information in it than its short length would seem to allow. A good book for basic accounting concepts.

Waite, Mitchell. *Computer Graphics Primer*. Indianapolis, IA: SAMS Books, 1979, 184 pp., $14.95. Programming information on how to draw shapes on different kinds of computers, how to create your own video graphics.

Magazine Bibliography

C

The articles listed below form a wide base of the current literature on the subject of graphs in general, and business graphics in particular. Items directly concerned with programming techniques, or those without any business focus, were not included. Some magazines will be available through your local library, and most back issues can be purchased from the publishers.

While some of the articles focus on Apple software, the items noted are available in IBM PC versions, in (perhaps) a slightly different form, so references to them are included here.

Following the article citations are the names and addresses of the most popular computer-oriented magazines, where you can order back issues.

Article Citations

Ahl, David H. "Evaluations of VisiTrend and VisiPlot from Personal Software," *Creative Computing Buyer's Guide 1982,* pp. 176–179.

Alker, Pauline Lo. "Accent on the Visual: Business Computer Graphics," *Desktop Computing,* 8/83, pp. 32–37.

Alesandrini, Katheryn. "Graphics that Dress for Success," *PC Magazine,* January 8, 1985, pp. 165–175.

Alperson, Burton L. "Beyond Bar Charts," *PC World,* 8/84, pp. 152–159.

Bayle, Elisabeth. "Picture This—and do it yourself," *Personal Computing*, 8/82, pp. 50–54, 58–64, 150.

Benoit, Ellen and Bernstein, Amy. "Graphic Detail," *Business Computer Systems*, 4/84, pp. 40–57.

Benson, Terry. "Graphics Capabilities for the Small Business," *Interface Age*, 2/82, pp. 66–69, 138–141.

Bishop, Jack. "Charting your Course on the PC," *PC Magazine*, January 8, 1985, pp. 177–185

Bonner, Paul. "Communicating with Presentation Graphics," *Personal Computing*, 7/83, pp. 110–119, 174.

Bonner, Paul. "Punching up your Presentation with Powerful Pictures," *Personal Computing*, 9/83, pp. 86–92, 209.

Bonoma, Thomas. "Thumbing Through Disk Magazines," *Microcomputing*, 1/84, pp. 28–36.

Bonoma, Thomas. "Probing a pfs Crash," *Microcomputing*, 2/84, pp. 22–27 (also includes brief reviews of BPS Business Graphics and Chartman IV).

Breiger, G.R. "VisiPlot and VisiTrend (review)," *Microcomputing*, 3/82, pp. 199–200, 210.

Brevdy, Mary. "Microsoft Chart (review)," *InfoWorld*, January 14, 1985, pp. 56–60.

Bryan, Shawn. "Statpro XT Brings Serious Statistical Tools to Micros," *Business Computer Systems*, 1/85, pp. 98–100, 104.

Burlbaw, Edward. "VisiPlot (review)," *Peelings II*, 2/82, pp. 31–32.

Burns, Diane and Sharyn Venit. "Business Graphics on a grand Scale," *PC Magazine*, December 25, 1984, pp. 228–241.

Burns, Diane and S. Venit. "Samurai Image Processor," *PC Magazine*, January 8, 1985, pp. 199–204.

Busch, David D. "A Decision for Business Graphics," *Microcomputing*, 1/84, pp. 58–60.

Campbell, Mary. "How to Design Better Spreadsheet Forecasts," *Lotus*, 5/85, pp. 73–77.

Campbell, Mary. "Designing a Trend Analysis Report, *Lotus*, 6/85, pp. 41–46.

Casella, Phillip. "Graph, a graphics program for the Apple from SPC (review of PFS: Graph)," *InfoWorld*, 8/2/82, pp. 54–55.

Celentano, Joseph P. "1-2-3 Graphics Made Easy," *PC World*, 8/84, pp. 271–275.

Chin, Kathy. "Business Graphics: Integrated vs. Stand-Alone," *InfoWorld*, Volume 5, # 45 (10/83), pp. 52–54.

Cleveland, William S., along with Persi Diaconis and Robert McGill. "Variables in Scatterplots look more highly correlated when the scales are increased ," *Science*, 6/82, pp. 1138–41.

Cobain, Bernard. "Olivetti PR 230 Jet Printer," *CAP*, 12/83, pp. 70.

Crider, Bill. "Professional Presentations," *PC World*, 8/84, pp. 248–254.

Cusick, Elizabeth. "Better Business Graphics," *Popular Computing*, 8/85, pp. 28–35.

Derfler, Frank J. "Graphics Software Comes of Age," *Microcomputing*, 4/84, pp. 32–34.

Derfler, Frank J. "Energize Your Graphics," (a review of EnerGraphics), *PC Magazine*, 5/1/84, pp. 171–178.

Derfler, Frank J. "A Day In The Life Of CADplan," *PC Magazine*, 5/15/84, pp. 216–224.

Diocco, John. "In the Third Dimension," *Business Computing*, 12/83, pp. 54–57.

Fiondella, Paul. "Videograms: a designer's description," *Popular Computing*, 11/83, pp. 114–117, 204–206.

Forbes, Ron. "Business Graphics Creates a Wealth of Information," *Business Software*, Sept./Oct. 1983, pp. 11–17.

Forney, Jim. "Video Wizardry with PC-Eye," *PC Magazine*, February 19, 1985, pp. 172–182.

Fowler, John. "PC Graphics Challenge the Mighty Cray," *PC Magazine*, January 8, 1985, pp. 205–209.

Free, John. "The Creativity Explosion in Computer Graphics," *Popular Science*, 6/82, pp. 80–83.

Freeze, Ken. "V-C-N Execuvision (review)," *InfoWorld*, October 29, 1984, pp. 62–66.

Fridlund, Alan J. "Grafix Partner (review)," *InfoWorld*, October 22, 1984, pp. 61–64.

Fridlund, Alan J. "Chartstar (review)," *InfoWorld*, March 25, 1985, pp. 45–46.

Gabel, David. "What's a graphics package like? (review of PFS: Graph)," *Personal Computing*, 2/83, pp. 102.

Gabriele, Rosemarie. "VisiTrend/VisiPlot (review)," *Popular Computing*, 3/83, pp. 166, 168, 171–172.

Gildewell, Richard. "Desktop Plotting: Getting Graphic on Paper," *Business Computer Systems,* 3/85, pp. 119–124.

Glau, Gregory R. "Graphs Make the Point," *inCider,* 2/83, pp. 136–141.

Glau, Gregory R. "Pick the Perfect Picture," *Desktop Computing,* 8/83, pp. 20–22.

Glau, Gregory R. "A Slice of Time," *inCider,* 8/83, pp. 40–45.

Glau, Gregory R. "Cash Flow Woes," *inCider,* 1/84, pp. 152–154.

Glau, Gregory R. "Selling Savings," *inCider,* 3/84, pp. 126–127.

Glau, Gregory R. "Taxing Times," *inCider,* 4/84, pp. 116–117.

Hamburger, Cindy. "60-Second Slides," *PC World,* 8/84, pp. 261–267.

Hansen, Jim. "A Tiger's Eye View of Computer Graphics," *Microcomputing,* 5/81, pp. 184–188.

Hansen, Jim. "Color Highlights Business Reports," *Desktop Computing,* 11/82, pp. 39–48.

Hart, Glenn A. "IBM Sets a New Standard," *PC Magazine,* December 25, 1984, pp. 171–178.

Hart, Glenn A. and Jim Forney. "Video Board Reviews," *PC Magazine,* February 19, 1985, pp. 121–171.

Heck, Mike. "Business Graphics for the IBM PC and Apple III," *Interface Age,* 10/83, pp. 124–126.

Heck, Mike. "PFS: Graph (review)," *Interface Age,* 5/83, pp. 86–91.

Heintz, Carl. VisiTrend is covered along with other Visi-products, *Interface Age,* 8/81, pp. 72, 148–149.

Herbert, Russel L. "Portable Graphics," *Portable Computer Magazine,* 8/83, pp. 56–60.

Hixson, Amanda. "VisiTrend and VisiPlot, trend analysis and plotting," *InfoWorld,* 5/3/82, pp. 34–36.

Jones, Gerald E. "Picture Processors: A Look at Business Graphics Software," *Interface Age,* 11/83, pp. 52–63.

Jones, Maureen. "Getting Good Graphs," *PC Magazine,* July 23, 1985, pp. 217–218.

Kass, Mark A. "Z-Soft's PC Paintbrush," *PC Products,* 5/85, pp. 125–128.

Keogh, Jim. "Power Presentations," *Personal Computing,* 10/83, pp. 56–68.

King, Elliot. "A Complete Buyer's Guide to Hard Copy Graphics," *PC Magazine,* 3/84, pp. 129-137, 194–196.

King, Elliot. "Business Presentations," *CAP,* 9/84, pp. 32–34, 36.

Kolata, Gina. "Computer Graphics comes to Statistics," *Science,* 9/82, pp. 919–20.

Lambert, Steve. "The Graphics Gallery," *PC World,* 12/84, pp. 180–187.

Lang, Laura. "Effective Slides from your IBM," *CAP,* 9/84, pp. 38.

Latamore, Bert. "A Graphic Display," *Desktop Computing,* 12/82, pp. 8–15.

Li, Lindsay. "Drawing Conclusions," *Business Computer Systems,* 4/84, pp. 115–130.

Loceff, Michael. "Computer Graphics . . . a Picture is worth 1K words," *Interface Age,* pp. 66–68, 124–128.

Lord, Ken. "Six Color Graphics Tools," *Desktop Computing,* 8/83.

McClain, Larry. "A Guided Tour of Business Graphics," *Popular Computing,* 11/83, pp. 86–96, 156–157.

McCune, David. "More Color than Big Blue," *PC World,* 8/84, pp. 168–174.

McLamb, Ken. "Persuasion made easy with Powerful Presentations," *Personal Computing,* 2/82, pp. 34–39.

McMullen, John and Barbara. "Videoshow 150 (review)," *InfoWorld,* March 11, 1985, pp. 36–37.

Mamis, Robert A. "Integrated-7: Graphics Shine, But It Doesn't Do Windows," *Business Computer Systems,* 4/85, pp. 94–102.

Martellaro, John. "PFS GRAPH (review)," *Peelings II,* Volume 4, Number 4, 1983, pp. 16–18.

Meinel, C. "Computer graphics on every desk," *Technology Review,* 10/82, pp. 74–75.

Myers, E. "Computer Graphics: Boom in Business Graphics," *Datamation,* 4/81, pp. 92–99.

Orloff, Richard W. "GeoGraphics," *PC World,* 1/85, pp. 148–155.

Personal Computing. "Graphics for the executive (covers PFS: Graph)," 5/82, pp. 190–192.

Personal Computing. A section about the Executive Briefing System, 8/82, pp. 51–52.

Personal Computing. A brief mention of PFS: Graph, 8/82, pp. 58.

Petrosky, Mary. "Presentation Software Sales Up," *InfoWorld,* July 8, 1985, pp. 34–37.

Post, Dan W. "Graphwriter for Good Graphics," *Interface Age,* 10/83, pp. 105–108.

Powell, David. "Buyer's Guide to Low-Cost Plotters," *Popular Computing*, 11/83, pp. 120–122.

Powell, David B. "VideoShow Hones Your Image," *Popular Computing*, 2/85, pp. 113–116.

Puglia, Vincent. "Pretty Pixels," (Review of ExecuVision), *PC Magazine*, 3/6/84, pp. 143–146.

Quinet, Linda. "Making Marketing Data Meaningful," *List*, 8/84, pp. 44–46.

Ramsdell, Robert E. "The Flexibility of VisiPlot (review)," *Byte*, 2/82, pp. 32–36.

Raskin, Robin and Tom Christopher. "PC Systems for Pie Chart Picassos," *PC Magazine*, January 8, 1985, pp. 187–197.

Rosch, Winn. "Fast graphs: quick, colorful and easy," *PC Magazine*, Vol 2, # 1.

Rosch, Winn. "Graphix Plus a Whole Lot More," (Review of Graphix Plus), *PC Magazine*, 5/1/84, pp. 179–183.

Ross, Steven C. "Charting the Future with pfs:GRAPH (review)," *inCider*, 4/83, pp. 84–89.

Rubin, Charles. "High-Powered Presentation Graphics," *Personal Computing*, 4/84, pp. 65–74.

Rubin, Charles. "Visual Decision Support," *Personal Computing*, 2/85, pp. 101–109.

Runchal, Akshai K., Jacob Treger, and Clement J. Tam. "Pick of the Plotters," *PC World*, 8/84, pp. 132–142.

Sandler, Corey. "Business Graphic's Business Graphics," *PC Magazine*, Vol. 2, #

Schnell, John. "Getting a Grip on Graphics," *PC Magazine*, 4/17/84, pp. 165–169.

Shamoon, Sherry. "The Bank is a True Believer in Slick Slides and Charts," *Management Technology*, 12/84, pp. 42–45.

Shea, Tom. "Personal Computer Graphics: Pushing Technology to the Limit," *InfoWorld*, Volume 5, Number 51, 1983, pp. 34–36.

Shelton, Joe. "Ventures with VisiCalc (includes VisiPlot/VisiTrend)," *Softalk*, 7/82, pp. 115–116.

Shelton, Joe. "Ventures with VisiCalc (covers Apple Business Graphics)," *Softalk*, 7/82, pp. 115–118.

Shotwell, R. "Computer Graphics: new picture possibilities for publishers," *Publisher's Weekly*, 6/4/82, p. 32.

Skiba, Mark. "Correspond in Color," *PC World*, 11/83, pp. 217–222.

Softalk. "At 3.3, VisiCalc Spawns a Family (review of VisiPlot/VisiTrend)," 6/81, pp. 31–32.

Solomont, David and Donna Stein. "Computer Graphics: Productivity Picture," *Business Computer Systems,* 12/82, pp. 41–44.

Stinson, Craig. "Ventures with VisiCalc (includes VisiPlot and VisiTrend)," *Softalk,* 7/81, pp. 14–17.

Stryker, Timothy. "What you didn't know about NEC Spinwriter," *Microcomputing,* 10/82, pp. 32–37.

The', Lee. "The Graphics Side of Printers," *Personal Computing,* 5/85, pp. 123–131.

Waese, Jerry R. and Jim Heid. "Teledin," *Microcomputing,* 1/84, pp. 62–64.

Waldman, Barry. "Computer from the Launching Pad," *PC Magazine,* 5/1/84, pp. 185–188.

Waite, Mitchell, and Christopher Morgan. "IBM PC Graphics Primer," parts I, II, III, *PC Magazine,* Vol. 1 # 12 +

Wilcox, David L. "The Boom in Business Graphics," *PC World,* 8/84, pp. 54–61.

Williams, Gregg. "A Graphics Primer," *Byte,* 11/82, pp. 448–470.

Young, Jeffrey. "Computer Graphics: Toys or Tools?," *Personal Computing,* 2/85, pp. 53–59.

Magazine Addresses

Byte
P.O. Box 372
Hancock, NH
03449
(603) 924-9281

Business Computer Systems
Cahners Publishing
221 Columbus Avenue
Boston, MA 02116
(617) 536-7780

CAP
Computer Accessories and Peripherals
2900 Bristol Street
Suite A107
Costa Mesa, CA 92626
(714) 751-2533

Compute!
Small Systems Services, Inc.
625 Fulton Street
P. O. Box 5406
Greensboro, NC
27403
(919) 275-9809

Computer Buyer's Guide and Handbook
Computer Information and Publishing, Inc.
Box 1563
FDR Station
New York, NY
10150

Computer Shopper
P.O. Box F
Titusville, FL 32780
(305) 269-3211

Creative Computing
Ziff-Davis Publishing
One Park Avenue
New York, NY 10016
(212) 725-3500

Desktop Computing
Wayne Green Inc.
Peterborough, NH 03458
(603) 924-9471

inCider
CW Communications/Peterborough
Peterborough, NH 03458
(603) 924-9471

InfoWorld
1060 Marsh Road, Suite 200C
Menlo Park, CA 94025
(213) 926-9544

Lotus
Lotus Development Corp.
One Broadway
Cambridge, MA 02142
(617) 494-1192

Management Technology
12th Floor, 135 West 50th Street
New York, NY 10020
(212) 247-6540

Microcomputing
Wayne Green Inc.
Peterborough, NH 03458
(603) 924-9471

Micro Co-op Newsletter
610 East Brook Drive
Arlington Heights, IL 60005
(312) 228-5115

Micro Discovery
5152 Katella, # 102
Los Alamitos, CA 90720
(213) 493-4441

PC Buyer's Guide
Ziff-Davis Publishing
20 Brace Road, Suite 110
Cherry Hill, NJ 08034
(212) 503-5444

PC Magazine
Ziff-Davis Publishing
One Park Avenue
New York, NY 10016
(212) 725-4694

PC Products
Cahners Publishing Company
221 Columbus Avenue
Boston, MA 02116
(617) 536-7780

PC World
555 DeHaro Street
San Francisco, CA
94107
(415) 861-3861

Personal Computing
Hayden Publishing Company
50 Essex Street
Rochelle Park, NJ
07662
(201) 843-0550

Popular Computing
P.O. Box 372
Hancock, NH 03449
(603) 924-9281

Small Business Computers Magazine
Ziff-Davis Publishing
One Park Avenue
New York, NY 10016
(212) 725-3500

Softside
Softside Publications
6 South Street
Milford, NH 03055
(603) 673-0585

Softalk
Softalk Publishing Company
11160 McCormick Street
Box 60
North Hollywood, CA 91603
(213) 980-5074

Software
Fast Access
2803 Ocean Park Blvd., Suite K
Santa Monica, CA 90405

Index

A

@IF function, 288, 295
Absolute cell address, 290
Accountant, 132, 176, 177, 184, 203
Accounting, 4, 105
   fee, 151
Accounts:
   old, 103, 104, 126, 128, 198
   overdue, 125
   past-due, 110
   payable, 97, 99, 105, 107, 108, 122, 185, 260–263
   receivable, 3, 5, 58, 89, 90, 96, 97, 99, 101, 103–105, 107, 108, 110, 122, 125, 127, 178, 189, 190, 192, 197, 201–203, 260, 261
Accumulated savings, 274
Acid test ratio (see Ratio, acid test)
Ad:
   budget, 157
   campaign, 165
   television, 168
Advertising, 1, 2, 5, 24–26, 37, 52, 149, 150, 152, 158, 164–167, 169, 170, 171, 173, 174, 235, 282
Agency, collection, 129
Air conditioning, 157, 158, 279
Analytical graphics (see Graphics, analytical)
Area chart (see Graph, area)
Assets, 86, 104, 177, 182, 183, 188, 189, 191, 192, 201, 203, 263
   current, 104–106, 184–188, 201, 202, 258
   fixed, 189, 190, 201, 203
   liquid, 86, 190
   quick, 105, 106
   total, 203
   turnover rate, 192, 193
Attorney, 64
Auto cost, 155
Average:
   collection period, 178, 197–199, 202
   volume, 82
Axis:
   X, 7
   Y, 7

B

Bad debt (see Debt, bad)
Balance Sheet, 104, 110, 200, 205, 206, 256
Banker, 176, 196, 201
Bar chart (see Graph, bar)

BASIC, 288
Basis:
   calendar year, 13, 22
   cost (see Cost, basis)
   draw, 78
   per mile, 29, 30
   retail (see Retail, basis)
   square foot, 52
   yearly, 22
Beil, Donald H., 282
Benefit, fringe (see Fringe benefits)
Bid, 1, 47, 64, 65, 67, 82 (see also Estimate, Proposal, Quotation)
   dollar value, 114
   volume, 64–68, 115
Bill:
   electricity, 158
   energy, 267
   telephone (see Telephone, bill)
Bonus, 132
Border, 16, 37
Brand of equipment, 110, 119
Break-even line, 46
Budget:
   ad (see Ad, budget)
   forecast, 4
Builder, 81
Building, 86
Business, 154
   cycle, 23
Buyer's remorse, 269

C

Calendar year basis (see Basis, calendar year)
Callback, 128
   rate, 51, 121, 122
Calls, service, 30, 38
Campaign, ad, 165
Capital, 254
   invested, 183
   owner-invested, 138
   working (see Working capital)
Cash, 189, 190
   condition, 82
   flow, 1, 2, 43, 186, 187, 200, 205, 223, 224, 226
   net, 223
   sales, 197
Cause and effect, 170
Change:
   percentage of, 37, 46, 56
   proportional, 36
   rate of, 144
   seasonal (see Seasonal change)
Charge:
   late (see Late charge)
   minimum, 69

Charges:
   electricity, 156
   finance (see Finance charge)
   gasoline, 156
   telephone (see Telephone charge)
Chart:
   area (see Graph, area)
   arithmetic, 36, 78
   bar (see Graph, bar)
   column, 3, 7, 28, 31, 32–35, 38 (see also Graph, column)
   map, 36
   pictorial, 36
   pie, 26, 38
   semilogarithmic, 36, 37
   stacked, 38
      column, 31
   window, 26, 248
Checks, payroll, 133
Clock thermostat, 273, 274
Cobb, Douglas Ford, 292
Code, department, 79
Collection:
   agency, 129
   period, 126, 200 (see also Average collection period)
   terms, 94
Collections, 123, 124
Collins, Mr. and Mrs. Floyd, 276
Color, 4, 16, 38
Column chart (see Chart, column)
Column-Width, 284
Commission, sales, 47
Communication, 10, 27, 265
Compensation insurance, workman's, 142
Competitors, 75
Construction, 76
Contracting work, 75, 78
Contractor, 47, 59, 61, 75, 76, 79, 81, 82
   general, 80
   heating, 80
Contracts, 47, 61, 63, 75, 80, 82, 126
Corporation, 203
Cost, 2, 69, 72, 74, 83, 93–95, 107, 109, 132, 173, 180, 267
   auto, 155
   basis, 132
   credit, 126
   cumulative, 273
   delivery, 148
   direct, 44–47, 57, 147, 150
      labor (see Direct labor)
   electricity, 157, 160
   interest (see Interest cost)
   labor, 72, 74, 75, 92, 93, 117, 133, 135–141, 146–148, 216
   material, 131, 135–137, 146, 147
   of goods sold, 233, 234
   operating (see Operating costs)
   overhead, 83

319

INDEX

payroll (*see* Payroll cost)
per mile, 150
postage, 51, 150
sales, 47, 48, 57, 83, 107
telephone, 149
total, 44, 93
truck, 5, 28, 150
  repair, 5, 28, 30
utility (*see* Utility cost)
variable, 146
warranty repair, 128
Credit, 91, 97, 124, 195, 200, 262
  cost, 126
  policies, 94
  risk, 126
  sales, 126, 197
  terms, 86
Creditors, 107, 108, 254
Cumulative:
  costs, 273
  data, 34, 35, 38
Current:
  assets (*see* Assets, current)
  liabilities, 104–106, 184, 185, 187, 193, 201, 258
  ratio (*see* Ratio, current)
  revenue, 41
Customer, 69, 86, 101, 103, 109, 117, 122, 128, 230
Cycle:
  business, 23
  operating, 184

D

Data:
  cumulative (*see* Cumulative data)
  historical, 8
  time series, 11
Database, 281
Day, kilowatt-hours per (*see* Kilowatt-hours per day)
Debt:
  bad, 101, 127
  long-term (*see* Long-term debt)
Decrease, percentage (*see* Percentage decrease)
Defective merchandise, 110
Deferred payroll, 220
Deficit, 94, 106, 107
Delivery, 131
  cost, 148
Department, 10, 74, 162, 173, 212–214, 216, 226 (*see also* Division)
  code, 79
  sales by, 51, 52, 69
  service, 60
Depreciation, 109, 256, 257, 263
Descriptive graph, 37
Detached slice, 27
DIF File, The, 282

Direct:
  cost (*see* Cost, direct)
  labor, 60, 131, 132, 135, 139, 140, 142, 146–148, 208, 211–213, 221, 226, 247
  mail, 168, 169
  payroll, (*see* Payroll, direct)
Display, 52
Division, 57 (*see also* Department)
Dollar, value bid, 114
Dollars:
  per hour, 249
Dot-matrix printer, 7, 10
Draw basis, 78
Dun & Bradstreet, Inc., 200, 248

E

Earning:
  power ratio (*see* Ratio, earning power)
  retained, 253
Edwards, James Don, 178
Effect, 170
Efficiency, 277
  energy, 230
  operating, 276
Electrician, 80
Electricity, 154, 157, 159
  bill, 158
  charge, 156
Electronic air cleaner, 276, 279
Employee, 1
Energy:
  bill, 267
  efficiency, 230
  savings, 278, 279
EPSON MX-80F/T, 10
Equipment:
  brand, 110, 119
  rent, 132
Equity, 201, 253, 255, 257
  owners (*see* Owners equity)
  ratio (*see* Ratio, equity)
Estimate, 47, 64, 82, 109, 110, 112, 128, 129 (*see also* Bid, Quotation, Proposal)
Expenses:
  labor, 110
  maintenance, 275
  office, 150, 155
  prepaid, 105
  sales, 47, 49
  telephone, 117, 150
  utility, 155, 157, 158

F

Fee:
  accounting, 151
  legal, 129

File-handling system, 117
Finance:
  charge, 124, 127, 197
    expense account, 127
Financial:
  health, 76
  ratio (*see* Ratio, financial)
  statement, 108, 135, 177, 248
Financing, 122
Fixed assets (*see* Assets, fixed)
Flow:
  cash (*see* Cash flow)
  of funds statement (*see* Statement, flow of funds)
Fonts, 293
Forecast, 9, 42, 57, 58, 90, 91, 159
Freight, 110, 117, 131, 132, 144, 148, 150
Fringe benefits, 4, 60, 72, 117, 206, 208, 216–220, 226, 227

G

Gallons of gasoline, usage (*see* Usage, gallons of gasoline)
Gasoline, 148
  charges, 156
General:
  accounting, 3
  contractor, 80
Graph:
  area, 34, 38, 267
  bar, 3, 7, 28, 32, 33, 35, 38
  column, 31, 33
  descriptive, 37
  high/low, 36
  line, 1, 12, 24, 33–35, 38, 87
  presentation quality, 10
  scatter, 3, 36
  stacked bar, 31
  window, 26
Graphics:
  analytical, 8, 37
  historical, 8
  persuasive, 10, 37
Grid line, 16, 37, 38, 119, 145, 152, 153, 159
  horizontal, 17
  vertical, 17
Gross:
  margin, 108
  profit (*see* Profit, gross)
  sales, 43
Group, product (*see* Product group)
Guarantee, 116

H

Heat pump, 119
Hercules graphics card, 292
Hermanson, Roger H., 178

INDEX

High/low graph (*see* Graph, high/low)
Historical data, 8
Honeywell, 274, 276
Horizontal grid line (*see* Grid line, horizontal)
Hour:
  dollars per, 249
Hours:
  worked, 211, 212
How Accounting Works: a Guide for the Perplexed, 177

I

IBM PC, 2, 3, 281
IBM PC/XT, 282
Income:
  statement, 131, 132, 136, 177, 200
    (*see also* Profit/loss statement)
  taxes, 256
Increase, percentage (*see* Percentage increase)
Inflation, 24, 42, 43, 57
Ink jet printer, 4
In-shop work, 69
Installation, 131
Insurance, 72, 229
  workman's compensation, 142
Integrated software, 281
Interest, 122
  cost, 190
Inventory, 3, 52, 60, 67, 79, 104, 105, 133, 177, 182, 184–186, 189–192, 233, 244
  turnover, 59
Invested capital, 183
Investment, 188, 191, 203, 253–255
Invoice, 78, 88, 122, 155, 198

J

Job mix, 252
John Wiley & Sons, 33

K

Kensiki, Peter R., 178
Kilowatt-hours:
  per day, 34, 158
  usage of (*see* Usage, of kilowatt-hours)

L

Labor:
  cost (*see* Cost, labor)
  direct (*see* Direct labor)
  expenses, 110
  outside repair, 72
  percentage (*see* Percentage, labor)

problems, 72
  repair, 60, 82
  revenue, retail, 72
  sales, 126
    retail, 74
  warranty repair, 128
Lag, 25, 92, 165, 166
Late charge, 122, 123
Lead, 94, 165
LeBlond, Geoffrey T., 282
Legal fee, 129
Legends, 19, 37
Level:
  noise, 271, 272
  sound, 272
Leverage, 254
Liabilities, 104, 177, 188, 193, 201, 263
  current (*see* Current liabilities)
Line:
  break-even (*see* Break-even line)
  chart (*see* Graph, line)
  graph (*see* Graph, line)
  grid (*see* Grid line)
  horizontal grid (*see* Grid line, horizontal)
  trend (*see* Trend line)
  vertical grid, 17
  zero (*see* Zero line)
Liquid, 5
  asset (*see* Asset, liquid)
Liquidity ratio (*see* Ratio, liquidity)
List, mailing, 168
Loan, 176
Location, 10, 43, 52, 57, 162, 173
  sales by, 51
Long-term debt, 185, 202, 253–259
Loss, 136, 191, 192
Lotus Development Corp, 6
Lotus 1-2-3, 6

M

Machine, office, 86
Machinery, 190
Mail:
  direct (*see* Direct mail)
  order, 83
Mailing list, 168
Maintenance, 150
  expenses, 275
  preventive, 30
Manager, 85
  office, 163
Manufacturer, 72, 119, 146, 270, 272
Manufacturing, 148
Map chart (*see* Chart, map)
Margin, gross, 108
Marketable securities, 105
Markup, 126
Material, 82, 93, 132, 133, 136–140, 146, 148 (*see also* Cost, material)
  sales, 126

Media, 165
  sales by, 167
Merchandise, defective, 110
Mile, cost per (*see* Cost per mile)
Minimum charge, 69
Mix, job, 252

N

Net:
  cash, 223
  profit (*see* Profit, net)
  receivables (*see* Receivables, net)
  value, 263
  worth, 183, 188, 190, 201, 202
Noise level, 271, 272

O

Office:
  expenses (*see* Expenses, office)
  machine, 86
  manager, 163
  salary, 154, 160, 162–164, 173
  staff, 152
  supplies, 132, 149, 173, 176
Old accounts, 124
1-2-3, 6
Operating:
  costs, 267, 273, 275, 276
  cycle, 184, 185
  efficiency, 276
  loss, 191
Options, 273
Order:
  mail, 83
  sequential, 14
Outside:
  repair labor, 72
  services, 131, 132
Overdue accounts (*see* Accounts overdue)
Overhead, 8, 26, 45, 47, 62, 74, 93, 95, 107, 146, 151–154, 157, 162, 163, 171, 177, 180, 202, 206, 223, 224, 247
  costs, 83
  reverse, 172
Overlay, 13, 14
Owner-invested capital, 183
Owners equity, 202, 203, 254, 255, 258, 262

P

PC, 5, 6 (*see also* IBM PC)
Pacific Institute, 33
Painting crew, 80
Past-due accounts (*see* Accounts, past-due)

INDEX

Payable, accounts (*see* Accounts, payable)
    ratio (*see* Ratio, payable)
Payables, 96, 99
Payback period, 275
Payroll, 2–4, 75, 92, 247
    checks, 133
    cost, 4
    deferred, 220
    direct, 4
    taxes (*see* Taxes, payroll)
People, service, 69
Percentage:
    changes, 37
    decrease, 43, 77, 78
    increase, 43, 77, 78
    labor, 140
    of:
        change, 46, 48, 56
        sales, 8, 140
Performance, sales, 68
Period:
    collection (*see* Average collection period)
    lag (*see* Lag)
    lead (*see* Lead)
    setback (*see* Setback, period)
Periodicity, 13, 14
Per mile basis, 29
Persuasive graphics (*see* Graphics, persuasive)
Pictorial chart (*see* Chart, pictorial)
Pie chart (*see* Chart, pie)
Plotter, 4
Plumbing, 80, 83
Policies, credit (*see* Credit policies)
Postage cost (*see* Cost, postage)
Prepaid expenses, 105
Presentation:
    quality graphics, 10
    sales (*see* Sales, presentation)
Preventive maintenance, 30
Price, wholesale, 143
Price-earnings ratio, 203
Printer, dot-matrix, 7, 10
PrintGraph disk, 6, 293
Product group, 79, 117
Profession, 64
Profit, 10, 41, 47, 51, 58–60, 70, 83, 138, 146, 152, 177–183, 188, 191, 192, 201, 202, 213, 214, 216, 220, 224, 226, 248, 249, 252, 254
    gross, 59, 93, 131, 202
    net, 131, 183, 202, 205
    sharing, 249
Profit/loss statement, 58
Projection, 5, 23, 112, 141
Proportional changes, 36
Proposal, 47 (*see also* Bid, Estimate, Quotation)
Prospect, 10
    sales (*see* Sales, prospect)

Q

Quality of accounts receivable, 126
Que Corporation, 282
Quick:
    assets (*see* Assets, quick)
    ratio (*see* Ratio, quick)
Quotation, 82, 112, 114, 128, 265 (*see also* Bid, Estimate, Proposal)

R

Raise, 144, 172
Rate:
    callback, 144
    turnover (*see* Turnover rate)
Ratio, 4, 175, 176
    acid test, 2, 106, 108, 175, 185, 186, 200
    current, 105, 106, 108, 184–188, 201
    earning power, 193
    equity, 203
    financial, 178
    liquidity, 105–108
    payable, 99, 101
    price earnings, 203
    quick, 175, 185, 200
    receivables, 99, 101
Real estate, 229
Receivables, 58, 88, 90, 91, 96, 99, 199
    accounts (*see* Accounts receivable)
    net, 105
    ratio (*see* Ratio, receivables)
Relative cell address, 290
Remodeling, 79
Remorse, buyer's, 269
Rent, 149, 151
    equipment, 132
Repair, 110, 150
    costs:
        truck, 5, 28, 30
        warranty, 128
    labor, 60, 82, 119
        outside, 72
        warranty, 128
    service, 59
    work, 69, 72
Reston Publishing, 282
Retail, 44, 101, 232, 235, 236, 243, 244
    basis, 132
    labor:
        revenue, 72
        sales, 74
Retailer, 229, 230, 231, 239
Retained earnings, 253
Revenue:
    current, 41
    retail labor, 72
Reverse overhead, 172
Risk, credit, 126
Robert Morris Associates, 200

S

Salary, 72, 110, 132, 164
    office (*see* Office salary)
Sale, 110
Sales, 2, 3, 65, 69, 70, 72, 86, 87, 89–92, 94–97, 99, 104, 107, 108, 112, 114, 120, 121, 128, 131, 132, 144, 146, 149, 150, 152, 156, 164, 167, 170–172, 174, 180, 190, 192, 195, 203, 206, 207, 209, 213, 220–222, 225, 226, 231, 232, 233, 235–238, 243, 247, 251, 255, 258, 261, 266, 282
    by:
        department, 51
        location, 51
        media, 167
    cash, 197
    commission, 47
    cost of (*see* Cost sales)
    credit (*see* Credit sales)
    department (*see* Department, sales by)
    expenses (*see* Expenses, sales)
    gross, 43
    labor (*see* Labor sales)
    material, 126
    percentage of (*see* Percentage of sales)
    performance, 68
    per square foot, 52, 53, 55, 57
    presentation, 265–267
    prospect, 10
    retail labor, 74
    technique, 5
    total, 9
    trend, 39, 42
    value, 247
    volume, 66, 67, 109, 116, 147, 148
Salesperson, 10, 47, 58, 60
Salmonson, R.F., 178
Savings, 267, 273
    accumulated, 274
    energy (*see* Energy savings)
Scale, 5, 15, 20, 38, 68, 70, 87, 101, 119, 137, 138, 152, 159
Scatter graph (*see* Graph, scatter)
Schmid, Calvin F., 33
Seasonal change, 250, 251
Seasonality, 160
Seattle, Washington, 33
Securities, marketable, 105

INDEX

Semilogarithmic chart (*see* Chart, semilogarithmic)
Sequential order, 4
Series:
 time, 23
 data, 11
Service, 60, 69, 82
 calls, 30, 83
 department, 60
 people, 69
 repair, 59
 technician, 51, 60, 69, 72, 75, 110, 119–122, 128, 251
Services, outside (*see* Outside services)
Setback period, 274
Shade, 38
Shading, 21
Sharing, profit, 249
Sheet, balance (*see* Balance sheet)
Slice, detached, 27
Social Security, 141
Software, integrated, 281
Sound level, 272
Spreadsheet, 58, 65, 99, 112, 114, 197, 236, 281
Square foot:
 basis, 52
 sales per, 52, 53, 55, 57
Stacked:
 bar chart (*see* Graph, stacked bar)
 chart (*see* Chart, stacked)
 column chart (*see* Chart, stacked column)
Staff, office (*see* Office staff)
Statement:
 financial (*see* Financial statement)
 flow of funds, 2, 177
 income (*see* Income statement)
 profit/loss, 58
Statements, 129
Statistical Graphics, 33
Subcontract, 80
Subcontractor, 81, 277
Supplies, office (*see* Office supplies)
System, file-handling, 117

T

Taxable, 82
Taxes, 60, 147, 223, 227
 payroll, 4, 141–143, 148
 unemployment, 141
Tax form, 205
Technician, 60
 service (*see* Service technician)
Telephone:
 bill, 150, 174
 charge, 156
 costs, 149, 155
 expenses (*see* Expenses, telephone)
Television, 169
 ad, 168
Terms, 124
 collection, 94
 credit, 86
Thermostat, clock (*see* Clock thermostat)
Therms, usage of, 158
Three-dimensional, 36
Tice, Lou, 33
Time:
 series, 23
 data, 11
 travel, 63
Times interest earned, 196, 202
Tires, 150
Title, 17, 37
Total:
 assets (*see* Assets, total)
 costs (*see* Costs, total)
 sales (*see* Sales, total)
Travel time, 63
Trend, 2, 3, 22, 24, 103, 131, 135, 139, 140, 147, 153, 154, 157, 160, 180, 193, 199, 200, 239, 240, 244, 248, 252, 259
 line, 9, 23, 24, 38, 42, 44, 55, 57, 58, 62, 65–67, 70, 72, 74, 76, 82, 112, 115, 116, 122, 125, 128, 152, 155, 159, 222, 225, 238, 268
 sales, 42
Truck, 86, 148
 costs (*see* Costs, truck)
 repair costs (*see* Costs, truck repair)
Turnover:
 inventory, 59
 rate, 233–235, 244
 assets (*see* Assets, turnover rate)

U

Unemployment taxes, 141
Usage of:
 gallons of gasoline, 158
 kilowatt-hours, 158
 therms, 158
 utility, 5
Using 1-2-3, 282, 288
Utility:
 cost, 150, 154, 156, 173
 expenses (*see* Expenses, utility)
 usage, 5

V

Value:
 dollar bid, 114
 net, 263
 sales, 247
Variable cost, 146
Variables, 286
Vertical grid line, 17
Volume, 109
 average, 82
 bid (*see* Bid volume)
 sales, 66, 67, 147

W

Warranty, 59, 60, 131, 175, 275
 repair:
  cost, 128
  labor, 128
Webb, Walt, 249
Wholesale, 44, 51, 59, 229, 232, 242
 price, 143
Wholesaler, 79, 230, 243
Window chart (*see* Chart, window)
Windows, 24, 25
Work:
 contracting, 78
 repair, 69, 72
Working capital, 104, 108, 154, 158–260, 263
Workman's compensation insurance, 142
Worth, net (*see* Net worth)

X

X axis, 7

Y

Y axis, 7
Year basis, calendar (*see* Basis, calendar year)
Yearly basis (*see* Basis, yearly)
Yellow Pages, 164, 168

Z

Zero line, 14, 20, 30, 32, 38, 42, 46, 47, 55, 95, 115, 125, 144, 147, 153, 200